THE BIOPOLITICS OF STALINISM

THE BIOPOLITICS OF STALINISM

Ideology and Life in Soviet Socialism

Sergei Prozorov

EDINBURGH
University Press

To Marina and Pauliina, in captivation

Edinburgh University Press is one of the leading university presses in the UK. We publish academic books and journals in our selected subject areas across the humanities and social sciences, combining cutting-edge scholarship with high editorial and production values to produce academic works of lasting importance. For more information visit our website: www.edinburghuniversitypress.com

© Sergei Prozorov, 2016

Edinburgh University Press Ltd
The Tun – Holyrood Road
12 (2f) Jackson's Entry
Edinburgh EH8 8PJ

Typeset in 11/13 Adobe Sabon by
IDSUK (DataConnection) Ltd

A CIP record for this book is available from the British Library

ISBN 978 1 4744 1052 6 (hardback)
ISBN 978 1 4744 1053 3 (paperback)
ISBN 978 1 4744 1054 0 (webready PDF)
ISBN 978 1 4744 1055 7 (epub)

The right of Sergei Prozorov to be identified as author of this work has been asserted in accordance with the Copyright, Designs and Patents Act 1988 and the Copyright and Related Rights Regulations 2003 (SI No. 2498).

CONTENTS

Preface	vii
Introduction	1
1 Postcommunist Stalinism: The Resurrection of the Effective Manager	13
The First Destalinisation: Getting Rid of the Sovereign	13
The Second Destalinisation: The Betrayal of the Revolution	19
The Red Emperor: The Product of Destalinisation	21
The Architect of Whatever	25
Transcendental Stalinism	30
2 Stalinism in the Theory of Biopolitics: A Brief Genealogy of a Reticence	38
Biopolitics and Socialism: Reciprocal Blind Spots	38
Foucault and Soviet 'Racism'	40
Is There a Revolutionary Biopolitics?	46
Agamben: Stalinism and the Integrated Spectacle	50
Esposito: Biopolitics and the Eclipse of Democracy	56
Biopolitics and Ideology: Giving Form to Life	60
3 The Great Break: Making Socialism Real	71
The Inactuality of Socialism	71
The Second Revolution	78
The War on Nature	84
The Soviet Katechon	93
Death to the Dying	97
Fedorov's Biopolitics of Resurrection	105
Bogdanov's Biological Communism	111
Anti-Immunity: Accelerating the Apocalypse	118

4	High Stalinism: Retreat, Simulacrum, Terror	127
	The Great Retreat: The Apocalypse Deferred	127
	The Negative Synthesis of Real Socialism	136
	The Great Simulacrum: Socialist Realism and Real Socialism	142
	The Limits of Simulation	146
	The Great Terror: Explicating the Senseless	150
	The Unreforgeable: The New Logic of Enmity	159
	Immanent Annihilation	165
5	Deathly Life: The Subject of Stalinism	171
	A Brief History of the Stalinist Subject	171
	The Diarist and the Dupe	176
	The Terrorised Subject	181
	Destructive Plasticity	185
	The Barren Life of Sofia Petrovna	191
	The Living Dead	198
6	Shalamov, or the Negative Experience	202
	The School of the Negative	202
	The Return of History as Horror	207
	Bitter Indifference	214
	The Ethics of Survival	220
	The Inhuman	227
	Revival	231
	Writing after the Gulag	235
	Shalamov in the Age of Anticommunism	243
7	A Real Renewal of Life: Towards an Affirmative Biopolitics	254
	Living Socialism Otherwise	254
	Diffuse Socialism	260
	Socialist Lives in the Absence of Socialism	269
	Immanence and Barbarism	273
	A Captivated Life	281
Conclusion		289
Notes		296
Bibliography		313
Index		331

PREFACE

This book was born out of a persistent unease about the status of the idea of communism in the postcommunist world. Having grown up during the Perestroika period, in which the official Soviet ideology that I was just beginning to be indoctrinated into quickly and almost majestically transformed itself into a laughing stock, I have found it difficult to dissociate the communist idea from its historical failure. It was impossible in 1991 to read Lenin, Trotsky or even Marx himself without relating them to the ruins of the Soviet order all around us. Yet, the usual explanations of this failure seemed to me to be at best problematic. Starting from the early 1990s, two types of such explanations have been offered. The first, associated with the theorists of totalitarianism, put the blame for the horrors of the Gulag camps, the societal degradation and the eventual economic collapse of the USSR directly on the idea of communism. This utopian idea of radical equality allegedly led to a horrendous social experiment, in which countless lives were sacrificed to the ideal that is, depending on the version of this theory, impossible, impractical or undesirable. The idea of communism appears to take us straight to the Gulag.

While such a definitive explanation was undoubtedly tempting amid the ruins of the Soviet order, it was ultimately unsatisfying. After all, most of the inmates of the Gulag were faithful communists, many of whom ended up there after carelessly voicing their view that the Soviet government had actually betrayed the communist idea. Moreover, observing the opulent and aloof lifestyle of the party *nomenklatura* in the late socialist period led one to conclude that these inmates had been correct and that the connection of the aging and jaded 'socialists' of the day to the revolutionary aspirations of socialism was at best tenuous. Perhaps, then, it was not the idea itself that led straight to the Gulag, but, as various 'revisionist' accounts suggested, the faults in its realisation: the idea of communism was still correct, valid and valuable; it was just implemented badly. It is easy to see why this view was enthusiastically embraced both inside and outside the former USSR: it allowed one to admit the obvious disastrous failure of the Soviet project and still retain one's communist commitments. However, such a stance also had its costs. What does it mean that the communist idea was 'implemented badly'? What exactly was bad in the process of its implementation? Was it the implementers who were either not communist enough (being too petty-bourgeois or populist) or overzealously communist (in contrast to their more mild-mannered European counterparts)? Or was it the population, which the implementers sought to transform into communists, but who fell short of the ideal, disappointingly sticking to their old ways and thereby undermining the project of realising the utopia? Perhaps it was the country itself, too vast and largely inhospitable, difficult to control in any manner other than the most cruelly autocratic one. And what does it mean that the implementation of communism in the USSR went wrong? Does it mean that communism was implemented only halfway or so, leaving the utopia incomplete? Or was the implementation process entirely perverse, producing something wholly other than communism and thereby betraying the idea? Was the product of the Bolshevik Revolution a particularly shoddy version of what was still recognisably socialism or was it something wholly other that was socialist in name only (fascism, Russian traditionalism, and so on)?

It would be easy to continue with these questions, but the point is clear. Once the blame for the disaster of the Soviet experiment is transferred from the idea of communism to the process of its implementation, there appear manifold possibilities of insulating the idea from contingent empirical faults in its realisation, all of which, however, have the same side effect. As a result of such insulation, we end up with a strictly transcendent status of communism as something that inevitably goes bad in every attempt to realise it anywhere on Earth. As Michel Foucault has sardonically put it à propos of the habit of the Western left to 'put inverted commas round Soviet socialism in order to protect the good true socialism': 'Actually the only socialism which deserves these scornful scare-quotes is the one which leads the dreamy life of ideality in our heads' (Foucault 1980a: 136). Ironically, having sought to salvage the idea of communism from the dreary ruins of the Soviet Union, one ends up not that far from the argument of the theories of totalitarianism: if every attempt to realise the idea of communism ends up a disaster, there surely must be something wrong with the idea itself.

Thus, twenty-five years after the demise of Soviet socialism, we remain stuck in a frustrated oscillation between blaming the idea, blaming its flawed implementation and, finally, blaming the idea *for* its flawed implementation. Getting out of this impasse around the postcommunist status

Preface

of the communist idea was the first motive for writing this book. The second was more down-to-earth and had to do with the tendency towards the rehabilitation of Stalinism in Putin's Russia, a rehabilitation that, at first glance paradoxically, coincided with the decline of the Communist Party and the Left more generally. After a decade of efforts at destalinisation in the late 1980s and early 1990s, which quickly went beyond Stalin's person to target the entire Bolshevik ideology, Stalinism came back in vogue in the late 2000s. Yet, this time it was largely stripped of all ideological attire. Instead, Stalin became valorised as, in the already infamous phrase from an official history textbook, an 'effective manager' who successfully got things done, e.g. built factories and canals, organised collective farms, won the war and, perhaps most importantly, transformed the poor and chaotic post-revolutionary Russia into a socialist superpower. While Lenin was associated with the revolutionary overthrow and destruction of the old regime (making it hard for him to score any points with the present one), Stalin became a symbol of the successful transformation of socialism from a force of revolutionary destruction into a positive social order. What Stalin the effective manager allegedly attained was then the actual implementation of the communist idea, its translation into a real *form of life*. Ironically, while the Left of various orientations continued to practise the old 'good idea, bad implementation' routine with respect to Soviet socialism, the new Stalinists, many of whom never claimed leftist credentials to begin with, applauded precisely the implementation itself, while the idea was left to gradually decline into irrelevance: 'The communist idea was probably junk, but at least Stalin managed to implement it in reality.' It was this paradox of the valorisation of Stalinism from a non- or even anticommunist position that made me seek a new perspective for analysing this experience.

As often happens, what I was looking for turns out to have been right under my nose all along. The valorisation of Stalin's effective management in isolation from the ideological orientation of his regime clearly resonated with the problematic of biopolitics that I had been working with for many years in other contexts. This problematic, which was originally developed during the 1970s by Michel Foucault but has since then been addressed in a variety of theoretical orientations or schools, extends the study of political power from the traditional functions of the defence of territory and the enforcement of the law towards the projects of positive management of the vital processes of the population. A narrow reading of the concept of biopolitics tends to identify it with a variety of sociomedical governmental interventions that seek to positively influence the life of the population by enhancing longevity, increasing birth rates, lowering mortality rates, and so on. While such interventions are certainly central to the government of life, the primary focus on these techniques has often served to occlude the specificity of Soviet socialism by demonstrating the superficial similarity of social and medical governance in the USSR to other modern states, either liberal or authoritarian, and relegating the explanation of the evident differences between them to the vaguely defined domain of ideology.

Instead, a broader reading of the concept, which I have developed in earlier works and elaborate on in this book, goes beyond the focus on strictly biological (physical, natural, and so on) aspects and rather inquires into the *forms of life* presupposed and effected in the rationalities of government. Rather than separate biopolitics from ideology, my approach poses the question of *how ideology itself becomes biopolitical*, that is how its ideas are to be translated into life in governmental practices. This understanding of biopolitics will permit us to isolate the specificity of Stalinism in comparison with the better-known cases of liberalism and Nazism. While both of these modes of biopolitics were primarily oriented towards the *protection* of life defined either in economic or in racial terms, socialism in its Stalinist version was driven by the desire to *transform* life, devaluing the present forms of life in the name of what they were to become. Consequently, while the violent tendencies in liberal biopolitics and the suicidal paroxysm of Nazi biopolitics may be understood in terms of the excess of protection that ends up threatening what it was meant to secure, the violence of Stalinism cannot be grasped in terms of this logic. Instead, it arose out of the drive to force the ideal of communism into lived reality, which took the form of forcing the existing forms of life *out* of existence, withdrawing protection from the lives that conflicted with the form to be imposed on them.

In this book we analyse the articulation of the biopolitical project of Stalinism during the late 1920s and its implementation in 1929–32, the period that has received the name of the Second Revolution or the Great Break. This period was characterised by the extreme assault of the regime on the remnants of pre-revolutionary Russia in the form of forced industrialisation, Cultural Revolution and, most infamously, the collectivisation of agriculture. We shall argue that the extreme violence and the tremendous human cost of these projects were not coincidental but rather essential to their function of forcing socialism into lived reality, which required the negation of those forms of life that conflicted with this idea. The possibility of lethal violence was inscribed into the very logic of the construction of socialism and, given that the Bolshevik regime dispensed with democratic and legal safeguards against such violence very early on in its existence, the conversion of Soviet biopolitics into a 'thanatopolitics' of mass murder was not a contingent failure of this project but its integral part.

This conclusion also permits us to offer a new perspective on the question of the Stalinist subject. Since the late 1990s there has been a growing interest in Soviet studies in the questions of subjectivity and subjectivation under Soviet socialism. While the Cold War era literature on totalitarianism tended to view the Soviet regime as utterly dominating and even destroying the subject, contemporary theories, often influenced by Foucault, choose to affirm the positive productivity of the Soviet regime with regard to the subject, all but validating the regime's own claim to have produced the 'New Soviet Person'. Yet, just as the biopolitical orientation towards the positive management of life does not exclude the thanatopolitical assault on the living, so the process of subjectivation may incorporate the destruction of subjectivity and in the extreme case of the Stalinist terror may even be entirely contained in this destruction. There is no contradiction between the admission of the productivity of the Stalinist regime and the interpretation of its product in strictly negative terms of the obliteration of the anterior subject. The biopolitical productivity celebrated by contemporary Stalinists ultimately comes down to the production of the living dead. It is with demonstrating the lifeless and lethal character of this productivity that any future attempt at destalinisation must begin. It is ludicrous to affirm the biopolitical achievements of Stalinism while lamenting its high human cost: this cost, be it the executed, the starved, the tortured or the terrorised, *was* the supreme achievement of the regime, 'real socialism' having little reality outside of the atrocities committed in the process of its construction. The violence of Stalinism was not a price paid for the attainment of socialism but part of its substance, the new world easily recognisable as a degraded version of the old one.

What is, then, our conclusion on the status of communism in the postcommunist period? Was it the idea itself or its flawed implementation that made Soviet socialism such a dismal failure? Our focus on the biopolitical conversion of socialism in the Stalin era evidently points to the aspect of the implementation, yet rather than elaborate the familiar formula 'good idea, bad implementation' with endless caveats and specifications, we might rather improve it by shortening it: 'the problem with the idea of communism was that it was implemented'. When communism becomes a project to be implemented, a positive order to be constructed in governmental practices, the quest for the transcendence of the old world gives way to its destruction in the immanence of the real.

Does this mean that communism should remain a mere abstract ideal with no relation to real life and forever barred from every attempt at actualisation? Is there any other possibility to realise the communist idea other than implement it as a governmental project that destroys far more than it can ever produce? Can there be a biopolitics that does not end up producing death in the name of a new, different, better life? The final chapter of the book relocates the discussion of Soviet socialism to the theoretical field of *affirmative biopolitics*, increasingly important in philosophy and social sciences. Our genealogy of the Soviet biopolitical project suggests that in order to conceive of an affirmative biopolitics it is necessary to radically rethink the relation between idea and life, dispensing with the 'constructivist' approach that seeks to implement the former in the latter. Instead, drawing on the experimental practices of fashioning a new life in the Soviet Russia of the 1920s, which disseminated throughout the society without coalescing into a form of life or social order, we propose to approach this relation in terms of *diffusion*, whereby the idea acquires a tentative vitality by gripping or captivating living beings who thereby become its vehicles as long as they remain positively affected by the idea in question. While we are all familiar with such 'life-changing experiences', we tend to discount them as fleeting and transitory in comparison to the grand attempts of political regimes at building new social orders. Yet, this perspective deserves to be reversed. In fact, an open-ended diffusion in the practices of those captivated by it is the only vitality that the idea can have. The manifold experiments in the 'new life' in the pre-Stalinist USSR were the *only* instances of real socialism and the monstrosity that was 'built' after these forms were destroyed in the late 1920s and early 1930s had little to do either with socialism or with life. The only socialism there can be exists in the practices of the socialists that sustain it as long as this idea positively affects their existence.

Of course, the same applies to any other idea, including liberalism, democracy or capitalism, that were ventured to be 'built' in postcommunist Russia with similarly disappointing results. What this book seeks to contribute to the ongoing debate on affirmative biopolitics is the simultaneous affirmation of the need to abandon the drive for the perfect way of life and the conviction that this abandonment does not condemn us to a resignation and accommodation to the ways of life predominant in our present. The dismal failure to actualise the idea of communism in the Soviet project should not lead us to renounce ideas, however radical, and attempts to change our selves, however ambitious. There is a particularly sad irony in the fact that the demise of Soviet socialism, a regime that lived off disempowerment and despair, tends to produce similar effects of disempowerment and despair today, as all alternatives to the global hegemony of capitalism appear discredited. Yet, such a conclusion is not at all warranted. In his testimonial Gulag prose Varlam Shalamov combined visceral hatred of Stalinism with a firm conviction that the Revolution had been a historic attempt at the 'real renewal of life' that was subsequently betrayed, 'cast aside and trampled upon'. Rather than discredit this drive for the real renewal of life, the horrendous experience of Stalinism paradoxically verifies it. It is precisely because such a monstrosity as Stalinism took place and left an indelible mark on Soviet and post-Soviet lives that the possibility of a different form of life remains the decisive political question.

The research for this book was funded by the Academy of Finland Research Fellowship during the period of 2010–15. I am thankful to the administrative personnel of the Academy and my site of research, the Department of Political and Economic Studies at the University of Helsinki, for their helpful and efficient work that made this fellowship period both pleasant and productive. I am particularly grateful to Esa Järvinen for his assistance in managing the project finances.

Early versions of some of the chapters in this book have been presented as conference papers, guest lectures and talks. I am thankful to my colleagues, whose comments and criticism were of great help in improving the final version: Alexander Astrov, Bill Bowring, Susanna Lindberg, Artemy Magun, Simona Rentea, Jemima Repo, Yevgeni Roshchin, Lauri Siisiainen, Nick Vaughan-Williams. I am particularly grateful to Mika Ojakangas, who read the entire manuscript in serial instalments and offered perceptive and challenging comments throughout the writing process.

Helsinki
May 2015

INTRODUCTION

Since Putin's advent to power the Stalinist period has been subjected to a controversial reassessment in Russia. After the destalinisation of the late 1980s to early 1990s, in which the public revelation of the Stalinist terror served to weaken and ultimately destroy the legitimacy of the Soviet state, recent years have been marked by the tendency towards a certain rehabilitation of both Stalinism as a historico-political phenomenon and Stalin as a statesman in both political and academic discourse. On the official level this rehabilitation became particularly evident in the context of the seventieth anniversary of the Molotov-Ribbentrop pact in 2009, whose occasion was used by the Russian government to assert its commitment to the Stalinist interpretation of World War II and criminalise its alleged 'falsifications'. The extremely negative official reaction to the 2009 Resolutions of the Organization for Security and Cooperation in Europe (OSCE) Parliamentary Assembly and the European Parliament on the remembrance of the victims of Stalinism and Nazism also demonstrated the increasing gulf between Russian and Western positions on the Stalinist period.

Moreover, public opinion polls in Russia have repeatedly demonstrated positive assessments of Stalinism. In 2008 Stalin came a close third in the widely publicised television show *Name of Russia*, in which the nationwide audience voted for their favourite figure in Russian history. In 2013 he came third in the Levada Centre poll of the public's favourite leaders of Russia in the twentieth century, narrowly losing to Lenin and Brezhnev (Arutyunyan 2003). According to the findings of the 2013 study by the Carnegie Endowment, destalinisation, initiated during the Perestroika period, has been a manifest failure, as *more* people support Stalin today than at the end of the Soviet period (De Waal et al. 2013). According to the study, 21 per cent of the Russians have 'respect' for Stalin and 47 per cent agree or 'mostly agree' with the statement 'Stalin was a wise leader who brought the Soviet Union to might and prosperity'. Twenty-two per cent of the respondents claimed that Stalin's terror was 'politically necessary' and 'justified by the historical circumstances'. Nonetheless, only 18 per cent said 'definitely' or 'probably yes' to the question of whether they wanted to live in a country ruled by a person like Stalin (ibid.). The 2015 Levada Centre poll showed that the number of Russians who consider the Stalinist terror 'justified' by the achievements of the period had risen from 25 per cent in 2012 to 45 per cent, while the number of those who consider Stalin a 'criminal' had decreased from one-third of the respondents in 2010 to a quarter of the respondents in 2015 (Colta Editorial 2015).

The figures become even more telling when the respondents are not asked about their personal preferences but requested to list 'great historical figures'. While in 1989 Stalin was only no. 11 in this list, with 12 per cent of mentions, in 2012 he moved up to the top spot with 49 per cent. During the same period Karl Marx moved from the third spot (35 per cent) down to the miserable no. 33 (4 per cent), while Peter the Great demonstrated admirable continuity, remaining in second place with 38 per cent. Interestingly, the negative evaluation of Stalin was lowest not only in the oldest age cohort (19 per cent for those 55 and older), which might be expected, but also in the youngest (19 per cent for those between 18 and 24) (De Waal et al. 2013). These figures demonstrate that the rehabilitation of Stalin and Stalinism since 1989 is nothing short of remarkable, supporting the claim that 'capitalist Russia is seemingly catching socialist Stalin fever all over again' (Miks 2013).

It is important to note that this rehabilitation is not restricted to the leftist sector of the political spectrum but transcends and neutralises ideological divisions, its greatest leap (from 35 per cent in 2008 to 49 per cent in 2012) coinciding with the period of the decline of the Communist Party of the Russian Federation (CPRF) (see De Waal et al. 2013). While in the 1990s a positive revaluation of Stalinism was a marker of a reactionary political discourse in the margins of the political spectrum, during the Putin period this revaluation has moved to the mainstream. Pro-Stalinist sympathies no longer indicate one's belonging to the left, however defined, nor even one's nostalgia for the Soviet period, but have been successfully incorporated into the defence of the contemporary, ostensibly capitalist order.

This resurgence of Stalinism is frequently explained in terms of the revival of imperialistic and expansionist sentiments, which treat Stalin in conservative and traditionalist terms as the creator of the 'Soviet empire', as opposed to Lenin as the revolutionary destroyer of the Russian empire. On the basis of a highly selective reading of the Stalinist period, both the apologists and the critics of the postcommunist rehabilitation of Stalinism present an image of Stalin almost completely dissociated from the ideology of Soviet socialism but rather entirely continuous with the imperial tradition of Russian history. This 'imperialist' reading of Stalinism is forcefully argued in the ever-growing sensationalist pseudo-historical literature on the Stalin period, whose titles indicate both the substance and the quality of the argument: *Stalin the Victor* (Oshlakov 2010), *Stalin and the People* (Zemskov 2014), *The Great Stalin* (Kremlev 2011), *Stalin: The Red Monarch* (Bushkov 2011) and, curiously yet not entirely unpredictably, *Stalin and Christ* (Nad 2011). Yet, even the better specimens of this approach inevitably obscure the key events of the period, from the collectivisation of agriculture to the Cultural Revolution, which are unintelligible outside of the ideological content of the socialist project. Why would a conservative recreator of the Russian Empire undertake an unprecedented overhauling of the rural way of life, destroying, along with millions of its bearers, the very tradition he was supposedly interested in reconstituting? By the same token, why was the expansion of the empire during and after World War II accompanied by the programmes of radical social engineering in the controlled territories that were counter-productive both politically and economically? Even if they do point to a real mutation of the socialist project in the Stalinist period, the traditionalist explanations fail to account for its conditions of possibility, mystifying the puzzle instead of resolving it. The more Stalinism is separated from the ideological context of socialism, the more uncanny and inexplicable it becomes.

In a 2010 article Alexei Tsvetkov isolated no fewer than five 'images' of Stalinism that survive in the postcommunist context: first, there is the *orthodox-socialist* Stalin as the Great Bolshevik who continued the Leninist revolutionary project without leftist excesses, modernised the economy and won World War II, but whose project was betrayed by the conservative bureaucracy after his death. Second, and against this image, there is Stalin as the *gravedigger of socialism*, the traitor to the cause of the Revolution and the destroyer of the Bolshevik Party, under whose savage reign socialism degenerated into state capitalism and imperialist chauvinism. Third, Stalin is represented as a traditional *Russian Emperor* who renounced communist cosmopolitanism and egalitarianism in favour of the construction of a new version of the perennial Russian Empire. Fourth, this image is reversed in favour of the representation of Stalin as a traditional *Eastern despot*, supported by the masochistic rabble that found enjoyment in its own subjugation. Finally, Tsvetkov introduces the figure of a '*postmodern* Stalin', theorised by refined intellectuals as the personification of a radically logocentric politics operating through the medium of language and hence capable of the total transformation of the world as a linguistic reality (Tsvetkov 2010; see also Dobrenko 2007; Groys 2011).

It is interesting to note that in this set the first and second, and the third and the fourth images are mutually exclusive and serve to cancel each other out: Stalin is either a true socialist or the gravedigger of socialism, an almost holy Emperor or a despicable despot. Rather than provide a positive and determinate notion of Stalinism, these two conceptual pairs rather demonstrate the problematic status of every claim about Stalin as a socialist *or* an imperialist. All that ultimately remains is the 'postmodern' image of the logocentric demiurge that is wholly detached from the real and the material. And yet, ironically, as we shall argue in this book, it is precisely in this dimension of lived reality that the reasons for the persistence of Stalinism are to be found. Thus, we shall add to Tsvetkov's list another figure that will subsume his five images by relocating them into a different interpretive frame.

We shall argue that the postcommunist remnant of Stalinism is not ideological but *biopolitical*. Inaugurated by Michel Foucault's genealogical research on the governance of sexuality, crime and mental illness in modern Europe, the problematic of biopolitics has recently developed into a much wider research orientation, addressing the rationalities of power over living beings in a variety of spatial and temporal contexts. The study of biopolitics is not limited to the empirical investigation of power relations in such areas as public health or sexuality, hygiene or the upbringing of children, but rather pertains to the *mode* in which political power takes life as its object, the manner in which power engages with life, for example as an object of protection, regulation, transformation, and so on. To speak of Stalinism in biopolitical terms is not merely to focus on its medical or social policies but to emphasise the centrality of life to its governmental rationality as a whole. The fundamental task of Stalinist politics was not to maintain or fortify the rule of the Bolshevik Party over the Soviet society, a goal already largely attained by Stalin's predecessors, but to make socialism, the ideal of the Bolshevik doctrine, a *positive form of life*. While Leninist and post-Leninist politics could be understood in *ideo*-cratic terms of seizing and maintaining state power through ideological predominance and the aspiration towards a different society, Stalinism may be termed *bio*-cratic in its ambition to give real existence to this ideological alternative, to make socialism no longer a matter of doctrine but rather a form of life. From this perspective, the specificity of Stalinism consists less in its fidelity or its betrayal of Leninist socialism but rather in its translation into biopolitical terms that attempted to make socialism *real*.

Introduction

The term 'real socialism' became widespread in the Brezhnev period and referred to the socioeconomic order that existed in the USSR and its satellite states in Eastern Europe. The reality of that socialism, which was increasingly uninspiring and dreary, was contrasted with the radical leftist utopias that by the 1970s became as unpalatable to the Soviet regime as they originally were to the capitalist states. Somewhat paradoxically, the reference to 'real socialism' sought to legitimise this disappointing order of things by proudly emphasising its reality: however drab and inefficient this order was, at least it was real. Yet, in the 1920s the reality of socialism was not yet a consolation prize but a fundamental task of the Bolshevik Party that was victorious in the revolutionary seizure of power and its defence in the Civil War but not much else, its early efforts in 'war communism' quickly abandoned for the New Economic Policy (NEP) of compromise with capitalism. Making socialism real, translating the precepts of the doctrine into life – this was the biopolitical problem, to which Stalinism was a complex, paradoxical and ultimately catastrophic solution. As we shall argue, it is this biopolitical dimension of Stalinism rather than its specific ideological content that has survived the previous attempts at destalinisation and is undergoing a rapid rehabilitation today. While the contemporary regime in Russia does not get very enthusiastic about the promotion of proletarian intelligentsia, collectivising agriculture, the construction of canals and other Stalin's policies, it nonetheless valorises Stalinism as a regime that was effective in their realisation, successfully producing socialism as a positive form of life.

This book was born out of the conviction that the studies of Stalinism and the research on biopolitics that have remained almost entirely without contact might both benefit from being brought together. The introduction of the biopolitical problematic to the studies of Stalinism provides a fruitful theoretical perspective for the interpretation of the empirical findings of historical research on various aspects of the Stalinist period, from consumption to terror, from the governance of sexuality to the regulation of science. Even more importantly, it isolates the dimension of the government of life, which might provide a more appropriate context for the key current debates on the period, concerning for example the Great Retreat of the mid-1930s, the causes of the Great Terror, the nature of Stalinist subjectivity. Finally, the focus on the biopolitical dimension of Stalinism permits us to understand the contemporary process of Stalin's rehabilitation in Russia, which is all but inexplicable from a strictly ideological perspective: why is an ostensibly right-wing conservative regime so fixated on the builder of socialism?

Conversely, engagement with Stalinism would be fruitful for the study of biopolitics, which has all but ignored the Soviet experience. The case of Stalinism exemplifies a biopolitical rationality that is in many ways diametrically opposed to the more familiar Western modes of biopolitics, both liberal and fascist. While the canonical studies in Western biopolitics tend to focus on naturalism as the fundamental principle of biopolitical rationality, operative in relation either to the economy (liberalism) or race (Nazism), Soviet biopolitics, whose goal was the construction of socialism as a new form of life, was strongly *anti-naturalist*, characterised by the drive to transcend (quasi-)natural states of affairs in every aspect of life. While the naturalist orientation of Western biopolitics led it to adopt a *securitarian* approach, whose task was the protection of life as it is, albeit often through negative means, the *transformative* orientation of Soviet biopolitics entailed that no value was granted to life as it was but only to what it was to become. Canonical studies of biopolitics usually target its securitarian logic, whose excesses lead to violence against life in the name of its own protection. Yet, the Stalinist case, in which the securitarian logic plays comparatively little role, was marked by even greater violence precisely as a result of its transformative ambition. Critical approaches to biopolitics would certainly benefit from considering this at first glance anomalous case, whose logic, as we shall argue, is not at all peripheral to the Western ontopolitical tradition but rather its essential component. While much of critical scholarship today tends to warn against excessive desire for security, our conclusions will rather demonstrate the ominous consequences of a 'constructivist' disposition that ventures to produce a form of life, social order or a type of subjectivity in governmental practices. Consequently, our analysis of the specific case of Stalinism will also permit us to articulate a perspective on affirmative biopolitics that is quite different from those currently discussed in the literature.

As an attempt at articulating the theory of biopolitics with the studies of Stalinism, this book is not a historical study but an interpretive treatise, which relies on a wealth of existing historical research in the elaboration of a theoretical argument about the Soviet biopolitical rationality during the Stalin period. Rather than introduce any new facts about the period, we shall analyse the phenomena and processes that are well-known to any student of Soviet history (collectivisation, Cultural Revolution, the Great Terror, the socialist realist canon, and so on). Yet, the perspective that we shall adopt is rather different from the prevailing approaches in Soviet studies today (see David-Fox 2004; Lenoe 2010: 213–42). While our study has certainly benefited from the insights of theories of totalitarianism, revisionist social history, the modernity school and the studies of Soviet subjectivity, the biopolitical perspective opens up a new terrain of analysis, inquiring into the ways governmental rationalities venture to access and dominate life. The differences between the contending approaches to Stalinism, which emphasise ideological domination from above and social forces from below, macro-level rationalities of modernisation and micro-level techniques of self-fashioning, become less important in this context, since we are no longer interested in isolating one explanatory factor (such as ideology or the rationality of modernisation), but rather attempt to trace the overall biopolitical rationality of Stalinism, whereby ideology was translated into lived reality in a combination of macro- and micro-level logics that need not be mutually exclusive. Rather than offer biopolitics as a new approach to Stalinism *alongside* the more established ones, our study offers an interpretive frame that makes these approaches more commensurable by relocating them to the new domain of the government of life.

The same can be said about our theoretical approach to biopolitics. In contemporary scholarship it is customary to distinguish the Foucauldian orientation to biopolitics as a historical phenomenon of modern governmentality (Foucault 1990a) from the Agambenian ontological reading of biopolitics as 'at least as ancient' as sovereign power (Agamben 1998). While Foucauldian studies tend to focus on historically discontinuous series of positive modes of the governance of life, the Agambenian orientation affirms the historical continuity of the negative operation of biopolitics as the reduction of positive forms of life to bare life. Yet, as we shall demonstrate, the two approaches are not incompatible, provided their functions are clearly distinguished. On the one hand, our analysis of the Stalinist project of producing socialism as a positive form of life during the 1920s–1930s is clearly aligned with the Foucauldian 'discontinuist' approach. On the other hand, our reconstitution of the radical negativity at the heart of the Stalinist project, including the mode of subjectivity it fashioned, resonates with Agamben's notion of bare life as the product of biopolitics. Rather than adjudicate between these approaches, we shall venture to demonstrate their commensurability in the analysis of concrete historical cases.

In the first chapter we address the postcommunist 'remnant' of Stalinism, which survived the demise of the USSR and has been undergoing rehabilitation under Putin. We shall trace the logics of the two 'destalinisations' in the Soviet Union (1956–64, 1985–91) and argue that it was the confluence of these two logics that enabled the revival of Stalinism in the postcommunist period. While in the Khruschev Thaw Stalinism was denounced as a personal deviation from and betrayal of 'true' Leninism and ascribed to pathological features of Stalin's personality, in the

Gorbachev period the denunciation of Stalinism gradually embraced communist ideology in its entirety, which was judged terrorist and criminal. If the logics of the two processes are superimposed on one another, Stalin appears as a traitor to a criminal system that deserved to be betrayed and hence as a positive figure, the saviour of Russia from the excesses of Bolshevism. This interpretation was ventured in the early 1990s in the 'red-brown' anti-Yeltsin opposition and subsequently embraced by the Communist Party of the Russian Federation and a variety of nationalist-leftist authors. A similar image was embraced during the Putin presidency, though, in line with the technocratic nihilism of the regime, Stalinism was no longer understood in terms of the synthesis of communism and nationalism, but rather in terms of the effective constitution and management of a new social reality. In this chapter we shall also address the complex and paradoxical orientation of Putinism to the Stalinist past, concluding that in today's Russia Stalinism in its biopolitical sense has become a quasi-transcendental condition of political discourse as such.

While Chapter 1 offers a historical introduction to the study, Chapter 2 provides a theoretical one. It addresses the puzzling status of Stalinism and Soviet socialism more generally in the canonical theories of biopolitics, where it has been largely ignored at the expense of liberalism and Nazism. We shall address the scant dossier of the remarks on Soviet biopolitics by the three key authors in the field – Michel Foucault, Giorgio Agamben and Roberto Esposito. We begin with Foucault's influential move of subsuming Soviet biopolitics under Western rationalities of government, rejecting the existence of anything like a properly socialist governmentality of life. We shall take issue with this argument, demonstrating that Foucault's genealogical scheme for the study of biopolitics actually admits of a possibility that he did not pursue, that is the biopolitics of class struggle, qualitatively different from the racist biopolitics he identified in Western governmentality. We then proceed to Agamben's theory of biopolitics, which was produced at the time of the collapse of the USSR and was understandably less interested in the socialist case. Agamben's famous claim about the 'inner solidarity' of democracy and totalitarianism in biopolitical terms leads him to deny any specificity to the Soviet case. Moreover, his critique of the revolutionary tradition of constituent power as complicit with the operations of biopolitics also demonstrates the impossibility of casting socialist biopolitics as an alternative to the Western traditions. Finally, we address Esposito's attempt to differentiate between totalitarianism and biopolitics as two paradigms for grasping the twentieth century. While Esposito criticises theories of totalitarianism for producing a

Introduction

concept that could never embrace both Nazism and communism, his own opposition of biopolitics and democracy as the key conflict of contemporary times produces a similar excess, as socialism is either subsumed under liberal and fascist biopolitics in a repetition of Foucault's gesture or implausibly associated with democracy. We then discuss the alternative pathway of inquiring into the biopolitics of socialism by focusing strictly on the empirical techniques of the government of life, addressed in the historical studies of the Stalinist period. While this research has yielded valuable results, it does not succeed in making Soviet biopolitics more intelligible, because the same techniques have different meanings and functions in different biopolitical rationalities. We therefore propose to approach the question of socialist biopolitics by addressing the *problematisation of life* at work within the governmental rationality of Stalinism: how does life function in the mode of political reasoning that defines the Stalinist project?

In Chapter 3 we begin this investigation by focusing on the emergence of the biopolitical project of Stalinism in the late 1920s as a result of the problematisation of the distance between the ideological and institutional hegemony of the Bolshevik Party and the underdeveloped, agrarian, capitalist society that it governed. Stalinism ventured to bridge this gap by producing socialism as a lived reality in the revolutionary project known as the Great Break, comprising collectivisation, industrialisation and the Cultural Revolution. The emphasis on the construction of socialism rendered Soviet biopolitics radically anti-naturalist, in contrast to the immunitary or *katechontic* logic of Western biopolitics that seeks to protect existing forms of life rather than bring new ones into being. We shall demonstrate that the paroxysmal violence of the Great Break owed precisely to this anti-naturalist disposition, which devalued existing forms of life as obsolete, paving the way for their negation and even annihilation. While this logic of biopolitics is evidently heterogeneous to Western biopolitical rationalities, it is not without precedent in the Russian cultural context. We shall briefly address its genealogical precedents in the philosophy of Russian Cosmism, particularly Nikolai Fedorov, and the biopolitical experiments of Alexander Bogdanov during the 1920s. The chapter concludes with an interpretation of the biopolitics of the Great Break in terms of the renunciation of immunitary rationalities in favour of an 'accelerationist' or apocalyptic orientation that exposes the society to unprecedented violence in order to clear the space for the advent of the new life.

Chapter 4 addresses the aftermath of the Great Break known as the period of High Stalinism. This period was marked by the tempering of the apocalyptic pace of the Great Break, which we analyse in terms of the three *negative inflections* of its rationality. First, the period was marked by a series of policy reversals that have come to be known as the Great Retreat: the rehabilitation of pre-revolutionary Russian history, the shift towards a pro-natalist family policy, the reaffirmation of hierarchy and discipline in schools and factories, the revival of conspicuous consumption, and so on. What unites these diverse tendencies was the emphasis on the return to order, stability and hierarchy after the flux of the Second Revolution. Whether we interpret this as the retreat from socialism or as the completion of its construction, in biopolitical terms this phenomenon exemplifies a compromise of the idea with the real, whereby the regime accepted the existence of certain pre-socialist forms of life and even relied on them for its own stabilisation and legitimation. Second, the aftermath of the Great Break was marked by the introduction of the official artistic canon, known as socialist realism, which authorised the representation of Soviet reality 'in its revolutionary development', as if socialism were already attained. The simulacrum of socialism thus produced served to crowd out the much more ambivalent reality of the Great Retreat and thus 'derealise' social life in the USSR by representing it as the triumph of the ideal. Finally, the mid-1930s were the period of the gradual unleashing of the Great Terror that peaked in 1937–8. While the violence of the Great Break was subordinated to the positive biopolitical project of constructing socialism, the Terror of the 1930s had no positive content: rather than exemplify the forcing of the ideal into the real, the compromise with it or its derealisation, the Terror was pure negation of the real and marked the transformation of biopolitics into thanatopolitics. It is the confluence of these three negative inflections that defined the remainder of the Stalinist period and arguably of the Soviet period as a whole.

In Chapter 5 we move from the macro-level of governmental rationality to the micro-level of subjectivation, addressing the mode of subjectivity produced in Stalinist biopolitics. The Soviet regime famously laid a claim to constructing a New Soviet Person as a new kind of political subject, though its actual productivity in this respect remains disputed among the scholars of Stalinism. While theorists of totalitarianism viewed Stalinism as crushing and dominating every aspect of subjectivity, more recent accounts of Soviet subjectivation tend to view the Soviet ideological discourse as positively productive in the Foucauldian sense. Our reading of High Stalinism permits us to combine the insights of both approaches: Soviet biopolitics was indeed productive, yet the subjectivity produced was purely negative, almost wholly contained in the destruction of the anterior subject. We interpret this mode of subjectivity with the help of Catherine Malabou's theory of *destructive plasticity*.

Introduction 11

Destructive plasticity refers to the capacity of the psyche to survive its own extinction, persist in the aftermath of a meaningless violent event that cannot be incorporated into and obliterates the contents of one's subjectivity. Malabou compares the behaviour of victims of brain damage and the survivors of 'sociopolitical' traumas and infers from the similarity of the respective symptoms the paradigm of a 'cool', disaffected, indifferent subject that has no content apart from the destruction of its anterior identity. This account of the terrorised subject resonates with Hannah Arendt's classic account of the totalitarian destruction of subjectivity yet attunes us to the fact that this destruction actually leaves a living remainder, the true New Soviet Person.

In Chapter 6 we elaborate our account of the Stalinist subject in a detailed reading of Varlam Shalamov's testimonial Gulag prose. The survivor of the dreaded Kolyma camps, Shalamov famously called the camp a 'totally negative experience', from which nothing positive could be learned. In contrast to Alexander Solzhenitsyn, who found in camp suffering the possibility of the strengthening of the subject through resistance, Shalamov rejected the possibility of any positive metamorphosis of the subject in the conditions of the camp. Instead, he analysed this experience as the gradual reduction of subjectivity to bare life, whose sole affective disposition is a bitter indifference to its own fate. In our analysis of Shalamov's *Kolyma Tales* we shall reconstitute his account of the destruction of subjectivity in the camps and the process of the partial revival of the camp survivor. We shall also address Shalamov's attempt to articulate a 'camp ethics' in the absence of any positive normative criteria, which he considered entirely inapplicable in the camp conditions. Finally, we shall address a puzzling paradox in Shalamov's work. While he was resolutely anti-Stalinist, Shalamov was never an anticommunist and, furthermore, retained his pride in having participated in what he called the 'real renewal of life' during the revolutionary period. While tendentious readings of Shalamov in contemporary Russia use his camp testimony to argue the well-worn thesis that all radical ideology leads to the Gulag, his own texts do not validate such a reading and are rather marked by the exigency for resuming the 'renewal of life' after the catastrophe of Stalinism. The testimony to the thanatopolitics of the camps thus ends up reframing the question of biopolitics in an affirmative key.

In Chapter 7 we shall outline the theoretical implications of our study of Stalinism for the contemporary debates on affirmative biopolitics in philosophy and social sciences. Our inquiry into Stalinism demonstrates that the negative conversion of biopolitics into thanatopolitics has to do not merely with the ideological content to be translated into life but primarily with the manner of its translation. To rethink biopolitics affirmatively is thus to rethink the relation between life and idea otherwise than in terms of forcing the latter into the former. The first step in this enterprise is reconceptualising our very notion of the real presence of the idea in life. Drawing on Quentin Meillassoux's distinction between modes of presence, we outline the logic of the *diffusion* of the idea in life, whereby its presence is real but incomplete or withdrawn, not taking an accomplished form of a new order. We then contrast this mode of presence with the 'ontology of effectiveness', whose ascendancy in the Western tradition Agamben has traced from the early Christian liturgy onwards. In this ontological disposition the real is grasped as an effect, a product or construct of a willed action. In contrast, the logic of diffuse presence does not produce stable effects that coalesce into a positive order, but rather transforms singular beings, in whose lives it is disseminated. The idea is not translated into life as the effect of the project of construction, akin to the Stalinist Great Break, but rather lives in its diffusion in the real. Our final step in the outline of affirmative biopolitics is to grasp this notion of the life of the idea. We rely on Michel Henry's phenomenology of life to advance the argument that the idea may only be said to 'live' insofar as it enters into life's own experience of auto-affection, if it succeeds in *captivating* a living being who thereby becomes a vehicle for this idea's tentative and transient diffusion. This is all the life that the idea can have: *contra* Stalinists then and now, the only 'real socialism' that ever existed was observable in the experimental practices of leftist activists in the 1920s, against whose disorderly plurality the Stalinist project was advanced in the first place.

The concluding chapter addresses the implications of this affirmative rethinking of biopolitics in the Russian postcommunist context. We argue that any future attempt at destalinisation must target less the ideology of communism than the biopolitical rationality that recasts ideas as constructible projects that can be forced into the immanence of life. And yet, the problematisation of any attempt to 'build' socialism or any other form of order should not entail resignation about the futility of radical transformation but rather a greater sensitivity to the way ideas may positively affect our lives rather than imperil them.

Chapter 1

POSTCOMMUNIST STALINISM: THE RESURRECTION OF THE EFFECTIVE MANAGER

THE FIRST DESTALINISATION: GETTING RID OF THE SOVEREIGN

Iosif Dzugashvili was called many names in his lifetime, 'Stalin' being only the most famous one. Before the Revolution Lenin once called him 'the wonderful Georgian' and his wartime Western allies called him 'Uncle Joe'. The cult of personality during his reign led to the proliferation of such grandiloquent titles as 'the Father of the Nations', 'the Coryphaeus of the Sciences' and 'the Architect of Communism'. His detractors were less grandiloquent, referring to him as 'the Super-Borgia', 'Genghis-Han', 'Caligula' or simply 'the pock-marked one'. What he was probably never called in his lifetime was 'an effective manager', a characteristic that seems at odds both with the acclamations of his supporters and the curses of his victims. Yet, this is how Stalin came to be known in 2009, after the history textbook edited by Danilov, Utkin and Filippov (2008) scandalously received the official endorsement by the Russian Ministry of Education for use in high schools nationwide (Brandenberger 2009). In the chapter on the Stalinist period in this textbook, authored by Filippov, Stalin was described as the effective administrator capable of getting things done and making things happen, the leader who restored order to post-revolutionary Russia and transformed it into a socialist superpower that challenged the Western world for almost half a century (Danilov, Utkin and Filippov 2008: 86–90). However crude and unsophisticated, such an interpretation of Stalinism explicitly manifests what aspects of Stalinism have been rehabilitated in the mainstream Russian discourse during the Putin presidency. While the attitude of the contemporary regime and its apologists to the 1917 Bolshevik Revolution is unequivocally negative, Stalinism as the era of the post-revolutionary construction of the new order receives a much more positive assessment, even as no representative of today's regime would subscribe to the ideological content of that order.

Indeed, the key characteristic of postcommunist Stalinism in Filippov's version is its ideological *vacuity*: Stalin is valorised as an 'effective manager' in the absence of any concern with what form of social order he actually managed.[1] What matters is effectiveness as such, the capacity of producing new realities whatever their ideological content is. This lack of concern with ideology is highly typical for the Putin regime, whose consolidation during the 2000s was characterised by the omnivorous combination of the most disparate trends from the entire political spectrum, which served to neutralise and disarm all ideological alternatives to the regime from the far left to the far right (see Prozorov 2008). Yet, the possibility of downgrading ideology in the interpretation of Stalinism was constituted long before the rise of Putin and must be understood in the context of the two attempts at destalinisation in Soviet history. Stalin the effective manager is what *remains* after the two destalinisations of the Khruschev and the Gorbachev eras. While today's revival of Stalinism leads many observers to lament the failure of these destalinisations, in this chapter we shall argue that it was precisely their success (on their own terms) that gave birth to the currently valorised remnant that we shall interpret in terms of biopolitics.

It is well-known that the Stalinist period was renounced twice in the history of the Soviet Union. The first destalinisation of the Khruschev period (1956–64), initiated with the secret speech at the 20th Party Congress and intensified with the 22nd Congress of 1961, targeted Stalin's 'cult of personality' and sought to put the blame for the Great Terror on Stalin personally so that he became cast as the *traitor* to the otherwise still noble cause. It is important to recall that the very concept of Stalinism was the invention of Stalin's critics. While once carelessly proposed by Lazar Kaganovich as an alternative to Leninism, the term never caught on with a positive connotation during Stalin's lifetime, since Stalin always chose to present himself as a Leninist. While Leninism itself was the construct of Lenin's successors, the concept of Stalinism was, from Trotsky's use in the 1930s onwards, deployed primarily by the opponents of Stalin.

In the late 1950s to early 1960s 'Stalinism' was introduced into the official Soviet discourse as a derogatory term by the party *nomenklatura* that itself actively participated in the most violent and destructive Stalinist policies, from the collectivisation to the Great Terror (Getty and Naumov 2010; Getty 2013), in order to mark the distance between the departed leader and the party elite that remained in office. Starting from the invocation of the 'cult of personality' in Khrushchev's 20th Congress

Speech, Stalinism was denounced as a largely *personal deviation*, the fault of an individual ruler and not the system.

> [Stalin], who absolutely did not tolerate collegiality in leadership and in work, acted not through persuasion, but by imposing his concepts and demanding absolute submission to his opinion. Stalin originated the concept 'enemy of the people'. This term automatically made it unnecessary that the ideological errors of a man be proven. It made possible the use of the cruellest repression, against anyone who in any way disagreed with Stalin, against those who were only suspected of hostile intent, against those who had bad reputations. Thus, Stalin sanctioned the most brutal violation of socialist legality, torture and oppression. (Khrushchev 1956)

Somewhat unexpectedly for a Marxist-Leninist, Khrushchev goes as far as to interpret these violations of socialist legality from a crudely psychological perspective, as determined by Stalin's proverbial suspiciousness or paranoia.

> Stalin was a very distrustful man, sickly suspicious. He could look at a man and say: 'Why are your eyes so shifty today?' or 'Why are you turning so much today and avoiding to look me directly in the eyes?' The sickly suspicion created in him a general distrust. Everywhere and in everything he saw 'enemies', 'two-facers' and 'spies'. (Ibid.)

Throughout the speech, Stalinist practices are contrasted with Lenin's way of doing things, which was characterised by modesty, collegiality, trust, and so on. It is therefore not surprising that at the end of the speech Khrushchev equates the abandonment of the cult of personality with the *return* to proper and authentic Leninism.

> [Comrades!] We must abolish the cult of the individual once and for all. We must correct the views connected with the cult in history, philosophy and sciences, and continue systematically the work done by the party's central committee during the last years, a work characterised by collective leadership and self-criticism. We are absolutely certain that our party, armed with the historical resolutions of the 20th Congress, will lead the Soviet people along the Leninist path to new successes, to new victories. Long live the victorious banner of our party – Leninism! (Ibid.)

Thus, the violence and strategic errors of Stalinism, including the disastrous first years after the German invasion, are dismissed as contingent effects of a defective personality, while the successes and victories of this period, including most crucially the victory in World War II, are reappropriated by the Party (or even the Soviet people in general). It is also the Party that leads the effort of the eradication of the Stalinist excess as a matter of a properly Leninist exercise in self-criticism. Anticipating possible questions about why this self-criticism only took place after Stalin's death, Khruschev ventures a dual response, simultaneously exonerating Stalin from some of the charges and demonising him even further.

> Some comrades may ask us: Where were the members of the Politburo? Why did they not assert themselves against the cult of the individual in time? And why is this being done only now? First of all, members of the Politburo viewed these matters in a different way at different times. Initially, many backed Stalin actively because he was one of the strongest Marxists and his logic, his strength and his will greatly influenced party work. After Lenin's death, especially during the first years, Stalin actively fought for Leninism against the enemies of Leninist theory and against those who deviated. At that time the party had to fight those who tried to lead the country away from the correct Leninist path. It had to fight Trotskyites, Zinovievites and rightists, and bourgeois nationalists. This fight was indispensable. Later, however, Stalin began to fight honest Soviet people. Attempts to oppose groundless suspicions and charges resulted in the opponent's falling victim to the repression. (Ibid.)

On the one hand, Stalin, for all his numerous personal faults, is not posited as a purely evil figure and his record is not entirely tarnished. For example, the terrorist violence of the collectivisation period that took the lives of millions or the terror against national diasporas in the late 1930s was never mentioned at all in the Report, so that all that Stalin was ultimately held accountable for is the terror against the Party itself – a fact that did not go unnoticed by later dissident writers such as Alexander Solzhenitsyn (Solzhenitsyn 2007: 20–4; see Toker 2000: 116). Even within this narrow sphere, Stalin's early 'struggles' in the aftermath of Lenin's death are deemed by Khruschev to have been fully legitimate. Stalin's fight against the left and right opposition in the late 1920s, which resulted in the total dominance of the Stalinist tendency in the Party, is deemed 'indispensable'. It is only later, probably after the February 1937 Plenum that unleashed the most extreme phase of the Great Terror, that Stalin began to 'fight honest Soviet people', including, no doubt, many of the Stalinists within the Party, who were accused of belonging to 'Trotskyites, Zinovievites, rightists, and bourgeois nationalists'. Yet, by that point, any attempt to criticise Stalin made one fall victim to the repression by being filed under these very categories. By maintaining the guilty status of the members of the opposition and refusing their rehabilitation, Khruschev and the party elite further depoliticised the Great Terror, making Stalinist violence a matter of a mistaken attribution to the thousands of innocents of the *real* guilt of the actual oppositionists (see Toker 2000: 49). If Trotskyites, Zinovievites and the representatives of non-Bolshevik parties were *in fact* enemies, then the struggle against them was entirely justified, as was the participation in this struggle of the surviving party elite, including Khrushchev himself, whose role in the Terror was far from insignificant. What was illegitimate was targeting 'honest Soviet people' in the framework of this struggle, the fault for which was Stalin's alone and not the Party's, especially since so many of the party members, particularly in its leading ranks, fell victim to Stalin's paranoia.

As a result of this move, the Party ended up entirely exonerated of Stalin's guilt and was even able to present itself as his primary victim to be pitied rather than blamed, especially insofar as it only needed to present this fact *to itself*, given that Khrushchev's speech remained secret and not published in the USSR until the Perestroika period. Moreover, the division of the victims of the Terror into true enemies and 'honest Soviet people' made it possible for the Soviet *nomenklatura* to grant or withhold rehabilitation in an ad hoc manner. Thus, for all its salutary effects in the revelation of the Stalinist terror and the rehabilitation of hundreds of thousands of its victims, the first destalinisation arguably *strengthened* the Soviet system and the Stalinist *nomenklatura* that ran it. Destalinisation removed from the Soviet system the quasi-transcendent sovereign instance that could never be fully incorporated into it and perpetually risked destabilisation by intervening into its smooth functioning. The decimation of the Party and Soviet government in the Great Terror demonstrated to the *nomenklatura* the fragile and hazardous character of its status as subjects to the sovereign. After the denunciation of Stalin and until the collapse of the USSR no transcendent figure of the sovereign ever again emerged in the Soviet order, which was instead characterised by the collective rule of the top party bureaucracy.

Indeed, the power of this bureaucracy was consolidated to such an extent that in 1964 it was able to remove Khrushchev himself from party leadership in an entirely peaceful manner without unleashing a new campaign of terror. Moreover, in the justification of this removal the party elite ironically made a reference to the very 'voluntarism' that Khrushchev criticised in Stalin's rule in the form of the 'cult of personality'. The first destalinisation thus marked the triumph of the immanence of bureaucracy over the transcendence of sovereignty, the closure and completion of the apparatus of Soviet government that no longer required a 'prime mover' to keep it running but could successfully run by itself. It was therefore only fitting that the denunciation of Stalin did *not* become a permanent part of the ideological self-image of the Soviet system: after the second run of destalinisation at the 22nd Party Congress in 1961 the references to Stalinism in the official discourse became ever more rare, while the process of the rehabilitation of its victims was all but halted, to be reactivated only after 1987.

On the other hand, the so-called restalinisation of the Brezhnev era did not amount to a full-scale rehabilitation of Stalin as a person or Stalinism as a system. While the regime certainly did become more forceful in its persecution of dissent, neither the scale nor the methods of this persecution amounted to anything like the Stalinist purges. The 'return' of Stalin into the official discourse pertained primarily to the recovery of the myth of his military genius as commander-in-chief in the Great Patriotic War and remained silent on the Terror, the violence of collectivisation and other contentious topics. Rather more interesting was the process of the re-appreciation of Stalin in Soviet society during the 1970s, not as part of the officially propagated ritual but precisely *in opposition* to it. We need only recall the well-known practice of taxi and truck drivers of displaying small portraits of Stalin on the windscreens of their vehicles to display their contempt for the current rulers, responsible for making the mess of things, whereas 'under Stalin such things [as the deficit of goods, street crime, prostitution, and so on] did not take place'. In the spontaneous ideology of the Brezhnev era, subsequently labelled the era of stagnation, Stalinism stood precisely for the *opposite of stagnation*, the time of extreme dynamism, development and mobility contrasting favourably with the dreary realities of the 1970s. Moreover, as the Soviet system started its terminal decline into inefficiency, corruption and moral decline, this spontaneous ideology tended to valorise the Stalinist period as 'at least orderly', when the state and the economy were functioning properly even if at the horrendous human cost.

Of course, such claims about the order and efficiency of Stalinism, which are entirely contrary to historical facts, could only be made when the Stalinist period became a distant memory, easily transformed into the stuff of fantasy. Irrespectively of whether it was authentic or fostered by the regime, this societal valorisation of Stalinism indicated the strength of the Soviet system, the sole alternative to whose stagnation was the terrorist paroxysm that, moreover, originally belonged to that system itself. It was as if the Soviet system offered to the population a perverse (non-)choice: *either us or Stalin* (who, come to think of it, is also one of us). Since even the truck drivers were really not very enthusiastic about choosing Stalin over Brezhnev and his decrepit successors, by the beginning of Perestroika in 1985 Stalinism was integrated in the Soviet ideological discourse as its 'inherent transgression', officially neither glorified nor condemned, while unofficially deployed as a false alternative to the system, a relic of the bygone age, whose grandeur may of course be valorised, but only at a safe temporal distance. In a tendency that would only become more pronounced in the postcommunist period, Stalinism was perceived by many to be a golden age, golden precisely because no one actually experienced it, which makes it readily available for the work of imagination that produces simulacra of order, abundance and justice.

THE SECOND DESTALINISATION: THE BETRAYAL OF THE REVOLUTION

The second destalinisation of the Gorbachev period initially began as a repetition of the Thaw of the late 1950s. The early revival of the criticism of Stalinism in 1987–8 formed part of Gorbachev's power struggle with the old party establishment and was initially a top-down policy, albeit enthusiastically supported by the intelligentsia: writers, journalists, academics, and so on (Popov 1987; Klyamkin 1987). At this early stage, Stalin was once again depicted as the traitor to the authentic socialist ideology and practice, embodied by Lenin. Yet, having started with rehashing the criticism of the cult of personality, the late-Soviet *nomenklatura* quickly went further than that. Unlike its 1950s predecessors, its members could not be accused of having been personally involved in the bloodbath of the purges, which made it safe to expand the criticism of Stalinism from being merely a personal deviation towards indicating the flaw at the heart of the Soviet system, that is the betrayal of 'authentic Leninism' by what in the ideological parlance of the time was called 'administrative command system' (Klyamkin 1987; Latsis 1988). While Khruschev's 20th Congress Speech addressed a personal issue which had already been resolved due to the death of the person in question, Gorbachev's anti-Stalinism became a resolutely contemporary affair, since the Stalinist system was held to have survived its architect and was only to be dismantled now in the project of Perestroika (see Gorbachev 1987).

What was at stake in this dismantling was at first still a return to authentic Leninism, although the content of this Leninism was quite different than in 1956. Starting from 1987, the alternative to the Stalinist command system was increasingly found in Lenin's NEP and, consequently, the first of the leading oppositionists to be rehabilitated in February 1988 were the Right, 'market-oriented' figures such as Alexei Rykov and Nikolai Bukharin. The gradual shift towards the market, planned in Gorbachev's economic policy, was legitimised by presenting authentic Leninist socialism as nowhere near as hostile to market principles as the Stalinist command system made it appear. In a similar manner, the democratisation of the Soviet system, undertaken by Gorbachev in 1987–9, was legitimised as the overcoming of the defects of Stalinism, which perverted the originally democratic intentions of Leninism.

Yet, this attempt to legitimise democratic and market-oriented reforms with reference to authentic Leninism ultimately backfired. As the state gradually yielded its monopoly on the discourse of destalinisation to the intelligentsia and the increasingly free mass media during 1988–9, it became difficult to contain the criticism of Stalinism within the paradigm of the 'betrayal of authentic socialism'. Instead, the rising anti-Stalinist discourse, including the voices of the dissidents of the 1950s–1970s finally entering the public domain (Vasily Grossmann, Alexander Solzhenitsyn, Varlam Shalamov), had no difficulty reconstructing the allegedly betrayed Leninism as the actual *origin* of Stalinism (see Selyunin 1988; Kozhinov 1988; Tsipko 1988). What in 1956 and in 1986 was construed as a betrayal of the original values of the Revolution now turned into the paradigmatic expression of these values: 'Stalin victoriously affirmed Lenin and Leninism, raised and fortified the Leninist banner over Russia' (Grossman 1989: 79). This is not a quotation from the Stalin-penned *Short Course of the History of the CPSU*, even though it could have easily come from there. These are the words from Vasily Grossman's *Everything Flows*, a novella originally written in 1961 and not published in the Soviet Union until 1989. Similarly to the more famous *The Gulag Archipelago* (Solzhenitsyn 2007: 19–39), Grossman's novella challenged the discourse of the Thaw in demonstrating the fundamental *continuity* between Lenin and Stalin with regard to the development of the dictatorial rule of the Party, the suppression of intra-party democracy, the contempt for civil liberties and the rule of law, the degradation of the revolutionary drive for emancipation into police-state repression – in short, the destruction of human freedom (Grossman 1989: ch. 25). In this account, which during 1989–91 became the mainstream position of the Soviet democratic intelligentsia, Stalinist terror was merely the most extreme manifestation of Soviet totalitarianism, whose foundations were laid as early as the Revolution of 1917, if not earlier, in the pre-revolutionary practices of the Bolshevik Party as the self-appointed vanguard of the proletariat (see Tsipko 1990; Kiva 1990; Sakharov 1991). From this perspective, a genuine destalinisation could only take the form of 'decommunisation', the liberation from the dictatorial reign of the Communist Party (see McCarland 1998).

In this manner, destalinisation stopped being the Party's regulated exercise in self-criticism but was mobilised by the emergent societal opposition against the regime itself. While in 1986–8 it was the reformist wing of the Communist Party that led the campaign for destalinisation and the return to authentic socialism of Lenin's times, in just two years destalinisation was reappropriated as the discourse of the anticommunist opposition, for which Stalinism was the only *real* socialism. While this identification of Stalinism with the essence of socialism is evidently not unproblematic from a historical perspective, what is more important for our purposes at this stage is its somewhat unexpected and paradoxical effect on the process of destalinisation. It was precisely the radicalisation and generalisation of the ideological battle in the late Perestroika period, whereby the critique of Stalinism was transformed into the critique of communism *tout court*, that paradoxically accounts for the *survival* of Stalinism in the postcommunist period.

THE RED EMPEROR: THE PRODUCT OF DESTALINISATION

While the Soviet system still existed, the articulation of Leninism and Stalinism in the negative figure of totalitarianism was a remarkably effective mechanism of its de-legitimation, permitting the societal opposition to rhetorically link the contemporary Communist Party, which *began* the process of destalinisation in the first place, with the worst aspects of the Stalinist terror. Yet, the demise of the regime and its official ideology in 1991 played a cruel trick on the destalinisers. Once the discourse of destalinisation was subsumed by the anticommunist ideology of the Yeltsin presidency, the violence and terror associated with Stalinism were generalised as the *modus operandi* of Soviet socialism from its very origin: Lenin's drive for the one-party dictatorship, the violent purges of non- and intra-party oppositions, the murder of the former Emperor and his family, the Red Terror of the Civil War, violent campaigns against the clergy and the intelligentsia all seemed to point to the Soviet system being 'terrorist' from the very beginning. Yet, starting from Khrushchev's 20th Congress Speech, one was accustomed to understanding Stalinism as the *betrayal* of socialism. What happens when the two logics of destalinisation are superimposed upon each other? Evidently, when Stalin is understood as the traitor to the socialist revolution and the socialist revolution is in turn understood in terms of the terroristic violence that characterised Stalinism, it becomes possible to recast Stalin as the *traitor of something that deserved to be betrayed*, that is the violent and terrorist logic of revolution as such.

If the Revolution itself was nothing more than the terror unleashed by the forces of pure negativity, what does it mean to betray it, as Stalin did, according to Khruschev and Gorbachev? Evidently, the betrayal of the revolutionary negativity can only consist in its *negation*, the return to order and stability after the violent excesses of the revolution, be these internationalist, atheist, regicidal or aesthetic. Yet, if this is the case, then Stalinism is separated from the generic notions of 'communism', 'socialism' or 'Bolshevism' that the postcommunist regime delegitimised as violent and terrorist. It then becomes possible to interpret the Stalinist 'betrayal' in the positive 'anticommunist' or 'anti-revolutionary' key, whereby, for example, the admission of Stalin's decimation of the Old Bolsheviks is immediately followed by the long list of violent crimes these Old Bolsheviks, from Tukhachevsky to Trotsky, have committed, from the repression of the Cossacks to the persecution of the Christians, from the armed reprisal against rebellious villages during the Civil War to the suppression of trade unions after it. Without necessarily explicitly saying as much, the anticommunist discourse made it appear that many of the victims of Stalinism actually *deserved* their fate precisely due to their commitment to the revolutionary ideology and practice that Stalin paradoxically both embodied (in the discourse of the anticommunist opposition) and betrayed (in the discourse of the 'destalinisers' within the Party). The same conclusion was reached more explicitly by the explicit apologists of Stalin in the anti-Yeltsin opposition of the early 1990s.

> In all its tragic ambivalence 1937 swept away from the historical stage all those who were ready to sacrifice Russia to their pseudo-revolutionary illusions, who reduced it to tinder for starting a worldwide fire. The repressions primarily targeted those who destroyed churches, collectivised the peasants and persecuted the Cossacks, asserted 'proletarian culture', trying to 'throw Pushkin off the steamship of modernity'. (Zyuganov 2008)

Indeed, if the problem with communism was its violent destruction of the traditional ways of life, then was not Stalin, with his abandonment of the early-Bolshevik iconoclasm and the restoration of many aspects of the pre-revolutionary social order in the mid-1930s, precisely the *solution* to this problem? In this manner, the ideological critique of communism stops serving the task of destalinisation but rather paradoxically and perversely supports the rehabilitation of Stalin: if the very idea of communism was so horrid, then why not give some credit to the leader who, while arising from the regime based on this idea, gradually distanced himself from it, replaced the entire Old Bolshevik elite with a new generation of leaders, rehabilitated traditional culture and even religion, and reincorporated the former imperial territories into the USSR? If it is communism as such that is the enemy, one could do worse than having Stalin among one's allies.

Postcommunist Stalinism

Moderate versions of this discourse were practised by the emergent Russian nationalist forces during the Perestroika period, which found the 'roots' of Soviet totalitarianism in the abstract character of the Marxist ideology that was allegedly imposed on Russian society in a violent manner that disregarded the 'organic' aspects of its historical development. From this perspective, Stalinism could be viewed as simultaneously the *expression* of this fundamental flaw of the communist ideology (for example in the policy of collectivisation) and its *correction* (for example in the rehabilitation of traditional culture, greater tolerance of religion, abandonment of cosmopolitanism, and so on) (see Tsipko 1990; Shafarevich 1990). In its most extreme version this discourse was practised by the 'red-brown' (communist-nationalist) opposition to the Yeltsin presidency in 1991–3, organised in the National Salvation Front and at its peak controlling over a third of the seats in the Congress of People's Deputies. This opposition movement, represented by such figures as Ilya Konstantinov, Victor Aksyuchitz, Sergei Baburin and Nikolai Pavlov, sought to resist the liberal reforms of the Yeltsin presidency by unifying communist and nationalist forces and the figure of Stalin was rhetorically mobilised as the personification of this left-right synthesis. The literary and journalistic work of Alexander Prokhanov, the editor of the oppositional newspaper *Den'* (published as *Zavtra* since 1993) was highly instrumental in this mobilisation. In Prokhanov's fiery rhetoric Stalin was reimagined as an almost divine figure, the 'Red Emperor' who restored the eternal Russian Empire after the tribulations of the Leninist revolution that had all but swept it away. The representation of Stalin in Prokhanov's innumerable editorials and novels was almost completely subtracted from the ideological content of Soviet socialism and was instead incorporated into the millennial list of Russian 'heroes', along with Alexander Nevsky, Ivan the Terrible and Peter the Great. The Soviet period was reinterpreted as the Fourth Empire that succeeded three previous incarnations of the Russian civilisation ('Kievan Rus', the Moscow Kingdom and Peter the Great's Empire). In line with this logic, Prokhanov was even able to posit Putin himself as the potential heir to Stalin, imagining him as the potential founder of the Fifth Empire (see Prokhanov 2013).

Despite the ultimate defeat of the National Salvation Front (NSF) in the confrontation with Yeltsin in October 1993, this construction of Stalinism survived in the discourse of the Communist Party of the Russian Federation (CPRF), which succeeded the NSF as the leading oppositional force during the 1990s. The 'left-patriotic' turn of the CPRF undertaken by its leader Gennady Zyuganov, the author of a book entitled *Stalin and Modernity* (2008), entailed a systematic downgrading of the revolutionary history of Soviet socialism and its recasting in statist if not outright imperialist terms, whereby pro-Soviet nostalgia coexisted harmoniously with regular lip service paid to Orthodox Christianity and Russian nationalism (see Zyuganov 2004). The gradual abandonment of Lenin in favour of Stalin as the preferred personification of the Soviet era testified to the Communist Party's preference for the 'traitor' over the revolutionary politics he apparently betrayed.

> [Stalin], more than anyone else in the political leadership of the USSR, understood that without the leading role of the state-constituting Russian people the multinational Soviet people had no chance of victory over the enemy in the coming trials. Starting from 1934 the Party and the government introduced a system of significant initiatives in the spheres of education and culture in order to restore the national pride of the Great Russians, Russian patriotism and the defence of Russian culture as the foundation of socialist culture. The main thing that happened in the 1930s in the spiritual life of the Soviet people was the return to the traditional popular foundations, starting from the rehabilitation of the family attacked during the 1920s. What really took place during the first Soviet Five-year Plans? Along with the construction of the mobilization economy there was the mobilization of the spiritual resources of our state, primarily those of Russian patriotism, Russian culture, that for centuries were the spiritual foundation of the unity of the peoples in the multinational country. The 'Russian turn' was the turn to the thousand-year-old Russian history, the recognition of the continuity of Soviet history with it. (Zyuganov 2009)

It is easy to see that this image of Stalinism interprets his 'betrayal' of revolutionary Leninism, a fact established in the Khruschev and Gorbachev destalinisations, in the positive terms of the negation of the negativity of revolution, the return to order and the resumption of the 'thousand-year-old history'. What Zyuganov admires in Stalinism is precisely his distancing from the revolutionary legacy: while he casts Stalin as 'a revolutionary and a patriot' (ibid.), there is precious little that is actually revolutionary in this image. While the image of Stalin constructed by Prokhanov and Zyuganov is admittedly extreme, the same discourse is practised in a tempered form in the more mainstream debates among historians. For instance, in an authoritative biography of Stalin, Svyatoslav Rybas views the Stalinist period in terms of the reconstitution of the Russian state after the turmoils of the Revolution, the return to order after yet another Time of Troubles, and downgrades the importance of the socialist project (Rybas 2010: 7–8).

Just as the images of Stalinism produced in the first and second destalinisations, this 'left-right' image of the Red Emperor may not stand up to historical scrutiny. As numerous studies have argued, Stalin's 'Great Retreat' from revolutionary socialism in the middle of the 1930s (Timasheff 1944; see Lenoe 2004; Hoffmann 2004) was not equivalent to the abandonment of socialism but to its reinscription in the new context of the stabilisation of the Soviet state, while his partial rehabilitation of Russian nationalism and Orthodox Christianity during and after World War II were motivated by instrumental considerations rather than major ideological shifts (cf. Van Ree 2002; Tucker 1992; Priestland 2007). The enthusiastic appropriation of Stalin by the self-styled Russian nationalists in the 1990s arguably tells us more about the Stalinism of these 'nationalists' than about the alleged nationalism of Stalin. Yet, what is more important at this stage is not the dubious character of the dissociation of Stalinism from socialism, which we shall return to below, but the very possibility of such a dissociation, which was established by the paradox of the second destalinisation, in which Stalin was cast as the criminal traitor of the system that was itself criminal and hence distanced from the very system he apparently personified. Once this move was made, it became possible to project the most heterogeneous ideological content onto Stalin and even, as we shall see in the following section, to valorise him in the absence of any such content whatsoever.

THE ARCHITECT OF WHATEVER

As we have argued in the Introduction, it was during the Putin presidency that the figure of Stalin made a comeback in the mainstream discourse, both governmental and public. While the Yeltsin presidency was largely consistent in upholding the anticommunist logic of the second destalinisation, the Putin presidency was marked by more complex and contradictory manoeuvres of affirmation and denial with regard to Stalinism.

Putin's restoration of the Soviet anthem (with new lyrics written by the same author, Sergei Mikhalkov) in 2000, the first year of his presidency, marked a turn towards the symbolic reappropriation of the Soviet heritage by the postcommunist regime. After a decade of scornful renunciation, in the 2000s all things Soviet were submitted to a more positive revaluation, be it through the official reappropriation of symbols and practices, the cultivation of nostalgia in mass culture or the postmodernist play with Soviet signifiers in literature and the arts. What was unequivocally denounced during Perestroika now became appreciated in its very equivocity: the Soviet period was too 'complicated' and 'ambiguous' to be simply brushed aside. The figure of Stalin was no exception to this tendency. In contrast to the direct valorisation of the kind practised by Prokhanov and Zyuganov since the early 1990s, the reappropriation of Stalin under Putin took the form of a careful balancing of the *pro et contra*, the positive and the negative aspects of the Stalin phenomenon.

> The rehabilitation of Stalin has proceeded cautiously and ambiguously. Putin's spin doctors did not deny that Stalin's regime had conducted mass arrests and executions but tried to minimise the importance of these events. They did so while emphasizing as far as possible the merits of Stalin as a military commander and statesman who had modernised the country and turned it into one of the world's two superpowers. Stalin once again became a legitimate positive figure on television and in political discourse after 2002. The Russian government discussed introducing into schools a new officially sanctioned history textbook with an approving mention of Stalin, and politicians spoke of the need to fight against 'the distortions of history' in teaching the next generation. (Gudkov in De Waal et al. 2013).

During his 2007 visit to Butovo, the site of numerous executions during the Great Terror, Putin explicitly referred to these events as 'insanity', stressing the need to make sure this tragedy is never forgotten (De Waal et al. 2013). In an even more explicit condemnation, Dmitry Medvedev, the caretaker president during 2008–12, claimed that despite his 'successes' Stalin had committed 'numerous crimes against his own people that cannot be forgiven' (Medvedev 2010). And yet, despite these critical remarks, the Putin regime never issued an unequivocal condemnation of Stalinism, balancing every negative statement with a positive one. Thus, for every condemnation of Stalin's Terror by Putin or Medvedev one could observe the official ceremony of laying flowers at Stalin's tomb by Boris Gryzlov, then Speaker of the Duma and leader of the United Russia Party, who suggested that Stalin's well-known 'excesses' should not be allowed to obscure his 'extraordinary' personality (see De Waal et al. 2013). In his 2008 televised call-in session Putin suggested that we should not rush to make any 'overall judgement' about Stalin: citing the disastrous consequences of Stalin's collectivisation, which took the lives of millions and utterly destroyed Soviet agriculture, Putin immediately added that 'we did, nonetheless, get industrialization' (Shuster 2009).

Putin also made use of the well-known rhetorical tropes of Stalinism in his own speeches, most famously in the aftermath of the Beslan massacre of 2004, when he called for strengthening the state: 'we have shown ourselves to be weak, and the weak get beaten' (Steele 2004). This was an unmistakable reference to Stalin's well-known 1935 speech, calling for catching up with advanced capitalist countries, and was widely interpreted as indicating Putin's turn towards a more repressive policy domestically and a more assertive one internationally (Service 2006: 272–3). After his return to the presidency in 2012 Putin also reintroduced two symbolic practices dating back to Stalin's times, which, without explicitly mentioning Stalin himself, re-established the continuity between the regimes at the time when the persecution of the civil society assumed such an intensity that comparisons with the purges of 1937 became abundant in the press. The first of these was the reintroduction of the title of the Hero of Labour, formerly known as the Hero of Socialist Labour, a title introduced in 1938 and first awarded to none other than Stalin himself. By the end of the Soviet system in 1991, when it was discontinued due to the disappearance of both socialism and the Soviet Union, this title had been awarded to over 20,000 people, over 100 of them lucky enough to receive it twice. In March 2013 Putin restored the title and on 1 May, the first Russian Heroes of Labour were presented with the award: two industrial workers, a farming machinery operator, a neurosurgeon and the famous conductor Valery Gergiev. During the same month, Putin supported the revival of official sports and fitness tests for school students, originally introduced in 1931 for all age groups of the Soviet population in the framework of the programme called 'Ready for labour and the defence of the USSR!' (*GTO* in the Russian abbreviation) (see de Waal et al. 2013).

Throughout the Putin period, one could observe a rather more enthusiastic rehabilitation of Stalin on the local and regional levels, which often went beyond what was possible during the 'restalinisation' of the Brezhnev era. In August 2009 the City of Moscow unveiled an inscription to Stalin in the entrance of the Kurskaya Metro station, which reads as follows: 'We were raised by Stalin to be loyal to the fatherland, [he] inspired us to labour and great works' (Shuster 2009). In 2013 Volgograd City Council, dominated by Putin's United Russia Party, voted to rename the city back to Stalingrad, albeit only for six days of the year, associated with the key dates in the Battle of Stalingrad during World War II (BBC Editorial 2013).

This tendency towards a more pronounced rehabilitation of Stalinism was followed on the federal level throughout Putin's third term, marked by the abandonment of the vestiges of the 'liberal' image and the increasing reliance on conservative and traditionalist forces against opposition in civil society in the aftermath of the mass protests against the rigged elections of December 2011 and March 2012. The repressive turn in state policy after these protests was often addressed in domestic and international media in 'neo-Stalinist' terms, whereby, for example, the arrests of oppositional activists and the attacks on non-governmental organisations were decried as the 'new 1937' (Gessen 2015; cf. Getty 2013: 269–92).

Putin himself laughed off this accusation during his annual televised call-in session in December 2013, responding to the question of Alexei Venediktov, the editor-in-chief of the Ekho Moskvy radio station, about his alleged use of 'Stalinist methods' in the following manner.

> I don't think we can see Stalinist elements here. Stalin [is known for] the personality cult and the mass violation of law, reprisals, prison camps – we see nothing like that in Russia today and I hope we will never see that again. Our people will never allow that to happen again. But that doesn't mean we should have no discipline, no law and order – and all people in Russia should be equal before the law. (Putin cited in Smith-Spark 2013)

Considering that what Putin referred to as the restoration of discipline, law and order was internationally condemned at the time as the 'unprecedented crackdown on civil society' (Smith-Spark 2013.), undertaken in the xenophobic atmosphere of entrenchment against all 'outside interference' in Russian politics, this self-dissociation from 'Stalinist methods' might appear dubious and even somewhat Stalinist in its duplicity. Yet, it is notable that despite Putin's clear break with liberal and centrist forces, he nonetheless felt the need to distance his reassertion of power from any comparisons to Stalinism.

The rehabilitation of Stalinism became even more pronounced after Russia's annexation of Crimea in response to the Ukrainian Revolution of February 2014 and the subsequent fostering of armed separatism in Donetsk and Luhansk regions in Eastern Ukraine. The annexation of Crimea, which was legitimised with reference to the protection of Russian-speaking minorities, was widely compared less to Stalin's territorial acquisitions than to Hitler's annexation of Austria, Sudetenland and Memel in 1938–9 (Zubov 2014). Nonetheless, Putin's brazen challenge to the post-Cold War international order and the increasingly repressive stance towards the opposition, branded as 'national traitors' (a calque from the German *Nationalverräter* used in Hitler's *Mein Kampf*), have lent additional credence to the interpretations of his third term as a new 'restalinisation'. Such interpretations were also fortified by the fact that the separatist paramilitary formations in Donetsk and Luhansk regions, assisted by Russian special forces and eventually regular army troops, were led by such openly Stalinist figures as Igor Girkin (Strelkov) and Alexander Borodai, both regular contributors to Prokhanov's *Zavtra* newspaper (see Martynov 2014). In summer 2014 it appeared as if the opposed sides of the political conflicts of the early 1990s, the 'red-brown' defenders of the Supreme Soviet and the new postcommunist elite that defeated them in October 1993, were on their way to merging into a single orientation.

In order to grasp the Putinite appropriation of Stalinism, we must recall the effect of the superimposition of the two logics of destalinisation. Insofar as the Putin regime kept its distance from both the Left of the CPRF and the Right of Russian Nationalism, the synthetic image of Stalin as the Red Emperor was evidently of little use to it. While this image was produced for the purpose of unifying the extremes of the political spectrum, which required the articulation of the 'Red' and the 'Imperial', the technocratic and pragmatic self-image of Putin, particularly during his first term (2000–4), was thoroughly at odds with such a synthesis. It would be difficult to find any evidence for Putin's valorisation of any specific achievements of Stalinism, for example the results of collectivisation, industrialisation and the Cultural Revolution, which were instead negated by the systematic dismantlement of the Soviet welfare state during Putin's reign. It would therefore be outlandish in the extreme to view Putin as a Stalinist in the *substantial* sense of the term.

And yet, while different from the 'Red Emperor' image in substance, Putin's rehabilitation of Stalin is conditioned by the same process of superimposing the two discourses of destalinisation and reappropriating the result of this imposition, that is Stalin's negation of the negativity of revolutionary socialism. The sole difference is that while Prokhanov, Zyuganov and other 'red-brown' oppositionists of the 1990s interpreted this negation in *determinate* terms, that is as the replacement of revolutionary negativity by something else (Russian nationalism, patriotism or imperialism), Putinism interprets it in *indeterminate* terms, whereby Stalin's negation of revolutionary negativity does not replace it with new, positive ideological content but simply suspends this negativity of revolutionary destruction in favour of positive and constructive activity of some sort. The object of valorisation is not any particular policy of Stalinism but simply the *fact* of the effective undertaking of these policies, 'getting things done' in the establishment of a new order of things. This is where we encounter Stalin as the 'effective manager', the 'builder' of socialism, taking the credit for collectivisation and industrialisation, the victory in World War II, the literal construction of the socialist society: new cities, factories, canals, statues, Luna Parks, school uniforms, musical comedies, and so on. In all this activity, Stalin stands at a clear distance from the egalitarian ideology of the October Revolution, associated primarily with Lenin, about whom Putin or any other key representatives of the regime have had precious little to say since 1999. With communism in terminal disrepute, the erstwhile 'architect of communism' is now simply celebrated as an architect of something positive, stable and relatively durable, whatever its ideological content might be.

This distancing of Stalin from communism has two effects that are beneficial from the standpoint of the contemporary regime. First, Stalinism is dissociated from the excessive negativity that is proper to every revolution and particularly the October Revolution (the weakening or destruction of statehood, the purge of elites, the decline of religion and traditional morality, and so on). It is possible to simultaneously justify or at least 'understand' Stalinist violence in the service of the reconstruction and strengthening of the state, and abhor Leninist revolutionary violence against the state, the tradition and established values. In this logic, the murder of Emperor Nicholas II and his family easily outweighs the murder of millions during the collectivisation and the Terror. Second, by virtue of its subtraction from the ideological content of the Revolution Stalinism ends up freed from any association with the eventual degeneration of this content into the senile idiocies of the Brezhnev era. Stalinism thus stands apart from both the revolutionary flux of 1917 and the dreary gerontocracy of 1977, even though there remains the inconvenience of 1937. It is now possible to be a Stalinist without being a socialist, a communist or even a vague and non-committal 'leftist', since what defines Stalinism is *not* the ideological content *per se* but rather its successful *translation into life* in a project of constructing a new positive order and managing it in an effective manner. In this way, the doubly negative image of Stalin produced in the two destalinisations, that is the traitor to the ideology that deserved to be betrayed, ends up inverted into the positive image of a builder and manager of a new positive order, who translated the flux of revolutionary negation that dissolved all traditional ways of life into the construction of the new, post-revolutionary form of life. While the Bolshevik Revolution was ultimately about destroying the old life, Stalinism is about building a new life, whose effective reality trumps its possibly questionable ideological content.

TRANSCENDENTAL STALINISM

While decidedly unorthodox, this 'de-ideologised' use of Stalinism has some historical credibility. The 'revisionist' scholarship in Soviet studies has long interpreted the Stalinist period as the era of grand societal transformation, in which socialism was constructed as a new reality. In her magisterial *Russian Revolution* Sheila Fitzpatrick succinctly sums up the difference of the Stalinist Second Revolution of 1928–32 from the October Revolution of 1917 precisely in terms of the former's far more extensive and intensive transformation of concrete forms of life.

> The structures of everyday life in Russia had been changed by the First Five-Year Plan upheavals in a way that had not been true of the earlier revolutionary experience of 1917–1920. In 1924, during the NEP interlude, a Muscovite returning after ten years' absence could have picked up his city directory (immediately recognizable because its old design and format had scarcely changed since the prewar years) and still have had a good chance of finding listings for his old doctor, lawyer and even stockbroker, his favourite confectioner (still discreetly advertising the best imported chocolate), the local tavern and the parish priest. Ten years later, in the mid-1930s, almost all these listings would have disappeared, and the returning traveller would have been further disoriented by the renaming of many Moscow streets and squares, and the destruction of churches and other familiar landmarks. Another few years, and the city directory itself would be gone, not to resume publication for half a century. (Fitzpatrick 2008: 149–50)

Fitzpatrick's description makes it possible to grasp why Stalinism appears simultaneously attractive and dangerous for the Putin regime. On the one hand, the 'effective manager' is precisely the image that Putin and his spin doctors have been trying to produce since his ascent to power in 1999, the image of a leader who can rein in the chaotic flux of the 1990s, end the apparently interminable 'transition' and produce a positive postcommunist order, be it the Fifth Empire that Prokhanov vainly hoped for or a 'liberal empire' once rooted for by Anatoly Chubais (2003). The example of a leader who successfully transformed society and instituted a new order in just a few years thus exudes an understandable attraction, which is further amplified by the possibility to uphold it without any commitment to its content. Once the productivity of Stalinism is separated from its socialist content, it is possible to affirm the former as a successful project of 'making socialism real', while negating the actual reality of this socialism. On the other hand, this formal affirmation of Stalin's 'effective management' is not without its risks. One cannot help but observe a profound difference between Stalin's project of radical social *transformation*, aiming at the creation of nothing less than a New Soviet Person, and Putin's technocratic, if not outright nihilistic, authoritarianism that has largely recoiled from transforming society and only sought to keep it *in its place*, devoid of any political subjectivity capable of challenging the regime's political monopoly (see Prozorov 2009b: ch. 2).

To return to Fitzpatrick's example, a visitor to Moscow in 2014 would not observe that many differences from 2004, aside from more signs of material affluence, increased police presence on the streets and greater media censorship. To the extent that Putinism shows an interest in the government of life, it has little to do with social transformation, but rather with the defence of traditional forms of life against corrupt and decadent Western influence. The regime's concern with issues of homosexuality, juvenile law, pornography, fitness, which became particularly shrill and intrusive during the 'Stalinist' third term, does not seek to produce new, ideologically defined forms of life, as Stalinism did, but to fortify traditional, morally valorised forms of life through the prohibition of all alternatives. For this reason, Putinism is best compared not to modern totalitarian regimes, characterised by at least the ambition of the total mobilisation of the population for the transformation of society, but rather to the traditional forms of autocratic rule, from which this element of mobilisation is largely absent. Even when the Putin regime did venture to mobilise mass support, as in the counter-demonstrations against the opposition in 2012 or in favour of the annexation of Crimea in 2014, these instances of mobilisation tended to be half-hearted, cautious and blatantly hypocritical, as if the regime treated even its own supporters as a potential threat. The closest analogues to Putinism are to be found not in the twentieth but in the eighteenth century or earlier, prior to politics' taking on the form of the mobilisation of the masses for historical projects or, perhaps, in the twenty-first-century post-historical condition where all such projects have lost their legitimacy and appeal (see Prozorov 2009b). Either way, the present regime shows few signs of any ambition to imitate the 'effective manager' in thoroughly transforming Russian society.

Yet, this modest biopolitical productivity of the regime in comparison with Stalinism may have disastrous effects for it. Just as in the 1970s Stalinism was viewed by many as an attractive alternative to the dreary stagnation of late socialism, today a neo-Stalinist project of a thoroughgoing transformation of Russian society may seriously undermine the Putinite stability. In August 2014 the Ekho Moskvy radio station organised a poll that asked the audience to choose their preferred presidential candidate between Putin and Igor Girkin, the Stalinist military commander of the self-proclaimed Donetsk People's Republic who became famous by the *nom de guerre* Strelkov (the Shooter). Strelkov won the poll by a wide margin among the phone respondents (64 per cent to 36 per cent) and a narrow one among online respondents (27 per cent to 22 per cent with 51 per cent undecided!) (Ekho Moskvy 2014). It is probably this unexpected victory that caused Strelkov's eventual flight from Ukraine back to Russia and his low profile ever since. Yet, after fifteen years of the valorisation of Stalin's effective management, it would not be very surprising to see the rise of new pretenders to the throne, who might be both more active biopolitically and more receptive to the ideological content of Stalinism than Putin himself.

In order to neutralise this potential threat, Stalinism must be simultaneously affirmed and negated, depending on the audience of one's discourse. The carefully dosed denunciation of Stalinism is addressed to the liberal opponents of the regime, whom the regime seeks to convince that any democratic concessions demanded by the opposition will only bring to power true Stalinists like Strelkov. Thus, the price for avoiding another version of the totalitarian terror is the maintenance of the present corrupt authoritarian system that keeps society in check without seeking to change the way it is. To the liberal opposition the regime thus offers a stark alternative, Putin *or* Stalin, which, for a liberal, is not much of a choice

It would, on the other hand, be a quick and easy choice for a *non*-liberal, such as the left-nationalist opposition that would happily seize on the possibility of going for a new Stalin, either a Red Emperor or an emperor of a different colour. For this reason, the regime presents this orientation not with an alternative but with an articulation: Putin *as* Stalin. The symbolic restoration of Stalinist titles and practices, the 'balancing' of the negative image of Stalinism and the imitation of Stalinist anti-cosmopolitan rhetoric are all part of this process of wresting Stalinism away from all those who might still want to imitate it *for real*. Of course, such an appropriation can only be partial, since no amount of official lip-service can erase the fact that the Putin regime presides over the *ruins* of the system created and managed by Stalin.

For this reason, neither of these two strategies actually succeed but inevitably lead to negative responses from the audiences. Faced with the false choice of Putin vs Stalin, the oppositional liberal never fails to remark that Putin himself *is* the contemporary embodiment of Stalin, which is *precisely* what Putin himself tries to prove to the left-nationalist opposition.

> The truth of the present historical moment is that the followers of Stalin and the successors of his political practice have won in the contemporary Russia. These are not old pensioners but rather the youth that has grown up in the atmosphere of restalinisation and absorbed all the clichés about Stalin. This is the regime that is now entering the state of fortification. (Pavlova 2013)

Conversely, the latter opposition treats with disdain the regime's fake Stalinism, insisting on its utter heterogeneity to whatever modern Stalinism is believed to look like – the point that the apologists of Putinism vainly try to communicate to the disbelieving liberals.

> What we have in front of us is not Stalin but a colonial administrator unsuccessfully posing as the sovereign. He does not develop the country but effectively transforms it into the source of raw materials for the West. This 'Stalin of today', whose ass the official patriots keep licking, has not punished a single participant of the grand robbery of our people. So do not tell us fairy tales about [Putin] as the Stalin of our time. Do not call the obedient slave by the name of the Red Emperor. (Kalashnikov 2013)

The regime's half-hearted negation of Stalinism is countered with its assessment as truly Stalinist, while its similarly inconclusive affirmation of Stalinism invites rejoinders that insist on the falsity of all the claims to affinity. Putinism *is not* Stalinism *and yet it is*; Putinism *is* Stalinism *and yet not*.

This perpetual oscillation between the affirmation and the denial of Stalinism is where we find ourselves today after the two destalinisations. The only permanent thing about this oscillation is the reference to Stalinism in the Russian political discourse, whereby the figure of Stalin throws its dark shadow over the entire political field. Ironically, this permanent reference coexists with the almost complete absence of anything like an 'empirical Stalinism', the ideological orientation that would affirm Stalin's positive programme of the construction of socialism. Stalinist communist parties have never succeeded in any elections since 1991: their strongest showing was the 4.53 per cent polled by the bloc called Communists and Working Russia for the Soviet Union in the 1995 Duma elections, while the explicitly named Stalinist Bloc could only manage a miserable 0.61 per cent in 1999. Today it would be difficult to find open proponents of the collectivisation of agriculture, the blowing up of churches or the use of slave labour in gigantic construction works.

That may be a consolation, but unfortunately it is the *only* consolation. The absence of 'empirical Stalinism' coexists with the forceful presence of what we might, by contrast, term 'transcendental Stalinism', which serves as the condition of possibility of political discourse as such. Political discourse in contemporary Russia is about Putinism being the last bastion against Stalinism or its most adequate modern version, about resisting Putin as the new Stalin or opposing him as the opposite of Stalin – in short, whatever is said in it has some reference to Stalin and Stalinism, even as the actual politics of the Stalinist period becomes increasingly distant and unintelligible. As a transcendental category, Stalinism readily provides us with interpretive keys for understanding contemporary events, hence the ease with which Putin's 2013 sacking of Vladislav Surkov was compared to Stalin's demotion of Yezhov at the height of the Great Terror (Latynina 2013) or the Pussy Riot trial was compared to the Moscow Trials of 1936–8 (Gessen 2012). The point is not whether these comparisons are justified, excessive or misleading, but that they inevitably arise in the political discourse that remains structured around the figure of the tyrant who died over sixty years ago.

This status of Stalinism in postcommunist Russian politics has important implications for any future attempt to resume the process of destalinisation, since it permits us to understand why the past and ongoing efforts to counter the rehabilitation of Stalinism have been so ineffective and even counterproductive. As long as these efforts take the form of the critique of the ideology of communism, they inevitably miss their target. The figure of the effective manager dissociated from the positive content of the social order he instituted is immune to such critique, since it is perfectly possible to agree with the destalinisers about the manifold flaws of socialism only to counter that Stalin's achievement consists precisely in constructing a stable and positive form of life despite these flaws and even correcting some of them in the process. It therefore makes little sense to oppose today's rehabilitation of Stalinism with the familiar anticommunist dogmata: today's Stalinists, be they the technocratic admirers of effective management or the apologists of the Red Emperor, show no interest whatsoever in the construction of socialism in one or many countries. Furthermore, destalinisation understood as an anticommunist ideological crusade not only misses its target but also hits the wrong one, endlessly bashing the ideas of egalitarianism, emancipation and social justice that were *already* perverted and negated in Stalin's time and continue to be perverted and negated under Putin.

Thus, any prospective destalinisation must confront postcommunist Stalinism on its own terrain, which calls for a different perspective. In our view, the theoretical perspective most appropriate for grasping this phenomenon is offered by the problematic of biopolitics. Even though, as we shall show in the following chapter, the canonical texts in this field have not addressed the Soviet experience or subsumed it under Western modes of biopolitics, this problematic is particularly fruitful for addressing Stalinism as the project of making socialism real, of translating ideological maxims into actual forms of life. The fundamental assumption of our study is that what constitutes Stalinism in its specificity is not merely the particular forms of life that were introduced in this period and have by now largely ceased to exist, but also the very logic underlying their institution. In other words, the familiar focus on the construction of *socialism* must be complemented by the attention to the *construction* of socialism.

Rather than dismiss the contemporary rehabilitation of Stalin's effective management in isolation from its ideological content as a laughable attempt to eat one's cake and have it, we propose to take it seriously as indicating a fundamental feature of the phenomenon of Stalinism, without the understanding of which we are resigned to the tired rehearsal of anticommunist maxims. An effective critique of postcommunist Stalinism is possible only on the terrain of biopolitics, where it must target precisely the productivity of Stalinism with regard to positive forms of life that it is presently credited with. Evidently, this does not mean replicating the isolation of biopolitics from ideology that sustains contemporary Stalinism. In fact, it is this isolation that makes it impossible to account for what is perhaps the most distinctive feature of Stalinism, the unprecedented scope and intensity of governmental violence. The artificial separation of ideology and governmentality makes it possible to perpetually shift the blame for the violence onto the other, whereby ideology would retain its purity by blaming the violence on its faulty application, while the apologists of 'effective management' would denounce the inherently violent character of the communist ideology yet continue to affirm the sheer efficacy of its implementation. As we shall demonstrate in detail in the following chapters, what defines Stalinism is the operation of the *conversion* of ideology into manageable reality, the biopolitical *realisation* or *effectuation* of ideological maxims. It is precisely at this intersection of ideology and governmentality that Stalinism reveals its productivity, which, as we shall demonstrate, is always simultaneously *bio*political and *thanato*political, ultimately producing death itself as a form of life.

The confluence of bio- and thanatopolitical rationalities has been the permanent focus of attention of the studies of biopolitics since Foucault's introduction of this problematic in the 1970s. In *History of Sexuality I* Foucault explicitly defined biopower not simply as the positive power to *make live* (as opposed to the sovereign power of making die) but also as the power to *let die* (1990a: 138; see also Foucault 2003: 247). He then elaborated the thanatopolitical aspect of biopolitics in his lecture course 'Society Must Be Defended', analysing it in terms of racism (2003: 239–63). Similarly, Giorgio Agamben's theory of biopolitics (1998) posited as its paradigmatic object the figure of *homo sacer*, a being that may be killed with impunity. Finally, Roberto Esposito (2008) analysed biopolitics in terms of the logic of immunisation, a negative mode of protecting life that introduces into it a measured dose of the very same pathogen, against which protection is needed. Given this interest in the coexistence and cooperation of the positive and the negative in biopolitical rationalities, it is puzzling that Stalinism has not received enough attention in the studies of biopolitics. In the following chapter we shall address this silence, starting from the investigation of Foucault's remarks on Soviet biopolitics and governmentality in the 1970s and then proceeding to the later studies of Agamben and Esposito. We shall then discuss the problems involved in the empirical studies of Soviet biopolitics from the perspective of the 'modernity school' in Soviet studies and outline our alternative approach to biopolitics as the problematisation of life in rationalities of government.

Chapter 2

STALINISM IN THE THEORY OF BIOPOLITICS: A BRIEF GENEALOGY OF A RETICENCE

BIOPOLITICS AND SOCIALISM: RECIPROCAL BLIND SPOTS

The problematic of biopolitics has become an increasingly influential research orientation in the social sciences, applied in a variety of disciplines to analyse the transformations in the rationalities of power over life in diverse spatio-temporal contexts. The two primary contexts for these studies have been liberalism, particularly post-World War II neoliberalism, and fascism, particularly German Nazism (see Agamben 1998; Esposito 2008a; Lemke 2011). What has been almost entirely missing is the third major political ideology of the twentieth century, that is socialism, particularly in its Soviet version (for exceptions see Collier 2011; Hoffmann 2011). There have been numerous studies of the positive and productive orientation of neoliberal biopolitics that governs lives through the mobilisation of the freedom of its subjects and the negative and destructive orientation of Nazi biopolitics that engages in paroxysmal violence in the name of the survival of the privileged race and ultimately threatens its very existence. Yet, the studies of biopolitics are all but silent about what was arguably the most ambitious project of the *positive* transformation of human lives, that is the creation of the New Soviet Person as the emancipated subject of socialist society, which at the same time unleashed the unprecedented *negativity* of terror against the very persons that were to be transformed.

The Soviet experience provides ample historical evidence of both the positive and negative aspects of biopolitics, its power to 'make live' and to 'let die' (Foucault 2003: 241). Nonetheless, aside from casual references to Soviet biopolitics in the work of Foucault, Agamben and Esposito, the theoretical literature on biopolitics has largely ignored the Soviet experience, while the empirical research in Soviet and Russian Studies has, with very few exceptions (such as Groys and Hagemeister

2005), largely ignored the problematic of biopolitics. This omission illustrates a wider lack of interest in the phenomenon of Stalinism in contemporary philosophy and political theory, which either subsume it along with Nazism under the ambiguous rubric of totalitarianism (Tismaneanu 2012; see Esposito 2008b, Losurdo 2004 for a critique) or dismiss it as a modern version of traditional Russian despotism that is of little philosophical interest (Pipes 2003). As Slavoj Žižek, who alone among major contemporary philosophers has addressed the problem of Stalinism at length (2002: 117–40; 2008: 211–52; 2005, 285–95), argued, Stalinism has not been subjected to the same philosophical critique that, from the Frankfurt School onwards, focused on Nazism as the obscene underside of Western modernity (Žižek 2002: 92–3). No such critique has been attempted in the Russian academic discourse, which focused either on setting straight the historical record of Stalinist terror or participated in the ideological polemic in the aftermath of the second destalinisation of the 1990s. Thus, despite the immensely rich historical research produced since the early 1990s, the phenomenon of Stalinism appears under-theorised and disconnected from the contemporary debates in political and social theory (cf. Edele 2010: 213–42; David-Fox 2004).

And yet, particularly in the case of biopolitics, this disconnection has proven highly detrimental, not merely because Stalinism offers an abundance of empirical examples of the exercise of power over life in a wide variety of spheres (hygiene, sexuality, legality, dancing, diet), but, more importantly, because this experience helps us address the central problem of the theory of biopolitics, which consists in explaining the persistent conversion of biopolitics into thanatopolitics, which arguably reaches its most extreme and paroxysmal point precisely in Stalinism. As a project of the post-revolutionary positive transformation of all social life along the lines of Marxist-Leninist ideology, Stalinism epitomises the assumptions of positive biopolitics about the amenability of the vital processes of populations to transformation by political power. The infamous slogans about the constitution of the New Soviet Person and the 'Soviet people' as a new 'historical community of human beings' clearly indicate the positive, literally constructivist character of the Soviet biopolitical project. At the same time, the actual experience of the construction of socialism, from the terror and the organised famine of the collectivisation to the anti-Semitic purge initiated by the Doctors' Plot of 1953, was remarkably violent, annihilating the very lives that were to be transformed into something new. Stalinism thus appears to be a case of an extremely productive or positive biopolitics that turned into an equally extreme thanatopolitics. It is precisely this extremity, whereby the *paradox* that arguably characterises *all* biopolitics collapses into a *paroxysm*, that makes the case of Stalinism indispensable for understanding the potentiality for violence immanent to biopolitics as well as the limits that restrain this potentiality within various modes of biopolitical government.

The justification for addressing the specificity of Stalinist biopolitics seems to be established firmly. Yet, since this justification should be evident for anyone with a minimal knowledge of Soviet history, there remains a puzzle of why the key theorists of biopolitics either ignored the Soviet experience or subsumed it under Western rationalities. Thus, before launching into the inquiry into the biopolitical rationality of Stalinism we shall address the scant dossier of the remarks on Soviet biopolitics by the three authors most associated with this problematic: Foucault, Agamben and Esposito. Perhaps the relative silence of these established theoretical perspectives will still be able to teach us something about both biopolitics and Stalinism.

FOUCAULT AND SOVIET 'RACISM'

Due to the centrality of Foucault's work as the inaugural discourse on biopolitics in political philosophy, we shall focus primarily on his treatment of Soviet socialism, which has since then been replicated in numerous studies (see, for example, Hoffmann 2011: 309–13). Since Foucault never addressed Russian or Soviet politics in any detailed manner, the textual corpus we are dealing with is necessarily scant, composed of brief forays in books, digressions in lectures, casual asides in interviews, and so on. The 1975–6 lecture course at the Collège de France called 'Society Must Be Defended' offers the most extensive treatment of the Soviet case in all of Foucault's writings, hence it will be the main focus of our analysis. Yet, while the textual corpus in question is scant, it is in no way incoherent, since, as we shall show, Foucault practised the same move of the subsumption of the Soviet experience under Western rationalities of government in a variety of contexts during the 1970s: from aesthetics to labour relations, from psychiatry to concentration camps.

Although Foucault's work on biopolitics only addresses issues of Stalinism and Soviet politics peripherally, it was clearly influenced by the events related to them. As Jan Plamper (2002) argued in a definitive analysis of the theme of the Gulag in Foucault's work, Foucault's genealogical turn towards the questions of power and government in the early and mid-1970s unfolded in the political context dominated by the publication of Solzhenitsyn's *The Gulag Archipelago* in French in 1974 (see also Kharkhordin 2001). It was this publication that accelerated the drift of French intellectuals, including Foucault, away from Marxism, and contributed to the rise of the 'anti-totalitarian' new philosophers (Bernard-Henri Lévy, André Glucksmann et al.), whom Foucault briefly supported. Moreover, the revelations about the Gulag in Solzhenitsyn's work led to the increased attention in France to the dissident movement in the USSR and Eastern Europe, which Foucault actively supported throughout the late 1970s and early 1980s and whose struggle for freedom of speech arguably influenced his turn toward the problematic of *parrhesia* in the lectures of the 1980s (Foucault 2011; see Szakolczai 1998: 251–5; Forti 2015: 269–72).

Nonetheless, despite its significance in the French intellectual-political context at the time, the Soviet case does not figure prominently in Foucault's analysis of biopolitics. The simplest explanation for this absence would be Foucault's proverbial Eurocentrism, discussed by numerous critics since the famous comment by Edward Said (1988: 9–10): 'his Eurocentrism was almost total, as if history itself took place only among a group of French and German thinkers'. And yet, such an explanation would be far too simple, since Foucault actually *did* discuss the Soviet Union in quite a number of articles, lectures and interviews of the 1970s. These texts suggest that the reason why Foucault did not analyse Soviet socialism as a specific case of biopolitics or governmentality was not his lack of interest in non-European history but rather his conviction that there was little about the Soviet case that was specific, idiosyncratic or unique. For Foucault, Soviet socialism was rather characterised by a puzzling persistence of the governmental technologies invented in late eighteenth- and nineteenth-century Europe. Whereas on the macro-level of state ideology and socioeconomic system the USSR obviously renounced Western capitalism, on the micro-level of disciplinary and biopolitical practices it continued to emulate its techniques. As early as 1971, Foucault argued that the Soviet Union

> adopted almost entirely the bourgeois value system. One gets the impression that communism in its traditional form suffers from a birth trauma: you would think that it wants to recapture for itself the world at the time it was born, the world of a triumphant bourgeoisie; communist aesthetics is realism in the style of the nineteenth century: Swan Lake, painting which tells a story, the social novel. Most of the bourgeois values are accepted and maintained by the Communist Party (in art, the family, sexuality, and daily life in general). (Foucault in Simon 1971: 196)

This proximity of Soviet socialism to the bourgeois 'value system' evidently serves as proof of Foucault's more fundamental theoretical thesis, established during the same period, that is regarding the irreducibility of power relations to the institution of state, their dissemination through a myriad of 'capillary' structures that need not coalesce around the state to have determinate political effects.

> In Soviet society one has the example of a State apparatus which has changed hands, yet leaves social hierarchies, family life, sexuality and the body more or less as they were in capitalist society. Do you imagine the mechanisms of power that operate between technicians, foremen and workers are that much different here and in the Soviet Union? (Foucault 1980b: 72–3)

In Foucault's view, despite the evident break with capitalist Europe in socioeconomic terms, the Soviet techniques of government were borrowed directly from its ideological antagonist, the only autochthonous addition being that of 'party discipline', whose genealogy has indeed been traced to the practices of Orthodox Christian communities (see Kharkhordin 1999).

> [It] is no doubt true that the Soviets, while having modified the regime of ownership and the state's role in the control of production, for the rest have simply transferred the techniques of administration and power implemented in capitalist Europe of the 19th century. The types of morality, forms of aesthetics, disciplinary methods, everything that was effectively working in bourgeois society already around 1850 has moved *en bloc* into the Soviet regime. Just as the Soviets have used Taylorism and other methods of management experimented with in the West, they have adopted our disciplinary techniques, adding to our arsenal another arm – party discipline. (Foucault 1994a: 64)

From this perspective, even the phenomenon of the Gulag, the paradigmatic site of Soviet biopolitics, appears as merely one more in the arsenal of governmental techniques borrowed by the Soviet regime from its ideological adversaries (see Engelstein 1993). Indeed, so strong is the affinity that Solzhenitsyn's metaphor of 'archipelago', applied to the network of Soviet labour camps, was transferred by Foucault (back) to the French context as a key concept in *Discipline and Punish* (Foucault 1977: 301; see also Foucault 1980b: 68). Foucault famously accounted for the birth of the Gulag with the help of the anecdote about the French criminologist Leveille advising the Russian government in 1892 to confine mental patients in Siberia.

> [Good] old Leveille had defined the Gulag. Deportation to Siberia already existed but I believe it must have functioned quite simply as exile for political prisoners. The idea that there could be set up there

a politico-medical – politico-penal-medical, or medico-politico-penal – confinement, with an economic function, which would allow the exploitation of the wealth of a still virgin country, that, I think, was a new idea. (Foucault 1988a: 181–2; see Plamper 2002: 269–70 for a critique)

In this manner, the Gulag is inserted into the Western genealogy of government as the 'intensification' of its logic and the grand opposition between liberal democracy and totalitarianism is rendered inoperative.

> After all, the organization of great parties, the development of political apparatuses, and the existence of the techniques of repression such as the camps – all that is quite clearly the heritage of liberal Western societies, and all Stalinism and fascism had to do was to stoop down and pick it up. (Foucault 1994b: 535; see also Foucault 1982: 209)

The Soviet experience is governmentally identical to the West despite being ideologically distinct from it and, given Foucault's interest in governmentality and a certain disdain for ideology, it is hardly surprising that the identity ended up more important than the difference.

Let us now turn to Foucault's more specific account of socialism from a biopolitical perspective. The two texts, in which the theme of biopolitics is discussed most extensively, are the 1975–6 lecture course 'Society Must Be Defended' (2003) and the first volume of *History of Sexuality* (1990), published in 1976. In the subsequent lectures at the Collège de France (1977–8, 1978–9) the concept of biopolitics became rather less accentuated. In *Security, Territory and Population* (2007) Foucault abandoned the perspective of the modern shift from sovereign power to biopower in favour of a more extended genealogy of government from early Christianity through the Reformation to the seventeenth-century doctrine of the *raison d'état* and eighteenth-century 'police science'. In *The Birth of Biopolitics* (2008) the term reappeared in the title, but hardly anywhere else, as Foucault concentrated on the analysis of liberal government as the 'basis on which something like biopolitics could be formed' (ibid.: 21), while repeatedly apologising for deferring the discussion of biopolitics itself, which never actually came, since the concept disappeared entirely from Foucault's writings after these lectures (ibid.: 78, 185). 'One would be incredibly hard-pressed to find in *The Birth of Biopolitics* anything remotely akin to a sustained analysis of biopolitics' (Hoffmann 2014: 57). Thus, the final chapter of the first volume of *History of Sexuality* and 'Society Must Be Defended' remain the texts, where the problematic of biopolitics is treated most elaborately, and in both of them it is explicitly discussed in terms of *racism*.

In *History of Sexuality I* Foucault uses the concept of racism to describe the Nazi regime as an articulation of the sovereign 'symbolics of blood' and the 'analytics of sexuality' associated with the rise of biopower (Foucault 1990a: 149–50). Foucault rejects any approach to Nazism as an abominable exception to the Western political tradition and instead treats it as a 'demonic' synthesis of sovereign and biopolitical techniques of government already operative in Western societies (Foucault 1988c: 71). The biopolitical logic of racism not only permits sovereign violence to survive in the climate hostile to it, but fortifies this violence by investing it with a wholly new function, no longer negative and repressive but rather oriented toward the preservation and improvement of the life of some races by annihilating the lives of the others, which pose a threat to it.

> [Racism] is primarily a way of introducing a break into the domain of life that is under power's control: the break between what must live and what must die. Its role is to allow the establishment of a positive relation of this type: 'the very fact that you let more die will allow you to live more'. The enemies who have to be done away with are not adversaries in the political sense of the term; they are threats, either external or internal, to the population and for the population. In a normalizing society, race or racism is the precondition that makes killing acceptable. Once the state functions in the biopower mode, racism alone can justify the murderous function of the state. (Foucault 2003: 255–6)

It is no longer a matter of what Foucault calls 'traditional racism' (ibid.: 258) that consists in mere animosity between different groups that plays no positive function in the ordering of a society. Nor is biopolitical racism merely a façade that conceals the immanent social antagonism by displacing it onto the enemy figure defined in racial terms – a quasi-Marxist account of racism that Foucault finds superficial. Instead, it is a matter of the transformation in the technology of power that is more fundamental than any ideological shift: racism is what permits the state to exercise its sovereignty by enfolding it in the biopolitical context, in which killing is only legitimate when it serves to enhance the survival and health of one's own race. Thus, the indistinction between the biopolitical preoccupation with fostering life and the thanatopolitical drive for annihilation that we observe in Nazism stops being paradoxical and is graspable as an expression of the logic of racism, according to which the life of any race is fostered by its purification from all otherness, which 'implies both the systematic genocide of others and the risk of exposing oneself to a total sacrifice' (Foucault 1990a: 149–50).

Yet, while this account of racism is quite plausible in the case of Nazism, can it be used for understanding Soviet socialism? In the final lectures of 'Society Must Be Defended', Foucault goes beyond his above-discussed empirical claims about the reliance of Soviet governmentality on the techniques developed during the rise of biopower in eighteenth- and nineteenth-century Europe. Socialism is now also racist in the much more fundamental sense.

> Socialism was a racism from the outset, even in the nineteenth century. No matter whether it was Fourier at the beginning of the century or the anarchists at the end of it, you will always find a racist component in socialism. (Foucault 2003: 261).

This is the case for two reasons. First, socialism has 'made no critique of the theme of biopower' and instead has taken over 'wholesale' the fundamental idea of modern biopolitics 'that the essential function of society or the State is to take control of life, to manage it, to compensate for its aleatory nature, to explore and reduce biological accidents and possibilities' (ibid.: 261). This means that as soon as a socialist state comes into being, it is a state 'which must exercise the right to kill or the right to eliminate, or the right to disqualify', [hence] 'racism is fully operational in the way socialist states (of the Soviet Union type) deal with the mentally ill, criminals, political adversaries, and so on' (ibid.: 262). Second, socialism is racist due to its emphasis on class struggle and the physical confrontation with the enemy, racism being the

> only way in which socialist thought, which is after all very much bound up with the themes of biopower, can rationalise the murder of its enemies. When it is simply a matter of eliminating an adversary in economic terms, or of taking away his privileges, there is no need for racism. Once it is a matter of coming to terms with the thought of a one-on-one encounter with the adversary, and with the need to fight him physically, to risk one's own life and to try to kill him, there is a need for racism. (Ibid.: 262)

While in the late nineteenth-century French context racism primarily characterised non-Marxist versions of socialism (Blanquism, anarchism, and so on) rather than strictly Marxist ones (both reformist and revolutionary), in the twentieth century it pertains primarily to the Soviet type of socialism, including the Stalinist and post-Stalinist USSR.

Thus, in Foucault's argument, the only biopolitical specificity that Soviet socialism possesses consists precisely in the *absence* of any specificity, in the paradoxical and deplorable fact that for all its ideological heterogeneity to the capitalist West it continued to rely on the biopolitical rationalities and techniques developed in it. This theme of the deficiency of socialism in its dependence on an alien logic of governmentality persists in Foucault's 1978–9 course *The Birth of Biopolitics*, notwithstanding the disappearance of every reference to racism in this course and the concurrent downgrading of the problematic of biopolitics in favour of the analysis of liberalism. In this course Foucault reiterates his by now familiar claim that there is no 'autonomous governmentality of socialism' (Foucault 2008: 93). Socialism might have a theory of the state, an economic rationality, a historical rationality, but when it comes to the rationality of government it remains reliant on those developed either in the liberal Europe or, perhaps even more so, on the pre-liberal rationalities of the police state (ibid.: 93; see also Foucault 2007: 311–31).

> [Socialism] can only be implemented connected up to diverse types of governmentality. It has been connected up to liberal governmentality, and then socialism and its forms of rationality function as counter-weights, as a corrective and a palliative to internal dangers. We have seen it function within governmentalities that would no doubt fall more under what we called the police state, a hyper-administrative state in which there is a fusion, a continuity, the constitution of a sort of massive bloc between governmentality and administration. Maybe there are still other governmentalities that socialism is connected up to; it remains to be seen. But in any case, I do not think that for the moment there is an autonomous governmentality of socialism. (Ibid.: 93)

Since the lectures do not pursue the theme of socialism any further, we are left with a diagnosis that is similar to the one made in the context of racism, yet, now that racism is out of the picture, somewhat more non-committal about what governmentalities socialism is actually 'connected up to'. Yet, what remains constant in Foucault's account is the subsumption of Soviet socialism under the European experience, the insistence on the 'unhappy symbiosis' of socialism with its ideological antagonists on the biopolitical terrain (ibid.: 94).

IS THERE A REVOLUTIONARY BIOPOLITICS?

We shall return to Foucault's argument about the racist character of socialism in the following chapters when we discuss the construction of enemies in Stalinist biopolitics. Yet, before challenging Foucault's account empirically, it would be helpful to point out that Foucault's own genealogy of racism in 'Society Must Be Defended' left open an alternative possibility of conceiving socialist biopolitics as an autonomous rationality. Let us briefly revisit this genealogy to locate this possibility that Foucault himself did not pursue.

In 'Society Must Be Defended' Foucault reconstitutes what he calls a 'historico-political discourse' that has functioned since the seventeenth century as an alternative to the more familiar discourses of political philosophy, focused on the problem of sovereignty, which Foucault was famously targeting at that stage in his work. In contrast to the abstract, ahistorical and impartial discourse of political philosophy, epitomised by Hobbes, this alternative discourse, whose emergence Foucault traces in seventeenth-century England (Edward Coke, John Lillburne) and early eighteenth-century France (Henri de Boullainvilliers), is historical through and through, arising within a particular struggle and taking up a position in it (Foucault 2003: 268–71). It is a 'counter-history', a history that does not celebrate, memorialise and reinforce sovereign power but rather seeks to undermine it by retelling the story of sovereignty as the narrative of submission and subjugation, told from below by those lacking in sovereign splendour and absent from the official history (ibid.: 66–76). Rather than represent society as a unity held together by the sovereign, this discourse casts society as always already *binary*, structured in terms of the antagonism between those in power and those lacking it, '[them] and us, the unjust and the just, the masters and those who must obey them, the rich and the poor, those who invade lands and those who tremble before them, the despots and the groaning people' (ibid.: 74).

This antagonism was framed in terms of the struggle of two so-called 'races' within a society. At this stage the concept of 'race' was not pinned to any 'stable biological meaning' (ibid.: 77) but rather designated a 'historico-political divide' between two groups in a society that did not share the same language or religion and only formed a united polity as a result of the conquest or subjugation of one by the other.

> Two races exist when there are two groups, which, although they coexist, have not become mixed because of the differences, dissymmetries and barriers created by privileges, customs and rights, the distribution of wealth, or the way in which power is exercised. (Ibid.: 77)

In contrast to the fictitious 'war of all against all' posited by Hobbes as the precondition for the institution of sovereign power, the counter-historical discourse posited real instances of war, such as the Norman conquest, as the actual foundation of state power and the real conflict between the conquerors and the conquered (for example the Normans and the Saxons in England, the Germanic aristocracy and the Gallo-Roman bourgeoisie in France) as the true substance of politics and history. We are evidently a long way from the modern notion of racism – if anything, the function of the counter-historical discourse in its original formulation is closer to what we would today call a 'revolutionary' discourse of emancipation.

Indeed, in Foucault's own genealogy, this counter-historical discourse served as one of the precursors of the revolutionary discourse in eighteenth-century France and beyond.

> What could the revolutionary project and the revolutionary idea possibly mean without this preliminary interpretation of the dissymmetries, the disequilibriums, the injustice and the violence that function despite the order of laws, beneath the order of laws, and through and because of the order of laws? Where would the revolutionary project, the revolutionary idea, or revolutionary practice be without the will to rekindle the real war that once went on and which is still going on? What would the revolutionary project and revolutionary discourse mean if the goal were not a certain, a final, inversion of relations of power and a decisive displacement within the exercise of power? (Ibid.: 78–9)

During the nineteenth century the counter-historical discourse split into two tendencies, the 'properly revolutionary' discourse of class struggle that maintained the historical orientation of the earlier discourse but replaced its 'races' with socioeconomically defined classes, and the 'properly racist' discourse, which replaced the historical approach with the quasi-scientific, biological and evolutionary one, thus recoding the historical war as the struggle of the race for existence. While the discourse of class struggle maintained its predecessor's function of *undermining* the stability of the state form, recovering and reactivating the historical war and the 'binary society' that gave rise to it, the racist, biologico-medical discourse began to serve the contrary function of the *stabilisation* of social order, recasting the binary society as a monistic one, which was threatened by heterogeneous elements that must be eradicated for the life of the race to be secure. As a result of this recasting, the state, which for the early counter-historical discourse was an instrument of the oppression of one race by another, becomes the 'protector of the integrity, the superiority and the purity of the race. The idea of racial purity, with all its monistic, Statist and biological implications: that is what replaces the idea of race struggle' (ibid.: 81). In this manner, counter-history ends up reclaimed by the traditional history of sovereignty and the *proto*-revolutionary discourse is converted into the *anti*-revolutionary discourse of state racism.

> Racism is, quite literally, revolutionary discourse in an inverted form. Whereas the discourse of races, of the struggle between races, was a weapon to be used against the historico-political discourse of Roman sovereignty, the discourse of race (in the singular) was a way of turning that weapon against those who had forged it, of using it to preserve the sovereignty of the State, a sovereignty whose lustre and vigour were no

longer guaranteed by magico-juridical rituals but by medico-normalizing techniques. Thanks to the shift from law to norm, from races in the plural to race in the singular, from the emancipatory project to a concern with purity, sovereignty was able to invest or take over the discourse of race struggle and reutilise it for its own strategy. State sovereignty thus becomes the imperative to protect the race. It becomes both an alternative to and a way of blocking the call for revolution that derived from the old discourse of struggles, interpretations, demands and promises. (Ibid.: 82)

Thus, the original discourse of the struggle of the races ends up split into the revolutionary discourse of struggle (without races) and the 'neo-Roman' counter-revolutionary discourse of the protection of the race. This split clearly suggests the possibility of two distinct forms of biopolitics correlative with these two strands: the biopolitics of class struggle (socialism) and the biopolitics of racism (Nazism). Instead, Foucault immediately effaces this difference by subsuming the former under the latter as its metaphorical version. While the Nazi discourse reinserts the biological logic of state racism into the mythical and archaic context of the war of the races, in the Soviet discourse the insertion of the theme of class struggle into the biopolitical context allegedly produces a quasi-scientific, medico-psychiatric interpretation of racism. What was at first constructed as an *alternative* to racism, whereby history was grasped as the conflict of classes without a racial dimension to it, somehow becomes a *form* of racism, apparently all the more insidious because there was no actual reference to race in it.

[Soviet racism] consists in reworking the revolutionary discourse of social struggles – the very discourse that derived so many of its elements from the old discourse of the race struggle – and articulating it with the management and the policing that ensure the hygiene of an orderly society. And the hoarse songs of the races that clashed in battles over the lies of laws and kings, and which were after all the earliest form of revolutionary discourse, become the administrative prose of a State that defends itself in the name of social heritage that has to be kept pure. (Ibid.: 83)

The question that has not been but can be raised within the Foucauldian genealogical framework is whether biopower must exclusively latch onto the state racism, which is only one descendant of the counter-historical discourse of race struggle, or whether it may also be exercised on the basis of the second descendant, that is the discourse of class struggle. After all, if racism was the 'inversion' of revolutionary discourse, what is the biopolitical content of that which it inverted? While, as we have seen, Foucault found the absence of an autonomous governmentality and biopolitics in socialism its key problem, explaining its internal contradictions and paroxysmal violence, this perception may well be the effect of a prior closure of biopolitics within the interpretive horizon of racism. Having excluded the possibility of a revolutionary biopolitics grounded in class struggle, one can either conclude that socialism lacks a biopolitical rationality as such or that it shares the rationality of racism with its ideological antagonists. Both conclusions are unhelpful for grasping the Soviet project and the governmental violence that accompanied it, the former effacing the specificity of this violence, irreducible to the traditional sovereign power of death, and the latter putting the blame for it on the rationality that, as we shall see below, was quite peripheral to this project.

AGAMBEN: STALINISM AND THE INTEGRATED SPECTACLE

The elision of the question of the biopolitics of socialism continues in the arguably most influential post-Foucauldian theory of biopolitics, developed in Giorgio Agamben's *Homo Sacer* series. The absence of any engagement with socialism in Agamben's work is much easier to understand than in Foucault's case: while Foucault posited the emergence of biopolitical rationalities of government as a historical event marking the 'threshold of modernity', Agamben has controversially argued that biopolitics is, first, at least as old as sovereign power and, second, coextensive with rather than opposed to it.

> The inclusion of bare life in the political realm constitutes the original – if concealed – nucleus of sovereign power. *It can even be said that the production of a biopolitical body is the original activity of sovereign power.* In this sense, biopolitics is at least as old as sovereign power. (Agamben 1998: 6; original emphasis).

While Foucault was primarily interested in the positive difference of modern rationalities of government from sovereign modes of rule, what interests Agamben in the problematic of biopolitics is the overall constellation whereby life is captured in political rationalities, the constellation that has evidently been there long before Western liberalism, the appearance of statistics, the invention of the population and other categories that were relevant for Foucault's historical account. In Agamben's argument, the relation between unqualified life (*zoe*) and political life (*bios*) strictly parallels the relation between natural sound (*phone*) and articulated language (*logos*): the former functions as the negative foundation of the latter, whose exclusion, domination or subjugation permits the constitution of a determinate form of language or social order: 'The living being has *logos* by taking away and conserving its own voice in it, even as it dwells in the polis by letting its own bare life be excluded, as an exception, within it' (Agamben 1998: 8). Biopolitics is then *ipso facto* as old as human language. The critics that repeatedly accuse Agamben of being 'ahistorical' are therefore ultimately incorrect: Agamben clearly traces biopolitics back to a historical event, albeit the one that took place long before European modernity or, for that matter, the Greek polis, but could be dated back to forty millennia ago (Agamben 2007a: 9), that is the emergence of the human being as a speaking being.

Evidently, if one adopts this perspective, then the differences between liberalism and socialism (or, for that matter, liberalism and Nazism) would appear to be so minor as to become almost invisible. And yet, Agamben's argument does not assert the utter immutability of the biopolitical logic throughout the history of political orders. While biopolitics is indeed as old as human history, something important still happens with the advent of modernity, which is the horizon within which both Nazi and Soviet totalitarianisms become possible. For Agamben modernity is a condition of *nihilism*, in which the devaluation of all positive forms of life (*bios*) leaves disconcealed the foundational status of *zoe* as the negative foundation of the political order and the sole possible object of political power. Given the bankruptcy of all positive forms of life, 'the only task that still seems to retain some seriousness is the assumption of the burden of biological life, that is, of the very animality of man' (Agamben 2004: 76–7). In modern nihilism *bios* and *zoe* are no longer separated as the positive (qualified) and the negative (unqualified) senses of life but are rendered *indistinct* in the manifestation of the negativity at the heart of every positivity.

> What characterises modern politics is not so much the inclusion of *zoe* in the *polis*, which is, in itself, absolutely ancient – nor simply the fact that life as such becomes a principal object of the projections and calculations of state power. Instead, the decisive fact is that the realm of bare life – which is originally situated at the margins of the political order – gradually begins to coincide with the political realm and exclusion and inclusion, outside and inside, *bios* and *zoe*, right and fact, enter into a zone of irreducible indistinction. (Agamben 1998: 9)

It is from this perspective that we should approach Agamben's controversial remarks about the 'inner solidarity of democracy and totalitarianism' in *Homo Sacer* (1998: 10). Totalitarianism exemplifies the most extreme manifestation of the biopolitical logic, whereby bare life as the object of sovereign power is no longer concealed under the veneer of the positive forms of good life but is revealed as such. 'Only because politics in our age has been entirely transformed into biopolitics was it possible for politics to be constituted as totalitarian politics to a degree hitherto unknown' (Agamben 1998: 120). Totalitarianism is therefore not a relapse of modern politics into a pre-modern or archaic violence but rather the most thoroughgoing expression of the nihilistic tendency at the heart of modernity itself.

> The totalitarianism of our century has its ground in this dynamic identity of life and politics, without which it remains incomprehensible. If Nazism still appears to us as an enigma, and if its affinity with Stalinism is still unexplained, this is because we have failed to situate the totalitarian phenomenon in its entirety in the horizon of biopolitics (Agamben 1998: 148).

Yet, what happens when totalitarianism is indeed situated in the biopolitical horizon? Agamben's response to this question has been rather ambivalent, oscillating between the maintenance of the difference between democracy and totalitarianism as distinct modes of biopolitics and the erasure of this difference in the argument for their 'indistinction'.

> [The] contiguity between mass democracy and totalitarian states does not have the form of a sudden transformation; before impetuously coming to light in our century, the river of biopolitics that gave *homo sacer* his life runs its course in a hidden but continuous fashion. It is almost as if, starting from a certain point, every decisive political event were double-sided: the spaces, the liberties and the rights won by individuals in their conflicts with central powers always simultaneously prepared a tacit but increasing inscription of individuals' lives within the state order. One and the same affirmation of bare life leads, in bourgeois democracy, to a primacy of the private over the public and of individual liberties over collective obligations and yet becomes in totalitarian states, the decisive political criterion and the exemplary realm of sovereign decisions. And only because biological life and its needs had become the politically decisive fact is it possible to understand the otherwise incomprehensible rapidity with which 20th century parliamentary democracies were able to turn into totalitarian states and with which this century's totalitarian states were able to be converted, almost without interruption, into parliamentary democracies. Once their fundamental referent becomes bare life, traditional political distinctions (such as those between Right and Left, liberalism and totalitarianism, private and public) lose their clarity and intelligibility and enter into a zone of indistinction. (Ibid.: 121–2)

On the one hand, democracy and totalitarianism remain distinct and it is possible to separate and presumably oppose the declarations of human

Stalinism in the Theory of Biopolitics

rights to racist policies of exclusion or extermination. In this case, we might speak of the *proximity* of the two on the basis of their shared biopolitical foundation, but not really of their indistinction. The history of modernity is then *double-sided* in the strict sense that it is possible to identify two distinct sides to it, that is the progressive emancipation of bare life and its subjection to governmental rationalities. On the other hand, Agamben leans towards a stronger and more controversial claim that brings democracy and totalitarianism so close together in an 'inner solidarity' (cf. ibid.: 10) that they become indistinct. In *Homo Sacer* this stronger claim is presented in a brief and elliptic manner that calls for interpretation.

> Democracy, at the very moment in which it seemed to have finally triumphed over its adversaries and reached its greatest height, proved itself incapable of saving *zoe*, to whose happiness it had dedicated all its efforts, from unprecedented ruin. Modern democracy's decadence and gradual convergence with totalitarian states in post-democratic spectacular societies, which begins to become evident with Alexis de Tocqueville and finds its final sanction in the analyses of Guy Debord, may well be rooted in this aporia, which marks the beginning of modern democracy and forces it into complicity with its most implacable enemy. (Ibid.: 10)

In this statement, the inner solidarity of democracy and totalitarianism is less a matter of their underlying identity than a result of the *degradation* of democracy. Yet, this degradation is itself rooted in the originary aporia of modern democracy, which, in contrast to classical democracy that was founded on the exclusion of *zoe* from *bios*, 'wants to put the freedom and happiness of men into play in the very place – "bare life" – that marked their subjection' (ibid.: 9–10). Agamben's scandalous invocation of 'inner solidarity' between the two regimes is thus not merely grounded in the familiar historical evidence of the fragility of democratic institutions (that is, it is not a 'historiographical claim') (1998: 10), but arises from his interpretation of both regimes as manifestations of modern nihilism. The key inspiration here is Guy Debord's famous theory of the 'society of the spectacle' (1994), which has been influential for the development of Agamben's thought since the late 1970s. For Debord, both totalitarian and democratic regimes were forms of what he called the spectacle, in which authentic existence is replaced by representation and the commodity-form colonises social life as such. Socialist totalitarianism exemplified a 'concentrated' spectacle, in which the sphere of representation was controlled by the state apparatus, while liberal democracy exemplified a 'diffuse' spectacle, in which this control was disseminated throughout civil society. In his later *Comments on the*

Society of the Spectacle Debord (2011) introduced the third figure of the 'integrated spectacle', a post-Cold War synthesis of democratic and totalitarian forms that combines enhanced state control with the proliferation of 'private' production of representations (see Agamben 2000: 73–89).

This theory is important for understanding Agamben's pessimism about democracy at the very moment of its apparent triumph at the end of the Cold War. What some commentators viewed as the 'end of history', whereby democracy became the 'only game in town', having triumphed over its totalitarian adversaries, was for Agamben the premonition of democracy's own decay.

> The substantial unification of the concentrated spectacle (the Eastern people's democracies) and of the diffused spectacle (the Western democracies) into an integrated spectacle is, by now, trivial evidence. The immovable walls and the iron curtains that divided the two worlds were wiped out in a few days. The Eastern governments allowed the Leninist party to fall so that the integrated spectacle could be completely realised in their countries. In the same way, the West had already renounced a while ago the balance of powers as well as real freedom of thought and communication in the name of the electoral machine of majority vote and of media control over public opinion, both of which had developed within the totalitarian modern states. (Agamben 2000: 81)

If the political history of modernity is approached in terms of the convergence of liberal democracy and totalitarianism in the form of the integrated spectacle of the global police state, then the phenomenon of Stalinism may be retroactively devalued as ultimately little more than a step in this abysmal process. Writing in the early 1990s, when the communist ideal and practice were utterly discredited, Agamben understandably found little of interest in it other than as a transitional stage towards the synthetic version of the spectacle that makes the formerly 'hidden' solidarity between totalitarianism and democracy fully manifest. As a form of totalitarianism, Stalinism both shares with democracy its biopolitical grounding and gradually converges with it as a result of democracy's degeneration under the condition of nihilism.

There is another important reason why Agamben refuses to consider Soviet biopolitics in its own right as distinct from the overall Western political tradition. In *Homo Sacer* Agamben briefly addresses the revolutionary discourse of communism in the context of his analysis of the ontological problematic of potentiality. The ontological distinction between potentiality and actuality is in the political context translated into the difference between *constituent power* (for example, popular sovereignty, revolutionary movements, and so on) and *constituted power* (of the state, law, police, and so on). While the prioritisation of actuality over potentiality would logically entail the complete exhaustion of constituent power in the constituted order that it establishes, the assertion of the ontological primacy of potentiality would presumably lead us to the affirmation of the irreducibility of constituent power. Antonio Negri, Agamben's critical interlocutor since the 1970s, has ventured precisely such an affirmation, separating constituent power as creative and revolutionary power of the multitude from the constituted power of the state or any other structure of authority.

> [Constituting] power is the act of choice, the punctual determination that opens a horizon, the radical enacting of something that did not exist before and whose conditions of existence stipulated that the creative act cannot lose its characteristics in creating. Sovereignty, on the other hand, arises as the establishment – and therefore, as the end – of constituting power, as the consumption of the freedom brought by constituting power. (Negri cited in Agamben 1998: 43)

Negri's argument belongs to the long series of attempts of the radical-democratic tradition to theorise constituent power in the manner that prevents its exhaustion in the constituted order to which it gives rise, the tradition whose twentieth-century paradigms include Trotsky's 'permanent revolution', Mao's 'uninterrupted revolution' and, most recently, Negri's own positive biopolitics of the struggle of the multitude against the Empire (Agamben 1998: 41–2). If socialism and communism could be posited as heterogeneous to the Western ontopolitical tradition, it would be precisely as examples of a political logic that privileges potentiality over actuality. Yet, for Agamben such an assumption of heterogeneity is ultimately illusory.

While Negri wishes to dissociate the potentiality of constituent power from the 'actualising' force of sovereignty, Agamben rather finds the ontological structure of sovereignty precisely in the Aristotelian concept of potentiality, which is always necessarily at the same time a potentiality for something *not to be*. While the conventional reading of sovereignty as supreme law-giving power emphasises the 'positive' dimension of potentiality ('I can'), to be worthy of its name this potentiality must be accompanied by its 'negative' counterpart ('I can *not*'), which refers to the possibility for the sovereign to *suspend* the law in the declaration of the state of exception. It is in this suspended state that potentiality can maintain a real existence without passing completely into actuality and this is precisely how sovereignty exists in the state of exception: 'the sovereign ban, which applies to the exception in no longer applying, corresponds to the structure of potentiality, which maintains itself in relation to actuality precisely through its ability not to be' (ibid.: 46).

It is thus impossible to oppose sovereignty as the actualising force of order to the constituent power of the multitude as creative potentiality. Sovereign power always already possesses all those features of potentiality and creativity that Negri and other thinkers in the radical-democratic and communist traditions try to reserve for the multitude, the people, the revolutionary party, the councils or any other embodiment of constituent power. Agamben's argument sheds light on the problem that has arguably plagued the entire history of revolutionary movements, whose victories, with important variations, largely led to the reproduction of the sovereign and statist logics that these movements initially targeted. Examples of French, Russian and Chinese revolutions are sufficient to observe how sovereign power recuperates the creative potentialities ostensibly advanced against it. In Agamben's interpretation, this repeated failure of radical politics has to do with its commitment to law and sovereignty in the guise of apparent opposition to them in the form of constituent power. 'Politics has suffered a lasting eclipse because it has been contaminated by law, seeing itself, at best, as constituent power (that is, violence that makes law), when it is not reduced to merely the power to negotiate with the law. The only truly political action, however, is that, which severs the nexus between violence and law' (Agamben 2005a: 88). Insofar as Soviet socialism did not sever this nexus, but, if anything, strengthened it in the Stalinist period, it is hardly surprising that it reproduced the fundamental logic of the Western ontopolitical tradition, including the nihilistic biopolitics that is its endpoint. Just as for Foucault, for Agamben socialism ends up a failed alternative to Western biopolitics that, rather than point to a way out of its lethal aporias, provides us with their hyperbolic paradigm.

ESPOSITO: BIOPOLITICS AND THE ECLIPSE OF DEMOCRACY

Roberto Esposito's theory of biopolitics, developed in his *Communitas – Immunitas – Bios* trilogy (2008a, 2010, 2011) and other works, follows Agamben in interpreting biopolitics in ontological terms, tracing its thanatopolitical turn to the immunitary logic of the protection of life by negative means. While Esposito's main works barely mention the socialist case and instead focus on Nazism as the extreme point of the immunitary tendency in the Western tradition, in his article 'Totalitarianism or Biopolitics?' (2008b) Esposito addresses socialism at length in his comparison of totalitarianism and biopolitics as two hermeneutic paradigms for understanding twentieth-century politics. He reads theories of totalitarianism, from Hannah Arendt to Jacob Talmon and François Furet, as problematic attempts to identify the origins of the catastrophes of the twentieth century. Arendt (1973) finds these origins in the decline of the Greek polis and the ensuing depoliticisation throughout the history of Western civilisation, which took a particularly intense and lethal form with the late nineteenth-century crisis of the nation-state, the emergence of imperialism and the appearance of racism as a political force. In contrast, Talmon (1970) (as well as, in different ways, Furet (1981) and Lefort (1986, 2007)) finds the origins of totalitarianism in the egalitarian excesses of democracy that give rise to formerly unseen forms of despotism (Esposito 2008b: 636–8). According to Esposito, both of these theories fail to provide a coherent account of a single origin (or set thereof) of the two distinct phenomena of Nazism and Stalinism that they subsume under the notion of totalitarianism.

Arendt's analysis traces the genealogy of Nazism in nineteenth-century European anti-Semitism, early twentieth-century imperialism and colonial administration and the post-World War I decline of the nation-state. Yet, while it is certainly plausible in the case of Nazism and other European fascisms, this account is difficult to apply to the Soviet case, since anti-Semitism and imperialism did not play the same role in revolutionary and post-revolutionary Russia as they did in Central Europe. Moreover, Esposito plausibly wonders

> how [we] are to hold together in a single categorical horizon a hypernaturalistic conception such as that of Nazism with the historicist paroxysm of communism. From a philosophical point of view, what does a theory of absolute equality—which is what communism at least in its principles purports to be—have to do with a theory and indeed a practice of absolute difference such as found in Nazism? (Ibid.: 637)

While in the famous concluding chapter of *Origins of Totalitarianism*, entitled 'Ideology and Terror' (1973: 460–79), Arendt does indeed attempt to hold the two together by subsuming racist naturalism and class historicism under her notion of the totalitarian ideology, the discussion of the origins of totalitarianism in the preceding parts of the book only seems to explain Nazi hypernaturalism and not Bolshevik historicism. Thus, Arendt's account of the origins of totalitarianism works much better as a genealogy of Nazism alone and, as Domenico Losurdo argued, the elements of this genealogy (such as racism, eugenics, imperialism, concentration camps, and so on) have a lot more in common with British and American liberalism than with Soviet Russia (Losurdo 2004: 38–41).

On the other hand, the theories that find the origins of totalitarianism in the alleged egalitarian excess of democracy that leads it to self-destruction have trouble subsuming under this scheme the experience of Nazism, which was hardly ever marked by the affirmation of egalitarianism.

> The totalitarian regime doesn't arise out of a defect but rather from an excess, a surplus, of democracy, from a democracy so radical, so extreme and absolute, and so full of egalitarianism as to break down its own formal limits and so to collapse on itself, turning into its opposite. (Esposito 2008b: 638)

Yet, if it is the egalitarian legacy of the French Revolution that somehow generates totalitarianism as an immanent perversion of democracy, then Nazism would clearly not belong to this genealogy and hence should not be counted as 'totalitarian'. Moreover, by positing totalitarianism as somehow immanent to democracy as its dream (equality) turning into its nightmare (the camp) (Esposito 2008b: 638), these authors unwittingly undermine the very opposition between democracy and totalitarianism that permitted grouping Nazism and communism together in the first place. If 'communism is both democracy's dream and its nightmare' (ibid.: 638), then its relation to the latter is much more complex than a frontal antagonism that characterises the relation of Nazism to democracy (cf. Roberts 2006: 17–23).

Dismissing both versions of the theory of totalitarianism as incoherent, Esposito then turns to biopolitics. Whereas the former approach remained tied to a unified interpretation of the history of modernity (that is, as the grand conflict between democracy and totalitarianism), the theory of biopolitics traces a radical disruption within history that takes place when life as such 'bursts into politics, thereby breaking apart its presumed autonomy, shifting discourse onto a terrain that is irreducible to traditional terms like democracy, power and ideology' (ibid.: 639). This disruption permits Esposito to rigorously distinguish Nazism from communism.

> [Nazism] isn't an ideology because it belongs to a dimension that is different from and subordinate to that of ideas, from which Marxist communism was born. Nazism isn't a markedly different species within the same genus, because it is situated outside Western tradition (a tradition that also includes the philosophy of communism among its offspring). Nazism isn't a political philosophy but a political biology, a politics of life and politics over life transformed into its opposite and for that very reason productive of death. (Ibid.: 640).

Stalinism in the Theory of Biopolitics

While the antagonism between liberalism and socialism pertains to and unfolds in the realm of ideas that *mediate* the access of power to life as such, Nazism is 'immediately biological' and it is this singularity of Nazism that renders the category of totalitarianism inoperative (ibid.: 641). The difference between Nazism and communism is not merely a difference between two ideologies but a difference between an ideology and a biology, that is, between things so incommensurable that they cannot be subsumed under a single concept.

Moreover, the attention to the biopolitical character of liberalism entails that the category of 'liberal democracy', conventionally used as the *antithesis* of totalitarianism, also becomes inoperative, insofar as the universalist and egalitarian connotations of democracy clearly conflict with the particularistic and naturalistic logic of liberal biopolitics.

> [When] the living or dying body becomes the symbolic and material epicentre of the dynamics of politics as well as its conflicts, we move into a dimension that lies not simply after or beyond democracy but resolutely outside it. Democracy is always directed to a totality of equal subjects, given the fact that they are separated from their own bodies and therefore understood as pure logical atoms endowed with rational will. This is why the onset of life into *dispositifs* of power marks the eclipse of democracy. (Ibid.: 643–4)

Thus, Esposito supplants the very opposition between democracy and totalitarianism by the dualism of democracy (which now includes communism as the 'paroxysmal fulfilment' (ibid.: 642) of the egalitarian promise) and biopolitics, which in turn is split between its *statist* form in Nazism and the *individualist* form in liberalism. The decisive political question of our time is, then, not the struggle between liberal democracy and left or right totalitarianism but between the egalitarian aspirations of democracy that constructs its subjects as 'disembodied subjectivities' and the biopolitical rationality of government that restores the 'bodily dimension' as at once 'subject and object' of politics (ibid.: 643).

Yet, even if we grant that the antagonism between biopolitics and democracy is indeed the definitive conflict of late modernity, where does Stalinism fit in this dualism? Surely it cannot be placed on the side of democracy, particularly in Esposito's own definition of it, given the abundance of historical evidence of the downgrading of 'disembodied subjectivity', be it legal or moral, in Soviet politics and the exercise of power directly and immediately on the 'bodily dimension', be it in military parades, shock labour campaigns, the Gulag camps or the NKVD torture chambers. Yet, it is also impossible to place it on the side of biopolitics, as Esposito defines it, since it is heterogeneous both to the individualist biopolitics of liberalism (due to its suppression of individualism) and the statist biopolitics of Nazism (due to its heterogeneity to the latter's racism and biologism). While in the dualism of democracy and totalitarianism Stalinism was illegitimately lumped together with Nazism, in the new dualism of democracy and biopolitics we at best end up repeating this gesture, whereby Stalinism becomes a metaphorical version of Nazi racism, and at worst lose sight of Stalinism altogether, since it becomes unsubsumable under either of the two categories. Just as the Cold War opposition of democracy and totalitarianism lacked logical coherence by permanently producing a remainder that could not be incorporated into it, the new dualism of democracy and biopolitics leaves a remainder of its own, a regime that is apparently neither democratic nor biopolitical.

Thus, the later theories of biopolitics follow Foucault's original elision of the question of socialist biopolitics. Socialism is always already subsumed, either together with Nazism as the totalitarian version of racist biopolitical rationality, or together with Western biopolitics as such as the hyperbolic paradigm of its degradation, or simply disappears as somehow not properly biopolitical at all.

BIOPOLITICS AND IDEOLOGY: GIVING FORM TO LIFE

If socialism performs a vanishing act in the existing theories of biopolitics, how may the biopolitics of Stalinism be grasped at all? An alternative solution would be to set theory aside and begin with the available empirical evidence, focusing, for example, on the regulation of life in the Gulag camps, the 1930s campaigns for hygiene or literacy, reforms and counter-reforms in family legislation, the militarisation of physical culture and sports, the regulation of abortion and the suppression of homosexuality, and so on. Since the early 1990s there have appeared numerous studies in Soviet history that focus on these and other practices from a variety of perspectives, not necessarily explicitly biopolitical in the Foucauldian or Agambenian sense (Hoffmann 2003, 2011; Hoffmann and Timm 2009; Starks 2009; Fitzpatrick 2002; Furst 2006). In this manner, the question of Soviet biopolitics is recast as a matter of concrete empirical investigation of the practices of population management in various domains. It should then be possible to avoid the problematic status of Stalinism in the theoretical discourse on biopolitics by finding a secure empirical basis in the actual governmental practices of the period.

Nonetheless, while most of the studies in this vein are certainly exemplary and helpful in enhancing our understanding of the Stalinist period, this 'empiricist' solution does not quite succeed in making Stalinist biopolitics any more intelligible, if only because it retains, explicitly or tacitly, the theoretical commitments whose problematic status we have just addressed. Starting with the presupposition of the radical difference between Soviet and Western societies in ideological terms, these accounts demonstrate that *despite* these differences the Soviet regime largely relied on the *same* rationalities and techniques of biopolitical regulation of populations and individuals as its Western antagonists. In the post-Soviet wave of the studies of Stalinism this approach, which has received the name of 'modernity school', was advanced against both 'totalitarian' and 'revisionist' theories in order to shift attention away from ideology on the one hand and political culture on the other, and focus instead on the governmental rationalities at work in the socialist project (Kotkin 1995, 2001; Hoffmann 2003, 2011; Holquist 2002; Hellbeck 2006). It interprets Stalinism as the period of the abandonment of the utopian experimentation with socialist forms of life in the early 1920s in favour of the top-down project of the construction of socialism in disciplinary and biopolitical practices. While the content of the experimental utopias of the 1920s certainly diverged from the mainstream of Western politics (but not its influential leftist subcultures!) (see Stites 1989), these new governmental practices were rather more resonant with the biopolitical tendencies in the West, precisely insofar as they often lacked any determinate ideological orientation but rather took the form of a generic 'modernising' or 'civilising' project.

> [Many] features of Stalinist culture reflected the ambitions of 19th and 20th century political leaders and social reformers to manage and mobilise their populations in ways unique to the modern era. In fact, the very notion of reshaping societies was a defining feature of European modernity. By the 19th century there arose in countries throughout Europe a new ethos of social intervention, by which state officials and nongovernmental professionals sought to reshape their societies in accordance with scientific and aesthetic norms. (Hoffmann 2003: 7)

> The Soviet Union was unavoidably involved in processes not specific to Russia, from the spread of mass production and mass culture to the advent of mass politics, and even of mass consumption, in the decades after 1890. World War I – during which the Russian revolutions took place – vastly deepened and broadened these trends among all the combatants. In Russia, the autocracy and empire gave way to a far more vigorous dictatorship and to a quasi-federal Union committed to a vague, ambitious, war-conditioned vision of anti-liberal modernity. Over the

next two decades, that vision acquired institutional forms which had some important resemblances to, and many important differences from, both liberal projects, such as the United States, Great Britain, and France, and other forms of anti-liberal modernity, such as Nazi Germany, fascist Italy, and imperial Japan. (Kotkin 2001: 113)

While the early Bolshevik utopianism posited the 'new man' in terms of the wholesale transcendence of the old forms of life, be it the family, religion or egotistic individualism, the Stalinist regime was rather more prosaic in producing 'new' men and women through literacy and hygiene campaigns, the regulation of sexual behaviour and child-rearing, vaccination and dental care (see Hoffmann 2003: 57–116). Insofar as studies of Soviet biopolitics focus on these governmental technologies, they are almost without exception led to conclude, as Foucault did in the 1970s, that Soviet biopolitics is not qualitatively different but may in fact be subsumed under Western biopolitics as a particular case of the more general paradigm of modern state interventionism alongside such other late-modernising countries as Turkey, Iran or Mexico (see Scott 1998: 87–101; Hoffmann 2003: 10; Kotkin 2001: 112–13).[1] Such familiar phenomena of the Stalinist USSR as economic planning, social welfare campaigns, disciplinary interventions or social surveillance are shown not merely *not* to be unique to the Soviet Union but also to have originated in the very capitalist societies that the Soviet model was apparently an alternative to. Of course, there were also numerous differences between the ways in which this state-led modernising project was undertaken, but these are easily explained with reference to the official ideology of Marxism-Leninism, in which these biopolitical techniques were contextualised.

> At the same time, the Soviet version of modernity certainly had features distinctive to itself. The norms and values promoted by the Soviet government had a particular anticapitalist, collectivist orientation. While socialist values were clearly a central component of Stalinist culture, the ambition to rationalise and reorder society was shared by intellectuals and social reformers throughout Europe in the 19th and 20th centuries. And the Stalinist use of traditional institutions and culture for modern mobilizational purposes similarly reflected the more general demands of mass politics after the First World War. Stalinist culture was a particular Soviet incarnation of modern mass culture. (Hoffmann 2003: 10)

It is important to note that the reiteration of the Foucauldian position on the absence of socialist biopolitics in the works of the 'modernity school' comes with a notable normative shift. For Foucault the absence of a 'properly socialist' biopolitics was (at least in the mid-1970s) a clearly lamentable fact that doomed 'real socialism' to the perpetuation of the violence that did not arise from its ideological *difference* from Western capitalism but rather from its biopolitical *identity* with it. In contrast, for the contemporary Foucauldian scholarship in Soviet studies this identity is a mere neutral fact that does not constitute a problem or a paradox. Moreover, the explanations for the exceptional violence of Soviet socialism are now sought not in the biopolitical techniques, whose operation is almost universal for the 'modern' period, but precisely in the idiosyncrasies of the ideology, with which they were articulated in the Soviet case: 'transformational ideologies and interventionist practices were mutually reinforcing. Social intervention was not necessarily harmful in and of itself. But when social intervention was combined with an authoritarian state, then it could result in lethal state violence' (Hoffmann 2011: 311). While for Foucault socialism was the ostensible other that disappointingly revealed itself to be somewhat the same (as the West) in the aspect of biopolitics, for the contemporary authors socialism was governmentally identical but disappointingly revealed its difference from the West in the aspect of ideology. Either way, there is no such thing as a specifically socialist biopolitics, for better (modernity school) or worse (Foucault).

It is easy to see that this reading of Soviet biopolitics ends up reinstalling the opposition between democracy and totalitarianism within the very discourse of biopolitics that Esposito praised for its neutralisation. As long as one considers biopolitical techniques in isolation from the ideology of a regime, one may safely expect to be able to point to the similarities between the Soviet Union and its ideological antagonists: after all, there are only so many ways to clean one's teeth or treat venereal disease, even if one is a Bolshevik. There is then no such thing as a distinct biopolitics *of* Stalinism, but only operation of biopolitics *in* Stalinism, which is similar to its operation *in* liberalism, Nazism, and so on. Of course, one shall also find that the Stalinist regime often utilised these biopolitical techniques differently, for example in a less effective and more violent manner, than Western societies. This difference may then be explained either by the *absence* of democracy, constitutionalism and the rule of law that tempered biopolitical interventionism in the West (ibid.: 310), or the *presence* of revolutionary ideology in Russia that intensified this interventionism beyond what was politically acceptable in Western societies (ibid.: 11–13). If Soviet biopolitics is similar to biopolitics in the West, then what accounts for the still important differences between Stalinism, Nazism and liberalism is good old ideology, which can transform otherwise innocuous regulatory techniques into a project of social genocide (ibid.: 238–304). Thus, in his magisterial study of Stalinist policies of 'cultivating the masses' David Hoffmann is able simultaneously to affirm the fundamental similarity between Soviet and West European policies and techniques in such fields as health care and surveillance, reproduction and education, forced population transfers and propaganda, and to explain evident differences between them by pointing to ideological divergences, which accounted for such things as the Soviet rejection of eugenics, the promotion of female participation in the work force or the collectivist orientation in the upbringing of children. Ideology is simultaneously downgraded as insufficient and rehabilitated as indispensable.

> The modern state practices and new technologies of social intervention that developed across the world assumed very different forms in particular social, political and ideological settings. In the Soviet case such differences included but were not limited to Marxist-Leninist ideology. (Ibid.: 3)

> Even given Marxism's historical teleology, Leninism's vanguardism and Stalinism's ferocity in dealing with purported enemies, it is impossible to discern the genesis of the Soviet system solely from Communist Party ideology. Many of the practices we consider Soviet in fact originated prior to the October Revolution. Soviet leaders subsequently attached these methods to their agenda of social transformation, but they did not invent housing inspections, the perlustration of letters, propaganda techniques, or concentration camps. (Ibid.: 311)

While the 'modernity school' in Soviet studies has been criticised from a variety of perspectives (Edele 2011: 227–43; Lenoe 2004; Martin 2000), in the context of biopolitics its main weakness consists in the division between ideology and governmental or biopolitical practices, which leads to the impoverished understanding of both. On the one hand, we end up with a reductionist understanding of biopolitics as almost literally 'biological politics', that is the governmental regulation of health and reproduction, hygiene, bodily conduct, physical demeanour and sexual practices, which may then be located in a variety of ideological contexts that are themselves apparently devoid of a biopolitical dimension. Of course, it is easy to see why one's interest in the power over life would be directed towards the broadly 'medico-social' aspects of government: after all, Foucault's own studies both before and after the explicit turn towards biopolitics (from *History of Madness* to *Care of the Self*) also privileged this empirical field and the very concept of biopolitics was advanced in the context of the *History of Sexuality*. Nonetheless, there is nothing historically novel or in any sense 'modern' about the governance of health, reproductive behaviour, physiological processes or bodily demeanour, which dates back to ancient history and about which we have ample evidence from the political thought of the Antiquity (Ojakangas 2011). The modern specificity of biopolitics cannot simply be defined by its object (the biological aspect of human existence) or domain (the medico-social field of intervention). Not every governmental regulation of infectious diseases, sexual deviance, hygienic practices or modes of appearances of its subjects is biopolitical; otherwise, biopolitics would be coextensive with human history as such.[2] It is certainly possible to make such a claim, as Agamben does from a very different perspective, but it would appear somewhat counter-intuitive coming from a 'modernity school'.

On the other hand, such an approach obscures the way ideology *itself* acquires a biopolitical dimension, rather than simply function as a context in which pre-given biopolitical rationalities unfold. In his study Hoffmann insists on the irreducibility of the governmental techniques in family, health or welfare policies to the precepts of Marxist ideology, tracing them back to the wider ideological field of nineteenth- and twentieth-century social engineering. This is undoubtedly true, yet if these techniques are not themselves 'nonideological' (Hoffmann 2011: 311) and were previously articulated in other ideological contexts, it is at least possible to pose the question of whether Marxist-Leninist ideology might have generated any biopolitics of its own, rather than merely recontextualise Western liberal or police techniques of government. While the modernity school presents a narrative of a largely uniform modern governmentality being given particular twists in disparate ideological contexts, it would be more helpful to inquire what biopolitical rationalities actually emerged out of these contexts themselves and how various ideologies problematised their relationship to life. In this manner, we will be able to identify much more precisely what is *modern* in, for example, the liberal, fascist or socialist government of life. As we shall demonstrate in the following chapters, the key feature of Stalinism is its attempt to produce a 'new life', proclaimed in Marxist-Leninist ideology, by radically transforming social reality. This problematisation diverged fundamentally and from the outset from liberal and Nazi modes of biopolitics, which, in their own distinct ways, oriented themselves towards securing life as it was, not producing life as it should be. Thus, Soviet ideology did not simply serve to modify the meaning or function of some biopolitical techniques but was rather *itself* to be transformed into one and it is this transformation that accounts for the specificity of Stalinism, including, as we shall see, its exceptional degree of violence.

Thus, instead of approaching biopolitics in terms of empirical techniques of population management, simultaneously separated from and contextualised in the ideological dimension, we propose to approach it as inextricably linked with the ideological or ideational aspect of politics, which determines the form, in accordance with which life is to be governed. The phrase 'giving form to the life of the people' was offered in 1936 as the very definition of politics by a Nazi scholar, Ottmar von Verschuer (Rose 2001: 2). While von Verschuer's vision of this life-forming politics unsurprisingly took the form of racial hygiene, racism is evidently not the only way to give form to the life of the people. For instance, the biopolitics of neoliberalism, which dispenses with the notions of both race and the people, continues to impose a particular, this time an entrepreneurial, form on the lives of the individuals it governs (cf. Lemke 2001: 202). Similarly, as we shall demonstrate in this book, Soviet socialism, which consistently denounced every form of naturalism and biologism, nonetheless possessed a clearly biopolitical orientation insofar as it ventured to fulfil its transcendent ideal in the immanence of social life.

The understanding of biopolitics in terms of the constitution of forms of life accords with Foucault's original articulation of this problematic, which, we must recall, was not restricted to any policy domain, let alone the biological aspect of life, but rather described a general rationality of power (Foucault 2008: 22). As Stephen Collier argued in his interpretation of Foucault's concept, there remains some confusion about 'what is designated as *bios* in biopolitics' (Collier 2011: 16). Using the example of Foucault's genealogy of liberalism, Collier argues that liberalism is biopolitical not because of its specific focus on the biological aspects of existence or its reliance on biological knowledge, but rather due to its general problematisation of social life as a quasi-natural reality that possessed its own rationality opaque to governmental practices and hence required a reorientation of government away from the ordering practices prescribed by the doctrines of 'police science' (Foucault 2008: 27–73). The *bio-* in liberal biopolitics refers precisely to this quasi-natural domain of 'lived social reality' *in its entirety*, without singling out anything like a specifically 'biological' aspect.

> Liberal and protoliberal thought could not have been concerned with the biological in the contemporary sense, since it simply did not exist at the time; and in the current usage the problems with which Physiocracy and British liberalism were concerned, and that were the focus of Foucault's analysis in these lectures, such as trade, patterns of habitation, urban conditions, means of subsistence, and so on, would be called 'economic' or 'social'. It is most accurate to say – and, in so many words, Foucault did say – that if a new figuration of 'Man' or 'anthropos', defined at the finitudes of life (biology), labour (economic activity) and language (sociocultural existence), emerged in the late 18th and the early 19th century as the object of the human sciences, then biopolitics designates the entry of this figure into the workings of political sovereignty. (Collier 2011: 17)

In this logic, the *object* of biopolitics must be expanded beyond the strictly biological understanding of life towards the entirety of human existence and its *domain* extended beyond the medico-social field of intervention, embracing the wider socioeconomic terrain.[3] What defines the specificity of biopolitics is then the specific *manner* in which power engages with life in this terrain. What changed in European modernity is neither the object nor the domain of power, which, as Agamben notes correctly, are 'absolutely ancient' (1998: 9), but the mode of *problematisation* of life in the rationalities of government, its ontological status, epistemic access to it, its ethical valuation, and so on (Foucault 1988b: 257–8; Deacon 2000). The ideas of liberalism did not merely function as a context for antecedent techniques of biopolitical regulation but thoroughly resignified these techniques and led to the invention of new ones, which functioned as solutions to the specific problems that liberalism had articulated in the domain of life. Biopolitics is then neither an alternative nor a successor to a purely ideological or ideational politics, but rather refers to the *reciprocal problematisation of life and idea*: how should life be lived in accordance with an idea, or how should a given idea be translated into life?

This operational definition of biopolitics occupies a level between the grand theories of biopolitics and the empirical analyses of governmental techniques. What we are interested in is not the empirical application of a ready-made theory of biopolitics (of Foucault, Agamben, Negri or Esposito), none of which have been able to address Stalinism in its specificity. Nor are we interested in the empirical study of predefined biopolitical techniques in the Soviet context, which would only lead to finding already familiar similarities and differences. The reader will therefore not find in this book many descriptions of Soviet manuals on parenting, bodily regimen in youth organisations, urban campaigns for hygiene and the regulations on alimony payments, all of which certainly have both a precedent in Western modernity and an indelible ideological originality of their own. Our concern is rather the investigation of the political rationality of Stalinism itself from the perspective of biopolitics, that is the reconstitution of the problematisation of life at work in the Soviet project of the construction of socialism. We thus continue to deal with what might be called the 'theoretical' dimension, yet it is not 'our' theory that we attempt to apply to the reality of Stalinism, but rather the 'theory' or at least the mode of political reasoning at work in Stalinist policies themselves that we seek to reconstruct.

While we share Collier's approach to biopolitics in terms of problematisation of life in governmental rationalities, we shall nonetheless take issue with his identification of this problematisation with socioeconomic policy in general. '[Foucault] might just as well have referred to an "econopolitics" or a "sociopolitics" or invented a more general term. But since he did not, and since biopolitics is an accepted term of art, I will stick to it' (Collier 2011: 17). This identification is understandable given Collier's privileging of the *Birth of Biopolitics* lectures over the more explicit and elaborate treatment of the theme in the earlier texts such as *History of Sexuality I* and 'Society Must Be Defended', which he dismisses as 'preliminary' and 'confused' (Collier 2009: 80; 2011: 16–19). Yet, as we have noted above, such a reading finds little textual support in Foucault's work. On the contrary, the few cursory references to biopolitics in *The Birth of Biopolitics*, which contrast with the rather more articulate notion in 'Society Must Be Defended' and *History of Sexuality I*, do not indicate any exit out of prior confusion but may simply reflect the loss of interest and prefigure the eventual abandonment of the term, which never occurs again in Foucault's texts after 1979. This abandonment evidently does not disqualify the analyses of biopolitics made in 1976 or later: after all, Foucault abandoned concepts all the time, some more definitively than others, which has not presented their fruitful application by his successors. Yet, it at least suggests paying more attention to the concept of biopolitics developed in the period when Foucault was most interested in the theme.

Moreover, while the problematisation of life discussed in the *Birth of Biopolitics* lectures is specific to liberal biopolitics and can hardly define the concept of biopolitics as such, Foucault's earlier account provides a more general conceptual matrix for addressing the governmental problematisation of life. What is essential to this matrix is the confluence of the productivity of power over life (making live) and the negative power of death (letting die). While, as we have seen, Foucault's privileged historical example of this confluence is racism, its significance is more general. As an object of problematisation, life always figures in biopolitical rationality in a dual manner, as both a problem and a solution, an end and a means, a *telos* and an instrument. Biopolitics does not simply stand in the service of *all* life, but may dispense with the life of some in the name of the life of others or even destroy one's life for one's own sake. Thanatopolitics is not extrinsic to biopolitics as its opposite or even as its perversion: while power is exercised in the name of life, it is not exercised in the name of any given life in particular, which rather functions as the object of rationalities that may well presuppose its elimination.

Thus, in any biopolitical rationality the notion of life figures in two different senses known since the Antiquity. While the life that serves as the *object* of governmental practices is unqualified life, literally any life

Stalinism in the Theory of Biopolitics

there is (*zoe*), the life that is the *telos* of political rationality is a qualified, determinate, positive form of life (*bios*). What defines biopolitics is then the transformation of unqualified life into qualified life in political rationalities, in which unqualified life is the object of politicisation that may be either positive or negative. It is easy to recognise in this definition Agamben's (1998: 8–9) concept of biopolitics as the *inclusive exclusion* of *zoe* into *bios*. As an object of politicisation *zoe* is obviously included in the realm of political life, yet precisely as an *object* it is included there in the marginalised, subordinated or suppressed position of being excluded, 'as if politics were the place in which life had to transform itself into good life and in which what had to be politicised were always already bare life' (ibid.: 7). Thus, for Agamben the elementary matrix of biopolitics, which has been there from time immemorial, consists in the negation of unqualified life in the process of its politicisation as good life. Biopolitics is never reducible to mere government of *zoe* for its own sake, since there is nothing in it that could guide or direct the activity of government, no content or qualification that politics could immediately appropriate as a value. Instead, even the most immediately 'biological' modes of governance such as Nazism had a clear idea of a privileged form of *bios*, in whose image *zoe* is to be transformed, maintained or secured.[4]

While Agamben's theory has been subjected to myriad criticism as misunderstanding, misusing or even abusing Foucault's original argument, the two perspectives are not incompatible as long as we clearly understand the different tasks they set out to achieve. Foucault famously opposed biopolitics to sovereignty as a novel form of power, which displaced the logic of sovereignty without completely dispensing with it (2007: 98–110). In contrast, Agamben's main focus is on sovereign power, whose essence he reconstitutes in terms of the biopolitical capture of life in a relation of inclusive exclusion (1998: 49–60). It is this originary capture that Agamben identifies as the *zero degree* of politics, of *all* politics, from which its historical forms analysed by Foucault (such as police science, liberalism and Nazism) derive. Zoe is *always* 'inclusively excluded' into *bios* as an object of politicisation, yet it is politicised in different ways in different historical periods. Conversely, while there have been numerous possibly incommensurable rationalities of governing life throughout history, they all arise from this elementary matrix of the inclusive exclusion of bare life. This explains Agamben's frequently criticised claim that even the most ostensibly 'progressive' forms of biopolitics (from universal health care to the legalisation of abortion) are necessarily grounded in the prior grasp of bare life by sovereign power (Agamben 1998: 9–11). If the sovereign capture of bare life is indeed the *zero* degree of biopower, then any *augmentation* of this degree in positive biopolitical practices may only conceal but never efface this capture.

While certainly different from Foucault's analysis, Agamben's approach actually addresses the same problem of the thanatopolitical conversion of biopolitics that Foucault articulated historically with his genealogy of racism. If we understand every positive mode of biopolitics as always already conditioned by holding bare life in its ban, then the reversal of biopolitics into thanatopolitics is fully immanent to biopolitical rationality itself. What remains to be understood, of course, are the specific conditions of this reversal, which depend on the way life and idea problematise each other in a historical rationality of government. As the following chapter will demonstrate, *contra* Foucault and contemporary Foucauldians in Soviet studies, Stalinism differs from the better-known liberal and Nazi modes of biopolitics, yet this difference can hardly be traced on the level of empirical techniques of the government of life, as if a specifically socialist governmentality could somehow invent hitherto unheard of ways to provide health care, regulate families or control deviance. Neither is this difference reducible to the superficial ideological colouring that singularises otherwise identical techniques of government. Instead, the difference in question consists in the specific way Stalinism politicises life, going beyond the demands for its protection or corrective intervention towards the affirmation of the possibility to attain a new life through the revolutionary negation of the old. In the following chapter we shall analyse this problematisation in a detailed account of the Stalinist Second Revolution of 1928–32.

Chapter 3

THE GREAT BREAK: MAKING SOCIALISM REAL

THE INACTUALITY OF SOCIALISM

The beginning of the Stalinist period may be conveniently dated to 1928, the year of the proclamation of the first Five Year Plan after Stalin's triumph over both the Left and the Right oppositions in the Communist Party. Eleven years after the Bolshevik seizure of power, the Soviet Union was about to embark on a gigantic project of the construction of socialism. This last sentence ought to give us a moment's pause. What *was* the Soviet Union during these eleven years, if it was not socialist? It was certainly ruled by a communist party, whose goal was the construction of socialism as the proverbial 'first stage of communism'.[1] This rule was strong enough to withstand the challenges of Civil War and the foreign intervention, and by 1928 the Bolsheviks no longer faced any domestic political challenge, even as they remained worried about the hostile capitalist encirclement.

Yet, when it came to the realisation of the programme of the construction of socialism, there were fewer reasons for optimism. It was not only that, as Viacheslav Molotov, Stalin's key associate, said, 'the revolution had taken place in a petty-bourgeois country' (Molotov cited in Kotkin 2014: 420), but that the country *continued* to be petty-bourgeois ten years after the revolution. In fact, the Civil War had all but wiped out the industrial proletariat that according to the Marxist canon was both the main agent and the beneficiary of the revolution. While the 'war communism' of 1918–20 was the first – and ultimately unsuccessful – attempt at the introduction of some primitive elements of communism in the conditions of civil war, the NEP marked a retreat from societal transformation, leaving the USSR in a curious position of an underdeveloped capitalist state ruled dictatorially by an avowedly communist party with no clear class basis (Roberts 2006: 230–3). In Lenin's lifetime the actual transition towards socialism as the first stage of communism did not arise as a practical policy goal – in contrast, the turn towards the NEP was canonically proclaimed as 'serious and long-term', suggesting that the socialist project entered a historical pause. In 1921 Lenin argued that Russia had only carried out a bourgeois-democratic revolution and had not yet got around to socialism (Kotkin 2014: 407). Nor was the question of the actual construction of the socialist order decided after Lenin's death: while the intra-party struggles of 1924–7 certainly revolved around the question of the best ways to go about the construction of socialism, they largely remained on the terrain of ideological doctrine, whose translation into life remained deferred (Van Ree 2002: 84–94; Kotkin 2014: 472–529). Thus, the dazzling celebration of the tenth anniversary of the Revolution could not conceal the unease about the postponement of the new life that it had promised.

In a magisterial study of the NEP era Vladimir Buldakov (2013) demonstrated the way this period of relative socioeconomic stabilisation, in which various elements of the pre-revolutionary socioeconomic order were rehabilitated, was also accompanied by the 'post-revolutionary frustration', the persistent concern about the realisation and, ultimately, the *realisability* of the socialist project, the wariness about the Revolution and the Civil War having been 'all in vain'. While the NEP is usually interpreted as a period of normalisation, the abandonment of extreme utopian fervour in favour of more pragmatic and realistic tasks of reconstruction (Hoffmann 2011: 200–3; Stites 1989: 116–19), Buldakov shows how this apparently self-evident stability was in fact viewed by many in Soviet society, especially the members of the Party, in rather more negative terms as testifying to the Revolution having run out of steam or even having been betrayed.

> What had happened to the revolution? Had the civil war been fought and won to hand power over to NEPmen and speculators? History's 'universal class' went hungry while kulaks could hoard immense stores of grain with impunity? Workers were sent to mines that collapsed on them – and was it all just accident? What was the self-proclaimed workers' state doing for workers? (Kotkin 2014: 696)

The NEP, which ironically consisted almost entirely in the return to the old economic policy, was perceived as marking nothing less than the death of the revolution. As Buldakov demonstrates, the reference to death should be taken quite literally in this context of the NEP era. The deaths of Lenin, and shortly thereafter of other leading Bolsheviks such as Felix Dzerzhinsky, Mikhail Frunze, Leonid Krasin and Viktor Nogin, added to the overall feeling of existential ennui, well captured by Walter Benjamin in his 'Moscow Diaries' (Benjamin 1978: 111–12, 129–30), a rather more uncanny preoccupation with death. The rise in the suicide rate in the mid- and late 1920s, the invention of new funeral rituals by the new regime, the popularity of various rejuvenation schemes and scams, the increasing hypochondria of Old Bolshevik leaders all testify to the 'postrevolutionary thanatomania' (Buldakov 2013: 115) of the NEP-era USSR, whose socialist orientation was perceived as lifeless and hence falling victim to the power of death. Both in the morbid preoccupation with it and the frantic attempts to avoid it, death was the permanent presence in the post-revolutionary society: 'It was as if the people were pondering the question of whether to die sooner or to go on living to see what the endless absurdity of existence will come down to' (ibid.: 170).

This is not to say that there were no attempts to attain socialism during the NEP. On the contrary, the aftermath of the Civil War was marked by a flurry of societal experimentation with new forms of life, from avant-garde art that sought to go beyond the representation of the world towards its actual transformation to worker and student communes that sought to embody the ideals of the Revolution in concrete forms of common dwelling, work and leisure (Stites 1989; Brovkin 1998; Buck-Morss 2002; Groys 2011). Nonetheless, the sheer pluralism of these efforts at constructing the New Soviet Person, which frequently contradicted and excluded one another, ensured that *none* of them was able to attain a hegemonic status and reorder Soviet society as a whole in the image of its ideological ideal. On the contrary, the endless debates between various groups, clubs and organisations about what constitutes a truly socialist form of life served to derealise socialism even further. Moreover, given that most of these experiments focused on cultural transformation, they functioned as forms of mediation that ventured to transform lives by learning and experimenting with new ideas. Perhaps the best summation of the logic of utopian experimentation in the 1920s is offered by Lenin's proverbial injunction 'Learn, learn, learn!' It is precisely by learning to live differently in different contexts, from communes to carnivals, learning new routines of time management at work or anticipating the communist future by reading utopian science fiction that Soviet citizens were expected to transform their very existence, shedding the degraded and corrupt forms of capitalist subjectivity and becoming New Soviet Persons.

This is where Stalinism comes in. As we have seen in Chapter 1, the aspect of Stalinism valorised in postcommunist Russia consists in the effective construction of the socialist order as a lived reality. It is certainly true that the defining feature of the Stalinist period is the advance beyond the political-institutional hegemony of the Bolshevik Party towards the actualisation of its positive programme in real life.

In less than a decade the Soviet Union was transformed almost unrecognisably from a backward and peripheral former empire into the world's only socialist state. It is therefore certainly fair to say that under Stalin the construction of socialism became a qualitatively different project (see Roberts 2006: 213–27). The mode of problematisation that generated Stalinism begins with the paradox of the Soviet Union being a non-socialist country governed by a socialist party and identifies a fundamental gulf in the Soviet reality between the transcendent idea of communism and the lived reality of Soviet society that remained fundamentally at odds with it. On the one hand, there was a doctrinal ideal stipulating forms of life proper to the victorious proletariat, which nonetheless remained largely lifeless in the society at large, particularly in the rural areas, where the overwhelming majority of the Soviet population continued to live. On the other hand, there was the givenness of lived reality in Soviet society which was somehow formless, particularly from the perspective of this doctrinal ideal: rather than correspond to any ideological form, the ways of life in the NEP-era Soviet Union were largely a result of the creative adaptation of the population to the chaos and deprivation of the Civil War (cf. Brovkin 1998). To articulate the *transcendence of form* and the *immanence of life* would be the task of the Stalinist project.

In Richard Stites's influential argument, Stalinism broke with the experimental politics of the 1920s in two ways (Stites 1989: 225–40). First, starting from the late 1920s the diverse and relatively autonomous social groups engaged in utopian experimentation became increasingly subordinated to the Soviet government and sometimes violently disbanded and prosecuted. Second, the pathos of utopian transformation characteristic of the 1920s gradually gave way to cynicism and opportunism, the resurgence of anti-egalitarianism and authoritarianism, which led to the dwindling of both negative ('iconoclastic') experimentation in arts, education, work and sexual life and to the increased cynicism about the more positive (egalitarian) experiments, from communes to proletarian culture. At the same time, these changes did not entail the abandonment of the transition to socialism but in many ways enabled its acceleration and intensification.

> Stalinism was not simply a negation of utopianism. It was a rejection of 'revolutionary' utopianism in favour of a single utopian vision and plan, drawn up at the pinnacle of power and imposed on an entire society without allowance for autonomous life experiments. (Stites 1989: 226)

Nonetheless, the authoritarian and violent character of this imposition does not efface its overall transformative ambition. We therefore find it difficult to agree with Stites's following claim, which appears to reduce Stalinism to a familiar form of pre-modern despotism.

> Stalinism did not aspire to transform human values; it accepted them as they were – and in the peculiar way that Stalin himself perceived them to be. There would be no pluralism and spontaneity, no separate experiments, and no belief in the inner goodness of man. Stalin's utopian design was a crueller mode of thinking based on view of man as sinful, evil, potentially criminal, lazy or stupid; it suggested, therefore, the arts of coercion, authoritarianism, brutality. (Ibid.: 226)

While it is probably possible to find historical examples that support this claim, it is hardly plausible as a general designation of the political rationality of Stalinism, particularly the early-Stalinist period of the Great Break (cf. Van Ree 2002: 114–35). Stalin's policies openly sought to transform human values through the reforging of criminals and class enemies through forced labour, the inculcation of socialist values through communes for juvenile delinquents, the transformation of hygienic standards through propaganda and inspections, the promotion of family values through a combination of rewards and punishments, and so on. While, as we shall see, Stalin did eventually come to accept certain pre-Soviet values 'as they were', this acceptance can hardly be generalised for the entire Stalinist period, since it so clearly contradicts the radical transformative pathos that Stites himself recognises at least in the period of the Second Revolution (Stites 1989: 227).

Thus, the difference between Stalinism and the 'revolutionary utopianism' of the 1920s must be formulated in a more nuanced fashion and it is precisely here that the notion of biopolitics becomes indispensable. What makes Stalinism biopolitical is its central question of the construction of socialism as a lived reality: how is it possible to transform a society governed by socialists into a society that is *itself* socialist? How is socialism possible in the domain of real being as opposed to utopian speculation? How does one proceed from reading socialism to actually living it? The specificity of Stalinism is then graspable in terms of the overcoming of the ideological approach to social transformation through learning and indoctrination by the properly biopolitical rationality that seeks to translate ideological precepts directly into the lives of its subjects. In this manner, a myriad of experimental attempts at the transcendence of the 'old world' through learning new forms of life gives way to the full forcing of *one* of these forms into the immanence of lived reality.

By ceasing all experiments with transcending conventional forms of life and instead attempting to create a new conventional form of life based on the communist ideology, Stalinism presented itself as a solution to the problem of the expiry of the Revolution that defined elite and mass perceptions of the NEP. As Buldakov (2013: 705) argues, it was the combination of the desire for stability and the mourning for revolutionary fervour that paved the way for Stalinism, which converted the messianic revolutionary drive that was in the mid-1920s primarily associated with Trotsky and the idea of world revolution into the project of the construction of socialism as a positive order of things. Stalinism was able to mobilise the waning revolutionary affect for the gigantic project of the construction of socialism, precisely because the society was aware of its waning and perceived it as problematic, even as it enjoyed the benefits of the new stability and abandoned the sacrificial drive of the Civil War (Kotkin 2014: 734). This is why, for Buldakov, the NEP cannot be considered a 'lost' or 'defeated' alternative to Stalinism, as it was sometimes presented during the Perestroika period (Buldakov 2013: 707; cf. Brovkin 1998). The ceaseless vacillations of the NEP actively generated Stalinism by forming a milieu in which the only solution to ineffective social experimentation would be a top-down biopolitical project: the transformative utopia of the Revolution had to be redeemed but within the immanence of socioeconomic reality. In Buldakov's argument, the genesis of Stalinism out of the 'post-revolutionary frustration' of the NEP took the threefold form of depression, aggression and repression' (ibid.: 718). The depression about the realisability of the revolutionary ideals gave way to the aggressive desire to 'repeat' the Revolution by forcing its maxims into reality, which was only possible through the 'repression' of all those apparently in the way of this forcing. 'From the faithlessness of the NEP grew a new faith, a faith in the leader' (ibid.: 661).

Since Buldakov does not utilise the biopolitical paradigm, his otherwise valuable interpretation of the descent of Stalinism obscures the relationship between the original revolutionary ideals and Stalinist rule, particularly during the period of the Great Break. Noting the obvious differences between the October Revolution and the Stalinist Revolution Buldakov opts for the interpretation of the latter as ultimately a fake revolution, a conservative project of stabilisation masking as the repetition of the authentic revolutionary negation. Thus, he argues that 'with the expulsion of Trotsky real revolution was dead, replaced by a new myth and a new leader' (ibid.: 594). Revolutionary flux was abandoned in favour of state-led recourse to purely archaic violence with no transformative content (ibid.: 684). Instead, in this chapter we shall argue that while the leader was indeed new, the myth in question remained the same and, rather than simply die, the Revolution was reinscribed in a different key that, instead of concealing its death, attempted to endow it with life for the second time.[2]

The Great Break: Making Socialism Real

It is well-known that Stalinism was characterised by very few innovations on the level of ideology, having freely borrowed various elements from both the 'leftist' and the 'rightist' oppositions of the 1920s (Van Ree 2002: 255–71; Tucker 1992: 526–49). Moreover, those innovations that could be partially attributed to it, most notably the idea of 'socialism in one country' (Kotkin 2014: 205), certainly did not have mass terror as their necessary outcome: on the contrary, in the post-revolutionary context they were perceived as moderate and normalising, a sign of a 'new maturity', in the famously misguided words of Boris Pasternak (cf. Žižek 2008: 211–14; Brandenberger 2012: 372–3). The true innovation and the true monstrosity of Stalinism do not lie in the ideological dimension but rather pertain to the biopolitical redeployment of the transcendent ideal of communism in the immanentist terms of the construction of the positive order of socialism, 'construction' becoming the privileged trope of the Soviet discourse from the late 1920s onwards. 'Socialism in one country' might have sounded disappointingly unambitious to the erstwhile proponents of world revolution, yet Stalinism would compensate for its modesty by endowing this socialism with reality.

> In October 1917 the working class defeated capitalism politically, having established its political dictatorship. Now the main task consists in the unfolding throughout the country of the construction of a new, socialist economy and thus finishing capitalism off also economically. The socialist industrialization of the country – this is the main point from which must begin the unfolding of the construction of the socialist economy. (Istoria VKP(b): 260–1)

Contrary to both its apologists and its detractors, Stalinism was neither a perversion of the utopian idea of communism by a caricaturised diabolical figure nor the realisation of the hitherto hidden obscene core of this idea. It was rather an attempt to *force* the transcendence of the socialist ideal within the immanent reality of Soviet society, which unleashed massive social dislocations that truly merited the name of the Second Revolution (Tucker 1992: 69–90). While the Revolution of 1917 was *political*, establishing the 'dictatorship of the proletariat' in the form of the Bolshevik party-state, the Second Revolution was manifestly *bio*political, translating these political changes into transformations in real life.

> The whole cultural system, comprising the organisation of the state, the ways of running the economy, the social structure, justice, the penal system, education, the visual and dramatic arts, literature and the daily life of the people, was in the throes of rapid change. (Tucker 1992: 93)

What distinguishes Stalinism from its Bolshevik predecessors and rivals, and what is celebrated in its contemporary rehabilitation in Russia, is its *daring* to force revolutionary transformation into life itself. It is thus only fair that its most sustained project bore the name of the Great Break (*veliky perelom*).[3]

> We forget just how wild was Stalin's gamble – as great or greater than Lenin's October coup, Brest-Litovsk, and the NEP. The Communist party, let alone the country, was not prepared for forced wholesale collectivization. Stalin could use the police to outflank the party but he also had to mount a high profile public trial [Shakhty] to fan the flames of 'class warfare'. Both collectivization and the class warfare campaign also required Stalin to outmanoeuvre his own inner circle, which looks easy only in retrospect. That all this upheaval, from the countryside to the mines and factories, was going to work out in Stalin's favour, however, was hardly guaranteed. He put everything on the line, including his personal power. (Kotkin 2014: 734)

Forcing revolutionary transcendence within the immanence of the social realm and thus making socialism no longer something learned but something lived – this is the biopolitical formula of Stalinism that, as we shall see below, accounts for its paradoxical and paroxysmal character.

THE SECOND REVOLUTION

The period of the Great Break (1928–32) is usually addressed in terms of three interrelated projects of societal transformation: the collectivisation of agriculture, industrialisation and the Cultural Revolution. In these projects the social reality of semi-capitalist agriculture, underdeveloped industry and the uncultured population was to give way to new forms of life: socialised (or nationalised) agriculture, rapid development of heavy industry, the development of proletarian culture and the rise of socialist intelligentsia.

While Soviet propaganda retrospectively converted the revolutionary policies of the Great Break into a historical necessity, at the time the choice of this direction, let alone its outcome, were far from determined, and the process of the Second Revolution unfolded in a chaotic and violent manner.

> [No] plan could have existed because actually attaining near complete collectivization was, at the time, unimaginable in practical terms. Collectivise one sixth of the earth? How? With what levers? Even the ultraleftist Trotsky had called a 'transition to collective forms' of agriculture a matter of one or two generations. Administratively the regime had attained

only a minimal presence in the countryside: outside the provincial capitals traces of the red banners, slogans, and symbols of the new order vanished and dedicated personnel were shockingly thin on the ground. At the same time, Stalin had concluded, that the impossible was a necessity. He would improvise a programme of building socialism: forcing into being large-scale collective farms, absent private property. (Kotkin 2014: 675)

While the term 'planned economy' might at first glance suggest a more orderly and less chaotic approach to economic activity, the opposite was the case in the Stalinist construction of socialism. The extreme ambition of the Great Break entailed that even planning was no longer a rational activity but a 'bachhanalian' (Tucker 1992: 97) or even 'Dionysian' (Rosenthal 2002: 237) project, a purposefully organised *disorganisation*.

[The] task of rapid industrialization was so daunting that without 'mad' Dionysian enthusiasm it might not have been undertaken at all. The Party adapted the warrior ethos of the Civil War to 'socialist construction', giving the Plan the aura of a military campaign and the pace of a forced march. Factories operated around the clock; loudspeakers blared forth statistics on production battles won, ambushes carried out, fortresses to be stormed, mobilizations to be completed, and targets to be destroyed. The press reported on 'campaigns' and 'fronts'. 'Deserters' were shamed or ridiculed. The war climate fostered zealotry and brutality and made it possible to deploy the masses in a way that might have been unacceptable in peacetime. In addition, war sanctioned the creation of an all-powerful state and an economy which disregarded civilian needs. (Rosenthal 2002: 247)

In his account of the Great Break Stephen Collier (2011) relies on the distinction between *genetic* and *teleological* planning in Soviet economic policy on the eve of the Second Revolution to demonstrate the divorce of planning from socioeconomic reality and, more generally, the devaluation of reality as such. The genetic planning approach, developed in the mid-1920s by such economists as Nikolai Kondratiev and Vladimir Groman, was grounded in the presupposition of the exteriority of socioeconomic processes to the state. The task of planning consisted in analysing the regularities of these processes in order to reconstitute their immanent laws of development, forecasting socioeconomic developments on the basis of these laws and modulating governmental interventions within the constraints of available resources. In contrast, teleological planning, most famously advocated by Stanislav Strumilin, took its point of departure from the *telos* of planning, from which it proceeded directly to the physical reality, in which the plans were to be implemented, without any concern for the limitations imposed by the immanent logic of the socioeconomic realm. The only constraints that this model recognised were physical rather than economic in character. 'Teleological planning did not recognise the distinction between the sphere of planning activity and an external environment or milieu. It simply assumed that the entire field of collective life could be subject to instrumental control by the state' (Collier 2011: 56).

While both approaches to planning affirmed state regulation of the economy, they did so on the basis of fundamentally different problematisations of its status. Teleological planning, which prevailed over the genetic approach in the preparation of the First Five Year Plan in 1928–9, explicitly rejected the limitations posed by the existing socioeconomic structures and processes as 'acceptance of the "generic inheritance of 300 years of Tsarism"' (Vaisberg cited in Collier 2011: 59). The idea that government must conform to, respect or even acknowledge the immanent laws of socioeconomic reality was thus delegitimised as 'creeping empiricism' (Rosenthal 2002: 276) that could only lead to the perpetuation of the legacy of backwardness. If the centuries of Tsarism are now to be transcended, why should the victorious new regime abide by the present features of the economy that are themselves determined by the discredited past? Instead, planning was to approach the entire socioeconomic reality as a *resource* for governmental mobilisation and regulation, a resource that is strictly physical and lacks any kind of rationality of its own (Collier 2011: 60). In this manner, Soviet economic policy could ignore the very existence of economy and society as realms of self-regulating processes.

> [The] teleological approach that took shape around the first five-year plan dismissed the strictures imposed by the putatively autonomous laws of society. *It insisted on the possibility of governing things in their immediate physical reality.* The principle of teleological planning was not exactly the domination of society. Rather it was that society, as such, was irrelevant to the considerations of total planning. (Ibid.: 62–3; my emphasis)

The name of the Great Break is evidently apt for this grand programme of social transformation that frees itself from any constraint or determination by reality, which instead figures in it solely as an object to be 'broken' to make a new life possible. Let us now briefly address the way this transformation unfolded in each of the projects of the Great Break. The forced industrialisation, implemented during the first two Five Year Plans, led to significant increases in coal and iron ore production and the establishment, frequently from scratch, of major new industrial complexes, such as Magnitogorsk and Kuznetsk, as well as new machinery, tractor and automobile plants. The rapid industrial development, particularly in heavy industry, came at the price of extreme social dislocation and led to a marked decrease in workers' living and working standards, since the product of this development was largely directed towards military production (see Kotkin 1995: 106–43; Tucker 1992: 101–15; Fitzpatrick 2002: 40–61; Khmelnitsky 2015). The workers' real incomes fell drastically during the early 1930s and their working conditions became poorer and more hazardous, particularly in the newly constructed complexes, where housing and hygiene conditions were at best rudimentary. The workers were also subjected to much more stringent production norms and harsher disciplinary measures, starting with the 1932 amendments to the Labour Code that made it possible to fire workers for one day's absence, intensifying with the 1938 introduction of compulsory 'labour books' and culminating with the 1940 legislation introducing criminal penalties for quitting a job or being late for work (see Fitzpatrick 2002: 8; Edele 2011: 196–7). During the Terror of 1936–8, even minor violations of work discipline would lead to the accusation of 'wrecking', immediately linked with political opposition and leading to long camp terms or even execution (Goldman 2011: 251–96). The camp system itself played not merely a punitive but also an active productive role in the industrialisation process, since major development projects, most notably the White Sea-Baltic Sea and Moscow-Volga canals, and the Baikal-Amur railway, relied on the use of the forced labour of camp inmates (Hoffmann 2011: 264–6).

The Cultural Revolution sought to overcome the pre-revolutionary 'cultural backwardness' through the development of universal school education and health care, literacy campaigns for adults, higher education for workers and the formation of the proletarian intelligentsia to replace the distrusted yet still necessary 'bourgeois specialists' (see Fitzpatrick 1974, 1992; David-Fox 1999). The cultural campaigns of this period sought to revive the militant spirit of the October Revolution and the Civil War and attacked all forms of non-revolutionary culture, both traditional and bourgeois, in the name of variably understood proletarian culture. As Sheila Fitzpatrick famously argued, the Cultural Revolution was a period of radical upward mobility and positive discrimination, whereby the purges of old professional elites and industrial managers cleared the way for the younger generations of 'promotees' (*vydvizhentsy*) from peasant and worker backgrounds (Fitzpatrick 1992: 16–35, 149–81). In its own way, therefore, this process redeemed the egalitarian promises of the 1917 Revolution by 'democratizing culture', equalising cultural opportunities, promoting the representatives of the formerly exploited classes to positions of authority, and so on (Fitzpatrick 1974: 33).

The other side of this process was the assault on 'non-proletarian' culture in all its forms. The campaigns led by the Komsomol and rank-and-file party activists united in professional and artistic associations of the militant left targeted 'alien class influences, bourgeois degeneration, petty-bourgeois wavering and blunting of revolutionary vigilance in the face of the more cultured class enemy' (*Pravda editorial*, 18 May 1928, cited in Fitzpatrick 1974: 42). In contrast to the utopian experimentation of the early 1920s that had largely similar goals, the Cultural Revolution of 1928–32 took an explicitly antagonistic form of 'class war on the cultural front' (ibid.: 34), combining violent militant action from below with party direction from above (cf. Priestland 2007: 39–44, 211). The 'warlike' character of the Cultural Revolution was also manifest in the criminal prosecution of professional and academic elites (the Shakhty Trial of 1928, the Industrial Party Trial of 1930, the Academics' Trial of 1931), the expulsion of students of non-proletarian backgrounds from schools and universities, the resumption of violent attacks on religion, censorship and witch-hunts in sciences and arts, and so on. The biopolitical orientation of this process is evident from the following claim: 'we have to drive out all trace of liberal culture-mongering from cultural work and conduct it as proletarian struggle for the real creation of a new culture' (*Pravda editorial*, 2 September 1928, cited in Fitzpatrick 1974: 42). 'New culture' could only attain the status of a 'real creation', if old culture, be it traditional peasant ways of life, the decadent 'jazz age' lifestyle of the NEP-men, the bohemian modernism of the urban intelligentsia or the technicist apoliticism of the specialists, could be *de*-created, sometimes in a painfully literal way.

Of course, the greatest 'break' was achieved in the process of collectivisation, which sought to and largely succeeded in radically transforming the forms of life of over 80 per cent of the population, from de facto private farming to forced employment in socialised or nationalised farms (see Conquest 1987; Viola 1999; Tucker 1992: 119–45; Edele 2011: 44–8, 172–9). While private farming had been routinely denounced by the Bolsheviks on ideological grounds since before the Revolution, in the first post-revolutionary years collectivisation remained a matter of minoritarian experimentation, less than 1 per cent of farm land having been collectivised in any way by 1928. According to Stephen Kotkin, the seizure of land by the peasants in and after 1917 constituted a veritable peasant revolution and throughout the 1920s it was all but unthinkable that the Soviet government would be able to reverse its results.

> [Stalin] would prove the mostly disbelieving Communist party wrong. Collectivization and the violent expropriation of better-off farmers (*dekulakization*) – Stalin's revolutionary shock of 1928–1930 – would

> turn out to be significantly more ramified even than Lenin's shock coup of 1917. What stands out in Stalin's action is not just his desire to launch a socialist transformation of the countryside, which all Bolsheviks expected to see eventually, but the fact that when the gamble met mass resistance and caused unfathomable ruin, Stalin *saw it through to completion*. No one else in or near the Bolshevik leadership, Trotsky included, could have stayed the course on such a bloody social-engineering escapade on such a scale. (Kotkin 2014: 421; original emphasis)

After just one year of Stalin's all-out drive for collectivisation, the percentage of collective farms rose to over 60 per cent, exceeding even the official designs of the Five Year Plan. The mobilisation of the peasant population for forced labour in state-organised and state-controlled structures not only swept away century-old communal traditions and ways of life of pre-revolutionary peasant Russia, but subjected millions of peasants to persecution, arrest, camp confinement, forced resettlement and separation of families. Mobilising the resentment of the poorest peasants and the young urban workers against the 'kulaks', Stalin's regime made a sharp turn to the far left at the very same time as it dealt a crushing blow to the Trotskyite leftist opposition that had advocated similar policies just a year before (ibid.: 676–85, 695). The revolution that was victorious in the cities in 1917 was now to triumph in the villages as well.

In his conversation with Prime Minister Churchill in August 1942 Stalin reportedly called the collectivisation 'a terrible struggle' that had been ever harder for him than World War II, since he had to face ten million antagonists among the peasants (Rybas 2010: 678). Violently crushing numerous attempts at resistance, the regime engaged in what amounted to the second Civil War, which was not over after the completion of the collectivisation in 1932 but flared up again in the form of top-down state terror in 1937–8, when the infamous 'mass operations' targeted former kulaks and village priests as well as their family members.[4] The most horrendous aspect of this civil war was the famine of 1932–3 in Ukraine, North Caucasus, Kazakhstan and other areas of the USSR, which claimed the lives of at least five million people. Whether the famine is interpreted as a consequence of disastrous economic policies or as an intentional act of genocide on the part of the regime, it remains by far the most lethal of all Soviet policies (Conquest 1987; Viola 1999; Edele 2011: 16–19; Wemheuer 2014). Yet, thanatopolitical effects are observable in all three projects of the Stalinist revolution, whereby the effort to produce a new lived reality takes the form of the negation of the given reality that conflicts with the prevailing ideological doctrine. 'The masses were regarded as objects to be reworked and transformed. In the fiery furnaces of the steel mills human nature would be smelted and recast' (Rosenthal 2002: 246). For the new socialist reality to emerge, the old society must cease to exist, sometimes only in terms of status (university professors reduced to unemployment and poverty) and sometimes in the brutely physical sense (millions of victims of repression, resettlement and starvation). In the remainder of this chapter we shall elaborate the relation between bio- and thanatopolitics in the rationality of the Great Break by comparing it with the problematisations of life at work in the Western modes of biopolitics, that is liberalism and Nazism.

THE WAR ON NATURE

Our brief analysis of the Great Break clearly demonstrates that the problematisation of life in the Stalinist project of the construction of socialism is fundamentally at odds with the problematisations constitutive of liberal biopolitics. In Foucault's well-known argument (2008: 61–70, 291–313), the key innovation of liberal governmentality is its ontological recasting of the social realm as a quasi-natural reality that is both anterior and exterior to political authority. For liberalism economy and society are never founded but are always already there as foundations of any possible politics and government (Burchell 1991: 134). The preceding European governmentalities of *raison d'état* and police science approached social reality as transparent and intelligible and hence subject to thoroughgoing governmental regulation that is in principle unlimited (Pasquino 1991: 111; Gordon 1991: 11). In contrast, liberalism followed the emergent human sciences in asserting a necessarily dense and opaque character of the socioeconomic realm that the state as a finite subject could never fully access (Foucault 2008: 61; see more generally Burchell 1991, 1996; Dean 1999: ch. 6). Nonetheless, despite this density and opacity, this realm is not chaotic but functions in accordance with its own immanent principles as a 'system of natural liberty' (Burchell 1991: 126–33). Governmental interventions that cannot fully access the logic of this system are bound only to tamper with it, undermining its own effective operation. From this ontological naturalism and epistemic agnosticism follows the central ethico-political tenet of liberal government: the suspicion that 'one always governs too much' (Foucault 2008: 319; 2007: 343–57).

This suspicion brings in both the problematisation of existing governmental operations as excessively restrictive and the imperative of founding government on the knowledge of the laws of economy and society. If authoritarian regulation that is detached from the immanent rationality of the social realm can only undermine its proper functioning, the activity of government must be reoriented away from voluntarist ordering toward the protection of the immanent workings of the system of natural liberty. The solution to the problem of 'governing too much' is thus not merely quantitative in the sense of minimising the scope of government, but also qualitative in the sense of adapting the techniques of government to the principles found in the quasi-natural reality of social life. Thus, the density and opacity of the liberal society do not prevent active governmental interventions in it, but rather reorient them towards an explicitly *securitarian* mode. 'Liberalism fosters the social by conceiving of the government of the state as securing the processes that constitute a society separate from the state' (Dean 1999: 147; see Foucault 2007: 349–57; 2008: 65–6). In this manner, liberalism may combine the self-critical ethos of problematising all government as potentially excessive with a specification of legitimate tasks for government that consist in securing the processes that are both ontologically and ethically prior to the acts of government themselves.

Evidently, the biopolitical problematisation at work in the Stalinist project of the construction of socialism is radically heterogeneous to this naturalist-securitarian approach. Insofar as it is animated by the quest for the revolutionary transcendence of the existing ways of life, socialism is opposed both to police science, whose aspirations for total *regulation* never entailed the drive for total *transformation*, and to classical liberalism, which sought to adapt the techniques of regulation to the immanent quasi-natural logic of socioeconomic processes. Our discussion of the abandonment of genetic planning on the eve of the Great Break clearly demonstrates the Soviet regime's repudiation of anything like natural laws of society. To the extent the Bolshevik ideology construed some aspects of the existing Russian reality as 'natural', this was not the harmonious and self-regulating nature whose immanent processes the government must secure, but rather the corrupted and debased nature that groans for the redemption from itself that the quasi-messianic revolutionary movement promises to attain (Dobrenko 2007: 75–82). In the words of Maxim Gorky, the founding father of socialist realism, 'nature is acting as our enemy and we must unanimously wage war against it as an enemy' (Gorky cited in Dobrenko 2007: 80).

> In the Union of Soviets, a struggle is taking place of the rationally organised will of the labouring masses against the arbitrary forces of nature and against the 'arbitrariness' in man, which in its essence is nothing more than the instinctive anarchism of personality, fed by centuries of pressure on it from a class-oriented state. (Gorky cited in Dobrenko 2007: 77)

> The war included the conquest of nature, an aspect of the Plan that melded Nietzschean, Fedorovian, and Marxist tenets with a Nietzschean apotheosis of will. Mountains were dynamited, primeval forests cleared, rivers straightened, and canals built, not just for economic reasons but as expressions of man's triumph over the 'elements', his subjection of the world to reason. (Rosenthal 2002: 248)

This aspiration towards the *transcendence of nature* differentiates socialist biopolitics not only from liberalism but also from Nazism, providing us with yet another reason to question the subsumption of the two regimes under the category of totalitarianism (Esposito 2008a; Losurdo 2004).

> Soviet power demonstrated permanently and on different levels of its political and economic practice a deep, almost instinctive aversion toward everything natural. The campaigns against genetics and psychoanalysis are as characteristic in this respect as the collectivisation of agriculture in the 1930s, aimed at uprooting the peasants and severing their traditional, intimate attachment to the earth. (Groys 2011: 122)

While Nazism sought to subject life to power by subjecting power to the biological normativity allegedly inherent in life itself, the Bolshevik revolutionary project ventured to subject and dominate nature, including human nature, by the power of ideas.

> Everything that is called culture arose from an instinct of self-defence and was created by the labour of man in the process of his struggle against stepmother-nature; culture is the result of man's striving to create, by the forces of his own will and of his own reason, a 'second nature'. (Gorky cited in Dobrenko 2007: 77)

This is why for Gorky and other socialist authors the Romantic idealisation of nature entailed little more than submissiveness to an arbitrary tyrannical power.

> In the relationship of poetry to nature, the things that have been heard most often and distinctly have been submissiveness and flattery. Praise of nature is praise of a despot, and in tone it is almost always reminiscent of prayers. Poets almost unanimously gloss over such bad tricks of nature as earthquakes, floods, hurricanes, droughts, and in general the various explosions and storms of its blind forces that destroy thousands of people and tear down the labour of their hands. Poets have never yet called mankind to fight against nature, for power over it, and while allowing themselves – not often – anger at two-legged despots, they have not raged at the blind tyrant. (Gorky cited in Dobrenko 2007: 81)

The Great Break: Making Socialism Real

It is this radical anti-naturalism of the Soviet project that throws doubt on Foucault's use of the notion of racism to describe Soviet biopolitical rationality, even in a loose, metaphorical sense.

> In Soviet State racism, what revolutionary discourse designated as the class enemy becomes *a sort of* biological threat. So, who is the class enemy now? Well, it's the sick, the deviant, the madman. As a result, the weapon that was once used in the struggle against the class enemy is now wielded by a medical police, which eliminates class enemies *as though* they were racial enemies. (Foucault, 2003: 83; my emphasis).

Yet, is this 'as though' justified: was the class enemy really 'a sort of' biological threat? After all, a principled rejection of racism even in its quasi-scientific and respectable eugenic guise was a permanent feature of the official Soviet discourse (Hoffmann, 2011: 105; Weiner, 1999: 1123, 1146–7). While there are evident limits to taking the proclamations of the Soviet discourse at face value, its hostility to racism was arguably not hypocritical and arose out of its ideological orientation that asserted the possibility and desirability of radical transformation of human nature, which logically made any naturalist essentialism the 'natural' enemy of socialism.

The distance of Stalinism from Foucault's concept of racism is best exemplified by the construction of the figure of the enemy during the Great Break. In Foucault's account, the enemy of Western biopolitics is constituted as the internal or external other, from whose contaminating presence or influence the racial self must be protected. Even when this other was assimilated to such an extent that it became all but indistinct from the self, its difference could be emphasised through rhetoric, mythologisation or pure fabrication. In contrast, the task of the Stalinist revolution was not the *protection* (of the race, nation, state, and so on) against the threat of the external or internal other but the *transformation* of society, which would abolish the existing hierarchies and distinctions between the self and the other. What is the enemy in this logic? It is clearly not the other than threatens the established way of life, but rather the personification of this way of life itself that, by holding on to it, thwarts the triumphant progress of the revolution. While the racist logic protects the given self against the threat of the other, the radicalised logic of class struggle at work in the Great Break attacks the given self *as* 'vermin', 'filth' or 'parasite' in the name of the otherness that it must *become*. The form of life that Soviet governmentality values and wishes to protect lies entirely in the future and the existing forms of life are only valuable as the sites of its eventual attainment. 'For the working class, the whole world, all of nature, is only material' (Gorky cited in

Dobrenko 2007: 78). Of course, as the violence of the collectivisation demonstrates, this mode of class enmity may well be at least as intense as racial enmity. Yet, even when class enemies (for example the representatives of the aristocracy, bourgeoisie or the clergy, uncannily termed 'the former people') were cast in the official discourse in quasi-biological terms as 'parasites', 'vermin' or 'filth' that could only corrupt the victorious proletariat and hence had to be excluded from the emerging polity through the deprivation of political rights, exile or incarceration (see Dobrenko 2007: 80–1; Weiner 1999: 1121), this exclusion did not operate in strict accordance with the naturalist and evolutionary logic of racism. The class enemy of the Great Break was not to be expunged or eliminated in a project of the purification of the race but rather transformed in what the official discourse of the time called 'reforging' (*perekovka*) – a violent project of correction that nonetheless stopped short of extermination.

The heterogeneity of socialist biopolitics to racism and to any form of naturalism more generally is best illustrated with an example from the field of biology, that is the fate of genetics and eugenics in Stalinist USSR, which changed drastically precisely in the period of the Great Break. Starting from the early 1920s, the Soviet regime took a strongly pro-Lamarckian position in the debate on genetics. The affirmation of the inheritability of acquired characteristics evidently vindicated the Bolshevik revolutionary project of the transformation of human nature through the modification of its environment. This Lamarckian orientation resonated with the interest of Soviet medical science in the 'positive' eugenics of the betterment of the human species through public health measures as opposed to the 'negative' eugenics of the forced sterilisation of the genetically unfit. Whereas the negative eugenic orientation clearly resonated with the ideals of racial purification underlying Nazi biopolitics, the positive programme appeared to converge with the revolutionary aspirations of socialism and the emerging social policies of the Soviet state. For this reason, in the immediate aftermath of the Revolution the Soviet regime embraced eugenics enthusiastically, both as a practical concern in the struggle against syphilis and alcoholism and as an ideal of social transformation more generally (Adams 1990; Rosenthal 2002: 195–202). Having triumphed over monarchy and the capitalists, the new regime could only be expected to revolt against heredity as well. In Trotsky's words, 'the human race will not have ceased to crawl on all fours before God, kings and capital in order to submit humbly before the dark laws of heredity and blind sexual selection' (Trotsky cited in Rosenthal 2002: 195). Similarly, in Bukharin's view, only the possibility of a positive-eugenic transformation ultimately legitimised the very project of the revolution as the transformation of the environment in order to improve the life of the human species: 'if we took the view that racial or national peculiarities are so persistent that it would take thousands of years to change them, then of course our whole work would be absurd because it would be built on sand' (Bukharin cited in Rosenthal 2002: 284).

The belief that positive eugenics was compatible with Marxism was also shared by many Western geneticists, such as Hermann Müller or Paul Kammerer, who were sympathetic to the Soviet Union and were lionised there in the 1920s. Eugenics was also positively viewed in much of the Soviet art and literature predating the Great Break. For instance, Sergei Tretiakov's celebrated play *I Want a Child* (1927) featured a protagonist who decided to have a child according to rational and politically correct principles, choosing a father that was both fit and proletarian, so that the baby would be genetically purged of the capitalist past (see Kiaer 2005). The project of artificial insemination was also discussed seriously in scientific circles as a means to increase the number of people with desirable heritable traits. Given the decline of the 'bourgeois family' after the revolution, women could now follow Tretiakov's protagonist in selecting the optimal sperm to produce the desired effects in their offspring, 'not necessarily from a beloved spouse' (Serebrovsky cited in Rosenthal 2002: 264). In Hermann Müller's later defence of eugenics the project of artificial insemination was elevated to the outright grandiose level.

> In the course of a paltry century or two, it would be possible for the majority of the population to become of the inner quality of such men as Lenin, Newton, Leonardo, Pasteur, Beethoven, Omar Hayam, Pushkin, Sun Yat Sen, Marx ... or even to possess their varied qualities combined. (Müller cited in Adams 1990: 194–5)

For Müller it was only in a classless society that eugenics revealed its full potential in improving humanity on the basis of universalism and egalitarianism: just as the proletariat appropriated the sphere of *production* after the October revolution, it must now appropriate the sphere of *reproduction*.

Nonetheless, starting from the late 1920s, eugenics quickly fell out of favour in the USSR, along with genetics more generally (Adams 1990: 180–1; Hoffmann 2011: 161–4; Rosenthal 2002: 264–5). During the Great Break eugenic research institutes, laboratories and specialised journals were shut down, while its practitioners were ridiculed and harassed. The drive of the Cultural Revolution for proletarian science made genetics suspect since it was originally associated with aristocratism and elitism. Moreover, the 'specialist-baiting' atmosphere of the time, marked by hostility towards bourgeois 'experts' of all sorts, made any idea of technical regulation of reproduction particularly suspect. Finally, much of the eugenic discourse emphasised the traditional role of women as mothers, which contradicted the emphasis in both the official and militant discourse on gender equality and the entry of women into the work force.

The greatest blow to Soviet eugenics and genetics came after 1933, when it became associated with Nazi racism and this association was used in the power struggle within Soviet biological science (Rosenthal 2002: 414–21). The phenomenon of Lysenkoism that has become the eponym for politically motivated pseudo-science arose out of the transfer of the principled anti-naturalism of Soviet governmental rationality into natural science itself. Trofim Lysenko, the long-time director of the Academy of Agricultural Sciences and the winner of two Stalin Prizes, made his name in the late 1920s by developing a technique of vernalisation, exposing the crops to high humidity and low temperatures, in order to increase the crop yield. While the actual success of this technique was debatable, in the conditions of famine in the early 1930s it made Lysenko a hero, particularly insofar as he differed from most biological scientists in having the correct proletarian background and a strong interest in politics (see Dobrenko 2007: 90–100).

Distinguishing himself from every version of genetics as biologically determinist and hence anti-Marxist, Lysenko claimed that nature could be entirely reshaped by human beings either by hybridisation or manipulating the environment. He was dissatisfied with the 'flat' evolutionism of Darwinism, since it excluded revolutionary leaps, and particularly dismissive of 'Mendelist-Morganist' genetics. The latter 'anti-revolutionary' science denied the possibility of 'controlling and purposefully changing the nature of organisms' by the 'appropriate change of the conditions of life of these organisms' and was therefore literally 'powerless' and 'fruitless' in contrast to the 'effective' Soviet revolutionary biology (Lysenko cited in ibid.: 97). Influenced by Ivan Michurin's experiments in creating new varieties of plants through grafting, Lysenko generalised and radicalised Michurin's relatively modest results into the apparent proof of the possibility of the human domination and control of nature, including, ultimately, human nature itself. This was to be achieved by 'slackening heredity'.

> Organisms with slackened heredity are more pliable, more plastic in the sense of acquiring new properties and characteristics needed by the experimenter. By raising the progeny of such pliable, plastic organisms in defined conditions from generation to generation, we get coordination of organs, functions, and processes; we get the new, relatively stable and reinforced, heredity of the organism that we need. (Lysenko cited in ibid.: 97).

Heredity would then be completely overcome and new species or combinations thereof could be produced: 'In our country, in any area of human activity, one may create miracles' (Lysenko cited in Rosenthal 2002: 414). Radicalising the Lamarckian position into a political standpoint, Lysenko opposed every version of genetics as contradicting the Marxist assumption of the irreducibly social character of human beings, who only become properly 'human' in a society and may therefore be completely (re)shaped by the socioeconomic system of this society.

> In our Soviet Union, comrades, *people* are not born. Human organisms are born, but *people* are created from organisms in our country – tractor drivers, motorists, mechanics, academicians, scientists and so on. And I am one of the people created in this way. I was not *born* as a human being. I was *made* as a human being. (Lysenko cited in ibid.: 416; original emphasis)

While his scientific credentials were allegedly dubious, Lysenko proved himself a master of translating ideological dogmata into pseudo-scientific discourse and intimidating his opponents by treating them as political enemies, 'kulaks' and 'wreckers' in science (ibid.: 416). As a result of his scheming, leading geneticists such as Nikolai Vavilov were arrested and executed during the Great Terror, while Lysenko developed a minor cult of his own that survived even the death of Stalin (see Krementsov 1996). In the postwar period he masterminded the grand project of the Great Transformation of Nature (*velikoe preobrazovanie prirody*), a series of frequently hubristic measures of land development, irrigation, the planting of shelterbelts that were supposed to improve the situation in Soviet agriculture after the famine of 1946–7. As with other Lysenko's enterprises, its success was questionable at best and the Great Transformation of Nature was abandoned after Stalin's death, along with all other designs for great transformations.

It is easy to see why the Soviet regime would reject genetic determinism, which put in question the very ambition of radical social transformation that would produce a new type of human being. It is also easy to see why it would be appalled by negative eugenics that blatantly contradicted the universalist egalitarianism of the official ideology and, moreover, was enthusiastically practised by the main ideological antagonist of the USSR at the time. It is more difficult to understand why even positive eugenics, based on Lamarckian principles, would fall out of favour during the Great Break and afterwards. In our view, for all its optimism regarding the transformation of humanity positive eugenics remained far too cautious about the possible speed of such transformation, quickly falling behind the dazzling tempos of collectivisation and industrialisation. This is why Lysenkoism radicalised this orientation to such an extent that it ultimately abandoned all concern with heredity as such. It was no longer a matter of modifying the nature of Soviet citizens through artificial insemination, making them resemble Marx and Omar Hayam 'in a paltry century or two'. Socialism could not wait that long and, according to Lysenko, it did not have to: if people were not born but were made, then it was possible to *re*-make them at any point in their lives, without the century-long process of managing heredity, and, moreover, the effects of such remaking would be inherited in accordance with Lamarckian principles, making it unnecessary to repeat the exercise of remaking in the future. While Lamarckism originally appealed to the Soviet regime due to its resonances with Marxism, it was eventually discredited as a version of 'biologism' (Rosenthal 2002: 285), which became a pejorative term from the Cultural Revolution onwards. The Stalinist politics of the transformation of life, that is *bio*politics, was, paradoxically at first glance, hostile to biology as such, viewing it as an obstacle or a limit to the radical transformation that should not take centuries but must take place in the here and now. Thus, the Soviet experiments with eugenics in the 1920s were filed away along with numerous other ineffective attempts at producing socialism in real life.

What remained was Stalin's own version, whose essence was, as we have seen, the forcing of the socialist ideal into the immanence of life by forcing out the existing forms of life. Lysenko's charlatanry was a perfect correlate to this policy in the field of science: while it had nothing to do with science as we know it, it provided the only possible 'scientific' version of this project, the *biological allegory of Stalinism*. As Dobrenko argues (2007: 92), Lysenkoism was not a matter of illegitimate extrapolation of ideology into biology but rather of the transformation of biology itself into a 'total metaphor'. It is therefore important to avoid the mistake of attributing to Stalinist biopolitics any influences from the field of biology. It was obviously *not* Lysenko who influenced Stalin, but strictly the other way round. Lysenko's 'socialist biology' was only successful in dominating the scientific field because it shared the fundamental problematisation of life with the Stalinist political project. Lysenko's affirmation of the possibility to create new species through the manipulation of the environment is merely a variation on the theme of forcing the transcendent idea into the immanence of life, which was also at work in such different settings as Makarenko's pedagogy, Strumilin's economic planning, Marr's linguistics, the productionist novel and the White Sea-Baltic canal. Rather than be in any way influenced or determined by biological knowledge, Stalinist biopolitics transformed the field of biology itself, but, as will be the case in other spheres, did so only negatively, leaving Soviet biology to degrade in the shadow of Lysenko's charlatanry.[5]

THE SOVIET KATECHON

The Bolshevik emphasis on the transcendence of nature may also be approached from a different perspective, namely the messianic character of the revolution. While the parallels between Bolshevik ideology and practice and various religious movements have often been used to question the authenticity or consistency of their communist commitments (Berdyaev 1937; cf. Halfin 2009), the connection between Bolshevism and messianism testifies less to the perversion of the scientific spirit of Marxism by archaic Russian superstitions than to the fidelity of the Russian Revolution to the spirit of Marxism itself, whose messianic character has only been fully illuminated in the political philosophy of the late twentieth century (Derrida 1994; Agamben 2005b). The 'revolutionary dreamers' of the 1920s embodied the ethos of messianism in trying to render inoperative the forms of life that past regimes construed as natural, essential or necessary and invent new forms of praxis that were purposefully, playfully and proudly cast as un- or anti-natural, from the use of bewildering acronyms to designate new Soviet institutions (Sovnarkom, Narkompros, Glavlit) to the invention of new revolutionary names for children (Vladilen, Oktyabrina, Dazdraperma). This experimentation with transcending the natural and affirming whatever the old world deemed contrary to nature was in perfect accordance with the logic of the radical reversal of the order of things in Pauline messianism: 'God chose what is low and despised in the world, even things that are not, to bring to nothing things that are' (1. Cor. 27–8, cited in Badiou 2001b: 47). Where the natural order once was, revolutionary messianism produces the radically new.

In the early Stalinist period this messianic orientation underwent an important transformation as a result of changes in the status of the communist ideal. As the messianic anticipation of world revolution dwindled after the end of World War I, the question arose of how the solitary revolutionary state may sustain itself in the hostile environment. Should the USSR pause and adapt to the capitalist world system (the NEP project) or continue on its path towards communism separately from the rest of the world (the solution eventually adopted by Stalin)? In the latter approach socialism was dissociated from the messianic idea of global transformation, of which the October Revolution in Russia would only be the triggering event, but rather began to define the positivity of the new Soviet state. For this state to maintain itself in the capitalist environment socialism had to cease to be a rallying cry for a global revolution and become a really existing form of order (see Van Ree 2002: 84–94). This new constellation permits us to understand the full significance of the much-maligned concept of 'real socialism', which refers precisely to the form of social order instituted in the USSR under Stalin and by Stalinist regimes in the post-World War II Eastern Europe. Insofar as by the late 1920s 'socialism in one country' became not merely a debatable doctrinal point but an empirical fact, it could only be sustained by converting the passion for the messianic transcendence of all natural orders into the real existence of a new immanent order as a 'second nature'.

As a result of this conversion in the mid-1920s the messianic understanding of socialism appears to give way to what we may call the katechontic logic. The concept of the katechon that first appears in St Paul's Second Letter to the Thessalonians refers to the restraining or delaying force that prevents *both* the coming of the Antichrist and the advent of *parousia* that is to follow it (see Schmitt 2003: 60; Agamben 2005b: 109–10; Virno 2008: 56–61; Esposito 2011: 52–79; Prozorov 2012). The katechon, originally exemplified by the Roman Empire, does not bring redemption to the society in the manner of the messiah or a quasi-messianic revolutionary party, but rather defers *both* redemption and catastrophe by maintaining the reign of the 'lesser evil' in order to make possible the eventual advent of the good. The doctrine of socialism in one country exemplified this katechontic logic by promising to sustain the new socialist state in the hostile capitalist environment but only at the price of deferring and indeed restraining the *parousia* of world revolution. In this logic the revolutionary ideal of the transcendence of nature must itself be attained within the immanence of the natural order of things so that socialism could be endowed with a real existence. By making socialism biopolitical the katechon would ensure its reality.

Yet, this is where things become complicated. The very ambition to make socialism real and thus sustainable as a form of life 'in one country' requires a radical overhaul of the real forms of life that characterised Soviet society on the eve of the Great Break, particularly in the rural areas, in which the Bolshevik revolution had actually resulted in the formation of a smallholders' market economy. During Stalin's fateful trip to Siberia in winter 1928, when he reached a decision on forced collectivisation, he gave an address to the local party bureau, arguing that Soviet economic development had reached a dead-end with the NEP. The only individual peasants that modernised their practices, using machines and fertilisers, were the well-off 'kulaks', whose very successes contradicted the ideological aspirations of the regime towards radical equality. 'The regime had become caught in a class-based vicious circle. The Bolsheviks desperately needed the peasants to produce good harvests, but the better the peasants did, the more they turned into class enemies, the kulaks' (Kotkin 2014: 676). The more successful the present NEP system was,

The Great Break: Making Socialism Real

the more distant socialism appeared, making it necessary for the regime to turn away from stimulating and sustaining its operation.

> [Could] we develop agriculture in kulak fashion, as individual farms, along the path of large-scale farms and the path of latifundia, as in Hungary, Eastern Prussia, America and so on? No, we could not. We're a Soviet country, we want to implant a collective economy, not solely in industry, but in agriculture. The whole Soviet system, all our laws, all our financial measures, all measures to supply villages with agricultural equipment, everything here moves in the direction of limiting individual-proprietor large-scale farming. [The Soviet system] cuts the kulak off in every way, which has resulted in the cul-de-sac into which our agriculture has now entered. Unification of small and tiny peasant household farms into large collective farms for us is the only path. (Stalin cited in Kotkin 2014: 671–2)

The construction of socialism in the countryside requires the destruction of the current smallholders' economy, including the kulak as a form of life. Thus, the katechon of socialism ends up protecting the *future* order by purposefully undermining the *present* one. It might appear paradoxical that this turn towards violent destruction came as a result of the abandonment of the messianic drive of world revolution, which would at first glance be expected to lead to a certain moderation of politics, its reorientation towards adaptive pragmatism and common sense, greater tolerance or even a re-appreciation of tradition, and so on. Indeed, this was how Stalin's ascent to power over Trotsky and the Left Opposition was first perceived by many representatives of the Soviet intelligentsia in the late 1920s (Bykov 2005: 515–19; 2008: 265–7). Yet, the hopes of many contemporaries that Stalin's policies would overcome the radical uprooting of the 1920s and proceed gradually by embedding the socialist project in the existing traditions were bound to be disappointed. Stalin's ascendancy over Trotsky did not bring about the moderation of the regime but rather its onslaught on the existing non-socialist forms of life in the name of converting the precepts of Soviet ideology into lived reality. Even though, as we shall see, this biopolitical assault of the Great Break was soon followed by the Great Retreat, characterised by a certain rehabilitation of the pre-Soviet forms of life, this very rehabilitation was soon accompanied by the genocidal terror of 1936–8. 'We now know that the apparent restoration of tradition is likely to lead to more victims than its destruction: restoration only pretends to heal dislocated joints but in fact it breaks one's arms' (Bykov 2005: 516). As the katechon of the socialist order, the Stalinist regime certainly defended social immanence against its evaporation in the world-revolutionary transcendence. Yet, insofar as the katechon was meant to sustain the *socialist* order, that realm of social immanence first had to be *made* socialist through the transcendence of all existing forms of life that conflicted with this ideal.

Since socialist lives admittedly cannot be created *ex nihilo*, they must be created out of the lives that are presently non-socialist: bourgeois, peasant, religious, individualist, and so on. How is this creation to take place? As long as transformation is thought in cultural terms of learning and indoctrination, it maintains a distance from the lives that are to be transformed in it and which are retained as immanent supports for the emergence of new political subjects. In Alain Badiou's contemporary reactivation of communist politics, these subjects are formed by incorporating their physical, living bodies into new 'bodies of truth', whereby particular desires and interests of the mortal 'human animal' are subordinated to the 'immortal' universality of political truths (Badiou 2009: 508–14). Evidently, this transcendence of the human animal's particularity is only possible *on the basis* of the same animal's physical body. 'The Immortal exists only in and by the mortal animal' (Badiou 2001a: 84). However extreme the content of its ideas, ideological messianism must necessarily presuppose the lives of the beings it targets as the condition of its own possibility.

Yet, what happens if this distance between the transcendent idea or 'truth' and the physical body is abolished in the biopolitical conversion of messianism, in which it is the human animal *itself* that must become socialist? In this case, the life to be created and the life to be transcended coincide without remainder, there no longer being any need for the immanent support of the transcendent truth, since the transcendent must itself become wholly immanent. The condition for this passage into immanence is no longer the preservation of the 'mortal animal' with its possibly deficient forms of life but rather its giving way to the New Soviet Person. The very same being that was promised the brighter future as a subject of a radically new life becomes the object of governmental violence that aims at nothing but fulfilling this promise, purging the old life away so that the new one might take root. The constitutive paradox of socialist biopolitics is that the combination of the immanentism inherent in any biopolitical rationality and the orientation towards transcendence that defines the communist revolution necessarily leads to the extinction of the very reality that is to be made socialist. The forcing of revolutionary transcendence within immanence ends up recasting transcendence in terms of empirical negation, whereby 'the things that are' are 'brought to nothing' through destruction and annihilation.

While the more conventional reading of the logic of the katechon (Esposito 2011: 57–64) approaches its function as the partial negation of order for the purposes of its preservation, the post-revolutionary Soviet katechon appeared to preserve the existing order solely in order to negate it itself. Whereas the utopian experiments of the 1920s dreamed of a total transcendence of 'old Russia' while leaving that very Russia intact as the material support for their imaginative quests, the Stalinist moderation of the pathos of transcendence rehabilitated 'old Russia' as the actual site for the construction of socialism, which eventually consigned it to empirical negation. It is not utopian radicalism but its biopolitically inflected moderation that eventually led to the paroxysmal violence of Stalinism.

DEATH TO THE DYING

We are now in a better position to address the question of the violent character of Soviet biopolitics through a systematic comparison of the Stalinist case with liberal and Nazi biopolitics. While Stalinist state violence is certainly extreme in comparison with any known case of liberal biopolitics, we ought not to forget that critical studies in the Foucauldian tradition have long emphasised the link between biopolitics and violence in liberal contexts. Despite the naturalist ontology at the heart of liberal biopolitics, the liberal orientation of *laissez-faire* never entailed the passive abandonment of an aboriginal reality to its own devices, but rather featured elaborate interventionist measures that sought to secure 'natural liberty' by taking necessary measures to correct its perversions. This 'corrective' aspect points to what Mitchell Dean and Barry Hindess have respectively termed the 'illiberality of liberalism' and the 'liberal government of unfreedom' (Dean 1999: 131–49, 2002a: 37–8; Hindess 2001: 93–5). According to these authors, liberal government historically identified within the 'natural' realm of society manifold categories of the population, whose properties or acts were deemed 'contrary to nature' and had to be rectified through governmental interventions, from the confinement of the mad to the correction of juvenile delinquents (Hindess 2001: 93–7). What unites all the objects of liberal interventions, irrespectively of whether they are deemed to be evil, mentally disabled, morally deficient or simply 'irrational', is their functioning in liberal governmentality as beings whose existence both belongs to nature and somehow violates its laws. On the one hand, these individuals and groups belong to the social realm, cast as ontologically and axiologically prior to government in the liberal mode of problematisation. On the other hand, however, their practices are not in accordance with the liberal vision of 'natural liberty' and thus require corrective interventions of liberal government that would restore the system of natural liberty to its proper functioning.

The orientation of liberal biopolitics towards security permits us to understand its corrective interventions in terms of Roberto Esposito's (2008a, 2011) influential notion of *immunisation*, that he presents as the paradigm of Western biopolitics. Similarly to the katechon discussed in the previous section, the politics of immunisation seeks to protect the community from its constituent negativity by mobilising this very negativity as an instrument of defence.

> [Immunity] reproduces in a controlled form exactly what it is meant to protect us from. Just as in the medical practice of vaccinating the individual body, so the immunization of the political body functions similarly, introducing within it a fragment of the same pathogen from which it wants to protect itself, by blocking and contradicting natural development. (Esposito 2008a: 8–9)

In a similar manner, liberalism violates its own limits so as to secure the operation of the system of natural liberty against the threats that this liberty appears to pose to itself. Insofar as natural liberty must logically presuppose the liberty of being contrary to nature and is thus a permanent danger to itself (Virno 2008: 31–4), liberal biopolitics is permanently mobilised for the protection of society from the threat of 'denaturation' that is inherent in it by practising a measure of this very denaturation itself in the governmental intervention of the kind that it otherwise frowns upon. In this manner, liberalism functions as a paradoxical agent of *re*-naturalisation, restoring the principles of natural liberty by repeatedly violating them in the name of their inviolability.

These interventions point to an inherent ambiguity in the central concept of liberal biopolitics: liberal society is simultaneously natural and artificial, both an antecedent reality, whose immanent rationality poses a limit to governmental action, and a positivity attained and maintained only through that action (Hindess 1996: 68–75). Liberal governmentality finds its very condition of possibility in the generalised 'illiberality' of corrective interventionism, which violates liberalism's own naturalist presuppositions but is nonetheless essential to its existence, functioning in the mode of the Derridean supplement, 'a strange difference which constitutes [liberalism] by breaching it' (Derrida 1998: 98). In Dean's reading, this paradox makes liberalism a potentially 'total' modality of government

> because its program of self-limitation is linked to the facilitation and augmentation of the powers of civil society and its use of these powers, in conjunction with the sovereign, disciplinary and biopolitical powers of the state itself, to establish a comprehensive normalisation of social, economic and cultural existence. (Dean 2002b: 129)

The Great Break: Making Socialism Real

The naturalisation of a certain artificial conception of society permits perpetual interventions in the name of its natural order, disavowing the constitutive and frequently violent character of these governmental practices. At the heart of liberal biopolitics we may therefore observe the aporia, whereby its naturalist ontology is always contaminated by the logic of supplementarity and every 'natural liberty' bears traces of 'corrective' interventions.

This critique of liberal governmentality that exposes its perpetual transgression of its own limits in the projects of immunitary re-naturalisation of the social realm attunes us to the implausibility of any simplistic contrast between liberalism and totalitarianism as between 'limited' and 'unlimited' government. Nonetheless, it would be equally implausible to efface all differences between, for example, liberal and Stalinist biopolitics on the grounds that liberalism does not respect its own limits. It would be more fruitful to focus on the specific role that this limit of 'natural liberty', however frequently violated, plays in liberal biopolitics. In the simplest of terms, liberal biopolitics intervenes in the society in order to secure its immanent functioning, which presupposes that this society must retain its self-identity, remain *what it is* in the course of and as a result of governmental interventions. The violent interventions of liberal government must therefore be limited to the cases when the object of government does not (appear to) follow its own natural laws, that is when its very existence is posited as a threat to the self-identity of the society as a whole. Of course, we should not complacently conclude from this that violent interventionism somehow becomes exceptional or peripheral to liberalism: since the natural character of the liberal society is *itself* an artifice, in principle anything can be found to violate it, from masturbating children to hysterical mothers, from welfare recipients to profligate governments. *Anything* but not *everything* – as long as there is at least *something* in the existing reality that government may graft itself onto as its foundation, the limit to the biopolitical negation of the given forms of life remains there.

The historical significance of the distance of Bolshevism from this liberal problematisation may be grasped with the help of a brief consideration of what socialism might have been in Russia in the case of the victory of the populist Socialist Revolutionary (SR) party that rivalled Marxism from the late nineteenth century until the October Revolution and posed the most serious challenge to the Bolsheviks in the aftermath of the Revolution (Smith 2011). The fundamental difference of the SR ideology from Bolshevism consisted in its valorisation of the Russian peasant commune as the site for the construction of the socialist order. In contrast, for the Bolsheviks the commune, or whatever remained of it in the aftermath of the late nineteenth- to early twentieth-century capitalist reforms of Sergei Witte and Petr Stolypin, was the locus of the most reactionary attitudes, entirely hostile to the socialist project (see Istoria VKP(b): 15). The Bolshevik attitude to the commune reflected their overall tendency towards the denigration of the existing reality as the condition of possibility of its revolutionary transcendence. For instance, Lenin's famous treatise 'The Development of Capitalism in Russia' (1967 [1908]) sought to prove, somewhat counter-intuitively, that capitalism was indeed sufficiently developed in Russia, so that it could then proceed to argue, on the basis of the Marxist logic, that its development was characterised by insurmountable contradictions that must eventually lead to its revolutionary negation. The socioeconomic reality was worth something only insofar as it harboured sufficiently strong contradictions that would threaten, or rather promise, its eventual disappearance. 'The catastrophic collapse of the old world, however debilitating for millions of real people, was taken as progress by the Bolsheviks: the deeper the ruin, the better' (Kotkin 2014: 231). In contrast, the SR valorisation of the commune (which was cautiously supported by none other than Marx (1881) himself in his letter to Vera Zasulich) located in the existing reality at least a kernel of a possible socialist transformation, which transformed their idea of the social revolution into a far less violent project. While the socialist-revolutionaries were anything but liberal in their substantive politics, their mode of problematisation of life shared with liberalism the naturalist ontology that connected the revolutionary project of transcendence to the immanence of human existence in a positive mode of securing and developing that which was already there, not accelerating the demise of that which is in the name of what is not yet there.[6]

Let us now briefly address Nazi biopolitics, which at least matched its 'totalitarian' twin in the scope and intensity of lethal violence. Without abandoning the naturalist ontology of life characteristic of liberalism, Nazism specified these naturalist presuppositions in racial terms. While classical liberalism claimed to protect the natural reality of economic exchange from corruption by governmental interference, Nazism claimed to protect the natural reality of the Aryan race from contamination by heterogeneous and alien elements in German society. Yet, precisely because the very naturality of this figure of race was at least as fictitious as liberal liberty, the elements it needed protection from multiplied infinitely and ultimately threatened to engulf German society as a whole. The violent paroxysms of Nazi biopolitics thus exemplify the most extreme form of Esposito's 'paradox of immunisation', whereby the desire to protect society from the negativity internal to it leads to the introjection of secondary or artificial negativity to such an extent that it ultimately threatens the society's survival.

> Immunity negates the power of negation, at least what it considers as such. Yet it is precisely because of this that immunity continues to speak the language of the negative, which it would like to annul: in order to avoid a potential evil it produces the real one; it substitutes an excess with a defect, a fullness with an emptiness, a plus with a minus, negating what it affirms and so doing affirming nothing other than its negation. (Esposito 2008a: 92)

Nazism found the German race lacking, that is harbouring the negativity of impurity, and sought to mend that lack through the negativity of a purifying violence, which ultimately turned suicidal: 'it is only by killing as many people as possible that one could heal those who represented the true Germany' (ibid.: 115). The extremity of the Nazi genocide is not a perversion of the idea of immunisation, but rather its logical conclusion, whereby the immunitary logic folds back on itself in an *autoimmune* manner: '[Nazism] strengthened its own immunitary apparatus to the point of remaining victim to it. The only way for an individual or collective organism to save itself definitely from the risk of death is to die' (ibid.: 138). From this perspective, the thanatopolitical conversion of Nazism into genocidal violence did not result from the absence of a restraining function of the katechon. On the contrary, the genocide was in itself an exercise of such restraining force, whereby the Nazi regime first made biological life the sole object of its protection and then sought to restrain the degenerate negativity it quite unsurprisingly found everywhere in the biological substance of the population. If the means of katechontic protection are always negative and if the danger is to be found everywhere in the population, then it is not surprising that katechontic protection ends up converted into a genocidal project of total negation. Thus, while Nazism certainly exemplifies an 'exasperated', 'paroxysmic', 'out of control' mode of the katechontic logic (Esposito 2006: 52–3), it does not leave the overall immunitary paradigm of biopolitics behind. The key difference of Nazism from liberal biopolitics consists in its construction of human nature in strictly biological terms, which renders its immunitary project no longer metaphorical but horrendously literal: 'What before had always been a vitalist metaphor becomes a reality in Nazism' (ibid.: 112). Yet, this shift from the metaphorical to the literal and from mediation to immediacy still takes place within the coordinates of the katechontic orientation.

Thus, both liberalism and Nazism deployed thanatopolitical interventions as 'secondary' immunising means of combating the negativity inherent in the social body, supplementing the ostensibly primary task of the positive augmentation of the vital capacities of respectively the economy and the race in accordance with their immanent natural laws. Only to the extent that these laws were held to be violated or endangered did the biopolitical rationality authorise violent interventions that sought to protect life from its immanent 'natural' negativity by the injection of secondary, 'artificial', negativity. This secondary negativity might at times slip out of control and endanger the survival of life itself, yet these paroxysms indicated biopolitics going *wrong*. For instance, the massive violence of liberal regimes in colonial territories could be understood as the betrayal of liberalism from *within* the liberal orientation (Losurdo 2011), while Hitler's 1945 Demolition Order that condemned the German population to death through the destruction of vital infrastructure was clearly a symptom of the ultimate *failure* of Nazism (Hoffmann and Timm 2009). While these paroxysms of immunitary biopolitics are indeed inherent in it as potentialities for thanatopolitical conversion, they are only accessible within these rationalities *as* paroxysmal, excessive and perverse. The naturalist presuppositions of the immunitary logic serve both to authorise corrective interventions and to condemn them when things get out of hand.

In contrast, the thanatopolitical conversion of Stalinist biopolitics may not be explained by the radicalisation of the paradox of immunity, since it is precisely the immunitary function that is *renounced* in the idea of forcing revolutionary transcendence into immanence. The anti-naturalism of Soviet biopolitics produces an uncanny reversal of the immunitary logic. While liberal and Nazi biopolitics are based on the idealisation of a particular existing form of life, which then functions as a standard for corrective interventions into other forms that do not accord with it, Soviet biopolitics is rather grounded in the imperative of the incarnation of the idea in life, the drive to give life to what does not yet exist. While naturalist modes of biopolitics may well deploy violence in order to protect what for them is a privileged form of life, there is *nothing* in the Stalinist biopolitical constellation that in principle deserves protection. Even the proletariat, in whose name the revolution had originally been undertaken, was radically diminished in numbers during the Civil War and was incapable of managing itself, let alone leading the country. In a clear contradiction to its own ideology, the Bolshevik Party had no basis in the Russian socioeconomic reality and hence faced *all* of this reality as an antagonist to be exposed to the violence of bringing a new life into being.

From the pre-revolutionary period until the Great Retreat of 1934 we would look in vain in the Bolshevik discourse for any valorisation of the existing forms of life in the Soviet Union, which were rather routinely vilified by the official discourse and, even more intensely, by the proletarian militants of the Cultural Revolution.[7] The village commune obscurantist and reactionary, the workers illiterate and disorganised, the intelligentsia decadent and disloyal – there was nothing in the Bolshevik biopolitical problematisation that could play the role of the market economy in liberalism or the racial substance in Nazism. Instead, the 'old world' was to be renounced completely in the name of a radical transformation that would genuinely break human history into two, the pre-communist era that would become 'pre-history' and the history of mankind proper that the construction of socialism would inaugurate. Contrary to both liberal and Nazi biopolitics that, at least in their ideological self-description, sought to capture and govern life according to its *own* immanent rationality, Soviet biopolitics was from the very beginning *hostile* to the very life it sought to govern. This hostility was particularly evident with regard to the peasant population (that is, the absolute majority of Soviet population on the eve of the Great Break), whose form of life was perhaps furthest away from the socialist ideal and therefore became the target of the most violent onslaught. The form of life practised by the overwhelming majority of the population was an obstacle to the actualisation of the revolutionary ideal and therefore a threat to the new life that the revolution promised.

Due to its renunciation of all naturalist presuppositions, the violence that seems counterintuitive in immunitary biopolitics is not at all paradoxical in the Soviet case. After all, the Internationale promised that the revolution would 'wipe the slate clean' so that the 'world would change its foundation' and 'whoever was nothing would become everything'. There is, then, nothing surprising about the hostility of the revolutionary project to life *as it is*, to the immanence of given forms of life that have attained a quasi-natural status or to 'mere life' understood as the confinement of humanity in its nature (Bykov 2008: 299). Moreover, the model for this 'change of foundation' had already been established by the political revolution of 1917, in which 'nothing' became 'everything' (and, conversely, the elites became 'former people') in the symbolic terms of positive and negative discrimination, abolition of ranks and titles, lustration, confiscation of property, and so on. Yet, as soon as we go beyond mere juridico-political reversal and venture to produce socialism as a positive form of life, the logic of the Internationale gets even more ominous. How can we change the foundation of the world in lived reality? What is the 'clean slate' if it is no longer a metaphor? Translated into biopolitical terms, the hostility to the existing world means that for nothing to become everything, something in the world would have to become *nothing*, that is, cease to exist. 'The absolute idealism of revolutionary engagement unleashed total instrumentalism in the elimination of obstacles hindering the new' (Sloterdijk 2012: 149).

This does not mean that Stalin and the Stalinists actually wanted to kill all their victims, but only that the possibility of extreme state violence was inscribed at the heart of the Stalinist biopolitical project. Of course, there were numerous factors that contributed to the particularly lethal outcomes of the Stalinist project: the experience of the Civil War that militarised the Party and the state, the structural paranoia of the Soviet regime about counter-revolution and the hostile international environment, the intolerance of internal opposition and factionalism, Stalin's personal suspiciousness and insecurity, the absence of due legal process, and so on (see Kotkin 2014: 649–52). While all of these factors made the regime's violent onslaught on the society more likely, what made it possible in the first place was the devaluation of the given forms of life in terms of the socialist ideal that led to the withdrawal of governmental protection from them.[8]

Thus, in a clear contrast to the logic of immunisation in both its moderate and extreme forms, the biopolitical rationality of Stalinism did not seek to promote, optimise, augment or even correct *what is* (however fictitious and artificial this given object turned out to be) but rather to *make be* (to create as positive reality that which was only present in the transcendent form of the revolutionary ideal). In the Stalinist problematisation the immanent reality of social life that liberalism and Nazism valorised as natural in their own distinct ways was devalued in its positive content by the very ideal which would come to replace it. If the existing reality of private property, individualism, religion, and so on is from the outset construed as obsolete and dying, then it can never pose a positive limit but only a purely negative obstacle to socialist transformation. The only thing that socialism promises to this dying reality is the actualisation of its death. This is why from the moment of its biopolitical conversion in the Great Break socialism became what Peter Sloterdijk (2012: 170) termed an 'exterminist' project.

Of course, our distinction between the immunitary or securitarian orientation of Western biopolitics and the transformative or constructivist orientation of Stalinism operates with ideal types of rationalities that were rather more intertwined in reality. After all, both the *homo economicus* and the *Volksgemeinschaft* that figure in liberalism and Nazism as objects of protection are not natural givens but constructs that first come into being in the very practices of their alleged protection. There is evident transformative violence in the governmental redefinition of all social life in racial terms, just as there is – undoubtedly lesser – violence in viewing all social life through the lens of entrepreneurial activity. As we have noted, the securitarian orientation of liberalism or Nazism did not preclude efforts at the positive transformation of those aspects of reality that were deemed contrary to nature. Conversely, the orientation of the Stalinist project towards radical transformation evidently did not exclude protective measures, particularly in relation to the newly emergent socialist realities: pro-natalist family policies, social hygiene and health promotion were as prominent in Stalin's USSR as they were in the capitalist West. While it would be entirely implausible to insist on the total separation of the two logics, it is nonetheless possible to identify the one that predominates in a given governmental rationality to such an extent that it authorises recourse to its opposite. The securitarian interventions of Stalinism had no autonomous basis akin to the naturalism and immanentism of Western biopolitics but were subordinated to the overall ethos of transcendence that was hostile to any form of naturalism. It would therefore be erroneous to look for precursors to Stalinist biopolitics in the Western models of the nineteenth and even the twentieth century. However, as we shall demonstrate in the following section, the Stalinist biopolitical rationality has an evident precursor in early twentieth-century Russian culture.

FEDOROV'S BIOPOLITICS OF RESURRECTION

We have demonstrated that the biopolitical rationality of Stalinism was based on the problematisation of the relation between the grand ideological vision of the communist revolution and the empirical lived reality that remained heterogeneous to it. The biopolitics of socialism is therefore by definition *transformative*, rather than securitarian, that is, it is oriented towards the transformation of life in accordance with certain ideological maxims or, amounting to the same thing, the translation of these maxims into lived reality. Its logic is therefore succinctly captured by a famous line from the Soviet song from the early 1920s: 'we were born to turn the fairy tale into life'. This formulation is a perfect summation of revolutionary socialism, which promises the attainment of freedom, equality and justice in this world through a fundamental reconstruction of the very foundations of social life. Yet, the genealogy of this logic is not exhausted by the travails of Marxism in Russia, since the ambition to turn a fairy tale into life also characterised diverse orientations in Russian philosophical, artistic, religious and scientific discourses before and after the 1917 Revolution. The idea of radical transformation of life in accordance with a certain idea or doctrine was affirmed by such diverse and irreconcilably opposed movements as symbolism, futurism, primitivism, theosophy, Proletkultism, and so on.

Of particular interest is the orientation that has received the name of Russian Cosmism. According to George Young (2012), the key feature that unites otherwise disparate approaches of religious philosophers such as Sergei Bulgakov and Pavel Florensky, natural scientists such as Vladimir Vernadsky and Alexander Chizhevsky, esoteric authors such as Alexander Svyatogor and Valerian Muraviev, is the principle of 'active evolution', the affirmation of the active role of humanity in the redemptive transformation of the world, the attainment of a new level of development or the overcoming of the human condition as we know it. Young defines Cosmism as a form of Promethean 'theurgy', in which thought, art and religion are endowed with an active transformative function as their contents are translated into lived reality. Cosmism is therefore distinct from the utopian genre in general, insofar as it emphasises the practical realisability of its ideals or at least attempts to make them realisable in principle.

> Active or self-directed evolution – holistic, anthropocentric and teleologically determined effort – are some of the terms that scholars have applied to all the Russian Cosmist thinkers, whether the given Cosmist is a poet, an artist, a theologian, a philosopher or a natural scientist. [Another characteristic] is the tendency to transform esoteric knowledge into exoteric, to turn elements of traditional occult wisdom into new directions in philosophy, theology, literature, art and science, a tendency that has allowed some critics of Cosmism to dismiss it as mere pseudoscience, pseudotheology and pseudophilosophy. A better way to describe [it] might be to regard it as occupying a unique borderland, a crossover area between science and magic. (Young 2012: 9)

The *transformation of the esoteric into the exoteric* is the key aspect of Cosmism as the precursor to socialist biopolitics. Russian Cosmists took up various aspects of Russian and foreign religious, occult or esoteric doctrines and tried to convert them into projects that could be realised in practice. Hence the attention of philosophers and esoteric thinkers among the Cosmists to the scientific aspect of their projects, and, conversely, the interest of Cosmist scientists in the grandiose designs that the science of the time deemed unrealisable. Insofar as the Cosmist movement sought to transform life within the terrain of life itself and not merely in the realm of ideas (Young 2012: 4–5), we may speak of this movement as proto-biopolitical, with an important proviso that while the movement in question was certainly *bio*-oriented, it was rather less *political*, insofar as its representatives neither had nor sought political power or influence. At the same time, the Cosmist movement was certainly sufficiently influential in Russian philosophical, scientific and artistic circles that it affected the Bolshevik orientation both before and after the Revolution (Young 2012: 193–217).

The key figure of Russian Cosmism from a biopolitical perspective is Nikolai Fedorov. Fedorov was born in 1829 as the illegitimate son of Prince Pavel Gagarin and was brought up by his father, having been separated from his mother at an early age. Throughout his life he maintained the role of the 'illegitimate' outsider, a nobleman without a title, a philosopher without a degree, a teacher without a job (Young 2012: 53) Having dropped out of the lyceum, Fedorov wandered all over central and southern Russia, taking on odd teaching jobs, seldom staying for more than a year due to conflicts with his superiors. It was during this period that he began developing his philosophy of universal resurrection that gradually gained popularity among such major figures as Tolstoy, Dostoyevsky, Soloviev and others. While Fedorov published precious little in this lifetime, his ideas quickly spread in oral form among the intelligentsia of Petersburg and Moscow and had an enormous influence on the most diverse fields of thought and practice, from Christian philosophy (Bulgakov, Florensky) to astronomy (Tsiolkovsky), from global history (Chizhevsky) to botany (Kuprevich), from poetry (Symbolism) to occultism (Theosophy).

Fedorov's grand project that he termed a 'common' or 'universal' task (*obshee delo*) was the resurrection of everyone who had ever lived on Earth. While this was definitely not a new idea and was in fact promised in various historical religions, Fedorov's version of the resurrection was clearly distinguished from all contemporaneous attempts to understand the overcoming of death in spiritual or religious terms (for example, in the work of such Russian philosophers as Soloviev or Bulgakov). While these and other authors sought to temper the radicalism of Fedorov's theses by reinterpreting them metaphorically, whereby resurrection pertained to the spirit alone or was a task projected infinitely into the future, Fedorov insisted that the resurrection was to be a real process accomplished in this world and resulting in the return to life of all who had ever lived. Notably, he called this project a 'task' or 'action' (*delo*), highlighting its practical orientation in contrast to the more contemplative orientation of other discourses on immortality. While his work was undeniably influenced by a wide variety of esoteric and religious sources (Young 2012: 81–6), Fedorov repeatedly attacked interpretations of his work that reduced his project to mystical, occult or esoteric ideas as dangerous distortions. The project of resurrection was to be undertaken within the immanence of lived reality, yet as a matter of the transcendence of this reality. Importantly in our context, Fedorov presented his project in terms of the confrontation and eventual victory over nature, the overcoming of its blind lethal force and putting it in the service of humanity.

For Fedorov every problem of human existence is ultimately derivative from the problem of death. Death or disintegration is a natural principle governing the existence of all things. Rather than associate nature with the vital principle, Fedorov saw in it primarily the power of death: the entire earth is a gigantic graveyard. Even the vital drive was devalued as ultimately leading to the 'animalisation' that Fedorov called 'pornocracy', a nihilistic surrender to sheer animality that is not much different from death (Fedorov 1970, vol. 1: 428). Similarly to Gorky, Fedorov was deeply critical of all naturalism, which he considered to be a Romantic idealisation, plausible only for the learned and the rich, who had no everyday contact with nature and were therefore able to aestheticise it. In truth, for those in direct contact within it nature was a matter of life and death and any nature worship was nothing but a 'death wish' (Young 2012: 60). Fedorov's anti-naturalism is easily understandable from the perspective of his key idea: if death is a natural phenomenon, then overcoming death entails a victory over nature. Yet, nature is not simply an enemy; if properly mastered, it can also become an ally in the struggle against death. Fedorov envisioned incredibly grandiose technological projects of rationally manipulating nature, such as controlling the Earth's electromagnetic field in order to escape the 'slavish orbiting of the sun', whereby the entire planet would become a spaceship that could be steered whenever one wished to go (Young 2012: 79). Yet, even though he called nature 'our temporary enemy but permanent friend' (Fedorov 1970, vol. 1: 239–40), the friendship in question is a rather asymmetric one, since nature remains both an object and an instrument of human interventions.

For Fedorov, the victory over nature would overcome not only death but also birth – in the 'reintegrated' world all who had ever lived would be restored back to life but no new beings would ever be born. The cessation of childbirth would indicate the triumph over nature in both its lethal and its vital power. Instead of creating new life, humanity would work on recreating all that had ever lived. Fedorov was notoriously hostile to the very idea of progress, which he viewed as mere acceleration of death and destruction. His ethics was oriented less towards a brighter future than towards correcting the extreme injustice of the past, whereby sons and daughters would return to their mothers and fathers the life that the latter had given them. Of the revolutionary ideas of liberty, equality and fraternity he only accepted the latter and even that was rethought in terms of the duty to one's parents, particularly fathers. The resurrection of our ancestors would reintegrate past and present humanity, overcoming every form of alienation.

> [The] earth will be the first star in heaven to be moved not by the blind force of gravity but by reason, which will have countered and prevented gravity and death. Nothing will be remote when in the integrated totality of worlds we shall see the integrated totality of all past generations. All will be kindred, nothing alien. This will be life ever new, regardless of its antiquity, spring without fall, morning without evening, youth without old age, resurrection without death. This day will be divine, awesome, but not miraculous, for resurrection will be a task not of a miracle but of knowledge and common labour. (Fedorov 1970, vol. 1: 203)

This is evidently a daunting project indeed, yet Fedorov emphasised that every little step along the way towards the universal resurrection would make the rest of the journey easier.

> Although the first resurrectee will be, in all likelihood, resurrected almost immediately after death, hardly ever having died, and after him will follow those, in whom very little decomposition is evident, nevertheless each new experience in this task will make subsequent steps easier. With each person resurrected, knowledge will be growing; it will peak in its task just when the human race arrives at the first person who died. (Fedorov cited in Young 2012: 49)

Moreover, since those resurrected would no longer die, they would have infinitely more time on their hands to pursue the studies necessary for resurrecting their ever more distant ancestors. It should eventually be possible to recreate whole persons from the tiniest particles of ancestral dust, which may be recovered on the moon or on other planets. Once the task of resurrection becomes truly universal and all other activities of humanity are subordinated to it, there is no limit to what humanity can do. At the same time, Fedorov proposed to start with more manageable and even modest projects, such as the establishment of local museums that would gather information on everyone who had ever lived. Whatever the scale of the project, what is crucial for Fedorov is the universality of the task, which can only be attained if it is taken up by the entire humanity that subordinates all of its activities to it. This is why Fedorov's political ideal was the unification of the world under one monarch who, somewhat unsurprisingly, was to be the Russian Emperor (Young 2012: 71–3).

The political dimension of Fedorov's project is arguably the least appealing part of his legacy. If the task to be realised is nothing less than the abolition of death, becoming God, the transcendence of nature, then it cannot be a matter of a free choice derived from one's particular interests but rather presupposes the unification of world society as a universal subject by a presumably enlightened Cosmist monarch. Moreover, as Young reminds us, a number of Fedorov's successors explicitly argued that 'active evolution' would necessarily involve failures to adapt, raising the question of what to do about those who failed to live up to the standards of the new life (Young 2012: 152–4, 236–7; see also Shlapentokh 1996). Since Cosmism was never articulated as a political project, this question was never addressed explicitly by any of its representatives, yet the potential for the purge of the old life by the builders of the new one is evidently there.

The originality of Fedorov's thought consists less in its main theme of immortality than in the active injunction to make this ideal practicable, produce resurrection as a *real presence*. The term 'projective knowledge' that Fedorov used to denote his mode of thought is therefore entirely appropriate. Knowledge is neither subjective nor objective, neither idealist nor materialist, but always irreducibly both, since it is contained in the subject's action on an object, the effective realisation of ideas in the material world (Young 2012: 79). The model of projective thinking was found by Fedorov in the Christian liturgy, which transforms mortal flesh into immortal substance. Yet, since the liturgy remains limited and incomplete, Fedorov sought to extend it 'outside the temple', whereby religion would join forces with science, art and other activities in attaining the goal of universal resurrection.

The level of ambition of Fedorov's projective thinking distinguishes his work from both his predecessors and his successors, who sought to develop his project in particular fields of art, philosophy or science, downgrading the universality of the task in question. Pre-revolutionary Russian art is most abundant in examples of the Cosmist disposition. We need only recall such movements as Symbolism with its goal of 'life creation' (*zhiznetvorchestvo*) (Ivanov, Blok, Bryusov), 'godseekers' (*bogoiskateli*) (Merezhkovsky, Gippius), 'Godbuilders' (*bogostroiteli*) (Lunacharsky, Krasin, Gorky), futurists (Kruchenykh, Khlebnikov, Mayakovsky) (see Rosenthal 2002: 33–111; Groys 2011: 26–7). In their own different ways all these movements sought to move beyond art into life as such, transform life through art, create a new type of human being, overcome the constraints of nature, attain a true life defined by various ideals, unite all of humanity with a common task, and so on. Yet, although all these projects certainly sounded grand and often produced brilliant artworks, in 'real life' they amounted to precious little. The attempts of both pre-revolutionary and post-revolutionary avant-garde to transform art into life and create a new type of subject paradoxically converged with what at first glance was their opposite, the modernist valorisation of the autonomy of art and the aestheticisation of life. Just as the 'life creation' of the symbolists amounted to little more than the aestheticisation of their public and personal lives (Young 2012: 178), so the 'new man' of the early Soviet avant-garde remained an aesthetic project that was rather distant from the life of the newly emancipated proletariat (Groys 2011: 19–32). Every attempt to transform art into life ended up translated *back* into art, where its products are still available for us to marvel at. Yet, at the time when the Russian society was already undergoing revolutionary transformation, the aesthetic experiments of the avant-garde were easily outstripped by a most ordinary local Party cell and were hence perceived as 'anachronistic, inappropriate and irritating' (ibid.: 30).

BOGDANOV'S BIOLOGICAL COMMUNISM

Despite its abandonment of the key idea of Fedorov's Cosmism, the Bolshevik Revolution followed the Cosmist movement in its radical anti-naturalism, universalism and authoritarianism. The problematisation of the inactuality of socialism that constituted the biopolitical rationality of Stalinism evidently resonates with Fedorov's dismissal of all prior doctrines of immortality as wilfully impractical, content with its infinite deferral or metaphoric displacement. While, as we have seen, the first post-revolutionary years were characterised by manifold experiments in socialism, many of them similarly impractical, at least one of these projects functioned as an important bridge between Fedorov's Cosmism and the Stalinist Great Break. This is Alexander Bogdanov's project of blood transfusion.

Bogdanov, a leading Marxist theoretician, practising medical scientist and erstwhile rival of Lenin for leadership in the Bolshevik Party, participated in the pre-revolutionary Godbuilders movement along with Maxim Gorky and such leading Marxist figures as Lunacharsky and Krasin (Rosenthal 2002: 70–93; Krementsov 2011: 33–53). The Godbuilders sought to complement the scientific Marxist analysis with a quasi-religious version of socialism, which would worship collective humanity as the subject of the transcendence of nature. Having subsequently distanced himself from the Godbuilders movement, Bogdanov retained its interest in myth creation as the essential part of the revolution, though his version of the myth was no longer religious but scientific or, more precisely 'science-fictional' – a genre that eventually flourished in 1920s Soviet Russia as the reflection of the ongoing social transformation. Bogdanov's 1908 novel *Red Star* described communist society as realised on Mars and offered a fictional version of the theoretical ideas he was developing at the same time (see Rosenthal 2002: 70–4). What made the novel stand out from the rest was Bogdanov's medical training, which made his science fiction more properly scientific, marked by a wealth of detail about the most minute aspects of the practical organisation of the new society. On one occasion in the novel the protagonist from planet Earth, Leonid, visits a Martian doctor and is treated to a lecture explaining why earthlings are so inferior to Martians in physical and cognitive abilities. The reason appears to be the technique of blood transfusion that the Martian doctor Netti terms the 'renewal of life' (Bogdanov 1984: 85–7). The simultaneous blood transfusion from one individual to another leads to the rejuvenation and increased viability of all those participating in the procedure. According to Netti, this admittedly simple method is not used on Earth due to the dominant individualist attitudes that make the vital fusion of individuals incomprehensible or unacceptable. In contrast, for the Martians it is a perfectly logical correlate to the collectivist ideals that this society lives by. For Bogdanov, blood transfusion took the ideal of collectivism down to the physiological level, translating communist ideological precepts about universal human fraternity into biological reality, which ultimately led to the production of a new type of being. As a result of regular blood exchange Martians evolved into a new kind of species with enlarged eyes and skulls, lower susceptibility to disease, a longer life span, diminished difference between the sexes, and so on. In psychological terms they exhibited faster reactions, better emotional control and higher cognitive abilities (see Krementsov 2011: 46–7).

Bogdanov's interest in blood transfusion did not remain restricted to science fiction, even though its more practical realisation had to wait until the mid-1920s. After the Bolshevik Revolution, Bogdanov, who had long since left the Party, turned his attention to cultural transformation and became one of the leaders of Proletkult, a non-party organisation promoting the formation of a properly proletarian culture. Supported by Lunacharsky and Bukharin yet distrusted by Lenin, Proletkult under Bogdanov's leadership sought to realise his pre-revolutionary theories, according to which only the proletariat itself could produce proletarian culture.[9] Bogdanov was deeply sceptical about the power of bourgeois 'specialists' in culture and science and sought to replace them by proletarians as soon as possible, which led to frequent accusations of class chauvinism and anti-intellectualism. Culture was no longer the province of a refined and gifted elite but was to be reclaimed by the proletariat and transformed into an instrument for a thoroughgoing reorganisation of life (Rosenthal 2002: 86–93). While it certainly produced important artistic movements, albeit often in the form of splinter groups, Proletkult was hardly successful in its main task, being at once too autonomous for the authorities and too experimental for the proletariat. It seemed like the only proletarian art that was produced in the framework of this movement was created by those who were already artists and not exactly proletarians at that. Cultural transformation was evidently more burdensome and less effective than the biological collectivism envisioned in *Red Star*.

After the Proletkult was disbanded in 1920, Bogdanov returned to his interest in blood transfusion. Having studied recent foreign research on the subject matter, during 1922–3 he enthusiastically began planning practical experiments in blood exchange with a narrow circle of associates, the first of which took place in February 1924, shortly after Lenin's death. Eventually, Bogdanov performed a blood transfusion on Leonid Krasin, his old acquaintance in the Godbuilders movement and now a senior Bolshevik official. Krasin was suffering from anaemia and the transfusion allegedly improved his condition so much that it aroused the interest of none other than Stalin himself. According to Krementsov, Stalin's interest in blood transfusion was due less to the appeal of Bogdanov's physiological collectivism than to more practical concerns. Krasin's illness was merely one in a series of Bolshevik leaders falling ill and dying during the middle of the 1920s – a phenomenon often described as 'Soviet exhaustion', nervous and physical fatigue in the aftermath of the struggles of the Civil War and postwar reconstruction (Krementsov 2011: 61–5, 85–6; Kotkin 2014: 576; see also Bernstein 2005). To recall Buldakov's argument discussed above, the fatigue in question was not a matter of being weary of revolution, which, after all, had long passed, but rather a result of the *retreat* of the revolution in the NEP. The Old Bolsheviks were nervous, impotent and dying, because in the NEP-era USSR their revolutionary struggle seemed to have been all in vain (Buldakov 2013: 114–15). Ironically, the technique relied on in the strictly medical treatment of this fatigue was also originally intended to address its true cause and fulfil the promise of revolution in real life.

Thanks to Stalin's interest and the support of the Minister of Health Care Semashko, Bogdanov was appointed director of the newly created Institute of Blood Transfusion, the first of its kind in the world. The institute was not run as a typical research institution but largely employed Bogdanov's comrades and blood exchange enthusiasts. Yet, the institute quickly became well-known all over Russia, since its project of enhancing viability through blood transfusion resonated with the theme of rejuvenation, which was the latest fad in Russian and European medicine at the time (Krementsov 2011: 73–9). Rejuvenation was practised through the transplantation of sex glands or the injection of extracts prepared from animal testicles, and leading Bolshevik figures were known to have benefited from such experiments (Shlapentokh 1996: 445). During 1926–7 Bogdanov attempted to theorise blood exchange as an alternative pathway to rejuvenation from the perspective of his 'tectological' universal science. He argued that in the course of blood exchanges the organism's viability increases due to the mutual compensation of the flaws or imbalances in individual organisms. Since blood is a 'universal' tissue that connects all other organs, tissues and cells, its chemical composition reflects the overall state of the organism at a given moment. Moreover, blood itself is the prime source of imbalance in the organism, which requires its periodic purification or renewal for which transfusion is the simplest method (ibid.: 84–5). Blood exchange not only prevents or slows the process of aging (by adding 'young' blood to 'old') but also leads to the general expansion of the organism's strengths and abilities, whereby it relies not only on its own viability but also on the strengths of all the others it is in common with through blood transfusion. 'Here begins what in the future will create physiological collectivism' (Baranovsky quoted in Krementsov 2011: 93). It appeared that the realisation of Bogdanov's utopia of *Red Star* on planet Earth was just around the corner.

Nonetheless, while many reviews of Bogdanov's project were glowing, the opinion of medical professionals was far more sceptical. Bogdanov's writings on the subject were routinely criticised as dilettantish if not downright absurd (Krementsov 2011: 94–7). In March 1928, Bogdanov participated in a blood transfusion experiment with a student who suffered from tuberculosis. While Bogdanov thought he was immune to the disease, both he and the student developed an acute adverse reaction to the transfusion and two weeks later Bogdanov died of renal and liver failure. Although his death was highly publicised and he was given a state funeral, his project was soon forgotten, his successors at the institute abandoning the idea of blood exchanges and dismissing Bogdanov's theoretical designs as scientifically crude and bordering on mysticism. Thus, the project of physiological collectivism was never realised, even as the technique of blood transfusions did spread throughout the Soviet Union in the aftermath of Bogdanov's death, albeit for much more modest medical or military purposes. During the Great Break, one of whose features was a thoroughgoing militarisation of economy and society, the government established a wide network of blood transfusion stations, instituted an elaborate system of organised donorship and established the world's first blood banks (Krementsov 2011: 105–9). Yet, important as these achievements were, they were a far cry from what Bogdanov himself intended to achieve through blood transfusion, that is rendering communism a biological fact.

This possibility was addressed in a rather less optimistic fashion in Mikhail Bulgakov's contemporaneous novella *Heart of a Dog* (1925), which remained unpublished until Perestroika. The main character of the novella, Dr Filip Preobrazhensky (his name appropriately derived from the Russian for 'transfiguration'), is a successful surgeon treating the party elite's 'Soviet exhaustion' through 'rejuvenating' injections of animals' sex glands, which allows him a lavish lifestyle in a seven-room apartment and a relative independence from lower-ranking and more equality-obsessed Bolsheviks, including one Shwonder, a hostile Marxist enthusiast and the chair of the housing committee. In one of his experiments, Preobrazhensky transplants to a stray dog the testicles and the pituitary gland of the recently deceased alcoholic Chugunkin. The dog, named Sharik, is rapidly transformed into a human being and is named Poligraf Poligrafovich Sharikov. Yet, the humanisation of the dog is not entirely successful, since Sharikov begins to behave in a crude and violent manner that is probably akin to the donor Chugunkin's disreputable lifestyle and retains some habits of a dog, most notably a fervent dislike of cats. Thanks to the efforts of Shwonder and other communist enthusiasts, Sharikov soon gets a rewarding job (strangling stray cats, no less!) and demands proper living space and other rights of the Soviet citizen at Preobrazhensky's apartment. Things go from bad to worse, and when Sharikov eventually denounces the professor to the secret police, Preobrazhensky and his assistant Bormenthal decide to reverse the operation, transforming the human back into the dog. When the suspicious Shwonder brings in the police and demands that they produce Sharikov, the professor produces the dog, to the surprise of the police and the disgrace of the hapless Shwonder.

During the destalinisation of the 1980s, this novella, whose publication in the 1920s was explicitly prohibited by none other than Lev Kamenev, was widely read as the satire of the transformative aspirations of the socialist revolution, whose aim of the liberation of the working class merely brought to power uncivil and violent brutes like Sharikov. In this reading, the negative figure of the novella was Shwonder, the communist enthusiast whose attempts to involve the former dog in the new Soviet way of life were bravely resisted by Preobrazhensky and Bormenthal. And yet, it is hard to ignore the problems with this reading: after all, it was not Shwonder who turned a dog into a man. Throughout the novella Shwonder remains blissfully unaware of Sharikov's origins, taking him for yet another proletarian beneficiary of the revolution. In contrast, Preobrazhensky is a much more influential figure than Shwonder, who seems not to be taken seriously by the authorities themselves, who gladly let the professor off the hook for his valuable services in their rejuvenation. While Shwonder exemplifies the unproductive, literally fruitless tendency in socialism, which fails to convert the emancipated proletariat into the class-conscious subject of its own transformation, Preobrazhensky does not merely stand for the successful rejuvenation of the Soviet elite, but demonstrates a more thoroughgoing biopolitical productivity, successfully transforming a dog into a man (and back again). While admittedly having nothing but contempt for the revolution and the Bolsheviks, Preobrazhensky is actually more useful for the Party than the windbag Shwonder, insofar as he can achieve in reality, through scientific experiment, what the latter only dreams about. It is Preobrazhensky rather than Shwonder that is the true 'effective manager' in the novella. And yet, Preobrazhensky understands that his achievement is dubious: the humanisation of the dog does not produce a more perfect human but rather the same imperfect being as the original donor. Moreover, he is clearly aware that Sharikov ultimately poses a danger for the likes of Shwonder himself, since the revolutionary enthusiasts would be wiped out by the very brutes they naively wished to emancipate. For this reason, at the end of the novel the professor reverses the experiment, turning Sharikov back into a dog. Yet, this conclusion still remains ambiguous, since all that this reversal shows is that Preobrazhensky is capable of *both* bio- and thanatopolitics: while Shwonder only engages in fruitless agitation, Preobrazhensky succeeds in both humanisation and dehumanisation. The ostensibly anticommunist surgeon ends up the true demiurge of the construction of socialism. While the novella never mentions Bogdanov, it issues a none too veiled warning about every attempt to make communism biological.

Bogdanov's project of translating the ideological maxims of communism into biological realities makes his approach paradigmatically biopolitical and thus a key precursor of Stalinism as we have defined it in this chapter. This is definitely not to say Bogdanov himself would have supported Stalin's Great Break or other policies. His relations with the Bolshevik regime were notoriously tense and it is doubtful that he would have survived even the Great Break let alone the Great Terror (Krementsov 2011: 114). What is at stake is rather the convergence of the logics of Bogdanov's eccentric designs for making communism physiological and the Stalinist project of the construction of socialism as a lived reality. For both Bogdanov and Stalin the attempts of the Proletkult and other revolutionary enthusiasts to attain socialism by inventing specifically proletarian art, science, work or housing arrangements were insufficient and ineffective. Bogdanov's interest in medicine led him to the discovery of the *shortcut* that, somewhat paradoxically, was supposed to produce communists without any need for any ideology of communism: blood exchanges would produce the universal brotherhood of men without any mediation by ideas or, rather, the idea of communism would itself be entirely actualised in the materiality of blood transfusion. Stalin's biopolitical shortcut follows a similar logic with far more grave consequences: the transcendence of the idea of communism is forced into the immanence of the real not by any medical technique but by forcing out the forms of life that conflict with it through unprecedented governmental violence. While Stalinism never attained the physiological level of Bogdanovism, it was infinitely more consequential in the actual transformation of human lives, even though, as we shall see, this transformation was primarily negative.

To sum up our brief genealogy of Stalinist biopolitics, there are evident resonances between Russian Cosmism and Soviet socialism (Shlapentokh 1996; Groys and Hagemeister 2005). Both were attempts to transform the real *within* the real, to overcome 'natural' principles (death or private property) within the domain of nature through scientific and technological means. Both posited a grand transcendent task (communism, immortality) and ventured to implement it within the realm of immanence. Both sought to convert the grand utopian idea into a series of gigantic, but still allegedly realisable projects, from the construction of dams and canals to the exploration of space.[10] Evidently, it is difficult to compare actual nationwide policies during the three decades of Stalinism with the idiosyncratic and outright bizarre designs of the Cosmists. For all its emphasis on practical implementation, Fedorov's 'common task' was never taken on as a political project and thus remained devoid of biopower. The same could be said about Bogdanov's blood transfusion, which, while receiving state support as a research project, was never mobilised by the state as a technique of government. The advantage of the Stalinist Second Revolution over these and other projects of radical transformation of humanity was its capacity to turn an ideological project into the policy of the authoritarian state supported by millions of organised enthusiasts. Whatever was lost in the utopian aspect (the resurrection of the dead, collectivism through blood exchange) was compensated for by the fact that the Stalinist project unfolded in a country of 170 million people, all of whom were affected by it, often in the painfully physical sense. In his classic study Groys argued that Stalin was more consistent and successful in realising the spirit of the Russian revolutionary avant-garde than the avant-garde itself: while the latter's ambition of turning art into life never managed to leave the sphere of the aesthetic proper, the Stalinist project actually did venture to transform life in accordance with its political-aesthetic ideal (2011: 67–74). The same goes for biopolitics: it was in Stalin's Five Year Plans, rather than the designs of the Cosmists and the Godbuilders, that the utopias of a new life were actually converted into government projects.[11]

ANTI-IMMUNITY: ACCELERATING THE APOCALYPSE

This brief analysis of the pre- and post-revolutionary precursors of Stalinist biopolitics demonstrates the centrality of the eschatological dimension to the project of the construction of socialism, which definitively separates it from Western biopolitical rationalities. As we have seen, immunitary biopolitics, both liberal and Nazi,[12] follows the katechontic logic of negative protection, in which the eschatological dimension is blocked and deactivated. These modes of biopolitics are constitutively *anti-utopian*: if protection of life may only be negative and the negativity that demands protection from is inherent in life itself, all that can be attained is always the *lesser evil* but never the Good as such.

> [Instead] of something good being acquired, something bad has been taken away. If life cannot be preserved except by placing something inside it that subtly contradicts it, we must infer that the presentation of life corresponds with a form of restriction that somehow separates it from itself. It must incorporate a fragment of the nothingness that it seeks to prevent, simply by deferring it. This is where the structurally aporetic character of the immunitary process is to be located: unable to directly achieve its objective, it is forced to pursue it from the inside out. In so doing, it retains its objective in the horizon of meaning of its opposite: it can prolong life but only by continuously giving it a taste of death. (Esposito 2011: 8–9)

Thus, in full accordance with the katechontic principle immunitary biopolitics fights evil with evil and in this manner defers the appearance of the Good. Of course, in its exercise of restraining power it makes a claim to transcendence, yet this can only be a transcendence that arises *out* of immanence, much as the Hobbesian sovereign that emerges out of the state of nature only to transcend it along with all of its subjects (Esposito 2010: 140–1; 2011: 86–7; see also Agamben 1998: 105). As Walter Benjamin famously remarked, this transcendence is ultimately fake, since the sovereign 'lord of creatures' itself remains a creature that embodies within its very power the nature that it claims to transcend (Benjamin 2003: 85). Yet, it is precisely because this transcendence can never succeed that the katechontic sovereign remains tied to the quasi-natural domain from which it emerges and which it must protect, if only negatively.

The Great Break: Making Socialism Real

In contrast, in socialist biopolitics transcendence does not arise *out* of immanence for the purposes of its protection but is rather forced *into* immanence for the purposes of its transformation. Socialism is the Good that is to be actualised within the domain of immanence, which calls for the negation of the forms of life that presently characterise it. Insofar as it is not valorised as a 'system of natural liberty' or a *Volksgemeinschaft*, but rather devalued in terms of the communist idea, anterior social reality is not worthy of protection, *even negatively*. While it certainly promises a 'new life', socialist biopolitics does not promise it *to* the 'old life' and its representatives, who are instead wholly *exposed* to the force of transcendence that takes the empirical form of existential negation. With immunitary protection withdrawn, the Soviet population ends up subject to all possible forms of negative intervention: confiscation of property, forced resettlement, camp confinement, organised starvation and, ultimately, 'liquidation' either 'as a class' (in 1928–32) or as 'enemies of the people' (1936–8). Since the logic of Stalinist biopolitics is wholly heterogeneous to the idea of immunity as negative protection, its exterminist violence comes as a perfectly logical consequence of its promise to transcend the way things are, which ultimately means that 'life as it is' would be no more. While the Soviet regime broke most of its promises, it at least fulfilled this one.

This eschatological drive of the Great Break entails a break with the katechontic logic that, as we have argued, accompanied the emergence of Stalinism in the mid-1920s as a project of 'socialism in one country'. Of course, the Stalinist USSR continued to be preoccupied with its holding out in the hostile capitalist environment and its obsession with security only grew more paranoid and murderous. And yet, its abandonment of the negative protection of society for its exposure to transformative violence in the name of the communist ideal points to the renunciation of the restraining function associated with the katechon. While the katechon defers the advent of the Antichrist, thereby also delaying the *parousia*, the *apocalyptic* longs for the *parousia* so much that it hurries the advent of the Antichrist or perhaps even takes this role upon itself (cf. Agamben 2005b: 62–5; Taubes 2004: 31, 103). In his 1942 discussion of the Nazi 'spatial revolution' Carl Schmitt termed this apocalyptic figure the 'accelerator' (*Beschleuniger*) (Schmitt 1995: 436; see also Hell 2009: 305). While in his postwar works, most notably the *Nomos of the Earth* (2003), Schmitt famously establishes himself as the defender of the katechon and even proclaims it as an article of faith (Schmitt cited in Meier 1988: 162), in this earlier text the katechon, exemplified by Great Britain, receives no positive evaluation and is rather treated as a negative force, an 'aging empire' that obstructs the progress of world history that for Schmitt at the time was embodied in the Third Reich. While Britain as katechon posed a barrier to change, the United States, which Schmitt considered to be a successor to the British Empire, failed to adequately play the role of the katechon, becoming entangled in contradictions that instead led the international order to its unravelling, thus becoming an 'accelerator against its will' (*Beschleuniger wider Willen*) (Schmitt 1995: 436), the true accelerator being of course the Third Reich as the 'young' imperial challenger to the Anglo-Saxon order.

In Schmitt's subsequent writings, the normative privilege between the two figures is completely reversed, the katechon evaluated positively as the guarantor of order and meaning and the accelerator approached purely negatively as an anomic force of dissolution and fragmentation. Yet, the brief positive reference to the accelerator in the 1942 text testifies to the possibility of the *devaluation of the restraining function* from within the otherwise katechontic logic of the valorisation of constituted order, which is precisely what takes place in Stalin's Great Break. The accelerator throws katechontic caution to the winds, yet *not* in order to destroy every constituted order in the hope for the Messianic Kingdom or world revolution, but rather to *fortify* this order by directly and immediately introjecting it with the Good that the messianic idea only promised and teased us with. This introjection cannot but take the form of the negative: 'that which is not' only attains being in the world by rendering inexistent that which is. Moreover, because the introjected negative is not even perceived as negative but rather as the Good itself, there is no need to limit its dosage, hence the autocritical disposition of avoiding 'governing too much', so characteristic of liberalism, could not possibly ever arise in the Soviet Union, which had explicitly renounced all formal limits to the exercise of power early on after the October Revolution.[13] Instead, the entire apparatus of government is reoriented from the 'conservative' task of securing, stabilising and restraining towards the acceleration, catalysation and forcing of the transcendent ideal into social immanence.

In studies of the Russian Revolution, the theme of apocalypticism usually arises in the context of the pre- and immediately post-revolutionary politics of the Bolshevik Party (Duncan 2000: 48–61), committed to revolution on the global scale and viewing Russia as the springboard for the wider revolutionary process, which, like every springboard, could well be sacrificed so that the world revolution could succeed. During the unravelling of the Soviet order during Perestroika, the Bolsheviks were routinely scorned for putting the utopian ideals of the world revolution above Russia's 'national interests', manifested in their 'anti-patriotic' stance in World War I, the 'treasonous' Brest Peace Treaty that surrendered over a third of Russia's territory to Germany, the Bolshevik funding of foreign communist movements during the famine in Russia in the early 1920s, and so on. It was as if the Bolsheviks cared much less about the country in which they had seized power than about using this power to accelerate the global revolutionary process, even if Russia itself were to perish in the preparation for it. In contrast, the Stalinist doctrine of socialism in one country allegedly marked the abandonment of these eschatological illusions in favour of a more realistic and pragmatic course of fortifying the socialist system within the USSR in a katechontic fashion.

This interpretation, which clearly accords with the contemporary 'effective manager' reading of Stalinism, completely ignores the Great Break and its horrendous social dislocations, which simply cannot be explained in terms of realistic and pragmatic policy designs. While the debates about the socioeconomic consequences of collectivisation and industrialisation show no signs of abating (Gregory 2003; Sanchez-Sibony 2014; Edele 2011: 193–210), it is clear that the shift from the NEP to the Great Break was not primarily motivated by economic calculations but rather by political considerations, which drove this Second Revolution forward despite massive social resistance and human cost. The katechontic tasks of securing and stabilising the Soviet state did not call for the civil war against the peasantry, which itself created a genuine security threat in 1930–2 and caused enormous instability in rural areas, or the shock industrialisation, which was disorganised and wasteful to an extreme degree (Kotkin 1995: 316–19; Edele 2011: 206–9; Fitzpatrick 2002: 40–64). 'Forced wholesale collectivisation only seemed necessary within the straightjacket of Communist ideology and its repudiation of capitalism. Nothing prevented the Communist dictatorship from embracing private capital, nothing, that is, except *idées fixes*' (Kotkin 2014: 725). Similarly, no pragmatic considerations of state consolidation could explain the vehemence of 'specialist-baiting' and assaults on traditional and bourgeois culture, both of which were politically and economically counter-productive (Fitzpatrick 1992: 115–47). In short, the Great Break makes no sense whatsoever from the perspective on Stalinism as a conservative-katechontic project that abandons the early Bolshevik apocalypticism that is usually associated with Stalin's arch-enemy Trotsky. Instead, it can only be grasped as the *intensification* of this very apocalypticism through the actual forcing of revolutionary transcendence into social immanence, notwithstanding its human costs, which were written off along with the old forms of life that were doomed to disappearance in the socialist world.

He would do it. Stalin would force the collectivization of Soviet villages and nomadic steppes inhabited by more than 100 million people between 1928 and 1933. At least 5 million people, many of the country's most productive farmers or herders would be 'dekulakised', enclosed in cattle cars and dumped off at far-off wastes. Those forced into the collectives would burn crops, slaughter animals and assassinate officials. The regime's urban shock troops would break peasant resistance but the country's inventory of horses would plummet from 25 million to 17 million, cattle from 70 million to 38 million, pigs from 26 million to 12 million, sheep and goats from 147 million to 50 million. Countrywide, nearly 40 million people would suffer severe hunger or starvation and between 5 and 7 million people would die in the horrific famine, whose existence the regime denied. (Kotkin 2014: 724)

While the paradox of immunitary biopolitics, theorised in different ways by Foucault, Agamben and Esposito, consists in the fact that every attempt to protect social reality against itself must make use of the very thing that endangers it, the paradox of Soviet biopolitics consists in the fact that its complete realisation would coincide with the complete annihilation of the lived reality to which it applied itself. If the Great Break were to succeed fully, the Soviet society would be completely *broken*. The violence of collectivisation provides perhaps the most staggering example of this thanatopolitical conversion of Stalinist biopolitical rationality. The introduction of collective farms as forms of life proper to the socialist order was not merely a grand military and police operation of forcing uncooperative peasants into new working arrangements, but unleashed a veritable orgy of symbolic and physical destruction of households, communities, churches, schools and, ultimately, persons filed under the perfectly elastic category of the 'kulak' (cf. Žižek 2008: 202–4).[14] The tragic fate of the Soviet rural areas, whose degradation persists throughout the postcommunist period, demonstrates the genocidal or, more precisely, *sociocidal* impact of the fusion of revolutionary transcendence and biopolitical immanence. It also demonstrates that this 'sociocide' was not an accidental aspect of Stalinist policy, to be explained away by conjunctural factors from Stalin's personality to the hostile international environment, but was rather the *essence* of the biopolitical project of the construction of socialism as a positive reality. As long as the domain of life that is the object of biopolitical government is not perceived as natural, *sui generis* and endowed with its own rationality, but is rather a priori devalued as the degraded, obsolete and already 'dying' remnant of the past, the production of the new is only conceivable as the negation that transforms the dying into the dead and only in this manner clears the space for the new life. This is why the construction of socialism was not merely a bloody but a *bloodthirsty* project. In the staggering words of Stalin's close ally Lazar Kaganovich, the Great Break consists in the 'radical destruction of all socioeconomic relations, accompanied by a technical revolution, and not the other way round' (Kaganovich cited in Priestland 2007: 207).

> Stalin made history, rearranging the entire socioeconomic landscape of one sixth of the Earth. Right through mass rebellion, mass starvation, cannibalism, the destruction of the country's livestock, and unprecedented political destabilization, Stalin did not flinch. Feints in the form of tactical retreats notwithstanding, he would keep going even when told to his face by officials in the inner regime that a catastrophe was unfolding – full speed ahead to socialism. (Kotkin 2014: 739)

Yet, what about the much-valorised positive and constructive impact of Stalinism? Stalin's apologists then and now never fail to produce long lists of his achievements in 'modernising' the Soviet society, providing universal access to health care and education and enhancing the population's health, literacy and social welfare. Our analysis of the Great Break as a biopolitical project permits us to counter these claims more effectively. It is not merely that these achievements are exaggerated, which they often are, or that they came at the horrendous cost of millions of lives lost in the famine and terror, which is also true, but rather that there is in the Stalinist mode of biopolitics no contradiction between positive transformative impact and the extermination of the lives to be transformed. Once it was articulated as a biopolitical project, the construction of socialism could not but proceed by the destruction of non-socialist 'socioeconomic relations' or positive forms of life, assisted by a 'technical revolution' that would sustain the new form of life. Were it the 'other way round', we would wait forever for socialism to be actualised, while technical progress perpetuated the old ways of life by rendering them *more* efficient and competitive (cf. Kotkin 2014: 724–5). Thus, just as governmental interventions were historically legitimised in liberal biopolitics as corrective operations against the forms of life that were contrary to nature, in Stalinist USSR positive techniques of government were enfolded and contextualised within the overall accelerationist orientation of Soviet biopolitics. From this perspective, eradicating epidemics and organising famines, support to families and their forced separation, fixing one's teeth and kicking them out, are not to be opposed as a salutary effect and its unfortunate 'cost', but rather viewed as two aspects of the same process of forcing in the new by forcing out the old, in which cost and effect become indistinct.

This leads us to suggest that the case of Stalinism might have offered Agamben a better example of what he intended to demonstrate with his controversial thesis about the camp as the paradigmatic nomos of modernity (1998: 166–80). During the Great Break the Gulag camps were incessantly publicised by the regime and its figureheads, such as the newly returned Gorky, as the prime sites of the construction of socialism. The construction in question was, first, literal, since camp inmates were engaged in all the major construction projects of the first Five Year Plans, and, second, figurative, pertaining to the socialist forms of life and their subjects, the proverbial New Soviet Persons. In this process of reforging, camp inmates were stripped of their positive forms of life (as kulaks, professors, priests, thieves, and so on) and subjected to forced labour and political indoctrination that would eventually transform them into model citizens of the new society. Whereas the colonial camps of Western powers and the Nazi concentration camps were, to varying degrees, exceptional in relation to the modes of government practised outside them, functioning as obscene supplements or dirty secrets of the respective regimes (Arendt 1973: 287–8, 434–59; Losurdo 2011: 114–15), until the late 1930s the Soviet camp was rather the *emblem* of the Soviet project, neither obscene nor secret in any way. The camp was where the biopolitical rationality of forcing transcendence into immanence was manifested most clearly and where this forcing encountered the least resistance, since not merely legal but also physical limits to the exercise of power were abolished within it. While the camp was certainly not a Bolshevik or even a Russian invention (Agamben 1998: 177; Plamper 2002; Engelstein 1993), it was only in socialism that it became, for a brief period in the late 1920s and early 1930s, the true paradigm of the society at large.[15] After all, starting from June 1934 any attempt to flee the Soviet Union became a criminal offence that could be punished by death penalty, which made it a restricted 'zone' not unlike a camp.[16]

The *History of the Construction of the White Sea–Baltic Canal*, the infamous volume produced by a brigade of leading Soviet writers and artists headed by Gorky in 1934, could not have appeared in liberal or Nazi regimes, which may have considered their camps a 'necessary evil', but never as the model of socioeconomic policy as such. Yet, this is precisely what Gorky, Shklovsky, Rodchenko and other key figures of Soviet art and literature ventured in their glorification of camp labour in the construction of the canal (Dobrenko 2007: 105–16). The plot of the book that would soon serve as a foundation for the socialist realist doctrine emphasised the transformation of class enemies, particularly kulaks and anti-Soviet saboteurs, into the heroes of socialist construction. While at the beginning of their terms the inmates are degraded as 'all the pus that the country had strained off' (Gorky et al. 1934: 69), at the end of the construction process they are presented as 'amazing builders' (ibid.: 320), thoroughly rehabilitated and transformed by labour. Comparing the White Sea camps with 'bourgeois prisons and camps', allegedly characterised by lawlessness and brute violence for solely punitive purposes, the authors both moralise and aesthetise the Soviet camp as the site of a positive, pedagogical transformation of the subject.

> [The] entire social pedagogy in the camps has grown out of the dictatorship of the proletariat, out of the laws of the socialist system. All of this complex, subtle and ramified system in fact consists in a single powerful thesis: in the camps we force people incapable of independently re-educating themselves to live the Soviet life, we push them until they begin to do this voluntarily. Yes, we force them by all means to do what millions of people in our country do by goodwill, experiencing happiness and joy. (Ibid.: 77)

The camp is the model of the Soviet order, in which the Stalinist biopolitical project could be managed more effectively. The camps of the Great Break were not death camps, even though hundreds of thousands certainly did die in them. They were rather sites for the construction of a new form of life, whose lethal character resulted from the devaluation of the lives of those confined in them as already obsolete. The socialist offensive could blindly pursue its elusive benefits since it had already dismissed the costs as negligible: 'And if it does not work, no big deal; the material is dirt cheap: criminals and the old intelligentsia that is dying anyway' (Bykov 2008: 289). The true horror of the Great Break is that its relapse into the frenzy of destruction did not take place as a matter of dysfunction or malfunction, the failure of an otherwise positive project. The rationality of the Great Break was from the outset constructed in terms of the radical indistinction between the positive and the negative, construction and destruction, forcing in and forcing out, life and death.

It is this indistinction that ultimately distinguishes Stalinism from pre-revolutionary biopolitical utopias, particularly Fedorov's project of universal resurrection. Of course, unlike Stalinism, Fedorov's Common Task remained a theoretical project that despite a great number of proponents never became an official ideology or even a party doctrine. We therefore do not know whether the attempts at the practical realisation of Fedorov's version of the forcing of transcendence within immanence would have ended up as murderous as Stalin's. Nonetheless, there is good reason to think that despite its authoritarian disposition, Fedorov's project would never have resulted in an abomination like Stalinism precisely due to the nature of its Common Task, that is the universal overcoming of death. The transformative exterminism that defined the Great Break is practically unthinkable in it, since there is nothing either in the present or the future that could possibly justify it. At stake in Fedorov's project was not some vision of a new life, in the name of which old life should be sacrificed as worthless. It was precisely 'new life' that was of no value for Fedorov, as long as old life continued to disappear into death and oblivion: what value is progress if it cannot bring about what all of humanity desires? Fedorov's mode of biopolitical problematisation is thus almost diametrically opposed to that of Stalinism: against the forcing *out* of old life in the name of the new one Fedorov affirmed the forcing of the old life, which had already passed into death, *back* into the world of the living.

It is not coincidental that the first, modest and realisable stage of Fedorov's project concerned the work of memory: since the task of resurrection pertains to everyone who ever lived, the first thing to do is assemble as much information as possible about everyone, since the tiniest and least important bit of information may be crucial in bringing this person back to life. In contrast, Stalin's regime undertook a veritable assault on memory by its ceaseless rewriting of history to accommodate the latest purge, whose victims were simply erased from official records, encyclopaedias, photographs, and so on. While Fedorov's biopolitics of resurrection began with active remembrance, Stalinism operated through active forgetting, complementing its work of extermination with artificial oblivion. It is not merely that one's long-gone ancestors were forgotten, as Fedorov lamented, but that many among the Stalinist generation were forced to renounce and forget their own parents and siblings. It is therefore incongruous, if not downright obscene, that many of today's Stalinists in Russia view Stalinism in quasi-Fedorovian terms as a colossal project of struggle against death (Young 2012: 235–42). Whereas Fedorov was obsessed with the impossible task of recreating one's ancestors from the long-settled dust, Stalin was obsessed by reducing the living themselves to dust. Only in this activity was he ever *effective*.

Chapter 4

HIGH STALINISM: RETREAT, SIMULACRUM, TERROR

THE GREAT RETREAT: THE APOCALYPSE DEFERRED

Great as it certainly was, the Great Break was never complete. The extreme biopolitics of the Second Revolution did not achieve a total forcing of the transcendence of the socialist idea within social immanence, which would have led to the total negation of anterior forms of life. The aftermath of the Great Break, often referred to as the period of High Stalinism,[1] was marked by a number of attempts to come to terms with this incomplete forcing of socialism into the real, which we shall address in this chapter.

On its own terms, the Great Break was an apparent success, particularly with regard to industrialisation, transforming the USSR from an agrarian country into an industrial power. During the four years in which the first Five Year Plan was fulfilled, the Soviet Union developed a formerly non-existing tractor and aircraft industry, built new automobile plants, power stations, railways and canals. And yet, all these accomplishments came at an exorbitant price. The collectivisation campaign in particular was an unmitigated disaster in humanitarian terms, killing hundreds of thousands during the institution of collective farms and the resettlement of kulaks and then millions during the famine of 1932–3. Moreover, collective farming, instituted at such a terrible price, proved grossly inefficient throughout the existence of the Soviet system, leading to permanent food shortages. Similarly, the forced industrialisation was marked by the decline of actual living standards of workers, their subjection to greater work discipline, the radical worsening of their work conditions and the growth of work-related traumas, diseases and deaths. It produced disastrous consequences in light industry, whose development was sacrificed for 'heavy industrialisation', primarily in the military sector, thus leading to chronic shortages of clothing, furniture and consumer goods. Moreover, even in heavy industry the revolutionary onslaught led to extremely wasteful use of and unintentional damage to foreign equipment (see Kotkin 1995: 58, 121–2, 269–70; Fitzpatrick 2002: 42–5, 171–8; Khmelnitsky 2015). Finally, while the costs of the Cultural Revolution in terms of loss of life or health were least destructive, its negative impact on Soviet science, education and arts could hardly be overestimated (see Priestland 2007: 249–51, 254, 260).

While many economists have since then argued that the achievements of Soviet industrialisation could have been attained in a more balanced manner, 'with far less turbulence, waste, destruction, and sacrifice' (Hunter cited in Tucker 1992: 203), such an approach ignores the fact that the Great Break was primarily *not* an economic but a political project, a genuine revolution whose methods *were* turbulence, destruction and violence. In the words of Dmitry Khmelnitsky (2015), economy itself became a 'taboo' during the Great Break.

> [It] will not do to simplify the collectivization as just another instance in the Russian state's infamous strong-arming of a predominantly peasant country because its agricultural season lasted a mere 125 days, perhaps half the length in Europe. Stalin was motivated by more than competition with more fortunate European rivals. Collectivization would give the Communists control over the vast countryside, a coveted goal no regime in Russia had ever had. But still more fundamentally, collectivization, like state-run and state-owned industry, constituted a form of ostensible modernization that negated capitalism. Thus did Stalin 'solve' the Bolsheviks' conundrum of how NEP Russia could become socialist Russia. (Kotkin 2014: 727)

Even if it were possible to achieve the quantitative targets of the Plan within the framework of the NEP, this would have done nothing for the qualitative task of the leap from capitalism to socialism, which required the actual destruction of the former. The process of collectivisation was so violent and its death toll so horrific, because its objective was not merely to finance industrialisation, ensure food supply or enhance agricultural productivity, but to 'deliver a crushing blow' against the kulaks, taking the class struggle to the village and winning it there. For this reason, if the blow was sufficiently crushing, collectivisation could be considered a success, even if it actually led to the *decline* in agricultural production (cf. Wemheuer 2014: 418; Kotkin 2014: 724–6). On the other hand, this Dionysian dimension of the Great Break was to be kept within limits and not become self-destructive, which would undermine the very existence of the society that was to be transformed and the very regime that was undertaking its transformation. The collectivisation process arguably marked the threshold beyond which the Bacchanalian drive would turn downright suicidal, threatening the Soviet regime either directly, as in the peasant uprisings in 1930–1, numbering over 10,000 a year, or

High Stalinism: Retreat, Simulacrum, Terror

indirectly, through the destabilising effects of starvation, mass migration from the villages, and so on (Tucker 1992: 182–4; Buldakov 2013: 299–300; Wemheuer 2014: 409–16).

It is therefore hardly surprising that the biopolitical experiment of the Great Break was gradually wound up during 1932–4,[2] its apocalyptic-accelerationist character abandoned in favour of a return to the katechontic logic. From 1934 to the end of the Stalin era the biopolitical rationality of Soviet socialism was subjected to what we might term three *negative inflections*. While the general task of the construction of socialism and the movement towards communism was never renounced by the Soviet regime until its demise, the modes of this construction no longer resembled the apocalyptic drive of the Great Break, where the transcendent Good was to be forced into social immanence immediately and directly. Instead, the Stalinist biopolitical rationality was fractured into three forms, all of which added a negative twist to the positive programme of the construction of socialism. These negative inflections should not be understood as negating the task of the construction of socialism *per se*, but rather the biopolitical mode of problematisation at work in this construction. While in 1928–32 we observed a paroxysmal attempt to create the new by negating the old, the three negations that together constitute the recognisable image of High Stalinism (1934–41 or, with some reservations, 1934–53) all proceed from the failure of this frontal approach and come to terms with this failure in their own distinct ways.

The first negative inflection is the process that has been known as the Great Retreat since the classic work by Nicholas Timasheff (1946) that continues to generate debates and controversies to this day.[3] In Timasheff's argument, by 1934 the Second Revolution had run out of steam and was abandoned in favour of what amounted to at least a partial restoration. This restoration took different forms in different areas: while the results of collectivisation and industrialisation were largely maintained and developed, the outcomes of the Cultural Revolution were inverted almost completely in the rehabilitation and rediscovery of traditional culture and its practitioners from Pushkin,[4] whom the prerevolutionary futurists had wanted to 'throw off the steamship of modernity', to Rubens, whose paintings of the 'fat ass of Venus' Malevich infamously demanded to be destroyed (Malevich, 1971: 68–72). In Timasheff's words,

> [The] masses could not be persuaded to enjoy the pseudo-art of the Communist Experiment. But they needed aesthetic stimulation, and its lack caused a sense of frustration, and was a source of unrest. The simplest

> solution of the difficulty was to repudiate the cultural experiment and
> to direct culture production towards the gratification of popular desires.
> (Timasheff 1946: 268)

Even if we disregard Timasheff's unkind view of the early-Soviet avant-garde, it is difficult to argue with his diagnosis about the failure of the new, experimental art to attract the interest of the masses.

Yet, the neoclassical or conservative turn taken by the regime was not merely a matter of a concession to popular desires, since in addition to rehabilitating 'lower' cultural forms, from crime fiction to jazz, the regime persisted in educating the masses in 'proper' culture. What changed was not the interest in acculturation, but the content of the culture in question. The militant campaigns for the development of 'proletarian culture' from below gave way to the top-down state policy of the 'acculturation' of the population, proletarian or otherwise, in a rather conventional understanding of culture that would certainly have been labelled 'bourgeois' during the Cultural Revolution: monumental architecture, neoclassical opera and ballet, nineteenth-century realist novel, and so on (Hoffmann 2003: 15–55; Brandenberger 2012: 370–1). As we shall argue below, the cultural doctrine of socialist realism, which was inaugurated in 1934 as the authoritative set of guidelines of what socialist art is like, was a far cry from the experimental and sometimes outlandish versions of 'proletarian art' and instead appropriated aspects of nineteenth-century realist and romanticist styles, albeit mobilising them for an entirely new purpose of representing revolutionary transformation of life. Other aspects of the retreat from the logic of the Cultural Revolution include the revival of folklore and 'national cultures', the restoration of hierarchies of authority in education and professional practices, the suppression of relatively independent proletarian cultural movements (Vpered, Proletkult, RAPP) in favour of state-controlled unions of writers and artists, and so on (see Dobrenko 2004; Hoffmann 2004: 662–3; Fitzpatrick 2002: 79–88; Clark 2011: 306–11; Rosenthal 2002: 325–49).

In the *economic* sphere the retreat from the apocalypticism of the Second Revolution consisted in the rehabilitation of 'specialists' after the infamous Shakhty and Industrial Party trials, the restoration of the authority of factory managers, the reintroduction of titles, ranks and other marks of status in industry, and the gradual shift to the use of economic incentives for workers, including the proverbial 'socialist competition' (Fitzpatrick 2002: 104–8). Since Stalin's 1931 'New Conditions' speech that halted the process of 'specialist-baiting' in industry, the regime began introducing higher wage differentials, abandoning the egalitarianism practised or at least declared since 1917.

The leadership's new emphasis on the need to fulfil plans within the constraints of existing resources encouraged it to move away from a revivalist faith in mobilisation towards a technicist emphasis on order and discipline. But it soon realised that money and market incentives had to supplement central decrees if the state was to impose discipline effectively. (Priestland 2007: 270)

In the sphere of *ideology* the retreat could be observed in the gradual downgrading of the themes of class war and proletarian internationalism and the cultivation of Russian patriotism (van Ree 2002; Tucker 1992; Brandenberger 2002; Brandenberger and Dubrovsky 1998). This development reversed the tendencies in the nascent Soviet historiography (the 'Pokrovsky School') towards a thoroughly negative and materialist reading of Russian history, which, moreover, emphasised the historical backwardness of the Russian Empire.[5] While during the 1920s nationalism, particularly 'Great Russian' nationalism, was suppressed as inherently chauvinist and imperialist, in the mid-1930s it was rehabilitated, particularly in the aspect of the glorification of the great 'state-building' historical figures from Yaroslav the Wise to Peter the Great. In his famous 1937 toast to the tsars who had enslaved the people but nonetheless built a great state (Brandenberger and Dubrovsky 1998: 880), which the Bolsheviks now reclaimed in the interests of the people, Stalin established a formerly lacking continuity between prerevolutionary Russia and the new regime and, in accordance with the new dogma of 'socialism in one country', synthesised revolutionary ideology with patriotic appeals to a 'fatherland'. The veritable explosion in historical novels and films (*Peter I*, *Alexander Nevsky*, *Minin and Pozharsky*, *Ivan the Terrible*), the cult of imperial military commanders such as Suvorov and Kutuzov and the relative depreciation of the formerly venerated heroes of the Civil War (ibid.: 881–2), the new emphasis on historical continuity in the teaching of history – all these phenomena are so at odds with the messianic spirit of the 1920s that posited a great divide between pre-revolutionary pre-history and the revolutionary present that it is difficult to downplay this shift as merely rhetorical (see Buldakov 2013: 598–9; Brandenberger 2002).

Even more striking were the changes in the sphere of *family values*, where the drive for the emancipation of women and the weakening of the traditional family as a patriarchal institution, still evident in the 1927 Family Code, was reversed in favour of a resolutely pro-family and pro-natalist policy, the complication of the divorce process and the criminalisation of abortion and homosexuality (Fitzpatrick 2002: 139–63; Hoffmann 2003: 88–116; Edele 2011: 163–92). In the immediate aftermath of the revolution the Soviet government tended to view the family as the obstacle to social emancipation and equality, and the first Soviet Family Code, passed in 1918, made both marriage and divorce remarkably easy to obtain for both parties. Traditional family values were ridiculed as 'petty-bourgeois philistinism' and were particularly shameful for the younger generation that prided itself on its sexual emancipation. Instead of the bourgeois family that enslaved and degraded women and promoted selfish individualism, Bolshevik leaders affirmed the idea of a romantic union based on radical equality, in which both parties actively participate in socioeconomic transformation. The regime also significantly relaxed the regulation of sexuality, legalising abortion, making available a variety of contraceptive devices and introducing elements of sexual education, particularly with regard to the prevention of venereal disease. While Lenin and other Bolshevik leaders stopped short of supporting the more radical ideas of sexual emancipation advocated by, for example, Aleksandra Kollontai, they nonetheless endorsed the overall orientation towards the diminution of the status of the family in social life.

Starting from the middle of the 1930s, Stalin's regime reversed most of these policies, opting for a strong pro-natalist course, motivated by the need to increase the birth rate after the calamities of World War I and the Civil War. This turn required support for and a strengthening of the family as the 'basic unit' of the socialist society in the manner that recalls the right-wing dictatorships in the Europe of the 1930s (Hoffmann 2003: 103). Thus, in 1936 the Soviet state banned abortion, other than for a strictly limited list of medical reasons, removed all contraceptive devices from sale and remoralised motherhood as women's 'duty' (ibid.: 99–101). It introduced a variety of family allowance schemes, invested in maternity and child care facilities, introduced higher alimony payments and actively enforced their payment, introducing prison sentences for delinquent fathers. It made divorce procedures more complex and expensive and undertook a massive propaganda campaign glorifying marriage, restoring the practice of wedding ceremonies with rings, dresses and nice-looking certificates (ibid.: 104; see also Fitzpatrick 1999: 141–3). What used to be branded 'petty-bourgeois philistinism' became part of official ideology and attacks on the family were in turn branded 'petty-bourgeois leftism' (Hoffmann 2003: 104). It is important to note that while the new pro-family course was definitely a retreat from the emancipatory orientation of the 1920s, it was not a retreat *back* to the pre-revolutionary patriarchal family, since the state did not simply leave the traditional family to its own devices but rather mobilised its traditional image for its own purposes and actively intervened in family affairs to ensure the stable reproduction of Soviet society: 'The family model promoted by the Soviet state heightened people's familial obligations but undercut their rights and autonomy as family members. The family was to serve the state not provide a sphere free from state intervention' (ibid.: 108).

Another key aspect of the Great Retreat is the radical reorientation of the regime's approach to *law*. While canonical Marxism affirmed the progressive withering away of the state and the disappearance of the law as the tool of class domination in the course of the transition towards communism, the new Stalinist orthodoxy emphasised the need for the strengthening of the state in conditions when socialism, according to the 1936 Constitution, was already 'constructed'. Stalin's ominous thesis about the intensification of class struggle amid the successful transition to socialism entailed the need for the strengthening and the expansion of the state, particularly its security apparatus. Similarly, in the conditions of the intensified class struggle, law, rather than wither away or decline into insignificance, was rehabilitated and entrenched as 'socialist legality', in which 'law is raised to the highest level of development. Our laws are the expression of the will of our people as it directs and creates history under the leadership of the working class' (Vyshinsky cited in Head: 108). Contrary to the precepts of Marxism, law was no longer analysed as the reflection of commodity exchange relations or the interests of the dominant class but rather, in a curious appropriation of legal positivism, 'as a set of normative prescriptions to be enforced by whatever regime was in power' (Head 2008: 150). Moreover, in line with the above-discussed aspects of the Retreat, this 'socialist legality' was characterised by the overturning of all the early post-revolutionary experiments with 'proletarian law' in favour of what was originally dismissed as obsolete bourgeois law: the categories of 'crime' and 'punishment' were restored along the principles of the sanctity of marriage and contracts, individual responsibility and fault (Head 2008: 108; Newton 2014: 74–99). Yet, in contrast to the operation of 'bourgeois law' in liberal democracies, this 'socialist legality' remained the *instrument* of, rather than a *check* on, government, becoming a key tool in the purges and show trials of the 1930s.

The orthodox-Marxist position of the post-revolutionary period was represented by such legal scholars as Yevgeny Pashukanis, who, in his 1924 book *General Theory of Law and Marxism*, affirmed the inevitability of the decline of law in a socialist classless society (see Head 2008; Bowring 2014: 48–75; Newton 2014: 100–27). For Pashukanis, law was inherently linked to the commodity exchange relationship and thus reached its highest point of development under capitalism as the instrument of the resolution of conflicts between the private interests of individuals. From this perspective, there was no such thing as proletarian or socialist law, and progress towards socialism necessarily presupposed the gradual extinction of the legal form as such in favour of technical and administrative regulation of the planned economy. To the extent that law survived in the USSR, it was as a means of regulating the continuing commodity exchange relationship persisting under the NEP and hence it was 'bourgeois' law despite its deployment in the interests of the proletarian state (Head 2008: 128). The attempt to develop an alternative form of proletarian or Soviet law was, despite all the appearances of revolutionary radicalism, reactionary, insofar as it posited the 'immortality of the legal form' (Pashukanis cited in ibid.: 128) Pashukanis's position, which was decidedly in the mainstream of Soviet legal scholarship in the early 1920s, became heresy in the 1930s, when Soviet law was no longer theorised as the temporary remnant of bourgeois law, a necessary evil for managing the contradictory period of the NEP, but rather as a properly socialist phenomenon with a positive function in the formation of the new order. The theory of the eventual extinction of the legal form under socialism was in this period relentlessly renounced by, among others, Pashukanis himself, which did not spare him from execution by the NKVD as a Trotskyite in 1937, incidentally without a proper trial (see Head 2008: 153–67).

Finally, the retreat from the revolutionary pathos of the Great Break was also noticeable in the most minute details of *everyday life*, such as in the field of consumption of material goods and public leisure. Stalin's infamous phrase 'Life has become more joyous, life has become more cheerful!', uttered at the Stakhanovite Conference in November 1935, ushered in the celebration of consumption and leisure that Sheila Fitzpatrick called a veritable 'consumer goods pornography' (Fitzpatrick 2002: 90). What was significant in this celebration was not merely the relatively modest improvements in the supply of goods and services after the famine of 1932–3 and the decline in commodity production during the Great Break. More important was the shift in the official discourse from the ascetic Puritanism accompanying the militant drive of the Great Break, in which any concern with material abundance was politically suspect, towards a tolerance and even a cultivation of consumption through advertising. As Anastas Mikoyan, the party official in charge of provisioning, exclaimed to what was probably universal assent, 'what kind of happy life can we have if there is not enough good beer and good liqueurs?' (Fitzpatrick 2002: 91)

The production of champagne, considered 'a symbol of material well-being', increased manifold in the mid-1930s, the beverage allegedly becoming affordable for any 'honest toiler'. Other products formerly considered bourgeois, such as perfume, stockings or rugs, became advertised as attributes of a 'cultured lifestyle'. The military style of clothing that Bolsheviks retained from the glory days of the Civil War gave way to civilian suits (ibid.: 92–3). Finally, the forms of leisure, previously associated with the pre-revolutionary era or the reviled NEP period, underwent a thoroughgoing rehabilitation: tennis, jazz, restaurants, comedy films, the New Year holiday as surrogate Christmas, amusement parks, carnivals all made a remarkable comeback in the mid-1930s after having been consigned to oblivion in the Great Break, creating an impression of a re-bourgeoisiment or a 'second NEP' (Fitzpatrick 2002: 93).

Of course, this revalorisation of consumption and leisure was largely restricted to the Soviet elite, that is, party members, the loyal intelligentsia and the Stakhanovite worker aristocracy, even though the advertising machine in Soviet newspapers and radio was, somewhat paradoxically, aimed at society at large. In fact, this advertising did not serve an economic function, since few, if any, of the advertised products were available to the general consumer and, when available in newly opened 'commercial stores', were prohibitively expensive. The function it served was an educative one, inculcating the public with good taste and 'culturedness' by informing them about the existence of washing machines and ketchup, frankfurter sausages and Camembert cheese, English suits and silk ties, and so on. The *Book of Tasty and Healthy Food*, a 1939 collection of recipes curated by Mikoyan himself, is a good illustration of this tendency. With a print run of eight million copies, this infamous book offered numerous recipes of culinary delights, the ingredients for most of which were never available to an average Soviet citizen in 1939 or, for that matter, any other year of the Soviet regime. Nonetheless, it had an important educative function, teaching the population about the 'cultured' diet and cooking in much the same manner as the party ideologists taught about the communist society to come. So strong was the resonance that the society to come gradually came to be defined *in terms of* the presently inaccessible commodities, Mikoyan's 'happy life' with 'good beer and good liqueurs', which eventually sealed the fate of the Soviet project.

The culmination of this process of the production and consumption of images of commodities rather than the commodities themselves was the All-Union Agricultural Exhibition (AAE), organised in 1939 and subsequently transformed into the Exhibition of the Accomplishments of the People's Economy (VDNKh). Valorised at the time as the greatest Soviet 'wonder' and becoming the setting of choice for numerous pre-war era films, most notably Grigory Alexandrov's *Radiant Path* (1940), the AAE celebrated the abundance of Soviet agricultural production in the conditions of a nationwide food deficit. While the goods displayed at AAE were ostensibly real, they were largely produced for the purposes of their exhibition and not actual consumption (even by privileged elites) (Dobrenko 2007: 303). Thus, the sausages, cheeses and furs displayed at the exhibition were in a strict sense objects of contemplation, as were most of the other objects of conspicuous consumption rehabilitated in the Great Retreat (Ryklin 2007: 186).

THE NEGATIVE SYNTHESIS OF REAL SOCIALISM

The production and consumption of the images of abundance intensified after the solemn proclamation of the completion of the construction of socialism, made by Stalin in 1934 at the 17th Party Congress and subsequently enshrined in the 1936 Constitution that formally abolished the revolutionary dictatorship of the proletariat and inaugurated a classless society. It is this formal accomplishment of socialism that the scholars critical of the Great Retreat thesis offer as the explanation of all the changes discussed above. According to Hoffmann (2004), the transformations outlined by Timasheff in the 1940s did not signify the abandonment of socialism but the consequences of its victorious completion.

> The evolution of Stalinist culture in the mid-1930s was precipitated not by an abandonment of socialism but by its purported realization. At the 17th Party Congress in 1934, party leaders declared that socialism had been built. According to them, the First Five-Year Plan and the collectivization drive had created an entirely socialist economy and had eliminated the exploiting classes and the remnants of capitalism. The achievement of socialism permitted the use of traditional institutions and culture to support and further the new order. The family, previously suspected of perpetuating bourgeois beliefs, could now be trusted to promote socialism among children. Monumentalist art and architecture, formerly instruments of the old order, now helped legitimate the new socialist order and symbolised its accomplishments. Patriotic appeals, elsewhere used to foment bourgeois nationalism, in the Soviet Union inspired defence of the socialist motherland. (Hoffmann 2004: 653; see also Hoffmann 2003: 2–3)

In Hoffmann's argument, the attainment of the tasks of the Great Break made its revolutionary and iconoclastic pathos no longer necessary and its targets, from bourgeois intelligentsia to traditional tastes in art, no longer dangerous, which paved the way for the new 'style' of Stalinism that sought to secure, stabilise and develop the already built socialist edifice. While this argument is certainly plausible and not that distant from Timasheff's original diagnosis, which never asserted that the Great

Retreat marked the outright *abandonment* of socialism (see Lenoe 2004), its credibility ultimately depends on whether one takes at face value Stalin's claim about the completion of the construction of socialism in 1934.

The debate on whether Stalinism was 'really' socialism dates back to the intra-party struggle of the late 1920s and has not lost its vivacity ever since (cf. Malia 1996; Tucker 1992; Lewin 1994; Kotkin 1995). Of course, any such debate is in principle interminable, forever doomed to oscillate between two unsatisfactory solutions to the problem of the correspondence of an empirical phenomenon to a theoretical concept. One attempt at resolving the dispute abandons the problem of correspondence by opting for *historical nominalism*: 'If Stalin called it socialism, it must be socialism' (Lenoe 2004: 725; cf. Dobrenko 2004: 682; Roberts 2006: 220–1, 230–3). According to this approach, insofar as contemporary China is ruled by the Communist Party, its socioeconomic system must in some sense be 'communist', though we would be at pains to point out in what sense this is so. However crude, this is indeed the option we use habitually with (proper) *names*. Thus, we usually do not question whether the ideology of the US Republican Party corresponds to any known variety of political republicanism or whether the UK Labour Party actually stands for the interests of the working classes, however defined. Only in rare and particularly incongruous cases, such as Vladimir Zhirinovsky's Liberal Democratic Party in Russia, do we tend to invoke this name with an obligatory smirk, but we *still* continue to invoke it, since this is quite simply what this party is *called*, not what it *is*. The problem with this nominalist understanding in the case of Stalin's socialism is that it deprives Hoffmann's claim of much of its weight: if socialism is whatever the regime wants to call the existing order, the fact of its 'having been built' is a result of a purely arbitrary decision that need not have any foundation in reality and may be as simulative as the AAE. We may then plausibly argue that rather than *result* from the successful construction of socialism, the process that Timasheff termed the retreat was the *signified*, for which Stalin's socialism was the ill-chosen signifier. Stalin's 'socialism' was then quite simply the *name* for the Great Retreat.

We may alternatively go beyond nominalism by treating socialism as a *concept*, which introduces a myriad of possible modes of definition: socialism may be defined in political, economic or social terms, as a form of rule or as a way of life (cf. Lenoe 2004: 725–6; Dobrenko 2004: 681–3). For instance, according to Kojève's (2001: 118) original definition of capitalism in terms of the exploitation of labour (the extraction of surplus value from the worker), Stalin's USSR was not merely *not* socialist, but rather the only twentieth-century country where paradigmatic nineteenth-century *capitalism* still existed. Alternatively, if we follow Hoffmann in defining socialism in terms of 'planned economy, state ownership of the means of production, and the Party's vanguard role in leading the country toward communism' (Hoffmann 2004: 652), then Stalinism certainly satisfies this definition. What is less satisfying is the definition itself, whose generality is not very helpful if we want to understand the specifically Stalinist mode of socialism: planned economy certainly did not require collectivisation to proceed the way it did, while the Party's vanguard role did not necessarily call for the Stalin cult and the decimation of the party elite during the purges of the late 1930s (cf. Kotkin 2014: 739; Roberts 2006: 232). Because of this generality, Hoffmann's definition easily subsumes *both* the Great Break and the Great Retreat (as well as the NEP, Brezhnev's stagnation and at least the early phase of Gorbachev's Perestroika). Yet, this only means that 'socialism' includes extremely different political and economic forms, including the one that Timasheff theorised as the partial retreat from socialism.

Despite this controversial character, the concept of the Great Retreat is helpful insofar as it permits us to grasp the evident policy discontinuity in early 1930s USSR. The shifts which we have described have not merely been perceived as steps away from socialism in the émigré press and scholarship but by Soviet society itself, including many among the soon-to-perish party elite and intelligentsia (Brandenberger 2012). While the assessment of these shifts varied from the consternation of doctrinal communists to the relief of the intelligentsia, they all agreed that an important change was taking place in the relation between the official ideology of the regime and the concrete forms of life in Soviet society. In our view, this change is best understood in biopolitical terms as the move from the accelerationist biopolitics of the direct forcing of the socialist ideal within the immanence of social life to a negatively inflected biopolitics that secures and fortifies the effects of this forcing by numerous reversals, compromises, qualifications or restorations.[6] We might well be dealing with something like 'socialism' in both cases, yet in the Great Retreat socialism takes a decidedly different form from the apocalyptic and sacrificial pathos of the Second Revolution with very important implications for the non-socialist forms of life in Soviet society. The 'socialism' of the Retreat was no longer a lethal force of the ideal that attacked the real in order to take its place but rather the partly realised ideal awkwardly seeking its accommodation within the real.

On the other hand, our approach to the Great Retreat as the negative inflection of socialism *within* socialism highlights the fact that however much the regime backtracked in 1934 and afterwards, it neither managed nor intended to *fully* reverse the policies of the Great Break and return to the practices of the NEP, let alone the pre-revolutionary period. The 'non-socialist' practices that were restored or revitalised in the Great Retreat did not survive the Great Break intact, if only because socialism remained the overarching context within which jazz and tennis, champagne and carnivals were reinserted, and in which they acquired new meanings: traditional authority of managers or professors intertwined with that of security police, economic incentives for workers conditioned by their incorporation into the Party, imported consumer goods available only in the restricted stores for the party *nomenklatura* or on the black market, the study of pre-revolutionary history used to legitimise Stalin's rule, and so on. Hoffmann is therefore entirely correct in viewing the term 'retreat' as inappropriate to describe the events of the mid-1930s, if we use the term in the sense of a usually forced or involuntary *return* to a past position or policy, especially as a result of a challenge, danger or threat (Hoffmann 2003: 89). Yet, the term begins to appear more appropriate, and indeed fortunate, if we consider its other meaning as an act of *withdrawal* into a safer, more secluded or more hospitable location such as 'a countryside retreat', 'retreat into the library'. It is in this sense of the cessation of the violent leap forward of the Second Revolution and the withdrawal of the regime into secure self-immanence, its avoidance of violent confrontation, that the term 'retreat' is more than appropriate to grasp the negative inflection of socialist biopolitics, which did not simply abandon or reverse this project but rather sought to partially negate its exterminist and self-destructive tendencies (cf. Roberts 2006: 227).

It is precisely in this context of social stabilisation and normalisation that Foucault's thesis on the reliance of the Soviet regime on nineteenth-century Western governmental technologies, addressed in Chapter 2, must be situated. Foucault's acerbic remarks about the valorisation of *Swan Lake*, narrative painting and the social novel in the USSR all refer to the period of the Great Retreat and would be barely conceivable in the iconoclastic context of the Cultural Revolution of the late 1920s. While Foucault was certainly correct about the use of Western governmental technologies by the Stalinist and the post-Stalinist regimes, he was wrong to infer from it the absence of any autonomous socialist biopolitics or governmentality. The fact that 'non-socialist' governmental technologies were deployed in the Soviet Union does not testify to some deep-seated inner contradiction of socialism, let alone its hidden 'racism', but simply to the retreat from its dominant rationality, that is, that of forcing socialism into life, which, as we have shown in Chapter 3, was grounded in a problematisation of life and ideology that was strikingly different from both liberalism and Nazism. In fact, in the middle of the 1930s the critics of the Great Retreat among the Old Bolshevik intelligentsia accused the proponents of the new patriotic line of 'simplistic, pseudosocialist racism' (Brandenberger 2012: 386). Rather than subsume socialism under racism, it would therefore be more fruitful to approach the Soviet recourse to ostensibly racist biopolitical techniques as a partial and tentative negation of properly socialist biopolitics practised in the Great Break.

In 'Society Must Be Defended' Foucault alludes to the idea of the retreat in Soviet socialism in his rhetorical question: 'And what if Rome once more conquered the revolution?' (2003: 84) However contested Timasheff's notion of the Great Retreat remains in Soviet studies, this question may be answered in the affirmative with regard to Stalinism. Yet, there remains a more specific question: did *'Roman' biopolitics*, which Foucault defined as racist, conquer *revolutionary biopolitics*, or did 'Roman' biopolitics conquer the revolution that had not produced any biopolitics of its own? While Foucault opts for the latter answer, our analysis in the previous chapter leads us to the former. The Great Retreat then becomes intelligible as the moderation of the biopolitical assault on the existing forms of life, their incorporation into the new order as the instruments of its stabilisation and the reorientation of governmental rationality from transforming society to securing the newly established order. It is this concern with security, conspicuous by its absence in the Great Break, that explains the recourse of the Soviet regime to the techniques borrowed from Western governmentality, for which the rationality of security, reflected in the immunitary orientation, has been constitutive (Foucault 2007: 11–87). The turn towards patriotism, the restoration of traditional structures and symbols of authority, the strengthening of families – while all these changes certainly had their own sector-specific rationalities, they are also understandable as attempts to stabilise the society whose radical transformation nearly destroyed it.

Nonetheless, despite the evident reduction in state violence after 1932, this negative inflection of the biopolitical project of the Great Break did not result in anything like a positive synthesis, but rather contributed to the proliferation of negativity. On the one hand, the rehabilitation of the forms of life formerly held subject to transcendence and effacement appeared to negate the properly revolutionary character of the Second Revolution, which appeared to the more radically minded observers as the second edition of the NEP (see Priestland 2007: 270–6). It is no coincidence that ten years before Timasheff's book a rather similar argument was made from a wholly different normative standpoint by a no lesser authority on socialism than Leon Trotsky (2004 [1937]: 206–19), for whom Stalinism marked the betrayal of the revolution by state bureaucracy that had become the new ruling class and restored traditional institutions to secure its hold over the society. On the other hand, the reinscription of 'bourgeois' forms of life in the socialist context negated their very status as bourgeois by subjecting them to the rituals of ideological hegemony, the hierarchies of the authoritarian party-state or the restrictions of the planned economy. If the Great Break had indeed succeeded in breaking the pre-socialist society to a significant degree, then what re-emerged in the Retreat were damaged, destitute and perverted versions of pre-Soviet forms of life.

A similar view has been offered by Vladimir Buldakov (2013), for whom Stalin's 'conservative modernisation', admired by contemporary Russian Stalinists, was no modernisation at all, but a project of stagnation and even degradation from the very beginning. As we have noted in the previous chapter, Buldakov's analysis does not mark out the specificity of the Great Break and treats the Stalinist period almost as all of a piece. While it would be hard to reconcile with the transformative drive of the Great Break, his interpretation is perfectly valid for the Retreat of the mid-1930s and helps us understand its negative character. While Timasheff originally viewed the Retreat as the welcome return to good sense after the mad flux of revolutionary experimentation, and contemporary authors such as Hoffmann view it as a successful adaptation of traditions to the newly attained socialism, Buldakov emphasises how the 'synthesis' of socialism and tradition was from the outset a *negative synthesis*, which brought together the *worst* aspects of both. 'The newborn system incorporated the worst features of the old, adding to them the vices of vulgarised innovations' (Buldakov 2013: 709). The Retreat enabled the survival or revival of pre-Soviet forms of life in a degraded and twisted form, resulting in the appearance of phenomena that belong neither to capitalism nor to socialism (ibid.: 693–4). To use a simple example, the distribution of consumer goods on the black market or restricted shops does not do credit either to capitalism or to socialism but in fact is a perversion of *both* ideologies. Nonetheless, it became a permanent feature of the Soviet order until its very demise, arguably contributing to the longevity of the economic system by compensating for its inability to ensure the supply of food and consumer goods. By the same token, the persistence of many social practices of the peasantry, from religious belief to spousal abuse, after their move to the cities clearly disproved the official claims about the 'culturedness' of the New Soviet Person, instead becoming recognisable, if disagreeable, attributes of that very person itself.

As a result of the Retreat there was born that uncanny phenomenon of Soviet society, which was neither strictly socialist nor bourgeois, neither public nor private, and so on (see Kharkhordin 1999: 270–6). While the Retreat arguably helped sustain the Soviet order during and after World War II, when the regime went even further in rehabilitating Russian nationalism, religion and traditional values (see Furst 2006), it made it increasingly difficult to invoke Soviet socialism as a positive reality, inflecting it with shadow supplements that simultaneously sustained and undermined the socialist state. In order to conceal the manifestations of this constituent negativity of the newly built socialism the Stalinist regime resorted to the second mode of the negative inflection of its biopolitical project, the production of simulacra of socialist forms of life.

THE GREAT SIMULACRUM: SOCIALIST REALISM AND REAL SOCIALISM

The period of the Great Retreat was characterised not only by the reversal of the policies of the Cultural Revolution in favour of the rehabilitation of traditional culture and art but also by the establishment of the first official Soviet artistic canon – the doctrine of socialist realism. Starting with the 1932 Decree 'On the Reconstruction of Literary and Art Organisations', which dissolved all independent artistic and literary associations and grouped all Soviet writers and artists into official unions, the regime abandoned its earlier policy of relative neutrality in the struggle between various artistic groups and directions, monopolised the control of the sphere of art and sought to lay down the regulative principles of Soviet art. The doctrine of socialist realism was officially inaugurated at the 1934 Congress of Soviet Writers and remained the official Soviet canon until the Perestroika period. Socialist realism was famously defined as 'truthful, historically concrete representation of reality in its revolutionary development' and specified in terms of four principles: proletarian orientation, typicality, realism and partisanship (Tertz 1960: 148).

This deceptively simple definition deserves attention since it pertains directly to the relation between transcendence and immanence that in our argument defines the Stalinist biopolitical rationality. Despite repeated emphasis on the *mimetic* aspect evident in the calls for 'truthful representation' and 'realism', Soviet aesthetics strictly delimited socialist realism from any form of 'naturalism', dismissed as a merely photographic representation of empirical facts as they are (see Dobrenko 2004: 798–9). This denigration of naturalism resonates with the general anti-naturalist orientation of Stalinist governmentality addressed in the previous chapter. If the task of socialist government is radical transformation, then the natural, however defined, can only be an object of or an obstacle to this transformation. What is to be represented truthfully and concretely is then *not* the brute facticity of the real but rather the 'typical', which Georgy Malenkov defined at the 19th Party Congress as

> that which most persuasively expresses the essence of a given social force. From the Marxist-Leninist perspective, the typical does not signify some sort of statistical mean. The typical is the vital sphere, in which is manifested the party spirit of realistic art. (Malenkov cited in Groys 2011: 50–1)

The typical is thus dissociated from the mean or average, most frequent or familiar, and instead pertains to the *essence* of phenomena, which remains inapparent and must be brought into appearance by artistic representation, as long as the latter is animated by the 'party spirit' that alone intuits the essence of things correctly (see Lahusen 2005).

The paradoxical requirement of the realistic representation of the invisible is intensified by the demand that this reality must be represented 'in its revolutionary development'. Rather than represent reality 'as it is', in the facticity of its being, the socialist-realist artist must represent it in its *becoming*, as something-to-come which does not yet exist but will be brought into existence by the policies prescribed by the party spirit. This principle paves the way for the proliferation of quasi-Romantic themes of heroic, if not outright superhuman, efforts of Soviet workers in the construction of socialism, for which, as the slogan of the decade said, 'nothing is impossible'. As long as the object of representation in socialist realism was the invisible essence of reality in its revolutionary becoming, this canon became thoroughly separated from reality as such, much as teleological planning in the economic sphere during the Great Break was divorced from economic realities and defined solely in terms of its internal consistency. Moreover, the similarities between socialist realism and teleological planning do not end here, since they are variations on the theme of the construction of socialism through the denigration and ultimately the derealisation of empirical reality. Socialist realism is the planned economy of art, while planned economy is socialist-realist art in the sphere of industrial or agricultural production. This parallel also permits us to understand the character of the *product* of socialist realism: the representation of the typical essence of the socialist reality-in-the-making was nothing other than a *simulacrum* of socialism, a strictly phenomenal appearance without any foundation in being.[7]

While, as we have seen in the previous section, the Great Retreat introduced negativity into the empirical reality of Soviet socialism, the construction of simulacra of Soviet forms of life sought to negate this negativity by the compensatory production of images of socialism the way it would be. Yet, in this process the biopolitical project of Stalinism remained in the terrain of the negative: the aesthetic discourse of 'socialist realism' produced simulacra of socialist forms of life, including the New Soviet Person, at the cost of the utter derealisation of life itself (Dobrenko 2007: 10–19). In order to grasp this derealisation let us compare the doctrine of Socialist Realism with the militant artistic tendencies of the Great Break that sought to produce proletarian art. Whereas the 'industrial novels' of Marietta Shaginyan, Fedor Gladkov and Valentin Kataev, or 'productionist' works in other art forms affirmed the asceticism and self-sacrifice of revolutionary labour in the service of future socialism (ibid.: 149–52), the socialist realist novels of writers such as Vsevolod Kochetov, Galina Nikolaeva or Vasily Azhaev dealt with same themes of labour and the construction of socialism from a melodramatic and almost hedonistic perspective: 'the new life is no longer being built only for the future; rather, the future (communism) is gradually moving into today's happiness' (Dobrenko 2007: 246–7; see also Heller 1995). Labour was no longer valorised as the force of the revolutionary transformation of nature and society, but rather aesthetised in itself, divorced from properly economic considerations, whereby what was produced in socialist production was 'production' itself, which did not have to yield any product beside itself (ibid.: 256). The aesthetisation of labour went hand in hand with the effacement of the very question of economic efficiency: as Dobrenko incisively remarks, the Soviet Union 'did not produce footwear, clothing, dwellings or food products, but rather made "cast iron and steel", "factories and blast furnaces" and waged a "harvest battle". The product itself ceases to be self-sufficient, the process of producing it becomes self-sufficient instead' (ibid.: xviii).

At first glance, the claim that labour no longer transforms reality resonates with the logic of the Great Retreat, which we have interpreted as a compromise of the ideal with the real. Yet, the function of socialist realism was not to assist, affirm or represent this compromise but rather to *efface* its every trace, whereby the actuality of the retreat from socialism was crowded out by the representation of socialism as already attained. The familiar images of real socialism, from the happily toiling collective farmers to the marching Young Pioneers, are products of this aesthetic project that did not simply seek to beautify the reality that was not entirely socialist but rather ventured to wholly replace the non-socialist reality with a simulacrum of socialism.

> If we were to remove Socialist Realism – novels about enthusiasm in industry, poems about the joy of labour, films about the happy life, songs and pictures about the wealth of the land of the Soviets, and so on – from our mental image of socialism, we would be left with nothing that could properly be called socialism. Nothing would remain but dreary workdays, routine daily labour, and a life of hardship and inconvenience – the same reality that can be attributed to any economic system. Thus once we 'distill' Socialist Realism, there is nothing 'socialist' left in the residue. Therefore we may conclude that Socialism Realism produced socialism's symbolic values by de-realizing everydayness. (Dobrenko 2007: 4–5)

In Dobrenko's argument, the Stalinist regime compensated for the deficiencies in real social transformation, which for him consisted in the construction of a modern 'disciplinarian society' (2004: 686; 2007: 30–4), with the massive mobilisation and deployment of aesthetic resources that produced a simulacrum of Soviet society 'in its becoming'. The incomplete and contradictory character of socialism as a lived reality led to the state totalisation of the *representation* of lived reality in the future anterior. Socialist realism is thus not merely an aesthetic doctrine, but rather a political rationality that authorises the production of aesthetic effects that both *simulate* the socialist forms of life, whose actual formation is deferred into the future, and *conceal* the difference of the actual lived reality from this simulative representation by 'derealising' this reality. This is what makes this inflection of the Stalinist project negative.

> The goal of Socialist Realism is the production of socialism via the reworking of reality into an ideologically consumable product. But a side effect of this operation is the de-realisation of everydayness: available reality must cease to exist in order to appear in the form of socialism. (Dobrenko 2007: 14)

It is easy to see the parallels between this doctrine and the immediately prior rationality of the Great Break. Socialist realism undertakes the same assault on reality, the same war on nature that the Great Break practised in the villages, at construction sites and universities, yet rather than annihilate living beings this assault takes the form of effacing all that is real in lived reality. In the words of Albert Camus, 'the real object of socialist realism is precisely that it has no relationship to reality. Reality is openly put at the top of the list, but only so that it is easier to destroy' (Camus cited in ibid.: 14).

Thus, the deficit in the production of real commodities was balanced by the production of socialism itself as an aesthetic phenomenon, the sole sphere of production in which deficits never occurred (ibid.: 256).

Following this logic to its extreme conclusion, Dobrenko makes a radical claim that the aesthetic effects of socialist realism were the *only* reality socialism ever had.

> [In] Socialist Realism itself one must see 'real socialism', considering that Socialist Realism is almost the only reality of socialism, since extra-aesthetic reality had nothing specifically socialist in it. The rest of reality remained voiceless, unarticulated and therefore lacking any means of expression. The more socialism realised itself, the more life was de-realised. The mechanism for realising socialism and simultaneously de-realising life was what we call Socialist Realism. (ibid.: 19).

This staggering claim establishes a direct connection between an aesthetic project, apparently furthest away from biopolitical considerations, and the biopolitical project of the construction of socialism that we have focused on in our study. While the Great Retreat negated the exterminist biopolitics of the Great Break by moderating the attempt to force transcendence into immanence, negating the purity of the ideal by the toleration of the messiness of the real, the socialist-realist simulacrum negated it by derealising the messy and unwieldy 'real life' by its saturation with the aesthetic representations of the socialist ideal. Socialist realism is thus also in some sense a biopolitical project, since it produces the very forms of life that the revolution aspired to. The happy life of the emancipated Soviet toilers as the 'new historical community of human beings' was right there – on the canvasses of paintings, in the melodies of songs and symphonies, in the pages of novels, on the radio and on cinema screens. The New Life, whose construction required the destruction of millions of lives, was all around one in the USSR: it could be heard, seen and even touched, yet it still remained *unreal*.

THE LIMITS OF SIMULATION

While it is impossible to doubt the achievements of the Stalinist state in the aesthetisation of socialism, we must also bear in mind the *limits* of this strategy. It has become fashionable in recent years to focus on the purely discursive or aesthetic aspects of the Stalinist regime (Halfin 2009; Hellbeck 2006; Dobrenko 2007; Kaganovsky 2008), analysing the productive powers of official discourses, rituals and modes of representation. Yet, while these approaches are often influenced by Foucault, it appears that they often suffer from what a prominent commentator on Foucault once called the 'illusions of realization and effectivity' regarding the operations of power (Gordon 1980: 246), whereby Stalinism is credited with immense biopolitical productivity, producing subjects and forms of life out of nothing. Yet, the only sphere in which such creation *ex nihilo* is possible is that of language. It is thus not surprising that the claims about the productivity of Stalinist power ultimately turn to the discourse of socialist realism as the prime site of the construction of socialism: 'The transition to "socialism" was accomplished, to a large extent, discursively' (Dobrenko 2007: 31).

> This will to radical artificiality inscribed the Soviet Communist project in the context of art. The Russian proletariat was to be freed from the alienated work it had to carry out under the conditions of capitalist exploitation, with the goal of becoming a collective artist creating a new world – and at the same time recreating itself as its own artwork. Where nature was, art should be. (Groys 2011: 122)

However, contrary to the illusions of the revolutionary avant-garde, one cannot create new men or women by works of art, especially not in the sense of the immanent conversion of transcendent ideals that Soviet biopolitics sought to attain. The product of socialist realism remains unreal in two senses: first, its representation of socialism is entirely divorced from the reality characterised by the Retreat and, second, the proliferation of these representations derealises this very reality, rendering it invisible and ineffable. Nonetheless, the task of derealisation may never be completely achieved: to recall the fundamental thesis of psychoanalysis, whatever is foreclosed in the symbolic returns in the real. While we shall address the specific manner of this return in the following section, what is crucial at this stage is the impossibility of completely effacing that very 'dreary life of hardship and inconvenience' that, according to Dobrenko, remains when one subtracts socialist realism from real socialism. Indeed, Dobrenko recognises the persistence of the modicum of non-aesthetised reality in Stalinism, for example in his claims about the 'principal event' of Stalinism being the formation of a disciplinarian society, the economic foundation of Soviet society being state capitalism and the 'violent death of the Russian village' as the 'root of the Stalinist terror' (ibid.: 30–3). Yet, this reality beneath the veneer of socialist realism is ultimately downgraded in his study in favour of the detailed analysis of the veneer as *itself* real.

> Socialist Realism is a highly aesthetised culture, a radically transformed world. Nothing could break through its texture of pure aesthetics. Aesthetics did not beautify reality, it was reality. By contrast, all reality outside of socialist realism was but the wilderness of everyday life, waiting to be rendered fit to be read and interpreted. (Ibid.: 4)

In contrast to this reduction of real socialism to socialist realism, we propose to treat the Great Retreat and the Great Simulacrum of socialist realism as two distinct, if intertwined, strategies of responding to the sociocidal impact of the Great Break: the negation of the ideal through compromise with the real and the derealisation of the real through the production of the simulacra of the ideal. The fact that the concessions and backtrackings of the Retreat unfolded simultaneously with the institution of the socialist-realist canon testifies to the insufficiency of the purely aesthetic approach to the construction of socialism. The forcing of socialism in the real during the Second Revolution was not simply abandoned for its idealised simulacrum in the sphere of art but also partially negated in the real for a more moderate course of peaceful coexistence with some pre-Soviet realities. Of course, the strategies of the retreat and the simulacrum often merged, as in, for example, the rehabilitation of consumption that for the absolute majority of the population took the form of the consumption of the *images* of Soviet commodities: Mikoyan's *Book of Tasty and Healthy Food* was indeed a true masterpiece of socialist realism. Yet, other policies of the mid-1930s, from the ban on abortions to the restoration of ranks and titles in the army and the professions, from the revalorisation of Russian tsars to the dismantling of egalitarian arrangements in industry, could not be subsumed under the simulacrum of socialist realism and often contradicted it explicitly. Thus, for all the fascination with the aesthetic productivity of Stalinism, the very character of this productivity ultimately marks the *failure* of the Stalinist project, whose original objective in the Great Break was, after all, never merely aesthetic.

As we argued in Chapter 3, the difference of Stalinism from the utopian experimentation of the 'revolutionary dreamers' of the early 1920s consists in its attempt to convert the ideological content of the revolution into the lived reality of socialism. If, as Dobrenko argues, this lived reality was solely representational, discursive or aesthetic, this only means that the biopolitical project failed to reach its goal or, perhaps, stopped short of reaching it in order to avert a suicidal catastrophe. Either way, Stalinism ends up suspended in the same abyss between the transcendence of the revolutionary idea and the immanence of lived reality, in which the revolutionary avant-garde originally dwelled. If the grandiose programme of the production of a New Life and a New Person comes down to the production of numerous artworks that are, to put it mildly, an acquired taste, how can we possibly distinguish Stalin from Malevich, Khlebnikov or Tatlin, the representatives of the avant-garde who also tried (and failed) to create a new life by aesthetic means?[8] If the aesthetic simulacrum were all there was to socialism, might we not suggest that the Suprematists, the Futurists or even the Proletkultists might have done a better job of it? The emphasis on the total *aesthetic* productivity of Stalinism obscures the fact that what it actually sought during the Great Break was *biopolitical* productivity, of which the simulacrum of socialist realism was a negative inflection, a dose of unreality inscribed within the project of making socialism real. While it is undeniable that socialist realism was about the only Soviet product of which there was no shortage and which proved to be one of the most durable, we must not lose sight of the fact that this product was always the second-best option for the regime itself.

Thus, in the High Stalinism of the mid-1930s we observe the coexistence of degraded pre- or non-socialist forms of life with the aesthetised forms of 'real socialism', aggressively promoted by the state and enacted in a myriad of official rituals, which, by virtue of their coercive and simulative character, contributed to the further degradation of social life. Having halted the offensive of the Great Break, Stalinist governmentality sought to compensate for its low biopolitical productivity with something like a *symbolic overkill*, the incessant production of aesthetic commodities that would crowd out the contradictory realities of the 1930s. Yet, this aesthetic overproduction could never completely cancel the distance between the splendour of socialist realism and the dreariness of real socialism. On the contrary, the more immense and awe-inspiring the simulacrum of socialism was, the more distant it became from the grim reality.

It is in this gap that we must locate the essence of Soviet socialism as such: rather than view either the retreat or the simulacrum as primary, we should approach them on the same terrain as two strategies of coming to terms with the aftermath of the Great Break. If the simulacrum had been primary to the reality of the retreat, we would have observed a fully successful derealisation of life or, perhaps, the ascent of the Soviet population to a purely 'spiritual life', oblivious to material realities. In contrast, if the retreat had been primary and the simulacrum had been merely an ornamental camouflage, we would observe a more cunning strategy of the formal maintenance of the socialist order by hollowing out its entire content, something that was arguably achieved in contemporary China. Yet, since these two strategies were of equal status as second-order adaptations of the biopolitical rationality, neither could triumph over the other, leaving the immanent order of the Soviet society torn between the retreat and the simulacrum. It is this split that accounts for the perennial instability of the Stalinist regime that in the mid-1930s reached the paroxysmal point of the Great Terror.

THE GREAT TERROR: EXPLICATING THE SENSELESS

Any discussion of High Stalinism would not be complete without an analysis of the unprecedented deployment of state violence during 1936–8 that became known as the Great Terror. The number of victims of the Terror remains a contentious point among historians, yet despite having been brought down from the dozens of millions spoken of during the Cold War (Solzhenitsyn 2007; Conquest 2007), even the most conservative assessments (Getty and Naumov 2010: 241–5) estimate the number of executions to exceed 680,000 people during 1937–8 alone. This staggering figure is only the tip of the iceberg. The number of arrests, imprisonments and deportations during the 1930s is estimated at over three million, and the body count goes up even further if one includes the victims of wartime deportations, the 'Sovietisation' of the western regions of the USSR before and after World War II and the postwar famine of 1946–7 (Hoffmann 2011: 238–9; Edele 2010: 40–5).

Nonetheless, what makes the Terror of the mid- and late 1930s unprecedented is not the body count *per se*. The Civil War of 1918–21 and especially the collectivisation of 1928–32 actually exceeded the purges of 1936–8 in terms of deaths, though not in terms of state-sanctioned executions.[9] What makes the purges unprecedented is rather the fact that they occurred not in the context of civil wars (against the political opponents or the peasantry as a class) but rather amid the ostensible *stabilisation* of the regime, testified to by both the retreat from the militancy of the Great Break and the painstaking construction of the simulacrum of the already-built socialism.[10] The purges unfolded in the aftermath of the promulgation of the 1936 Constitution, which proclaimed the completion of the construction of the socialist order, restored the rights of the former 'exploiting classes' and formally introduced universal and direct suffrage. In its abandonment of the principle of the dictatorship of the proletariat and the restoration of civil and political rights to the former bourgeois classes, including the ex-kulaks, the Constitution was a good example of the logic of the Great Retreat, while its declarations of wide-ranging social and economic rights and benefits in health care, education, housing, pensions and leisure exemplified the operation of the simulacrum of the 'better and joyous life' under the new order. In everyday life terms the purges came unexpectedly at the end of the 'three good years' of 1934–6 after the mishaps and tragedies of the Great Break (Fitzpatrick 2002: 7). These 'good years', while still difficult in economic terms, were nonetheless characterised by the sense of newfound stabilisation, the hopes for improvement in living conditions and the development of Soviet leisure culture, from Stalin's favourite musical comedies to carnivals in Gorky Park, with Ferris wheels, bowling alleys and jazz bands (see Schlögel 2012: 372–86, 404–12, 433–43; Roberts 2006: 260–1).

It is in this atmosphere of relative optimism that the purges began after the assassination of Sergei Kirov on 1 December 1934.[11] Yet, this conjunction of the normality of the Retreat and the paroxysms of state violence is only a puzzle insofar as we remain committed to the understanding of the Terror in much of 'totalitarianism theory' as the logical consequence of the radicalism of the idea of communism, whereby we would expect the climax of terror to coincide with the periods of the most intense ideological radicalism, such as 1917–21 or 1928–32. Yet, the Soviet experience clearly shows that there is no necessary connection between terror and ideological radicalism: while the Great Break was *both* ideologically radical and extremely violent, the Terror of the late 1930s unfolded in the context of an evident relaxation of ideological dogmatism and was directed *against*, among others, ideological radicals among the former oppositionists (that is, Trotskyites and Zinovievites).

As Alain Badiou (2013) has argued in a recent review of the relation between communism and the Terror, the Terror was not the logical consequence of the affirmation of the idea of communism but rather a result of a *retreat* from this idea, which in Badiou's ethics of fidelity amounts to its betrayal. In the case of Stalinism this retreat had two aspects, the first pertaining to the objective aspects of the post-revolutionary trajectory in Soviet Russia and the second to the subjective orientation of the Soviet regime. First, as Badiou argues, the turn to the Terror was a result of the subsumption of revolutionary insurrection under the rationality of the state and, moreover, the state perpetually preoccupied with ensuring its own survival. As a result, in the aftermath of the Civil War the communist experiment, which was not essentially linked to the state and was even originally viewed as instrumental in the latter's eventual withering away, was sidelined in favour of the project of securing the new Soviet state in the atmosphere of anxiety, fear and search for enemies, which was fertile ground for the use of terrorist methods for resolving what Badiou, faithful to his erstwhile Maoism, calls 'non-antagonistic contradictions'.

> These circumstances were the worldwide slaughter of the inter-imperialistic wars, ferocious civil wars, and the aid given by foreign powers to the counterrevolutionary factions. They were the circumstances of an ongoing shortage of experienced, stoical political cadres, the best of whom were carried off early on in the whirlwind. All of this created a political subjectivity composed of a superego imperative and chronic anxiety. Uncertainty, ignorance, and fear of treason were decisive factors in what

> we now know about the climate in which the leaders made their decisions. This subjectivity in turn led to the main principle of action being to treat any contradiction as if it were antagonistic, as if it represented a mortal danger. The habit that developed in the civil war of killing anyone who was not with you became entrenched in a socialist state that was constantly amazed at having successfully prevailed. (Badiou 2013: 7)

Second, and more importantly, the recourse to terror was for Badiou the result of a subjective reorientation of the regime away from the experiment of creating new non-capitalist forms of life towards the competition of the Soviet state with its capitalist antagonists. This turn towards competition was a logical consequence of the doctrine of socialism in one country and the katechontic holding back of world revolution: if socialism and capitalism are expected to coexist for the foreseeable future, then the triumph of the former over the latter cannot take the form of a definitive victory and the destruction of the adversary, but only one of success in the competition with the adversary that stops short of the final battle. While the socialist revolution initially promised a life that was *otherwise* than in capitalist states, the logic of competition rather proceeded from the imperative of doing *better* than the opponent, which necessarily presupposed some degree of commensurability between the two systems: it would be impossible to adjudicate the competition between highly heterogeneous entities. The idea of competition thus necessarily introduces mimetic rivalry, whereby overcoming the opponent first requires becoming similar to it. Thus, rather than cultivate a form of life wholly other to capitalism, the Soviet Union ventured to defeat capitalism by beating it *at its own game*, which first required the massive mobilisation of all kinds of resources simply to 'catch up' with the capitalist West. It is this mobilisation, which was in principle unnecessary from the standpoint of the idea of communism but indispensable in the logic of competition, that, according to Badiou, legitimised the use of terrorist means.

> [The] main lesson learned from the last century's revolutions can be expressed as follows: competing with the adversary always leads to the mere semblance, not the real, of force. For the communist Idea is not in competition with capitalism; it is in an absolutely asymmetric relationship with it. As the dramatic conditions that accompanied their implementation clearly showed, the Soviet five-year plans and Mao's 'Great Leap Forward' were forced constructs. Slogans like 'catch up with England in fifteen years' implied a forcing, a perversion of the Idea, and ultimately the obligation of implementing Terror. Far from being a consequence of the communist Idea, Terror actually results from a fascination with the enemy, a mimetic rivalry with it. The effect of competition

with capitalism gradually leads to the Idea itself being purely and simply abandoned in favour of a sort of paradoxical violence that consists in wanting to achieve the same results as capitalism – whereas one actually wanted, and to a certain extent created, all the conditions necessary in order *not* to achieve the same results. (Badiou 2013: 10)

In this interpretation, rather than being incompatible with the Terror, the Great Retreat actually constituted its conditions of possibility. As soon as the regime recoiled from the grand biopolitical tasks of the Great Break into the compromise with the real that sought to stabilise and secure the Soviet state, socialism was no longer the radically incommensurable Other of capitalism, but its rival that had to borrow the latter's methods when these proved effective. Thus, when the Stalin Constitution of 1936 declared socialism to have already been attained, this socialism appeared quite similar to capitalism in the aspects of work discipline, submission to factory management, conservative family values, nationalist propaganda, and so on. The Terror was merely one more in the series of mobilising mechanisms by which the Stalinist system sought to beat capitalism by becoming more like it.

While Badiou succeeds in demonstrating the irreducibility of the Terror to the idea of communism, his interpretation of the Terror as the effect of the Retreat is insufficient and must be complemented with a biopolitical perspective. Badiou's reading of the retreat in terms of the statist conversion of the revolutionary project entails that the retreat in question took place as early as the Civil War period, making it impossible to distinguish between the Great Break and the Great Retreat, which for him were all part of the same ill-fated statist conversion of the idea of communism. Thus, in his account of the Terror Badiou uses the example of the first Five Year Plan and the slogan of 'overtaking England', which belong to the period that was in fact characterised by the very revolutionary drive that Badiou considers to have been extinguished and perverted. While Badiou equates the statist conversion of the revolution with the retreat from the revolution as such, in our view the true retreat took place in the mid-1930s, when the biopolitical ambitions of the Great Break were tempered in a compromise with the pre- or non-Soviet forms of life. Yet, similarly to Badiou's account, this retreat was *also* accompanied by terror, which we shall now analyse as a negative inflection of the Soviet biopolitical project.

In order to account for the rationality of the Stalinist terror we must distinguish between at least three main types of governmental violence during the period of 1936–8. The first and the best-known is the purge within the Bolshevik Party, which began with the assassination of Sergei Kirov and initially focused on the prosecution of Stalin's opponents among the Old Bolsheviks, already removed from the top positions in power after the defeat of the Left and Right oppositions in 1925–7. The first Moscow Trial in August 1936 sentenced to death Grigory Zinoviev, Lev Kamenev and fourteen other leading Bolsheviks, finding them guilty of the organisation of the 'Trotskyite-Kamenevite-Zinovievite-Leftist-Counter-Revolutionary Bloc' and the conspiracy to assassinate Kirov. The second trial, held in January 1937, focused on the 'anti-Soviet Trotskyite Centre', featuring such prominent former members of Left and Right Oppositions as Karl Radek, Yuri Pyatakov and Grigory Sokolnikov. In this trial, the main focus was on sabotage and 'wrecking' in industry, where many of the accused occupied leading administrative positions. In June 1937 a secret trial of the leading Red Army commanders, including Mikhail Tukhachevsky, Iona Yakir and Ieronim Uborevich, took place, where the top military officials were found guilty of 'right wing Trotsky-ite military conspiracy' against the USSR and executed. The purge of the military was followed by the escalation of purges in the regions of the USSR, where most of the regional leaders were removed and prosecuted during the summer and autumn of 1937. Finally, the Third Moscow trial took place in March 1938, in which the accused, including the former leaders of the Right Opposition Nikolai Bukharin and Alexei Rykov, and the former NKVD chief Genrikh Yagoda, incidentally the organiser of the first trial, were grouped into the 'Right Trotskyite bloc' and found guilty of assassination attempts against Lenin and Stalin going as far back as 1918, the poisoning of Maxim Gorky as well as espionage for most European states. As a result of these trials, the entire 'Old Bolshe-vik' elite that led the Party during the Revolution and the Civil War were executed, with the notable exception of Stalin himself.

These four trials had much wider implications, leading to arrests, tri-als and executions of numerous party and military officials associated with the executed leaders, both in Moscow and in the regions. Moreo-ver, given the patron-client relationships between the party elite and the Soviet intelligentsia (Tucker 1992: 572–84), numerous Soviet writers, artists and intellectuals fell victim to the Terror due to their acquaint-ances among the purged elites: Isaac Babel, Leopold Averbakh, Vladimir Kirshon and others. More generally, due to the active solicitation by the NKVD of letters of denunciation, the Terror rapidly expanded beyond the top levels of the Party, government and trade unions, as these denun-ciations became a highly effective instrument for getting rid of unpopu-lar factory managers, advancing one's career by eliminating competitors, resolving private vendettas and family disputes, or simply redirecting the threat of the purge from oneself onto someone else (Goldman 2011). Similarly to top-level purges, in which the terrorisers (such as Yagoda,

Yezhov and other top NKVD personnel) could rapidly themselves become the terrorised, the spirals of accusation and counter-accusation tended to engulf everyone involved, as the accusers of 1937 were often hounded as 'bawlers' in 1938 by the rehabilitated victims of their denunciations. This logic of escalation through popular participation lends credence to the frequent comparisons of the Terror with suicide (Getty and Naumov 2010: 165) or an auto-immune disease (Goldman 2011: 297).

The enthusiastic participation of the Soviet population in the Terror led a number of authors to pose a provocative thesis about the connections between the Purges and the abortive campaign for democracy in 1937. Following the adoption of the 1936 Constitution, the USSR was to hold direct legislative elections to the newly established Supreme Soviet, which, for the first time since the Civil War, were to be competitive and based on universal, equal and direct suffrage, abandoning the discrimination of the former aristocracy and bourgeoisie, inscribed in the 1918 and 1924 Constitutions. Multi-candidate elections were also held in party organisations and trade unions (Goldman 2007: 95–132; Kharkhordin 1999: 157–63; Getty and Naumov 2010; Priestland 2007: 381–7). The Terror was the permanent backdrop to these experiments with democracy, insofar as the losing side usually lost more than seats and positions, their files transferred straight to the NKVD. While some authors focus on the use of the terror by the government in order to ensure that no former oppositionists, kulaks or priests get elected (Getty and Naumov 2010: 143–64), others trace the way the conjunction of election and purge made it possible for the rank-and-file to challenge local party and union leaders, remove ineffective or corrupt management and reassert themselves as the 'popular sovereigns' they were officially claimed to be (Goldman 2007). Though there are certainly numerous reasons for the regime's eventual abandonment of the idea of competitive elections, it is at least plausible that one of them was the fear of the terror spiralling out of control and engulfing the regime itself (Getty and Naumov 2010: 196–215; Goldman 2007: 252–62; Priestland 2007: 369–73). While archival research in the postcommunist period reaffirmed Stalin's key role in masterminding the purges, which was previously challenged by various authors of the 'revisionist' turn, we must also not forget this populist or pseudo-democratic dimension of the Terror (Rogovin 1998, 2009; Rittersporn 1991).

In contrast to the party and union purges related to the Moscow trials, the two other types of purges were secret and rarely involved the wider population as accusers or 'bawlers'. The *mass operations* of 1937, sanctioned by Order 00447, 'Concerning the operation of repressing former kulaks, criminals, and other anti-Soviet elements' (31 July 1937), targeted numerous categories of 'social aliens': from former kulaks (returning from the camps and forced resettlements of the Great Break period) to priests, from former White Army officers to beggars and prostitutes, from convicted criminals to members of the non-Bolshevik Left in the pre-revolutionary period. The Order provided quotas for arrests and execution for every region of the USSR, which were often overfulfilled by the regional authorities, eager to avoid a similar fate in the party purges. The number of those killed in the mass operations alone is estimated at 385,000 (Goldman 2007: 5). In his analysis of the Great Terror from the perspective of social modernity Hoffmann (2011: 278–94) discusses these operations in terms of 'excisionary' violence, a case of negative social engineering, in which particular social groups deemed dangerous or irredeemable are to be extracted from society and, ultimately, physically eliminated. Following Stalin's infamous thesis on the intensification of class struggle in the course of the successful construction of socialism, the regime renewed the attacks on the 'class aliens' in the middle of the 1930s, now subsuming them under the category of the 'socially alien' or 'anti-Soviet' elements, which included ostensibly non-political criminals or 'marginal elements'. In this manner, the process of class war that still characterised the Great Break was thoroughly depoliticised and transformed into a 'social cleansing' operation. As Hoffmann (2003: 76–87) demonstrated in an earlier study, this process also had its correlate in the party purges since the mid-1930s, where former oppositionists were routinely accused of excessive drinking, womanising, homosexuality or other forms of 'moral corruption'. Starting from 1937 this moralising tendency was intensified further still, leading to the construction of the irredeemable 'enemy of the people' that we shall address below.

Finally, the Terror took the form of *national operations*, targeting the diasporas that were deemed unreliable in the condition of a hypothetical war. In Stalin's logic, diaspora nationalities (Poles, Germans, Koreans, Finns, Romanians, and so on) were particularly suspicious, since they had another state that they could be loyal to, even if they had never visited that state and had no connections within it whatsoever. The national operations included forced resettlements (e.g. of Koreans from the Far East to Kazakhstan), arrests (e.g. of all Germans employed at Soviet factories) and executions (e.g. of alleged Polish spies). It is these operations that clearly accord with Foucault's notion of racism, as long as it is applied in a metaphorical sense. The same applies a fortiori to the post-World War II purges of Nazi collaborators in the newly annexed territories of the USSR or the anti-Semitic repression of 1948–53 (Hoffmann 2011: 295–301; van Ree 2002: 201–7; Weiner 1999: 1131–40; Barnes 2011: 231–9; Lowe 2012: 340–58; Gellately 2013:

193–208). These policies, whose scope and intensity only become fully known after the demise of the USSR and which could therefore not have been addressed by Foucault, were barely mediated by the socialist ideology of class struggle. Instead they confirm the regime's retreat from its principles that became particularly pronounced during and after World War II and during the early Cold War period, as geopolitical considerations of state security and international power politics repeatedly overrode the ideological concerns of the socialist project (cf. Weiner 1999: 1129–30). Of course, one should not overestimate the degree to which the 'ethnicisation' of the enemy obscured political and ideological criteria: Ukrainian nationalists belonging to the Ukrainian Insurgent Army (UPA), for example, were prosecuted as 'bourgeois nationalists' and not as Ukrainians, while the anti-Semitism of 1952–3 targeted specific individuals and groups as 'rootless cosmopolitans', while leaving many Jews in key positions in the Soviet state, army and industry. As Amir Weiner (1999: 1155) argues, '[excision], even when totalised, did not emanate from a genocidal ideology and was not practised through exterminatory institutions. Purification did not engage collectives as such but rather the individuals who comprised them.' Nonetheless, particularly the national operations against the diasporas clearly exemplify the move away from the ideologically based repression to the quasi-racist logic of purification of the Soviet society from heterogeneous elements.

These different aspects of the Terror evidently make it difficult to arrive at a single interpretation of this phenomenon.[12] The national operations lend themselves to an instrumental interpretation most easily: given the 'capitalist encirclement' and the memory of the Allied intervention in the Civil War, the Soviet regime had been anticipating a future war from its very inception, most notably in the 1927 'war scare', and used this anticipation to legitimise its increasingly repressive policies (Kotkin 2014: 619–21). Nonetheless, the fear of the 'fifth column' in the eventual war, which was offered as the justification of the Terror in the post-Stalin period by no less a figure than Molotov himself (2007: 156, 252) and was then repeated incessantly by lesser-known Stalinists then and now, cannot really explain the decimation of the army, the execution of the homeless or the purge of the Central Committee composed of faithful Stalinists, whose association with the left or right opposition dated back almost 10 years, if it could be established at all. How exactly can a country prepare for war by murdering over a million of its citizens and condemning another few million to forced labour? The scale and scope of the Terror was such that the 'fifth column' argument could only be meaningful if one posited the entire population as the potential enemy of the regime, which, of course, could then easily be reversed into casting the regime itself as the sole true 'enemy of the people' (cf. Tucker 1992: 625).

Other well-known explanations, such as Hannah Arendt's argument (1973: 389–458) about the Terror as the pathway to 'total domination', the revisionist thesis of Getty and Naumov (2010) about the origins of the Terror in the institutional power struggle between Stalin and the regional leaders, and the argument of the 'social modernity theory' about the Terror as an extreme form of modern social interventionism (Hoffmann 2011) fare little better, capturing some aspects of this phenomenon while being powerless in the face of others (cf. Roberts 2006: 221–3, 257–61). Perhaps this is the fate of all attempts to explain such a staggering phenomenon: since every explanation implies the possibility of justification (by endowing that which should not have been with *reason to have been*), the phenomenon that we consider unjustifiable must remain in some sense and to some extent inexplicable (see Levi 1991; Amis 2014: 303–10). There is, however, an evident danger in this position that consists in making the phenomenon in question so singular as to be entirely ineffable or even mystical, which perversely transforms the interpretation of the event into its mute adoration (see Rancière 2010b: 196–202). 'To say that Auschwitz is "unsayable" or "incomprehensible" is equivalent to *euphemein*, to adoring in silence as one does with a god. Regardless of one's intentions, this contributes to its glory' (Agamben 1999b: 32–3).

The ethico-political problem of explaining and justifying the Stalinist terror was the focus of Dmitry Bykov's acclaimed novel *Justification* (2003). The novel's protagonist's quest to understand the Terror ultimately leads him to the discovery of a secret project of the production of New Soviet Persons in the Gulag camps, the 'Golden Cohort' that was trained to withstand torture, hunger and deprivation in order to become elite soldiers in the upcoming war. The Terror is thus understood as the ultimate test of the Soviet population before the war, in which the weak were simply annihilated, while the strong were strengthened even further by their privations and mobilised for the selfless struggle for the USSR. While this grotesque biopolitical utopia initially appears to satisfy the protagonist's desire for the justification of the Terror and even provides a positive contrast to the sterile nihilism of the post-Soviet era that he inhabits, its utter falsity is revealed to him in his last moments before he accidentally drowns, without explanation and for no reason. The transcendence of life as such in the new life of the Golden Cohort did not produce superhuman heroes, but simply a heap of corpses.

> The human that he dreamed of overcoming was finally being overcome. And there was no one to ask for help, since he was falling into himself, into his own justification of tests, deaths, carnage, into his own recognition of their great secret meaning. The meaning was here, beneath and around him; all that he had accepted and justified swallowed him up. (Bykov 2003: 294)

While the search for explanation as justification ends in the character's death, apparently as meaningless as the Terror whose meaning he sought to establish, this ending of the novel does not leave the Terror entirely inexplicable or ineffable. The unjustifiability of the Terror, the falsity of every interpretation that views it as a misguided quest for overcoming the 'merely human', the exhaustion of every claim to transcendence in the pure nothingness of destruction – this, as we shall demonstrate in the remainder of this book, is, if not the best explanation, then at least the best *explication* of the Terror: it is explicable precisely and only *as* meaningless, failing utterly in whatever positive task it might have set itself. This meaninglessness and negativity are not the necessary failures of our understanding of this atrocious event, but belong to the essence of this event itself, i.e. their status is not epistemological but ontological. For this reason, the failure of every explanation must no longer be perceived as a failure, or at least not as *our* failure. It might not be possible to find out *why* the perpetrators of the Terror did what they did, but perhaps it is less important than establishing *what* they actually did, contrary to their own deluded or hypocritical claims about it. Thus, rather than attempt to elucidate the causes of or reasons for the Terror, we shall attempt to explicate it through its effects within the overall biopolitical rationality of High Stalinism.

THE UNREFORGEABLE: THE NEW LOGIC OF ENMITY

Let us begin by addressing the relation of the Terror to the biopolitical project of the Great Break. While the extraordinary violence of the Great Break was inscribed in the project of biopolitical transformation, the construction of a socialist society through the negation of non-socialist forms of life, the Terror of the mid-1930s manifestly lacked any such transformative objective, being solely punitive in the strictly negative sense. Unlike the violence of the Second Revolution, whose task was reforging and which was expected to yield new forms of life in the place of the old, 'dying' ones, the Terror simply attacked these dying forms of life (as well as many ostensibly new, socialist lives) without seeking to forge anything out of them, or, as we shall argue in the following chapter, forging a paradoxical form of life contained in death itself. In

1937 Stalin's regime no longer sought to transform former oppositionists through 'criticism and self-criticism', reforge former kulaks and priests into 'honest labourers' or remake the members of the suspected nationalities into true proletarian internationalists – instead, it focused on killing as many of them as possible and thoroughly dehumanising the others through slave labour in the Gulag. All that united such different victims of the Terror as regional party leaders, prostitutes, priests, Koreans, union leaders, Poles, army generals and street beggars was that their difference from the idea of the New Soviet Person no longer made them candidates for reforging but simply exposed them to death.

The best illustration of this shift is the drastically changed status of the camps in the mid-1930s. The celebration of the camps as sites of 'reforging' human beings, from kulaks or criminals, into heroic builders of socialism, described in the previous chapter, was completely abandoned in the mid-1930s. A good indication of this change was the official ban on the Gorky-edited book on the White-Sea Channel in 1937, as many of its co-authors also perished in the Terror (Dobrenko 2007: 105, 138; see Barnes 2011: 163–5, 255–6).

> [As] the 1930s progressed, optimism and openness about penal practices gave way to scepticism and secrecy. The early 1930s saw the initial restriction on the publication of criminal statistics in the open press. Prisoner transports were hidden as 'special equipment'. Prisoner correspondence was severely restricted. Released prisoners signed secrecy agreements, forbidding them to talk about the camps. Nobody could enter regions like Kolyma without special entrance permits. After 1936, the continued existence of criminality was an embarrassment for a polity that explained such problems in terms of the social milieu. A crossroads has been reached in 1936, when the adoption of the Stalin constitution was accompanied by the announcement that socialism has been built. (Barnes 2011: 256)

The public aesthetisation of the camp as the paradigmatic site of Soviet biopolitics gave way to the increased secrecy regarding the camps, while the arrests and executions during mass and national operations took place under complete secrecy, without involving regular police or army troops (Werth 2007).[13] Moreover, as Steven Barnes demonstrated, the 'redemptive' function of the camps that was an essential component of the discourse of reforging in the late 1920s and early 1930s was downgraded in the period of the Terror, which was reflected in the decrease of pardons and early releases and the increased recourse to harsher forms of punishment (*katorga* and 'special camps' for especially dangerous prisoners) as well as permanent forms of punishment without any possibility

High Stalinism: Retreat, Simulacrum, Terror

of redemption, such as permanent exile for the victims of the national operations and permanent deportations for special camp inmates (Barnes 2011: 164–73, 191–3). While the kulaks of the Great Break were to be 'reforged', violently if need be, in order to be transformed into proper Soviet citizens and eventually return to society, in 1937 the same kulaks were considered irredeemable and condemned to execution or lengthy camp terms that were often followed by additional terms and became de facto life imprisonment (ibid.: 34–5, 255). Similarly, the victims of the national operations were simply categorised as potential or actual spies for enemy powers, making terror a matter of 'cleansing' rather than reforging or reform (Barnes 2011: 93–8, 185–93). By the same token, while the defeated oppositionists of the late 1920s were usually expelled from the Party and exiled, with the possibility of eventual reinstatement and rehabilitation, the very same oppositionists had no hope for such a corrective punishment in 1936, when their political 'crimes' were usually accompanied by accusations of malicious 'wrecking', sabotage and destruction and the revelations of their moral failures, from drug abuse to homosexuality. In the high-profile show trials the evil character of the accused took on almost diabolical proportions, excluding the very possibility of reforging.

> The show trials of the 1930s demonstrated that seemingly quite normal persons were capable of strewing ground glass in the food of the workers, giving them smallpox and skin disease, poisoning wells and public places, infecting livestock with anthrax, and so on. Moreover, they did all this on a superhuman, unimaginable scale, accomplishing the most titanically destructive feats in many places at the same time. That the actions of the show-trial defendant defied ordinary human logic was usually even emphasised in the accusation because this inexplicability was evidence that his evil will was absolute and incorrigible and could only be subdued by physically eliminating the individual. (Groys 2011: 61)

Paradoxically at first glance, the reason why the Terror of the late 1930s was so murderous was precisely the officially proclaimed completion of the construction of socialism in the USSR, manifested in the 1936 Constitution's formal abolition of the 'dictatorship of the proletariat' and the cessation of class war (Tucker 1992: 441–78; Hoffmann 2011: 278–305). During the struggle for socialism in the Great Break, dissent, crime and social deviance were still interpreted in class terms as the effects of the persistence of the vices of capitalism, and corrective measures focused on the *transformation* of the class consciousness of the subjects in question. Once socialism was held to be achieved, it was impossible to cast undesirable behaviour as a mere remnant of capitalism, which could now only be the indication of active resistance to the socialist regime, which in turn was interpreted as the effect of one's defective, incorrigible or monstrous nature. In this manner, politics was criminalised and crime politicised, while both were subjected to a strong moralisation. In such a constellation the pettiest of crimes could be interpreted as a political gesture that, moreover, pointed to one's moral defect – a conjuncture that made recourse to violence almost inevitable. Whereas collectivisation posed the task of the liquidation of kulaks 'as a class', that is, their dispossession, resettlement and reform, the mass operations were content with the mere liquidation of former kulaks as individual beings (Hoffmann 2011: 292–3; see also Hoffmann 2003: 178–9).

This new constellation led to a fateful shift from the late 1920s logic of class enmity to the 1930s notion of the 'enemy of the people'. This term, whose genealogy dates back to the French Revolution, was brought into the public discourse in Stalin's speech at the infamous Central Committee plenum in February 1937, which launched the most extreme phase of the Terror (Goldmann 2011: 73–9). The 'enemy of the people' was no longer a class enemy, simply because the 'non-productive' classes had already been abolished during the dismantling of the private sector in industry and the successful collectivisation process in agriculture. Yet, neither was it an analogue of the Nazis' racial enemy, since it could no longer have a determinate identity of its own (for example, kulak, aristocrat, 'bourgeois specialist') that would individualise it and serve as the ground for its exclusion and annihilation. After the successful completion of the construction of socialism the enemy could only hide behind a legitimate identity of the collective farmer, worker, army general or member of the Central Committee.

This is why since the middle of the 1930s the enemy was usually presented in both official discourse and popular culture as the spy of foreign powers, engaged in 'wrecking' activities of almost diabolical proportions while maintaining the appearances of the ordinary Soviet citizen (see Goldmann 2011: 23–79). Rather than invoke a struggle for the protection of the race against an identifiable Other (Nazism) or the struggle between antagonistic classes in a divided society (the Great Break), the logic of enmity during the Great Terror called for the tireless disconcealment of the invisible enemy within the ostensibly united and harmonious society presented in the simulacra of socialist realism. This is why one's class (or other) identity neither resigned one to persecution nor spared one from it during the years of the Terror. Insofar as the enemy was now always a 'hidden' one, it was necessary not merely to show resolve and courage in confronting it, as it was during the Civil War or the collectivisation, but also to practise extreme vigilance, since *anyone at all* could be the enemy and no positive principle of distinction was of any use in revealing it. After all, the greatest proportional number of the 'enemies of the people' turned out to be found within the Central Committee of the Party itself, the majority of whose members ended up executed (Getty and Naumov 2010; Getty 2013). As a result, the entire Soviet people without exception found itself exposed as potentially its own enemy.

Thus, while, according to Stalin's famous dictum, class struggle intensified along with the progress of the USSR in the construction of socialism, this class struggle was certainly not the same in 1937 as in 1928. While the Great Break was characterised by an explicit antagonism between the state and the peasantry, the period of the Terror was marked by the disappearance of any identifiable agent of antagonism and the consequent dissemination of state violence throughout society: where there once were the Party and the kulaks, there now were the people and its enemies, and one could never be sure which category one belonged to.

> The phrase 'enemy of the people' was useful because it economically expressed a political situation, in which hundreds of thousands of people, arrested and sentenced by extrajudicial bodies, simply vanished. The term encompassed many possible offences and required no concrete proof of wrongdoing. As an accusation, it demanded no evidence of an actual crime or knowledge of previous factional debates. Unlike 'Zinovievite', 'Trotskyist' or 'rightist', all of which pointed to the victim's earlier adherence to a specific oppositional program, 'enemy of the people' was not associated with any prior political position. In this sense, it was the perfect figure of speech for a plenum that popularised repression by involving the rank and file in a mass campaign against authority. (Goldman 2011: 77)

In this new construction of the enemy as absolute yet invisible, diabolically evil yet perfectly ordinary in appearance, a foreign spy yet a long-respected neighbour, there was no longer anything surprising about the heroes of the Revolution and the Civil War, award-winning enterprise managers or celebrated writers suddenly being exposed as 'enemies of the people'. The presence of so many enemies in the top echelons of power in the USSR was not at all damaging for the regime, since all it pointed to was the failure to 'unmask' these enemies that necessitated the punishment of *new* enemies and stimulated more active efforts at unmasking in the future. Thus, the Terror acquired a self-propelling dynamic at the same time as it lost any meaningful ideological content.

> Stalin originated the concept 'enemy of the people'. This term automatically made it unnecessary that the ideological errors of a man be proven. It made possible the use of the cruellest repression, against anyone who in any way disagreed with Stalin, against those who were only suspected of hostile intent, against those who had bad reputations. On the whole, the only proof of guilt actually used was the 'confession' of the accused himself. 'Confessions' were acquired through physical pressure. Innocent individuals – who in the past had defended the party line – became victims. (Khruschev 1956)

The use of forced confessions became a defining feature of the Great Terror and deserves a detailed discussion beyond the scope of our study (see Halfin 2009). We shall merely note the key function of confession in the new constellation of enmity: since the enemy no longer had an objective basis in class or other predicates, its crimes could no longer be simply attested to by objective evidence. The enemy of the Great Break had nothing to confess: its opposition to the Soviet regime was objectively manifest in its very actions of resisting collectivisation or its very nature as a 'class alien'. In contrast, the enemy of the people in 1937 was a devious monster hiding behind the veneer of a regular Soviet citizen, hence the need for the investigative genius of the secret services in unmasking it. Yet, the true victory over the enemy does not consist in producing objective evidence of the enemy's actions or plans, but in the enemy's subjective *revelation* of its own enmity, whereby its very hiddenness and duplicity would come to be revealed in public discourse. In the plot of the show trials the enemy unmasked *itself* and then proceeded to leave its undeserved place in Soviet society, usually for the world of the dead.

In this manner, confession functioned as the exact obverse of the logic of reforging in the Great Break: the kulak, sentenced to a camp term, was expected to work his way back to freedom and *join*, for the first time, Soviet society as a rightful member. The victim of the Terror, who already occupied an (often privileged) place in Soviet society, forfeited it by confessing to being an enemy and thereby himself contributed to the purification of this society. Even if one was not sentenced to death and eventually made it out of the camps, the stigma of the enemy of the people was never replaced by the proud title of a reforged proletarian, if only because the official discourse made fewer and fewer references to the proletariat, let alone reforging. Indeed, the Terror's equivalent of the teleology of reforging was nothing but death, which purged the Soviet social body of the defective, the monstrous and the evil and thus restored the collective to its ideal state.

IMMANENT ANNIHILATION

We are now in the position to grasp the Great Terror as the third modality of the negative inflection of the Stalinist biopolitical project. While the violence of the Second Revolution was biopolitically directed towards the establishment of the socialist order as a lived reality through the negation of existing forms of life, the violence of the Terror was biopolitically senseless, that is, it served no transformative purpose on either the individual or the collective level. No social, economic, cultural or political transformation of any kind actually took place in 1936–8, when at least 1 per cent of the Soviet population was exterminated.

In his brilliant study of Stalinist 'politics of mobilisation' David Priestland distinguished between four ideal types of approach to the construction of socialism. The basic distinction is between 'technicism', founded on the primacy of economics and technology, and 'revivalism', characterised by the primacy of ideology and voluntarist charismatic politics. Within technicism Priestland distinguishes between elitist technicism (a top-down scientific and technocratic approach to socioeconomic transformation) and non-elitist or liberal technicism (a rationalist and gradualist approach, practised during the NEP and affirmed by the Bukharinist 'right' opposition prior to the Great Break). Within revivalism he similarly distinguishes between elitist revivalism (state-led and coercive construction of the socialist order that mobilises the proletariat and moulds its class consciousness) and populist revivalism (radical social transformation on the basis of quasi-democratic participation of the workers and the 'proletarianisation' of the state) (Priestland 2007: 41–9). The Stalinist period is then interpreted by Priestland as a series of shifts between these positions: from the moderate technicism of the NEP through the populist revivalism of the Great Break to the combination of elitist technicism and a non-Marxist 'neo-traditionalism' in 1932–5. In Priestland's interpretation, the eruption of the Terror in 1936 marked the regime's final relapse into populist revivalism that mobilised the rank-and-file workers and party members against the ruling class of state and party bureaucracy. The catastrophic consequences of this resumption of class struggle against the 'new class' led to the cessation of the Terror in 1938 and the complete abandonment of populist revivalist policies for the remainder of Soviet history.

While this approach appears to present the Terror as the second edition of the Great Break, Priestland also notes a number of key differences. First, unlike the Great Break, which dismantled the socioeconomic system of the NEP, the Terror left intact the order inaugurated by the Great Retreat (2007: 308–9). Second, in contrast to 1928 there was no longer any ambition of revolutionary transcendence – on the contrary, the Terror ensured that things would stay the same. Finally, in contrast to the class-based universalism of the Second Revolution, the Terror unfolded in the context of the revival of nationalism and patriotism, the increasing political and cultural xenophobia, and the anticipation of the new World War. Yet, these three differences immediately point to the radical negativity of the Terror, not merely with respect to its form (after all, as we have seen, the Great Break was just as or more violent) but also with respect to its content or *telos*. While the Great Break relied on negative means of implementing a positive project, it is difficult to see the Terror as a means towards any end at all.

A good illustration of the senselessness of the Terror is the well-known fact that even in the short time span of 1936–8 it engulfed the terrorisers themselves, making the distinction between the executioner and the victim problematic. In the argument of Alexander Etkind, 'if the Nazi Holocaust exterminated the Other, the Soviet terror was suicidal' (2013: 8). For example, Semen Firin, the head of the construction works at the White Sea-Baltic Sea Canal, under whose supervision hundreds of thousands perished in slave labour, was himself executed in 1937. Matvei Berman, one of the organisers of the Gulag, was arrested and executed in 1939 (Etkind, 2013: 8). The exemplary case is the fate of the NKVD during the Great Purge, which was one of the most 'repressed' institutions of the Soviet regime (Getty and Naumov 2010: 122–6, 165–7, 215–16; Rogovin 1998: 276–80; Rogovin 2009: 61–7, 205–13, 413–20). Genrikh Yagoda, the chief of the NKVD at the beginning of the party purge, eventually fell victim to it, being replaced by Nikolai Yezhov, under whose leadership the Terror reached its heights. In April 1938 Yezhov was himself removed from the leadership of the NKVD (and eventually executed in 1940), to be replaced by Lavrentiy Beria, under whom the Terror continued in a somewhat tempered manner. The arrest and execution of Beria himself in 1953 after the death of Stalin symbolically marked the end of the era of terror in Soviet history.

What is the relation between this senseless paroxysm of state violence and the biopolitical project of the construction of socialism? As we have argued, starting from the mid-1930s, the positive self-presentation of the Stalinist regime was split between the *retreat* from the revolutionary vision of socialism and the *simulacrum* of real socialism presented by socialist realism. The Terror could therefore not be a *method*, however erroneous or horrendous, of the construction of socialism, since the socialist edifice was already in place, albeit in the form of the split between the reality of the retreat from it and the simulacrum of its attainment. Nor was it a method in the *destruction* of socialism, a version of the counter-revolutionary Thermidor, since it maintained the selfsame

High Stalinism: Retreat, Simulacrum, Terror

edifice largely intact, even as it annihilated many of its builders. The negativity of the terror was directed neither towards construction nor towards destruction but must rather be viewed as a negative inflection of the prior attempt to construct socialism as a real form of life. It must therefore be investigated on the same plane as the previously addressed phenomena of the Retreat and the Simulacrum.

The Terror provided the ultimate solution to the problem that had plagued socialist biopolitics from the outset: how does one pass from the revolutionary ideal to the real immanence of the post-revolutionary order? The answer of the Great Break was the violent annihilation of anterior forms of life that cleared the slate for socialism as a positive form of life: *the ideal is forced into the real by the negation of the real*. The overly destructive and socioeconomically catastrophic impact of this project led to the partial negation of this negation: the *rehabilitation of the real in the retreat of the ideal* (the Retreat) and the *'derealisation' of the real by the aesthetisation of the ideal* (the Simulacrum). While these responses tended to limit and contain violence, either by backtracking on the socialist offensive or by relocating the construction of socialism into the aesthetic domain, the Terror paradoxically responded to the transformative violence of the Great Break with *more* violence, albeit the violence now detached from any transcendent ideals and reduced to purely immanent blood-letting. If the biopolitical project of the Great Break marked a forcing of the transcendence of the communist ideal within the immanence of social life, the Terror negated this violent forcing, not by the retreat from the negating action or the formation of the simulacra of its effects but rather by divorcing the process of negation from the transcendent ideal, making the annihilation of immanence itself wholly immanent. This is why it is entirely futile to attempt to explain the Terror by suturing it to the idea of communism. While the violence of the Great Break could still be understood as the correlate of the extreme character of the tasks that the regime had set itself, in 1937 there were no longer any such tasks in terms of which the terror could be justified or interpreted. On the contrary, this was the period when the symbolic dimension of politics, in which alone ideals may be posited and affirmed, momentarily faded into the background, setting the stage for a bloodbath that truly signified nothing.

> These events mark a drastic change in the pattern of Stalinist discourse. This period, that of blind terror, really marks the temporary eclipse of the discursive strategy altogether. It is as if the Stalinists, prisoners of their fears and iron discipline, had decided that they could not rule any longer by rhetorical means. The outbreak of this blind terror was not the culmination of previous rhetoric, it was the end or negation of discourse altogether. (Getty and Naumov 2010: 195)

This unleashing of negativity within social immanence in the absence of any forcing of the transcendent ideal may of course be articulated with the more conventional interpretations of the Terror. In accordance with the more 'intentionalist' explanations that emphasise Stalin's personal role in the Terror, it might be grasped as the regime's 'revenge' on Soviet society for failing to submit to the socialist ideal, which necessitated the retreat in policy and the reduction of socialism to an aesthetic project. In terms of the more 'structuralist' explanations, the Terror may be understood as the symptom of the failure of the construction of socialism as a positive order, which was manifested in 'acting out', hysterical and ultimately impotent violence that had no meaning or purpose but struck blindly at various groups in the Soviet society, from beggars to the General Staff, from national diasporas to the cultural elite, from the Central Committee to ex-kulaks, and was only ceased by the regime when it threatened to engulf the system itself (cf. Žižek 2002: 128; Sloterdijk 2012: 161–8). Either way, the Terror was a purely negative response to the negativity of the socialist biopolitical project and rather than overturn this negativity it augmented and escalated it. It therefore marks the final stage in the conversion of biopolitics into thanatopolitics. Devoid of a transcendent ideal to be forced into social immanence, governmental violence itself becomes strictly immanent and the political system is transformed into an exterminist machine: the violent forcing of the ideal into the real ends in the sheer destruction of the real.

The Great Retreat, the Great Simulacrum and the Great Terror – these three negative inflections of the biopolitical project of the Great Break constitute the biopolitical rationality of High Stalinism that defined the Soviet system until Stalin's death and perhaps even until the demise of the USSR. What makes the case of Stalinism so interesting yet difficult to grasp from a biopolitical perspective is the fact that the phenomena that constitute its familiar *positivity* (for example, the neoclassical style in architecture, socialist realist novels and films, party purges) are actually effects of the *negation* of a prior and much more radical project of the Great Break. While in the postcommunist period we are all accustomed to judging the utopian project of the construction of socialism a failure, this judgement was arguably made as early as 1934 by Stalin himself and his closest associates. What we have come to know as 'real socialism', proclaimed in the 1936 Constitution and glorified in the 1938 *Short Course of the History of the CPSU*, was in fact the combined effect of complex strategies that sought to, respectively, compensate for, conceal and avenge this failure. It is important to reiterate that these three inflections never amounted to anything like an explicit repudiation of the Great Break. On the contrary, they ensured that the Second Revolution could continue to be celebrated in socialist realist art at the same time as many of its architects were sent to concentration camps and its policies surreptitiously reversed. Furthermore, the negative inflections of a project as negative as the Great Break did not entail the self-cancellation of negativity in pure affirmation. While the original project of the construction of socialism was extremely violent, if not outright genocidal, its negation did not result in the amelioration of violence, but, during the Great Terror, in its liberation from any transcendent ideal and relapse into pure bloodbath. If Stalinism teaches us a lesson, it is not merely that utopian politics always results in violence, repression and disappointment, but also that the *negation* of utopia in the triumph of a moderate or pragmatic line may be no less violent or repressive and at least as disappointing.

What began as an apocalyptic project of transcending the natural order of things in the triumph of socialism as a positive, lived reality ended up in an uneasy compromise with this very order of things, covered up by the proliferation of simulacra of socialist forms of life and enforced by terror disseminated throughout the society. This combination of retreat, simulacrum and terror, first articulated in the mid-1930s, defines real socialism as we know it, and its subsequent development, including its eventual demise, may be grasped in terms of the eventual disarticulation of its terms (cf. Roberts 2006: 266–7). Once the terror subsided after Stalin's death and the simulacra of socialism grew worn out and ineffective during the Brezhnev era, all that remained of socialism was the retreat from it as such. The restoration of capitalism in 1991 was little more than the final victory of one of the tendencies of the mid-1930s. Boris Groys (2010) is thus entirely correct in suggesting that rather than being defeated in an ideological conflict, arms race or economic contest, Soviet socialism actually cancelled itself out by progressively abolishing all its forms except for the form of the retreat. From this perspective, the valorisation of Stalinism in contemporary Russia is certainly less surprising: the regime born out of the abandonment by the Soviet *nomenklatura* of its ideological simulacra in exchange for the private ownership of state property remains faithful to at least one of the policies constitutive of High Stalinism. The more comprehensive its official propaganda becomes and the less squeamish the regime gets in its recourse to violence, the less ambivalent its Stalinism will appear.

We have now reconstituted the biopolitical rationality of Stalinism on the systemic level. Yet, this interpretation leaves us with a puzzle. What kind of life was actually produced in the Great Break and its negative inflections, if both projects were characterised by extreme negativity and destruction? What did it mean to *live* the Retreat, the

Simulacrum and particularly the Terror? What was that New Soviet Person that Stalinism claimed to have produced? Was there a positive mode of subjectivity that corresponded to these rationalities or was all subjectivity extinguished by governmental violence? Addressing these questions requires moving from the level of the overall governmental rationality to the terrain of subjectivity, in which the new life was supposed to take hold. In Chapter 5 we shall venture a critical reinterpretation of the studies of Soviet subjectivity from a biopolitical perspective and articulate a negative mode of subjectivation, which produces the subject that survives its own destruction. Chapter 6 will then develop and elaborate this interpretation through a close reading of Varlam Shalamov's testimonial prose.

Chapter 5

DEATHLY LIFE: THE SUBJECT OF STALINISM

A BRIEF HISTORY OF THE STALINIST SUBJECT

Starting from the late 1990s, a series of works by Igal Halfin (1999, 2009), Jochen Hellbeck (1996) and other scholars of Stalinism made 'Soviet subjectivity' a popular research agenda in Soviet studies. Combining Foucault's late work on subjectivation and the techniques of the self (Foucault 1990b, 1990c, 2006) with the renewed attention to the specificity of Soviet ideology, allegedly overlooked in revisionist scholarship since the 1960s, these authors were able to provide a powerful, if highly contested, account of the process of subjectivation under Stalinism. In their argument, when Soviet individuals appropriated the official ideological discourse in the process of intense self-examination, they simultaneously integrated their existence into the process of great social transformation and incorporated this process into their own existence, thereby becoming properly historical subjects of the construction of socialism. The Soviet subject was neither destroyed by the totalitarian regime nor successfully escaped its grip but was rather produced by it as a positive form of life. The new 'subjectivity school' thus sought to advance beyond the approaches to subjectivity in totalitarian and revisionist theories, which we shall briefly consider before critically engaging with the contribution of the new approach itself.

Classical theories of totalitarianism approached communist ideology as an extraneous force that was imposed on the anterior, already formed subject, crushing and dominating it with the aid of the security apparatuses (see Brzezinsky and Friedrich 1965: 21–2). The biopolitical counterpart to this notion of the subject would evidently be the forcing of the transcendent ideal of communism into social immanence during the Great Break, in which anterior forms of life were devalued as obsolete and this obsolescence was then materialised in acts of governmental violence. In this account, Soviet totalitarianism, which, unlike Nazism, lasted for more than one generation, actually succeeded in deluding or forcing its subjects into submission, destroying their anterior freedom, atomising all existing community and solidarity, and thus perverting the very essence of human existence. This approach posits the Soviet subject as, on the one hand, already *preconstituted* along the lines of the subject of Western liberalism (Krylova 2000: 124–5) and, on the other hand, as always already *diverted* from this authentic mode of subjectivity as a victim of totalitarian indoctrination. The sole exception to this image of the thoroughly indoctrinated victim is the often discussed figure of the cynical careerist who used ideological maxims to promote his self-interest in the system (Krylova 2000: 128–30; see also Fainsod 1959: 479, 480; Inkeles and Bauer 1959: 314–19; Brzezinski 1967: 66).

Fittingly for a Cold War discourse, the totalitarian approach used the negative evidence of the destruction of subjectivity in Stalin's USSR to fortify the figure of the Western liberal subject. By presenting the image of the Stalinist subject as the perverse effect of total indoctrination, permeating not only the subject's consciousness but also the unconscious, and thus destroying in advance any possibility of resistance, theories of totalitarianism made a moral plea for the preservation of the 'free subject' of liberalism against this corrupting influence of the totalitarian ideology (see Krylova 2000: 127–9). Yet, it is certainly ironic that the only mode in which this liberal subject was present in the totalitarian society was not as the heroic subject of resistance, which was seen as all but impossible, but as the cynical manipulator of the system, who, after all, could only manipulate it by virtue of *not* being completely indoctrinated and hence to some extent 'free' from it.

After Khrushchev's destalinisation and the emergence of the Soviet dissident movement the totalitarian image of the Soviet subject as the duped believer in the ideological lie became less plausible and was replaced by a more complex idea of the subject that did not wholly subsume subjectivity under ideological indoctrination. The revisionist approach elaborated and generalised the image of the Soviet subject as the manipulator of the system, arguing that Soviet citizens appropriated the communist ideology in a pragmatic manner to advance their interests in the period of rapid transformation and unprecedented social mobility. Thus, the Soviet subject dutifully reproduced the ideological maxims of socialism but retained at least a minimal distance from it. In order to be able to rationally 'operate' the system for its own benefit, the subject must have had some understanding of its benefit that would be irreducible to that of the system. The subject was therefore conceived as from the outset split between the public façade and a private underside. In this manner, the revisionist approach took the image of the opportunist originally developed by the totalitarian school and purged it of all moral valuation, presenting an image of a rational subject making the best of it in the time of radical flux and uncertainty by adopting a double life, split between the formally loyal and obedient self, duly reproducing the official slogans, and the informal, hidden or secret self, existing at a distance from the system and its ideological maxims.

This double life need not necessarily result from a cynical opportunism and the desire to make one's way up in the system but might also arise from the desire for security, convenience or simple inertia. In particular, Vera Dunham's (1990) work on the restoration of 'middle class' values in Stalinist USSR challenged the totalitarian approach by making the Soviet subject seem very familiar from a liberal perspective, albeit still *negatively* familiar: endowed with individuality and the capacity for critical self-reflection, this subject nonetheless did not possess a moral conscience and the will to struggle for its liberation. Despite this crucial difference, the split subject of revisionism was far removed from the image of the totally indoctrinated victim, whose very humanity was perverted, if not annihilated entirely. To the extent that its passivity or opportunism were to be lamented, they were lamented as something 'all too human' rather than as the effects of dehumanisation. It is easy to see that this concept of the subject corresponds to our notion of the Great Retreat, in which the biopolitical imperatives of the construction of socialism were moderated in favour of a certain compromise with the real that allowed one to live at some distance from the very ideology that was being forced into one's life.

This reorientation paved the way for the analysis of the Soviet society that no longer highlighted its exceptional singularity but rather sought to understand its historical specificity on the basis of the idea of the subject that was in principle compatible with those employed for analysing Western societies. In the work of Moshe Lewin, Sheila Fitzpatrick and other authors of the revisionist orientation (Lewin 1994; Fitzpatrick 1992; Tucker 1973), the Stalinist subject was grasped as 'disoriented and unsettled, ignorant and confused, neurotic and unable to grasp the overwhelming and rapid historical change, by which he is interpellated in frequently contradictory directions' (Krylova 2000: 138). The subject's reliance on the Soviet ideological discourse was no longer a matter of a confident manipulation of a stable system but rather a matter of striving to attain some stability in the flux of the Stalinist Second Revolution that dissolved all existing social relations and identities. The Soviet subject was neither viewed as a dehumanised victim of total domination nor as a moral invalid devoid of all inner integrity but rather analysed in its often desperate attempts to adapt to the radical transformation of his environment. Yet, according to Anna Krylova, the promising avenues of research opened by this rethinking of the subject were soon closed off by the narrowing of the approach to, once again, the liberal image of the self-interested rational agent.

> Accepting the revisionist view of Stalinist society as mobile, chaotic, and socially fragmented, the discussants largely overlooked the inevitable product of these grandiose transformations—namely, the unsettled, fragmented subject. The totalitarian–revisionist debates of the 1980s created a conceptual paradox: a chaotic, fluid society and a unitary, self-centered, Soviet superman negotiating through history unencumbered by its calamities. The liberal paradigm still governed the subject of Soviet studies. (Krylova 2000: 140)

The situation did not change radically during the 1990s despite the collapse of the Soviet system and the opening up of the Soviet archives to the researchers. The key innovation during this period was the attempt to reinscribe the behaviour that totalitarian theory viewed as a sign of moral deficiency and revisionism viewed as evidence of pragmatic adaptation as acts of 'creative resistance' on the part of Soviet individuals (Kotkin 1995: 154). Stephen Kotkin's magisterial *Magnetic Mountain*, which was the first to introduce an explicitly Foucauldian perspective to the study of Stalinism, did not impose any a priori definition of the subject onto the reality of Soviet socialism. Instead, it '[let] people speak as much as possible in their own words' (ibid.: 21), tracing the way Soviet subjectivity emerged in this discourse. Kotkin's study of the transformation of everyday life in the Stalinist industrialisation at the site of the construction of Magnitogorsk, one of the gigantic projects of the 1930s, revealed the extent to which the process of subjectivation under Stalinism was neither a matter of the totalitarian domination of subjectivity nor the pragmatic and adaptive use of it but rather a matter of self-fashioning through a complex engagement with the system, in which resistance played as much of a role as obedience and internalisation.

> The kinds of lives that the urban participants came to lead and the identities they formed involved eager participation in, frequent circumvention of, and resourceful, albeit localised resistance to the terms of daily life that developed within the crusade of building socialism. One resists, without necessarily rejecting, by assessing, making tolerable, and, in some cases, even turning to one's advantage the situation one is confronted with. An appropriate analogy is to the Japanese martial art of judo. Even when the weight of the force against one is seemingly overwhelming, as was the case with the Soviet state, the possibility remains to sidestep and thereby use that heavy force against itself. (Ibid.: 21–2)

While this approach certainly enabled a more nuanced treatment of the process of subjectivation, it also introduced an ambivalence quickly noted by Kotkin's critics (Krylova 2000: 143–4; Halfin and Hellbeck 1996: 459): if resistance is no longer frontal and explicitly political but rather utilises the official discourse of 'speaking Bolshevik' (Kotkin 1995: 198–236), how is it possible to tell apart resistance and obedience, internalisation and manipulation in the practices of the Soviet subject? If the subject in question dutifully participated in 'shock work' and 'socialist competition', aspired to be a Stakhanovite and condemned the 'Trotskyite-Zinovievite bloc', was this an indicator of obedience, as would appear at first glance, or of some obscure version of resistance? If it was the latter, then how was this resistance different from the cynical manipulation of the system through the hypocritical reproduction of its slogans? The image of 'creative resistance' is always at risk of splitting back into the two familiar categories of totalitarian indoctrination and cynical opportunism. In Kotkin's case, the latter option is much more accentuated, since he is at pains to demote the totalitarian image of the Stalinist subject as the 'believer', completely indoctrinated and lacking any exteriority to the ideological content: 'It was not necessary to believe. It was necessary, however, to participate as if one believed – a structure that appears to have been understood, since what could be construed as direct, openly disloyal behaviour became rare' (Kotkin 1995: 220). It is evident that this account of the Soviet subject resonates with the second negative inflection of socialist biopolitics analysed above – the Great Simulacrum, in which subjectivation took the form of one's entry into and mastery of a purely symbolic form of life regulated by the canon of socialist realism.

The other option, the resurgence of the totalitarian image of the believer, is arguably represented by the more recent work on Soviet subjectivity, exemplified by Jochen Hellbeck and Igal Halfin, who continue the Foucauldian line of inquiry initiated by Kotkin but develop it in the opposite direction. In contrast to Kotkin's approach to ideology and the Soviet discourse ('speaking Bolshevik') as a strategic resource for the subject, deployed in a covert judo-like confrontation with the powers that be, Hellbeck argues that ideology was rather 'a living tissue of meaning that was seriously reflected upon' (Hellbeck 2006: 11). While it has become customary in Soviet studies to assert the fundamental split between the public and the private at the heart of the Soviet subject, making the latter domain the only possible site of authentic freedom (and a problematic one too, due to its closing off from any dimension of publicity or sociality!), Hellbeck's study of Soviet autobiographical texts, primarily diaries, reveals how intolerable [Soviet subjects] found a condition of 'dual soul', how little appeal a retreat into private life had to them and how they applied mechanisms of rationalisation in attempts to restore harmonious notions of themselves as part of socialist society. (Ibid.: 11; see also Kozlova 2005).

Thus, Hellbeck rejects the familiar approach to studying Soviet reality by 'reading between the lines' and proposes to focus on the lines themselves, analysing Soviet ideology as a 'living and adaptive force, operating on living persons who engage their selves and the world as ideological subjects' (ibid.: 13). Rather than read Stalin-era diaries as an indication of the crushing and dominating force of Soviet ideology that perverted authentic subjectivity or as proof of the Soviet subjects' skilful manipulation of the official terms of discourse, Hellbeck reads them as the expression of a fundamentally authentic 'urge to ideologise one's life, to turn it into the expression of a firm, internally consistent, totalizing *Weltanschauung*' (ibid.: 13). While Kotkin was content with analysing the strategic game of power and resistance, in which one of the resources was 'speaking Bolshevik', irrespectively of whether this speech was authentic or fake, Hellbeck takes the Soviet discourse much more seriously as contributing to the formation of Bolshevism as a form of life, 'living Bolshevik' – hence his persistent reference to this ideology as *itself* somehow alive or rather coming to life in the practices of the subjects (ibid.: 11, 31, 362). While the Foucauldian orientation of these studies is explicitly invoked only with regard to Foucault's later work on self-fashioning, it is hard not to notice its resonance with Foucault's *earlier* work on biopolitics: what is the translation of ideology into life through its mobilisation as an instrument of self-fashioning, if not the very principle of biopolitical government, different both from the authoritarian imposition of ideology as a purely formal set of rules, no internal commitment to which is needed, and the totalitarian use of that ideology to extinguish subjectivity as such in the production of automatised obedient selves?

THE DIARIST AND THE DUPE

In his determination to read the reproduction of the maxims of Soviet ideology in the Stalin-era diaries as the expression of newly constructed socialist selves, Hellbeck credits Soviet biopolitics with immense productivity, presenting its ambition of the establishment of the New Soviet Person as a *real achievement* (ibid.: 356–61). And yet, this is evidently a risky move, since it appears to take for granted both the entire symbolic edifice of Soviet ideology and its capacity to translate itself into the lives

Deathly Life: The Subject of Stalinism

of its subjects. This leads to a number of problems. First, as Hellbeck's critics have noted, there is a danger here of replicating the theses of the theory of totalitarianism, albeit *with a positive sign* (Etkind 2005: 176). As Eric Naiman argues, the approach that takes the subject's internalisation of the ideological discourse as the expression of its will or desire risks 'reading totalitarianism as it would "want" to be read' (Naiman 2001: 311), or making it look *even better* than it did itself (Etkind 2005: 176), that is, as productive rather than destructive, positive rather than negative. While the Soviet biopolitical discourse did not shun from the violent tropes such as 'reforging', 'remoulding' or 'remaking', the use of the neutral term 'subjectivity' and the emphasis on voluntary *self-fashioning* through the innocuous activity of diary-keeping conceal the violence of the Soviet regime even more than it cared to do itself in its own ideological simulacra. In the concluding chapter of his study Hellbeck explicitly links the Stalinist mode of self-fashioning to the general European tendency for the 'aesthetization of politics', both on the left and on the right (ibid.: 361). Yet, his account tends to downplay the fact that this aesthetisation could only be maintained with the help of not merely symbolic but also physical violence, which, moreover, often elicited the very same knowledge as the one that was produced by the diarists in an apparently voluntary manner. Against this distortion of the Soviet project, Etkind argues that the primary site for the production of autobiographical knowledge in the USSR was not the diary but the police or other bureaucratic interrogation, which sought to elicit from the subject highly individualised knowledge and used whatever means necessary to obtain it.

> One might wonder why the new paradigm of Soviet subjectivity has not produced heart-breaking research on tortures and confessions. The most welcome confessions were those where the content had not been induced or predicted by the torturer and his superiors. One can argue that pain was inflicted in order to produce 'subjective,' 'sincere,' even 'free' confessions. One cannot argue, however, that these are the same 'sincerity' and 'freedom' that we, modern people, understand by these terms. (Etkind 2005: 180)

The second problem that both Etkind and Naiman note in their critiques of the 'Soviet subjectivity school' is that the account of the subject offered in these studies is 'so psychologically impoverished as to call into question the idea of the human subject at all' (Naiman 2001: 313; see also Etkind 2005: 173–4). Indeed, even if one grants that the reproduction of the official discourse in autobiographical writing was an exercise in subjectivation, then the subject thereby produced is both *shallow* (constituted by the appropriation of the surface of the official ideology) and *hollow* (lacking any interiority aside from the external discourse he or she has appropriated). In fact, the use of ideological discourse in the process of self-fashioning attunes us to the fundamental shift in the function of ideology in the Soviet regime. While before the revolution ideology functioned as a critical concept, something to be unlearned and thrown off one's back as 'false consciousness', under Stalinism it became a positive concept, something to be learned and reproduced in one's daily life as an acquired language. Yet, this entailed the need to 'un-learn' prior ways of speaking or living and learning them anew, which resulted in a thorough de-naturalisation of both life and language, which cannot but have been traumatic for the subject. Thus, Naiman suggests that rather than speak of the successful production of subjectivities through the adoption of the official discourse we should rather speak of Soviet individuals as 'damaged by discourse' (Naiman 2001: 315), 'abridged' by the reduction of their subjectivity to a two-dimensional discursive frame: 'Hellbeck's heroes seem to have become more alienated from themselves than were any 19th century Marx's exploited workers' (ibid.: 315).

Similarly, Etkind approaches Hellbeck's subjectivation in terms of the wider biopolitical tendency of Soviet socialism to aspire to the transformation of human nature, yet, in contrast to Hellbeck, views this transformation as an utter failure, yielding only negative results. Hellbeck is only able to ignore or downplay this failure by remaining on the level of the *text* of the diaries, for all his interest in the translation of ideology into life. As a result, subjectivity is approached as a purely discursive fact – a rather more modest vision of the Stalinist project than the one aspired to by the Stalinists. Yet, discourse is not all there is to life, even when it seems to crowd out life itself by being dutifully invoked in one's every practice. The ambition of Stalinism to produce a new life was not at all metaphorical, which perhaps accounts for the regime's *own* rather less enthusiastic assessment of its success.

> Actually, the project was not about letters at all. It was about flesh, and human nature, and power over the flesh. New Men had to live, struggle, and replace the old men, people as they really were, who for this very reason became 'enemies of the people.' The Soviets were proud of their military victories and technological successes, but throughout the greater part of their history, even they were self-critical about their achievements in the formation of the New Soviet Man. Still, Hellbeck and Halfin compare 'Soviet subjectivity' with modern or 'liberal' subjectivity. But 'Soviet subjectivity' is a failed project, and always was; 'liberal subjectivity' is an everyday reality. Essentially, comparing them is like

comparing one person's desires to another's accomplishments. Hellbeck is right when he says that Soviet concentration camps were designed as construction sites for the building of the New Man. Is it not important that New Men were never built there, perhaps not even a single one? (Etkind 2005: 177)

Finally, the third problem pertains to the authors' explicit or implicit approach to the Soviet ideological discourse as the *only* one available to Soviet individuals as a means of subjectivation, as if 'Bolshevik' was the only language these individuals could speak (Naiman 2001: 312; Etkind 2005: 179). If such claims are taken seriously, this means that those opposing the Stalinist regime (such as Trotskyites, Orthodox Christians, nationalists, and so on) had no subjectivity or paradoxically had to rely for their subjectivation on the resources of the system that they fought (cf. Krylova 2000: 128). And yet, there is ample evidence of alternative modes of subjectivation, relying, for example, on traditional religious doctrines, village ways of life, the ethos of the pre-revolutionary bourgeoisie and intelligentsia, preserved, against all odds, in the Stalinist USSR. Moreover, the phenomenon of the Great Retreat may be grasped in part as a compromise with at least some of these modes of subjectivation to the detriment of the official 'socialist' one. Finally, from the Foucauldian methodological perspective that both Hellbeck and Halfin rely on, any claim for the exclusivity or predominance of a particular mode of subjectivation appears misguided from the outset: what about Foucault's favoured 'subjugated' or counter-knowledges, the anonymous resistances of 'infamous men' and the general thesis about the priority of resistance to power (1990a: 81–114)?

Thus, while it has succeeded in bringing the problematic of subjectivity into the mainstream of Soviet studies, the 'Stalinist subjectivity' approach suffers from the exaggeration of the biopolitical productivity of the Stalinist regime, which leads it to ignore both the extra-discursive violence at work in the production of the Soviet subject and the impoverished character of Soviet subjectivation. At the same time, it is difficult to agree with Etkind's criticism that takes the other extreme position of suggesting that 'new men' were never 'built' in the Stalinist USSR, in the camps or elsewhere, and that, therefore, the Stalinist subject is an illusion while the liberal subject is apparently the real thing. It would be easy to perform the same critique with regard to the liberal subject in Western societies, exposing it as a discursive artefact of governmental rationalities, which, as Foucault repeatedly suggested, were never realised completely while still producing certain real effects.

[These] programmes don't take effect in the institutions in an integral manner; they are simplified, or some are chosen and not others; and things never work as planned. But this difference is not one between the purity of the ideal and the disorderly impurity of the real, but that in fact there are different strategies which are mutually opposed, composed and superposed so as to produce permanent and solid effects which can perfectly well be understood in terms of their rationality, even though they do not conform to the initial programming. The fact that 'real life' is not the same thing as theoreticians' schemas does not entail that these schemas are therefore utopian, imaginary, etc. These programmes induce a whole series of effects in the real: they crystallise into institutions, they inform individual behaviour, they act as grids for the perception and the evaluation of things. (Foucault 1991: 81)

From this perspective, even if the New Soviet Person was not realised in full accordance with the blueprint, this does not mean that the project of its construction had no productivity whatsoever. Something, or rather someone, *was* indeed produced in the practices of translating ideological maxims into life, yet this effect of Soviet biopolitics cannot be simply *read off* the designs for its production (or even the reproduction of those designs in the diaries of Soviet subjects). As we have demonstrated above, biopolitical productivity always goes hand in hand with its negative, thanatopolitical correlate, and this confluence was particularly pronounced in Stalinism due to the explosive synthesis of revolutionary transcendence and biopolitical immanence in this project. For this reason, the Stalinist subject must be analysed not only in the official rationalities of its formation but also in the various modalities of its *de*-formation, be it the damage by discourse (Naiman) or physical torture (Etkind). Rather than overstate the biopolitical productivity of Stalinism by equating the subject with the discourse it reproduces, we must complement the analysis of the positive rationality of subjectivation with the negative, thanatopolitical underside that accompanies and conditions it. While, as we have seen, the existing theories of the Soviet subject may be viewed as corresponding, respectively, to the Great Break, the Great Retreat and the Great Simulacrum, what is manifestly missing in the literature on Soviet subjectivity is the theory of the subject corresponding to the Great Terror.

Pace Etkind, this focus on the radical negativity of terror must be distinguished from an outright *denial* of biopolitical productivity: the New Soviet Person was indeed produced under Stalinism, hence this project was not a simple failure; yet, this production operated as much, if not more, through negation, up to and including physical annihilation, as through positive (self-)fashioning. The very failure to create the New

Soviet Person in accordance with its positive model became an indelible feature of this person itself, who, as it were, incorporated its own negation into its identity. The ultimate paradox of subjectivation in Stalinist biopolitics is that it produced negation, destruction and ultimately death as themselves constitutive of a form of subjectivity. What totalitarian theory viewed as mere *destruction* of the subject must rather be approached in terms of the *production* of the subject that carries this destruction within itself as, ultimately, its sole essence. In the remainder of this chapter we shall elaborate this account of the Stalinist subject, focusing in particular on the dimension of terror, whose effects on the process of subjectivation we shall analyse with the help of Catherine Malabou's theory of traumatised subjectivity. In the following chapter we shall elaborate the analysis of the terrorised subject at the most abysmal site of their formation, that is, the Gulag camp, focusing on the 'negative experience' of the camps presented in the testimonial prose of Varlam Shalamov.

THE TERRORISED SUBJECT

As we have argued in Chapter 3, the extreme biopolitical offensive of the Great Break, which sought to translate into life the ideological content of socialism, including the model subjectivity of the New Soviet Person, proceeded through the negation of the lives that stuck to their old, obsolete or dying forms, be they that of kulaks, intelligentsia or non-proletarian artists. The positivity of the new Soviet subject, the builder of socialism, was thus from the very outset coterminous with the negation of everything non-Soviet within this very subject, which frequently led to the literal negation of the subject itself. Just as the construction of properly Soviet culture or agriculture ultimately took the form of the destruction of the existent culture and agriculture, so the positive content of the new subject of the Stalinist Second Revolution was necessarily contaminated by the negativity arising from the destruction of the previous forms of life. In line with Kaganovich's above-cited dictum about the Great Break, the builder of socialism was first and foremost the destroyer.

Just as the overall biopolitical project of the Great Break was submitted to three negative inflections to temper this negativity and endow the emerging order with a stable and durable existence, so the formation of the Stalinist subject after the suspension of the Great Break took the form of these three inflections. Since these inflections were deployed in Soviet biopolitics in an almost simultaneous manner during the mid-1930s, the Stalinist subject similarly experienced them together, though of course different individuals were more or less likely to experience particular inflections to a greater or lesser degree. It is this simultaneous operation of three distinct rationalities that makes the Stalinist subject such an ambivalent and problematic figure, as instantly recognisable as it is monstrous. This is the subject that knows the simulacrum for what it is yet continues to enact it, all the while engaging in doing things 'the old way', all of this taking place in the permanent danger of falling victim to state terror which it cannot but perceive as senseless despite its best efforts to endow it with meaning, be it secret, obscene or absurd.

While all three forms of negative inflection of Soviet biopolitics were at work in constructing the Stalinist subject, it is the permanent threat of senseless terror that accounts for its singularity. In the absence of terror we would be dealing with a relatively simple case of the interplay between the de facto retreat from the ideological maxims of the regime and the ever more intense simulacrum of these maxims in the monopolised public sphere. The subject, constituted in this interplay, would by definition be a *dissimulator*, ceaselessly moving between the unspeakable reality of the retreat and the domain of unreal speech, utilising its advantages in the latter for material gains in the former and the other way round. This view of the subject, constituted by 'closing off' a private domain of existence, whose rules were dictated by the reality of the retreat, from the ritualised public sphere (Kharkhordin 1999: 278) is familiar to us from the accounts of the *post*-Stalinist society, in which the threat of mass terror gradually subsided. In contrast, the subject of High Stalinism was irreducible to this figure of the manipulator of the public/private distinction, unwittingly created by the Soviet system, since its very existence was marked by the terror that was so random and meaningless as to preclude the very possibility of its manipulation. It is easy to see how one could successfully 'work the system' in the 1970s, when it became stagnant and thoroughly ritualised. Yet, in the mid-1930s (or, for that matter, during the war or in the postwar period), rather than successfully play the system, one was rather more likely to end up its *plaything*, as the system in question could annihilate or spare one's life for no apparent reason. Thus, while insisting on the simultaneous operation of all three logics in the constitution of the Stalinist subject, we must nonetheless assign a certain priority to terror as the key element in the Stalinist mode of subjectivation.

The same argument may be made with regard to the camp as the site of subjectivation. In the previous chapter we showed how the Gulag camp, which served as the model of the Stalinist biopolitical project during the Great Break, lost its exemplary function during the Great

Terror, becoming a strictly punitive structure with no ambition to produce 'reforged' Soviet subjects. Slave labour in the camps was no longer a path to redemptive transformation but rather a matter of the inmates' compensation for their wrongdoings (Barnes 2011: 36–41, 59–60). Of the three modes of the negative inflection of Stalinist biopolitics, two, the Retreat and the Simulacrum, played practically no role there. As sites of forced labour the camps barely benefited from the increased use of economic incentives, while the retreat in education, culture and family policies were of little relevance to the inmates. By the same token, while the inmates of the camps were in all likelihood exposed to socialist-realist art during their terms, they were no longer expected to internalise it in the manner prescribed for the general Soviet audience: precisely *as* convicted 'enemies of the people', the inmates were *missing* both from socialist-realist representation (in marked contrast to the literature and film of the late 1920s, when they were their privileged protagonists) and from its audience (by being removed from the Soviet society and its cultural sphere) (Barnes 2011: 58–9).

Of course, if we turn to the third modality of the negative inflection, that is, Terror, it is evident that it was not merely present in the camps but present to an extreme degree, never realised in Soviet society at large. As delimited zones of confinement, where one could not benefit from the relative stability and security offered by the Great Retreat and where the brutal reality of hard labour and violence resisted the socialist-realist derealisation of life, the camps were the sites where the murderous logic of the Terror was left to unfold freely. Of course, life outside the Gulag was also characterised by oppression, privation and violence, while labour was compulsory and often forced in Soviet society in general. Moreover, given the sheer number of Gulag survivors and returnees, their experiences affected and transformed Soviet reality 'on the outside' and continued to do so throughout the Soviet period. Finally, insofar as the threat of ending up in the camp was not restricted to any particular categories of the Soviet population but was disseminated throughout society, including the ostensibly loyal elites, the boundaries between the camps and the sites of 'normal' life were porous indeed. Thus, while the camp no longer served as the publicised model of the Soviet project, it remained too close to the norm to be categorised as an exception. As Leona Toker demonstrates in her study of the testimonial literature of the Gulag survivors, a paradigmatic relation between the camps (the 'zone' in inmate slang) and society at large ('the larger zone') was routinely established in these discourses as well. The whole of the Soviet Union was viewed as the giant prison with varying degrees of deprivation of freedom, of which the camp proper was the maximal.

> [The] camp is but a more condensed expression of the tendencies at work in the country as a whole. The uniqueness of its semiotic system, accountable for turning the camp into 'another kingdom' or 'a world apart', can be seen as a result of the dialectic leap from quantitative changes to a qualitative difference. (Toker 2000: 93)

If the Soviet subject was primarily subjectivised by terror, it is hardly surprising that it permanently experienced an uncanny proximity to the site, in which terror was given free rein and unfolded with maximal intensity.

Yet, how can terror function as a mode of subjectivation rather than the instrument of the destruction of subjectivity? While our argument on the centrality of terror in the formation of the Stalinist subject certainly resonates with the classical works of the theory of totalitarianism, it is important to emphasise an important difference. In our interpretation terror is not an outside force that *destroys* an already given subject, endowed with an identity, desires, interests, and so on, but a paradoxical mechanism of the constitution of the subject that destroys its identities, desires and interests without nonetheless eliminating the subject as such, which persists in the sufferance of this destruction. Moreover, while the theory of totalitarianism emphasises the role of ideology in the total domination of the subject, in our account of High Stalinism the role of ideology will, for evident reasons, be somewhat downgraded in comparison with the Great Break. As we have argued above, after the full-blown biopolitical assault of the Great Break the Soviet regime undertook a series of ideological compromises and concessions that weakened the degree of ideological domination (the Retreat). Further, it resorted to the increased ritualisation of ideological maxims whereby they were concentrated in the domain of representation (the Simulacrum). Finally, in contrast to the Great Break, in which violence was explicitly framed in terms of the ideological categories of reforging, dekulakisation or shock industrialisation, the paroxysmal violence of the Great Terror was barely explicable in ideological terms and rather exemplified the uncanny perversion of these terms themselves: such fiery insults as 'right-Trotskyite bloc', 'Judas Trotsky', 'White Guard shrimp', 'the lackeys of fascism', 'Bukharin-Trotsky gang' replaced all meaningful ideological discourse during the period of the Terror. While the theory of totalitarianism viewed Stalinism in terms of ideological domination that overwhelmed the subject with new doctrinal meanings, our approach to terror as a mode of subjectivation rather emphasises the fundamentally meaningless character of totalitarian violence.

DESTRUCTIVE PLASTICITY

It is the meaninglessness and radical contingency of the Stalinist terror that aligns the problematic of Stalinist subjectivity with Catherine Malabou's recent theory of the 'new wounded', the subjects of *trauma*. Drawing on a critical reading of psychoanalysis and the recent findings of neurological research, Malabou poses the question of the transformation of subjectivity by radically unforeseeable events such as brain damage. In contrast to the 'sexual' causality of psychoanalysis, for which the impact of any external event is necessarily *mediated* by the internal phantasmatic structure of the psyche, such different events as Alzheimer's disease, post-traumatic stress disorder, terrorist attacks and sexual abuse are, in Malabou's argument, characterised by a 'cerebral' regime of eventuality. This regime is defined by the sufferance of shock or violence that cannot be represented and symbolised by the psyche but rather results in its complete destruction (Malabou 2012a: 33). The similarity of the symptoms displayed by the victims of these very different events, such as displays of coldness, indifference and disaffection, permits Malabou to suggest a 'general theory of trauma', based on a cerebral etiology.

> [Both] subjects with brain lesions and those who have suffered types of trauma not linked with cerebral pathologies present identical behaviours. The behaviour of subjects, who are victims of trauma linked to mistreatment, war, terrorist attacks, captivity or sexual abuse, displays striking resemblances with subjects who have suffered brain damage. It is possible to name these traumas 'socio-political traumas'. Today, however, the border that separates organic trauma and socio-political trauma is increasingly porous. All trauma impacts neuronal organization, particularly the sites of emotional inductors. In all of these situations, the same *impact of the event* is at work, the same *economy of the accident*, the same relation between the psyche and the catastrophe. (Malabou 2012a: 10–11; original emphasis)

While sociopolitical traumas arguably differ from lesional ones in rarely occurring entirely by chance, contemporary traumas are, in Malabou's reading, also marked by the absence or, at least, the concealment of intentionality, taking 'two, apparently contradictory, forms: they appear either as perfectly unmotivated accidents or as the necessary blindness of natural laws; political oppression assuming the guise of a traumatic blow stripped of all justification' (ibid.: 11). The extreme contingency of a pure accident is here virtually indistinct from the extreme necessity of the laws of nature or social laws presented as naturally necessary.

Thus, in Malabou's theory brain lesions begin to function as a *paradigm* of all trauma: 'the most exceptional, the "most exemplary" of all examples and at the same time the most banal of all examples; both *the* example and *an* example among others' (ibid.: 156). Similarly to the status of the camp during the Great Break, brain lesions are both the concentrated expression of the overall logic of trauma and part of a wider series of traumas. 'Brain lesions are paradigmatic in the sense that they are the very example of violent, meaningless, unexpected and unforeseeable shock that transforms the identity of the subject, interrupts his relation to himself and permanently disorganises the process of his auto-affection' (ibid.:156). At the same time, they are examples of a more general model, which subsumes other traumas, in which no brain damage is involved. Just as the sexual etiology of psychoanalysis did not presuppose that all psychic events are determined by sexual factors, so the cerebral etiology does not suggest that sociopolitical traumas necessarily involve brain lesions.

It is this understanding of trauma that makes Malabou's account of its subjects, the 'new wounded', so helpful for our rethinking of Stalinist subjectivity. While the above-discussed studies of Soviet subjectivity address subjectivation in the late-Foucauldian fashion as 'care of the self', whereby the subject furnishes its positive identity through various versions of bodily regimen and spiritual exercises, Malabou's 'traumatic subjectivation' attunes us to a different and more fundamental dimension of subjectivity that eludes *both* the conscious techniques of the self, analysed by Foucault, and the subject of the unconscious, theorised by psychoanalysis. Malabou refers to this dimension as 'destructive plasticity' (2012a: 17–19; see also 2012b). While in its positive sense the concept of plasticity refers to the capacity of an entity to *receive* and *give* form, in its negative sense it refers to the possibility of the *destruction* of form. 'Destruction too is formative. A smashed-up face is still a face, a stump a limb, a traumatised psyche remains a psyche. Destruction has its own sculpting tools' (Malabou 2012b: 4).

Crucially for our purposes, the destruction involved in the trauma does not simply annihilate a form but rather produces a new form, which is nonetheless *entirely contained in destruction*: 'the permanent dislocation of one identity forms another identity – an identity that is neither the sublation nor the compensatory replica of the old form, but rather, literally a form of destruction' (Malabou 2012a: 18). While the Freudian unconscious was famously theorised as indestructible due to its positive plasticity, the effect of trauma is the emergence of the form of subjectivity wholly contained in its utter destruction or, in the biopolitical lexicon of our study, of a form of life exhausted in the negation of life.

> The core of subjectivity, when attacked, is quite simply at risk of dissolving. Within the Self, at the most elementary level, there is no repression, nor disavowal, nor formation of substitutes in the face of danger. Faced with a threatening event, the Self has only one way out – its own loss. (Ibid.: 45).

The subject of trauma is no longer a Heideggerian 'being-towards-death' but rather someone that 'has already been dead' and continues to manifest their own death as a positive form. In Freudian terms, we can no longer speak of the death drive but rather of the 'death of the drive' (ibid.: 20), which is nonetheless not the same as the death of the subject as such. On the contrary, psychic life survives the disruption of cerebral auto-affection and hence its own annihilation, yet it only does so by means of the birth of a new unrecognisable person, defined by disaffection or 'coolness', indifference to oneself and others (ibid.: 48). The identity of this new person is created through the loss of past identity and is wholly coextensive with it, which makes the psychoanalytic practice of regression that affirms the persistence of childhood in the adult radically ineffective. There is no past to regress to in this case, only a present without a childhood to return to.

> Even if Alzheimer's patients seem to 'fall back into childhood', it would still be possible to affirm that they return to a childhood that is not their own, to a childhood that is only a concept of childhood that consists in a set of stereotypical gestures and postures that pertain to everyone's childhood and thus to no one's childhood. A childhood without a child to live it. (Ibid.: 61).

The traumatised subject truly goes 'beyond the pleasure principle', beyond both love and hate, and consists wholly in the 'work of the death drive as the formation of death in life, the production of individual figures that exist only within the detachment of existence' (ibid.: 199; see more generally ibid.: 195–9). Malabou finds in this figure of the subject the paradigm of a 'negative possibility'. While we are more accustomed to associate possibility with affirmation (even if it is the affirmation of the negative!), there is another type of possibility, which is impossible to recuperate as a mode of affirmation but which is also not the same as a mere absence of possibility. While the modes of negation employed by psychoanalysis since Freud (repression, denegation, disavowal, and so on) are all ultimately convertible into affirmations through various forms of interiorisation, the negative possibility that Malabou elucidates consists in the negation that cannot be interiorised, in the complete effacement of the old subject and the birth of a new one, which is in no sense a *re*-birth but the unprecedented coming of the other that remains wholly other. The subject of trauma is the subject that has actualised the possibility of its own non-existence.

> The negative possibility, which remains negative until it is exhausted, never becomes real, never becomes unreal either, but remains suspended in the post-traumatic form of a subject who misses nothing – who does not even lack lack, as Lacan might have written – remains to the end this subjective form that is constituted starting from the absence from the self. No psychoanalytic development of negativity is currently able to approach this possibility. (Malabou 2012b: 90)

Thus, we end up with the idea of a subjectivity constituted as a result of a traumatic experience, devoid of sense and wholly contained in the similarly senseless survival of its own destruction. For Malabou, it is thus senselessness that has become the dominant feature of contemporary politics.

> [We] have entered a new age of political violence in which politics is defined by the renunciation of any hope of endowing violence with a political sense. The dissimulation of the reason for the event is the new form of the event. The increasingly radical effacement of the distinction between accident and crime, between the disastrous incidents and war, the multiform presence of the absence of any responsible instance or author makes the natural catastrophe of contemporary politics into a daily occurrence. (Malabou 2012a: 155)

'Coolness', which characterises the symptoms of the 'new wounded', is now generalised as the principle of contemporary political reality as such.

> [The] impact of social war is just as forceful as a brain lesion and no less violent than being struck by a bullet or an iron bar. Even if such blows do not always occur as sudden events but tend to be more continuous or harassing, their sense, like that of a brain lesion, remains dissimulated beneath an absence of sense – social conflict without dialectic, as anonymous as a natural catastrophe – an absence that reveals the very coolness of the political and the social today. (Ibid.: 160)

This staggering account may certainly appear excessive in its insistence on the senselessness of violence and suffering as the defining feature of the contemporary conjuncture in global politics. At the same time, Malabou's diagnosis is highly pertinent to such specific instances of political violence as the mass terror practised by the totalitarian regimes of the twentieth century. The idea of a constitutively traumatised subject resonates with Alexander Etkind's recent attempt to elaborate Agamben's notion of bare life in the context of Soviet totalitarianism as 'tortured life'.

> This is life that has been stripped of meaning, speech, and memory by torture. [It] is created by destitution but this is a kind of destitution that is generated by the purposeful efforts of the state and its institutions. This life can survive and recover but the posttraumatic consequences are unavoidable. (Etkind 2013: 29)

Furthermore, Malabou's theses about the contemporary political conjuncture fully accord with Hannah Arendt's famously harrowing description of 'total domination' with its triple destruction of subjectivity in the totalitarian regimes of the middle of the twentieth century (1973: 437–59).

> Total domination, which strives to organise the infinite plurality and differentiation of human beings as if all of humanity was just one individual, is possible only if each and every person can be reduced to a never-changing identity of reactions, so that each of these bundles of reactions can be exchanged at random for any other. The problem is to fabricate something that does not exist, namely, a kind of human species resembling other animal species, whose only 'freedom' would consist in 'preserving' the species. (Arendt 1973: 438)

This description is analogous to Malabou's account of a traumatised subject, which, as we have seen, is devoid even of some of the 'reactions', particularly affective or emotive ones. In Arendt's account, the process of the 'destructive formation' of this subject takes three steps. The first is the killing of the 'juridical person in man' (ibid.: 447) through putting certain categories of population outside the protection of the law, placing concentration camps outside the legal system and exposing their inmates to arbitrary violence. The second step consists in the 'murder of the moral person in man, by making martyrdom impossible' (ibid.: 451). In Arendt's account, both Nazi and Stalinist regimes sought to remove the possibility of making one's death meaningful as the final act of resistance and hence freedom. This took place through the use of threats against family members to ensure obedience and even complicity in mass murder, and the oblivion of the victims through the prohibition of grief and remembrance (ibid.: 452). The final step towards total domination consists in the complete destruction of individual identity through privation, humiliation and torture. 'The aim of all these methods is to manipulate the human body – with its infinite possibilities of suffering – in such a way as to make it destroy the human person as inexorably as do certain mental diseases of organic origin' (ibid.: 453).

Thus, Arendt appears to have arrived at Malabou's conclusion fifty years earlier. Although the parallel between political violence and mental diseases is not elaborated in *Origins of Totalitarianism*, Arendt even alludes to the problem of the ineffectiveness of what she calls 'psychological' attempts at interpreting this condition, which resonates with Malabou's wariness of the psychoanalytic approach to subjectivity: 'Conceivably some laws of mass psychology may be found to explain why millions of human beings allowed themselves to be marched unresistingly into the gas chambers, although these laws would explain nothing else but the destruction of individuality' (ibid.: 455). Similarly to Malabou's account of the 'coolness' of traumatised subjects, Arendt highlights the production of apathetic and disaffected subjects, 'marionettes without a slightest trace of spontaneity' as the key goal of totalitarian regimes (ibid.: 456–7). What distinguishes totalitarian regimes from all the tyrannies of the past is, for Arendt, the fact that they establish 'conditions under which people no longer wish to live' (ibid.: 442), in which they only survive as 'living corpses' (ibid.: 451). Finally, in just the same way as Malabou, Arendt emphasises the meaninglessness of all this violence, speaking of the 'utter lunacy' (ibid.: 453) of the camps as places where 'senselessness is daily produced anew' (ibid.: 457), even though she takes care to emphasise that this senselessness also establishes a perverse 'supersense' of ideology that crowds out any sense of reality. And yet, however sensible this supersense might appear to totalitarian leaders, their violence cannot but strike their victims as entirely senseless.

This was particularly true in the Stalinist terror, many of whose victims were ardent supporters of the very ideology, in the name of which they were imprisoned or executed. With the exception of thousands of *genuine* Trotskyites and other former oppositionists, as well as thousands of priests or White Army supporters, the *millions* of the victims of the Terror were, for all practical purposes, *Stalinists* in their ideological orientation, frequently occupying top positions in the Soviet elite: the majority of the Central Committee exterminated in 1937–8, almost *all* regional party leaders, the leadership of the Komsomol, and so on. As we have argued in the previous chapter, even if specific instances of the Terror (such as the national operations or the decimation of the Central Committee) lend themselves, with many caveats, to 'rationalist' or 'instrumental' interpretations, the overall sequence of 1936–8 is devoid of any overarching sense and rather resembles a natural catastrophe, with which it has indeed been compared (Wood 2005: 48).

Deathly Life: The Subject of Stalinism

The impact of the Terror on almost all categories of the Soviet population (the young and the old, city-dwellers and peasants, communists and non-members of the Party) was such that Russian society arguably has not recovered from it even in the post-Soviet period, which is yet another explanation for the transcendental status of Stalinism in Russian politics addressed in Chapter 1. Yet, in the studies of Stalinist subjectivity this traumatic character has been treated metaphorically at best, often slipping into a moralising discourse about repentance or subsumed under the Foucauldian art of self-fashioning, where it functions as the negative supplement of positive efforts to make (oneself) a New Soviet Person. Yet, before any self-fashioning may be traced in diaries, memoirs or oral histories, there is a question of how the sheer existence of one's self was affected by the Terror. If the subject, which was incited by the official ideology to work on itself and transform itself into a New Soviet Person, was already traumatised by the experience of collectivisation, arrest, denunciation, separation from its family, then it is not surprising that the end result of its 'work on the self' would fall far short of the ideal of subjectivity that the regime aspired to. And yet, this falling short does not indicate the failure of the regime's biopolitical productivity but demonstrates its success in producing desubjectivation as itself a form of subjectivity.

THE BARREN LIFE OF SOFIA PETROVNA

An exemplary account of the terrorised and disaffected subject of Stalinism is offered in Lydia Chukovskaya's *Sofia Petrovna*, a staggering novella depicting the plight of a mother whose son, Kolya, a successful engineering student, is arrested during the campaign against 'wrecking'. Initially active and optimistic in her pursuit of justice, Sofia Petrovna is gradually overwhelmed by the denunciations and arrests around her. Throughout the novella, she continues to believe the overall narrative about wrecking, espionage and the enemies of the people, considering her son's case, as well as the cases of some of her fellow workers and acquaintances, to be merely unfortunate mistakes. After venturing to defend her friend, Natasha, accused of wrecking for a minor typographical error, she is fired from her job. Natasha eventually commits suicide, while her son's friend Alik, who helped her in finding out the truth about Kolya's arrest, ends up arrested himself. Increasingly isolated and alienated, Sofia Petrovna finds out from the prosecutor that Kolya confessed to the charges of terrorism. At the end of the novel Sofia Petrovna receives a letter from her son, reaffirming his innocence and asking for her help. Yet, having failed in all her endeavours and having lost those who assisted her, Sofia

Petrovna gives up her struggle. She burns the letter in desperation and stamps out the flames on the floor. While this poignant ending of the novella is often interpreted as a matter of a mother's betrayal of her son, in a later afterword Chukovskaya explicitly refuses to exercise moral judgement and particularly assign guilt, dispensing with the entire legalistic tradition of ethics (cf. Agamben 1999b: 19–24).

> Sofia Petrovna isn't able to generalise from what she sees and experiences; and she's not to be blamed for that, because to the ordinary person what was happening seemed purposefully planned senselessness; and how can one make sense of deliberately planned chaos? Particularly when one is all alone: each person was cut off from anyone else experiencing the same thing by a wall of terror. There were many people like Sofia Petrovna, millions, but when people are denied all documents, all literature, when the true history of whole decades is replaced by fictitious history, then the individual intellect is cast back on itself, on its own personal experience, and it works less well than it should. (Chukovskaya 1994: 112)

While the complicity of Sofia Petrovna and millions like her in the Great Terror is evident, it is not to be evaluated as the act of a pre-constituted subject but rather as itself an *effect* of subjectivation. The silences, inactions and betrayals do not indicate what Soviet subjects 'have always been', as if their ethical flaws have been revealed by their failure to pass some kind of moral test. Any understanding of the Terror as a moral test is simply obscene and any morality that would *require* such a test deserves nothing but complete oblivion. Rather than show us the hitherto concealed (im)moral essence of the subject, the act of Sofia Petrovna indicates what she has *become* as a result of the trauma of terror. Sofia Petrovna does not betray her son in the moment of burning his letter: in this moment she *does not have* a son, her relationship with him having been extinguished as is the relationship with her own former self.

Let us return to Chukovskaya's fortunate designation of the period of the Terror as 'purposefully planned senselessness'. This definition corresponds almost to the letter to the sociopolitical traumas described by Malabou: unlike brain lesions, which may result from an entirely contingent accident, sociopolitical traumas induced by wars, terrorist acts, captivity, and so on are usually 'deliberately planned' yet *no less* senseless for that reason. In the absence of anything like a public sphere, in which the events of the purges could be freely discussed and made sense of, individuals affected by the terror (not only as a direct victim, but also as a relative, friend or colleague) find themselves isolated and alienated with nothing to fall back on other than their 'intellect cast back on itself', which cannot symbolise and absorb the shock of the meaningless event. Sofia Petrovna's stamping out of the fire that burned her son's letter is simultaneously the stamping out of her own psyche, the act of (self-)destruction in which another subject is born, albeit a subject whose identity is entirely contained in the death of the preceding one, whose form of life is nothing but the negation of an earlier life.

This is why this subject is only manifested in the *minimisation of its own manifestation*: withdrawal, indifference, disaffection. There is simply *nothing else* that could show itself in this subject that lives its own extinction. Having burned her son's letter, Sofia Petrovna does not take up the official mode of subjectivation by appropriating the narrative of wrecking and enemies of the people. At the endpoint of her struggles she does not renounce her past conviction of her son's innocence in favour of replicating the official proclamation of his guilt in her diary. While ceasing to *resist*, Sofia Petrovna does not begin to conform, obey or adapt but simply *desists*, her existence suspended in this state of desistence that is a far cry from the activist concepts of the Soviet subject as a cynical manipulator of the system, a rational self-interested agent, a tactical 'Bolshevik-speaker' or an enthusiastic diarist. Yet, neither is it possible to view Sofia Petrovna as a dupe of ideological indoctrination, since it is not clear what this indoctrination actually achieves in her case. Rather than surrender to the Big Other as the 'subject supposed to know', she 'does not want either to know or not to know' (Malabou 2012a: 215). We are familiar with the classical argument about totalitarian subjects as victims of ideological propaganda (cf. Arendt 1973: 341–64). Yet, in this case it is in fact propaganda *itself* that falls victim to the senselessness of the trauma, becoming wholly ineffective in relation to the indifferent subject who could not be bothered one way or another (cf. Arendt 1973: 392). The decline of ideological, or more generally symbolic, efficacy that marked the post-Stalinist period and was the key factor in the unravelling of the USSR could be traced back to the trauma of the Great Terror, which rendered the subject far too 'cold' for ideological indoctrination to ever be really effective.

It is important to note that Malabou's understanding of subjectivation does not pertain exclusively to the victims of sociopolitical violence, but also to the executioners.

> 'Making suffer' today manifestly assumes the guise of the neutrality and senselessness of a blow without author and without history, of mechanical violence, and of the absence of interiority – thereby adding another valence to the inexhaustible concept of the banality of evil. (Malabou 2012a: 200)

As Joshua Oppenheimer's brilliant films *The Act of Killing* and *The Look of Silence*, which focus on the perpetrators and victims of the 1965 genocide of communists in Indonesia, demonstrate so starkly, indifference and disaffection characterise serial killers and war criminals no less than their surviving victims. Sociopolitical violence produces a general 'coolness' in society, confirming the well-known yet still disturbing observation that 'after a while the mentality of the inmates is scarcely distinguishable from that of the camp guards' (Arendt 1973: 442, fn. 132). In the Soviet context, this thesis is supported by the testimonial prose of the Gulag survivors and victims of Stalinist terror, who emphasise that the violence exercised in camps and prisons rarely took the form of sadistic torture, enthusiastically administered by the executioners, but was rather administered in a callous and indifferent manner, demonstrating the same disaffection that this violence eventually produced in its victims (Toker 2000: 246–7; Shalamov 1994: 355).

The 'cool subjectivity' of traumatised and terrorised Soviet individuals may thus be approached as the real supplement to the ideal of the New Soviet Person, produced in the simulacrum of socialist realism.[1] While the latter construct was produced in conjunction with the demands for greater 'humanism' after the experiments of the 'productionist' art of the Great Break (see Dobrenko 2007: 150–60; Clark 2011: 105–36), the real human substrate was rather characterised by the dehumanisation resulting from the shock of governmental violence. Such frequently noted features of the Stalinist and the post-Stalinist subject as atomisation, the lack of empathy and solidarity, the indifference to the suffering of the other are a direct result of the violent practices of the Great Break and the Terror, in which any assistance to the prosecuted kulaks, 'enemies of the people' and their families was severely punished. The frightening evidence in the famous 1933 letter of Mikhail Sholokhov to Stalin that described the atrocities of collectivisation pertains not merely to the suffering of the 'de-kulakised' peasants themselves but to the forceful cultivation of the indifference of the others to this suffering, the destruction of empathy that produced every subject as fundamentally and devastatingly *lonely*.

> [It] was officially and strictly prohibited for other kolkhoz farmers to let the exiled into their homes to stay overnight or to get warm. They were to live in barns and cellars, in the street or in the gardens. The population was warned: whoever lets in an exiled family will be exiled with his family. And they were indeed exiled, even if some kolkhoz farmer, moved by the screams of freezing children, would let an exiled neighbour in to warm up. I saw what I could not forget until I die: in the Volokhovskaya village of the Lebyzshensky kolkhoz at night, in the frost and

terrible wind, when even dogs hide from the cold, the families of those thrown out of their homes sat in the streets and burned fires. Children were covered in rags and put on the ground that melted down due to the fire. Children's screams were all over the streets. In the Bazkov kolkhoz a woman with an infant was exiled. All night she walked around the village and begged to be let in with her child to get warm. No one did, fearing that they would be exiled themselves. In the morning the child died in mother's arms and the mother got severe freezing. (Sholokhov 1933)

While the trauma of the survivors of the exile is evident, we must not forget the much less intense but still effective trauma of the kolkhoz farmers, who were prohibited from exercising elementary charity, the punishment for human empathy being one's subsumption under the plastic category of the '(sub)kulak'. Besides its revolting cruelty, this prohibition testifies to the utmost senselessness of the collectivisation process, which did not target a determinate category of peasants perceived as enemies, but rather attacked the entire village population with unprecedented hostility that sought not to convert and mobilise but simply to force into submission through violent shock that destroyed the entire fabric of human relations, resulting in the production of the multiplicity of lonely disaffected subjects that, in a sadly ironic twist, was for some reason called a 'collective'.

In Arendt's classical account, loneliness is the human experience that totalitarianism feeds on and enhances to a horrendous degree. It should not be confused with either *isolation* or *solitude*. Isolation is characteristic of traditional tyrannies that sought to disempower human beings from acting in concert (Arendt 1973: 474). It only sought to destroy the public realm while leaving the entire realm of private life 'with the capacities for experience, fabrication and thought' intact (ibid.: 474). In contrast, totalitarianism also targeted these 'non-political' capacities of thought and experience, making impossible not only political 'action in concert' (*praxis*) but also the productive activity of humanity more generally (*poiesis*), leaving the human as nothing more than *animal laborans*, a creature capable only of labour – a horrendous possibility that, as we shall see in the following chapter, was indeed realised in the Gulag. It is this creature that is paradigmatically lonely, even if – and especially when – it is with others in the cramped spaces of the camp.

For Arendt, the condition of loneliness is not constituted by being actually separated from others, but is fully realisable *precisely* when the subject is cramped together with others without any space in between them, this space being the condition of any possible sociality: 'By destroying all space between men and pressing men against each other, even the productive potentialities of isolation are annihilated' (ibid.: 478). This is why the camp, characterised by overcrowding and the disappearance of private spaces, was the space where loneliness was manifested most starkly. Paradoxically at first glance, loneliness consists precisely in the impossibility of being solitary. 'In solitude, I am "by myself", together with my self, and therefore two-in-one, whereas in loneliness I am actually one, deserted by all others' (ibid.: 476). Loneliness is characterised not by the absence of others, but by the absence or at least the inaccessibility of one's own self *as* other, of being with or talking to oneself. Yet, insofar as for Arendt solitude is the condition of all productive human activity, of all thought and experience, insofar as 'all thinking, strictly speaking, is done in solitude and is a dialogue between me and myself' (ibid.: 476), then the lonely being suffers nothing less than the impossibility of thinking and experiencing and this impossibility is its entire substance. We are back to Malabou's figure of the 'cool subject' that survives and lives its own demise, the collapse of all its relationships, including the relation to itself.

> Destructive plasticity deploys its work starting from the exhaustion of possibilities, when all virtuality has left long ago, when the child in the adult is erased, when cohesion is destroyed, family spirit vanished, friendship lost, links dissipated in the ever more intense cold of a barren life. (Malabou 2012b: 90)

Insofar as its *modus operandi* consists in nullifying the anterior form of subjectivity, the traumatic mode of subjectivation associated with the Terror becomes a paradigmatic structure of Stalinist subjectivity. Of course, there were other types of subjects located along the continuum from the Retreat to the Simulacrum: cynical conformists and skilful manipulators benefiting from the unprecedented upward mobility at the time of the Terror, the 'new middle class', interested in cultivating their private sphere, the dutiful 'workers on the self' monitoring their progress in their diaries, 'dissimulating animals' engaging in illicit non-socialist practices while obediently enacting official rituals, and so on. Yet, whatever *else* the Soviet subject might have been, it was also always at the risk of being obliterated and continuing to live this obliteration.

In Alexander Solzhenitsyn's novel *In the First Circle*, the main protagonist, Innokentiy Volodin, a young diplomat, is initially presented as the model Stalinist subject, advancing in his career by skilfully navigating the gap between the reality of the retreat from socialism (evident in the world of abundance and privilege enjoyed in Volodin's professional and family circles) and the simulacrum of its achievement (maintained in his professional activities). His fateful decision to make a phone call to the US embassy regarding the Soviet attempts to acquire information on the nuclear bomb (in the long version of the novel (2009)) or to warn his family doctor against interaction with foreigners (in the shorter, 'lightened' version (1968)) quickly leads to his arrest by the secret police. Nonetheless, Volodin appears somehow prepared for this eventuality, since the shock of the arrest and the consequent humiliation in the Lubyanka prison pass quite quickly. He has no illusions about getting away with what he did and is aware that his entire identity has already begun to disintegrate: it is not a coincidence that a young guard processing him refers to Volodin's identity in the past tense, asking him: 'Who were you?' (1968: 549). And yet, immediately after his arrest Volodin begins calmly, or, perhaps, *coldly*, to adapt to his new conditions, devoting his attention to practical matters such as keeping his trousers on without braces (ibid.: 536). While it was impossible to be fully prepared for the intrusion of the traumatic experience of terror, in which case the impact of the trauma would be at least partially neutralised, the 'real possibility' of ending up the 'enemy of the people' was always integrated into the structure of even the model Stalinist subject, thanks to the numerous examples of the downfall of the top representatives of the Stalinist elite, from Yagoda and Yezhov in the 1930s to Kuznetsov and Voznesensky in the late 1940s.

Traumatic subjectivation need not have completely effaced other modes of subjectivation but may rather account for their survival in a damaged, ineffective or inoperative status. Was the coldness of the NKVD guard in the camp a result of his anterior propensity for evil or rather a result of traumatic damage that affected his relational capacities, resulting in his indifference to suffering, both his own and that of others? (Cf. Malabou 2012a: 202) The same question may be posed with regard to such diverse categories of subjects as dissimulating ex-kulaks, forging a new identity for themselves in perpetual fear of being found out, the members of Stalin's inner circle (Molotov, Kalinin, Poskrebyshev, and so on) whose wives were incarcerated in the camps, and, why not, Stalin himself, whose infamous coldness after his wife's presumed suicide in 1934 is often proposed as the psychological 'explanation' for the murderous purges. Insofar as it is impossible to exclude the Terror from the diagram of Soviet subjectivation, it serves, exactly in the same mode as Malabou's brain lesions, as both *an* example and *the* example of Stalinist subjectivity.[2] Against the current tendency in the scholarship on the Stalinist period to ignore or downplay the terror in the focus on the purely discursive or aesthetic aspects (for example, the study of artworks, diaries, lifestyles, and so on), Alexander Etkind has claimed that 'only violence – threats, purges, arrests, torture, show trials, executions, and the gulag' (2013: 31) could sustain the symbolic edifice of Soviet ideology, socialist realism or Stalin's personal cult, without which none of them would have attained either their power or their longevity. Thus, any explanation of these phenomena that elides the fact of terror as the permanent backdrop to the existence of Soviet individuals risks distorting and mystifying the Soviet subject as either a cynical operator or a naive dupe. While there was certainly a little of both in the Stalinist subject, there was *also* a heavy dose of senseless violence that affected or, better, *disaffected* the functioning of both these types.

THE LIVING DEAD

The paradigmatic status of terror in the Stalinist mode of subjectivation is particularly evident in the biopolitical context. Let us recall the fundamental paradox of socialist biopolitics that has accompanied us throughout this study. The Stalinist project of the conversion of revolutionary transcendence into the immanence of lived reality necessarily involved the empirical negation of the existing reality, the production of the 'clean slate' that would serve as the foundation for the new order. After the apocalyptic drive of the Great Break was partially halted, Stalinist biopolitics unfolded in the mode of three negative inflections of this project: retreat, simulacrum and terror. The first two modes are conceivable as departures from the original task of forcing the new model of subjectivity into life, which logically entails refraining from the negation of the existing forms of life. The Great Retreat was a compromise of the ideal project with the immanent reality that contradicted it, whereby various aspects of the reality to be negated were rehabilitated and incorporated into the new regime, permitting a degree of social stabilisation after the turmoil of 1928–32. The subject presupposed and produced in the Retreat was therefore the *subject of the past*, grounded in the pre-Soviet reality that withstood the attempt at its negation, though not without paying a heavy price of sociocultural degradation. The Great Simulacrum of socialist realism exemplified another kind of the retreat of the ideal before the real, whereby the former withdrew from the latter and turned back on itself, compensating for the lack of its real efficacy by the aesthetic derealisation of life itself. The subject presupposed and produced in this project was the *subject of the future*, a purposefully derealised model, whose empirical actualisation might well be deferred but whose aesthetic deployment serves to crowd out empirical actuality itself. The final form of negative inflection, the Great Terror, differed from the other two, since it no longer negated the real by the ideal, or the other way round, but, having dispensed with the ideal as such, made the work of negation wholly immanent, producing nothing but the real negation of the real.

At first glance, the paradigmatic product of this negation of the real would be a *corpse*, marking the final stage in the conversion of biopolitics into thanatopolitics. And yet, things are more complicated than this. In contrast to the explicitly genocidal drive of Nazism, the production of dead bodies (of any category of the population) was never part of the governmental rationality of Stalinism: while its body count is at least comparable to that of Nazism, Stalinism never attempted to exterminate an entire group, be it ethnic, social or otherwise. Surely, all 'enemies of the people' were to be exterminated, but these enemies came from all possible strata of the population and could not be identified by any other predicate than their enemy status itself. As a result, the thanatopolitical drive ended up disseminated throughout society, becoming rather less accentuated than in Nazism. And yet, even though it lacked Nazism's morbid fascination with the production of death, Stalinism was also thanatopolitical in its very essence and not merely in its effects. We may identify the subtle difference between the two by suggesting that whereas Nazism *converted* biopolitics into a thanatopolitical project of extermination, whereby power produced death *rather than* life (Esposito 2008a: 110–44), Stalinism operated through their *indistinction*, whereby power produced life *as* death or death *as* life.

During the High Stalinist period the Soviet biologist and Old Bolshevik Olga Lepeshinskaya developed highly idiosyncratic ideas about 'living substance' (1954), which became quite influential in the postwar period, when they were popularised by Lysenko, giving Lepeshinskaya a Stalin Prize, the title of Academician and even a token seat in the Supreme Soviet. Even at the time the notion of a pure living substance was suspect as a relapse into theories of autogenesis or spontaneous generation, a 'prescientific' biology of the likes of Paracelsus, who recommended creating a living child out of the putrefaction of human sperm first in a pumpkin and then a horse's stomach. What characterised pure living substance according to Lepeshinskaya was primarily *formlessness*.

> Living substance is a protoplasmic mass, not having the form of a cell, containing within itself in one form or another nuclear substance, but not having the form of a nucleus, rather being present in the protoplasm or in a diffused or atomised state. (1954: 85; see Dobrenko 2007: 87)

Living substance possesses vital activity but lacks all form of a body. Because of this indeterminacy, this substance exists on the borderline between life and death: for instance, viruses were theorised by Lepeshinskaya as both 'living creatures' and 'nonliving substances' (ibid.: 87–8).

In fact, what we observe in this figure is nothing other than bare life as the sheer facticity of *zoe* devoid of a determinate *bios*. In this figure of living substance form and content become indistinct since they ceaselessly pass into one another: 'it is the content but nothing contains it; it is form but it no longer forms anything, exposing, thereby, itself' (Agamben 2014a: 38). Yet, while Lepeshinskaya's revolutionary biology presupposed this living substance as the *object* of revolutionary transformation, whereby new forms are created out of vital formlessness, her figure of the living substance is far more apposite to describe the *product* of Stalinist terror. Living substance is not the origin that is then subjected to the formative activity of the revolutionary class, party or leader, which make a positive form of life out of it, but rather the effect of the destruction of every anterior form of life in governmental violence, which reduces forms of life to the threshold between life and death. The living substance is not something that precedes every form but what *succeeds* it, what remains when nothing remains of what a life was in positive terms. Thus, Lepeshinskaya's biological fantasy of pure living substance corresponds to the real biopolitical achievement of Stalinism: the subject that continues to live its own death.[3]

The prime biopolitical product of Stalinism is then not the corpse but the *living dead*, the irreparably damaged subject that suffers the shock of the terror that obliterates its psyche and yet continues to live its obliteration. The subject produced by the Stalinist terror is thus the *subject of the present*, insofar as its past has been erased and its future is a matter of indifference for him. In this manner, the Terror neutralised the impact of the potentially fatal contradiction between the Retreat and the Simulacrum, the persistence of the old amid the already attained new, by rendering this contradiction imperceptible in comparison to the shock of the trauma. It is then not surprising that as soon as the threat of terror subsided in the post-Stalin period, the contradiction between the reality of the retreat and the simulacrum of socialism became the primary corrosive and corrupting factor, undermining the Soviet system and leading to its implosion in the Gorbachev era, when the threat of terror became purely hypothetical. To the extent it is possible to speak of the effectiveness of the terror, this obscene effectiveness consists in applying to the subject's very being the shock of such magnitude that its surrounding reality, with all its insurmountable contradictions, becomes indifferent to it. The Stalinist subject was suspended between a past that was no longer its own and a future it no longer wanted in the present that contained nothing other than this suspension. In this manner, biopolitics did not *turn into* thanatopolitics in the sense of positive transformation of life relapsing into the negation of life, but rather became wholly indistinct from it. Stalinism *did* produce the New Soviet Person as a new form of life, yet this form has no content aside from the death of the old form. Rather than have the new form succeed the old one, the 'new' is here simply the annihilation of the old, the stillborn child that is the spitting image of its dead mother.

In his fiery and poignant essay on Stalinism Martin Amis argues that the 'new men' that the Soviet experiment ventured to create were indeed created, albeit not as models of physical and spiritual perfection but as figures of 'negative perfection', the complete and total triumph of negation that one observes in the Gulag.

> I knew that we would find them, the New Men. There they are, beaten, beaten and once again beaten, down on all fours and growling like dogs, kicking and biting one another for a gout of rotten trash.
>
> *There* they are. (Amis 2003: 81)

Chapter 6

SHALAMOV, OR THE NEGATIVE EXPERIENCE

THE SCHOOL OF THE NEGATIVE

Varlam Shalamov, born in 1907 in Vologda, was first arrested as a student in 1929 for belonging to a Trotskyite group and circulating Lenin's famous 'Letter to the Congress', in which he had criticised Stalin. Shalamov was then sentenced to three years at a camp in Solikamsk. It was during this period that the Soviet camp system was founded in the course of the Great Break, functioning as the tool of the reforging of class enemies through labour. The first organiser of the Kolyma camps, in which so many Trotskyites and other oppositionists eventually perished, was Eduard Berzin, who was himself executed in 1938 as a Trotskyite. The system originally instituted by Berzin in the Urals camps during 1929–30 was, according to many accounts, including Shalamov's own, still relatively humane, permitting early release for good work, providing decent supplies of food and salaries that could be used to support families 'on the outside' (see Shalamov 2005; 1994: 368–9).

After his release in 1931 Shalamov returned to Moscow and worked as a journalist before getting arrested again in January 1937. As a previously convicted Trotskyite, Shalamov was now an evident target of the Great Terror and was sentenced to five years at a camp in Kolyma in the Far East. At this time, it was no longer Berzin's reforging camp that operated through moral and material incentives, but a system of slave labour that was rather designed to unforge or destroy 'enemies of the people'. Moreover, political prisoners, especially those marked as Trotskyites, were used for particularly hard labour, were prohibited all communication with the outside world and were routinely abused by professional criminals that were entrusted with watching over them. In 1942 Shalamov's sentence was extended until the end of the war. During the following year he received another ten-year sentence for 'anti-Soviet agitation', which consisted in the claim that Ivan Bunin, an émigré author not sympathetic to the Soviet regime, was a classic

Shalamov, or the Negative Experience

writer. During his imprisonment in Kolyma Shalamov had to work in gold and coal mines in extremely adverse conditions of cold and hunger and had to endure both the punishments of the camp administration for failing to meet work quotas and the brutal violence of the criminal population of the camp. In 1946 Shalamov was so weakened and emaciated that he became what in the camp slang of the time was called a *dohodyaga* ('goner') – the Russian equivalent of the *Muselmann* of the Nazi camps, an emaciated inmate that occupies the borderline between life and death. Shalamov was saved by a doctor inmate who procured him a position as hospital attendant, which he occupied until his eventual release in 1951.

After Stalin's death Shalamov was allowed to leave the Magadan region and settled in a small town outside Moscow. In 1956, the year of Khruschev's Thaw, he was officially rehabilitated and returned to professional writing. During this period he completed his collection of short stories that has come to be known as *Kolyma Tales*.[1] Excerpts from the collection were first published in the West in 1966. In 1972 Shalamov denounced this publication in a letter to *Literaturnaya Gazeta*, possibly under pressure or in the hope that this would make possible the publication of his poetry inside the USSR. This episode contributed to the distancing of Shalamov from the Soviet dissident community, which he was from the outset heterogeneous to due to his strongly pro-revolutionary sympathies that contrasted with the increasingly anticommunist and conservative dispositions of the dissident intelligentsia.

Shalamov's health was ruined in the camps and for the rest of his life he suffered from pellagra with its 'three d' symptoms: diarrhoea, dermatitis and dementia. In 1979 he was placed in a nursing home, which to him resembled a camp and reactivated many camp practices, from hoarding bread to sleeping on bare mattresses. In 1982 he was moved to the psychiatric hostel after allegedly resisting wards. While being transported there, tied to a chair, he caught pneumonia and died two days after.

Shalamov's *Kolyma Tales* have been the focus of a myriad of studies from all possible perspectives – historical, philological, philosophical, and so on (Podoroga 2013; Ryklin 2007; Toker 2000: ch. 6). What the analysis of this chapter intends to contribute to these studies is the elaboration in the biopolitical context of Shalamov's well-known judgement on the camps as a *negative experience*.

> The camps are in every way schools of the negative. No one will ever receive anything useful or necessary from them – neither the convict himself, nor his superiors, nor the guard, nor the inadvertent witnesses, nor the camp administrators, nor their subordinates. Every minute of camp

life is a poisoned minute. There is much there that a man should not know, should not see, and if he does see it, it is better for him to die. ('Red Cross' in Shalamov 1994: 412)

The camp is a totally negative experience, down to the very single minute. A person only grows worse. Nor can it be otherwise. There is much in the camps that a person should not see. But to see the lower depths is not the most terrible thing. The most terrible is when one begins – forever – to feel those lower depths in one's own life, when one's moral measurements are loaned from camp experience. (Shalamov cited in Toker 2000: 180)

If the camp is a totally negative experience, what is the mode of being of the subject that undergoes it? What does it mean to experience negativity as such and go on living? A good starting point for this discussion is the contrast between the constructions of the Gulag in the work of Shalamov and Alexander Solzhenitsyn, perhaps the best-known representative of Soviet 'Gulag literature'. Shalamov's insistence on the total negativity of camp experience rejects every attempt to endow the camps with a redemptive or morally elevating function of the kind that we may find in Solzhenitsyn's *The Gulag Archipelago*, as well as his fictional works on Stalinism such as *In the First Circle* and *The Cancer Ward*. For Solzhenitsyn, the horrors of the camp were limit experiences that, while certainly destroying many personalities, also managed to strengthen others by stripping their existence of habitual superficies, petty concerns and common opinions. For Solzhenitsyn himself the camp entailed the final liberation from all illusions about Soviet socialism and the thorough reassessment of the entire revolutionary tradition and its ultimate abandonment in favour of a version of nationalist conservatism. It is thus possible to become different and even *better* in the camp through one's resistance to the dehumanising oppression that reigns there.

It is this possibility of maintaining or reconstructing one's subjectivity in positive terms in the conditions of the camp that Shalamov persistently denies. The camps make impossible any *positive metamorphosis* of the subject, whereby it becomes something else by abandoning or fleeing one's earlier identity, for example a conservative instead of a communist, a Christian instead of an atheist, and so on. The camps are only capable of what Malabou termed 'destructive metamorphosis', which is not constituted by *fleeing* one's own form but rather consists in assuming as the new form the very *impossibility* of flight (Malabou 2012b: 3–5). As the site of utter deprivation, escape from which was practically impossible (see Shalamov 1994: 373–9), the camp effected a purely negative metamorphosis whereby

> [the] only way out from the impossibility of flight [was] the formation of a form of flight. In other words, both the formation of a type or ersatz of flight and the formation of an identity that flees the impossibility of fleeing itself. Identity abandoned, dissociated again, identity that does not reflect itself, does not live its own transformation, does not subjectivise its change. (Malabou 2012b: 11)

The metamorphosis that takes place in the camps does not endow the subject with a new form but *de-forms* the subject as such: 'The only other that exists in this circumstance is being other to the self' (ibid.:11). It is certainly possible to become *other* in the camps and, as Shalamov's texts mercilessly document, this indeed happens in a span of a few days in the cold, hunger and hard labour in Kolyma. Yet, this otherness is nothing other than the *othering of the self from itself*, the deformation of the subject that, for lack of anything like a new form, becomes sedimented as a form of subjectivity in its own right. Evidently, in this destructive change it is impossible either to become *better* or even stay good: 'a person only grows worse'. Importantly, this utter negativity of camp experience does not merely concern inmates but also pertains to guards, administrators, doctors – whoever came into contact with this site of negativity.

> [There] a convict learns to hate work. He does not and cannot learn anything else. He learns flattery, lying, petty acts, and major villainies. He becomes totally engrossed in himself. His interests have narrowed, become impoverished and crude. Moral barriers have somehow been pushed aside. In camp a human being learns sloth, deception and viciousness. He rates his own suffering too highly, forgetting that everyone has his own grief. He has forgotten empathy for another's sorrow; he simply does not understand it and does not desire to understand it. He is morally crushed. His concepts of morality have changed without his having noticed this change. What will the guard tell his fiancé about his work in the Far North – the guard who often held human lives in his hands and who often killed people who stepped outside the forbidden zone? Will he tell her how he used his rifle butt to beat hungry old men who could not walk? ('Red Cross' in Shalamov 1994: 412)

This is why Shalamov refers to the camp as an 'enormous experiment in the corruption of human souls' ('Mister Popp's Visit' in Shalamov 1994: 478), which left no one untouched. Moreover, this corruption was irreversible – something Shalamov repeatedly emphasised in a number of stories. To survive the camp was to survive the corruption of one's soul and thus to go on living *with* a corrupt soul – this is why 'it is probably better to die' than to survive this experience and why survival is only possible through forgetting, which is precisely what Shalamov's work resists.

> A human being survives by his ability to forget. Memory is always ready to blot out the bad and retain only the good. There was nothing good in the spring 'Duskania' and nothing good was either expected in the future or remembered in the past by any of us. We had all been all poisoned by the north and we knew it. ('Dry Rations' in Shalamov 1994: 43)

Shalamov's insistence on the total negativity of camp experience is particularly illuminating from the biopolitical perspective, since it categorically rejects the biopolitical productivity that Stalinism was and continues to be credited with. For Shalamov, the form of life that is produced in the camp is merely the negation of life. The biopolitics of the Gulag is directly and immediately thanatopolitics; it does not produce anything positive even by accident. If Solzhenitsyn's account of redemption and self-realisation through suffering were plausible, it would have meant that in some perverse way the Stalinist project had *succeeded*, that it was indeed possible to become a 'new man', if not *thanks to* the governmental violence of Stalinism then *despite* it, by surviving it or fighting against it. In such an account the metamorphosis, however degrading or destructive, still appears to be ultimately redemptive, 'a strange salvation but salvation all the same' (Malabou 2012b: 12). Shalamov completely renounces this logic. The strongest who survive in Kolyma are still degraded and broken. What does not kill you does *not* really make you stronger; it only leaves you damaged. The camps do indeed immediately strip one of the superficies of worldly existence, yet what remains beneath them is not some kernel of authentic subjectivity but simply bare life devoid of any attributes other than its exposure to death. What is stripped off, discarded and destroyed is not merely the habitual and the superficial but the very positivity of worldly existence that defines a form of life (*bios*). 'The flight identity forged by destructive plasticity flees itself first and foremost; it knows no salvation or redemption and is there for no one, especially not for the self' (Malabou 2012b: 12).

In Shalamov's story 'In the Night' the protagonist, a doctor named Glebov, and his fellow inmate Bagretsov, are busy removing rocks from a large heap on a terrace by the hill. Glebov finds it difficult to respond to his friend's question about whether he was a doctor. His old identity has been destroyed but it is not clear what, if anything, has replaced it. Moreover, Glebov's 'remaining consciousness' is too weakened even to pose these questions.

The time when he had been a doctor seemed very far away. Had it ever existed? Too often the world beyond the mountains and seas seemed unreal, like something out of a dream. Real were the minute, the hour, the day – from reveille to the end of work. He never guessed further, nor did he have the strength to guess. Nor did anyone else. He did not know the past of the people who surrounded him and did not want to know. But then, if tomorrow Bagretsov were to declare himself a doctor of philosophy or a marshal of aviation, Glebov would believe him without a second thought. Has he himself really been a doctor? Not only the habit of judgement was lost but even the habit of observation. The consciousness that remained to him, the consciousness that was perhaps no longer human – had too few facets and was now directed toward one goal only, that of removing the stones as quickly as possible. ('In the Night' in Shalamov 1994: 12)

The purpose of removing the stones was to take the shorts off the body of a recently buried inmate. The shorts in question were 'like new' and thus tradeable for food or tobacco. However macabre the scenario appears, Shalamov's text is devoid of any negative judgement – compared with many others, this is a story with a genuinely happy ending: 'The dead man's underwear was warm under Glebov's jacket and no longer seemed alien. Bagretsov smiled. Tomorrow they would sell the underwear, trade it for bread, maybe even get some tobacco ...' (Ibid.: 14). Indeed, this is far from the dehumanisation that we shall encounter below. While Glebov and Bagretsov have no moral qualms about their endeavour as such, at least Glebov is not entirely indifferent to the content and context of his actions: he bluntly refuses to wear the dead man's underwear, even though this is a much safer way to get it inside the camp barracks. While Glebov's old identity has been destroyed and no new identity has emerged in its place, he nonetheless exists as an active and interested subject, albeit with a 'reduced' consciousness and moral sense oriented squarely towards immediate needs. Glebov occupies the top rung of the downward ladder of dehumanisation, every step downwards from which erases one's subjectivity while leaving intact its form.

THE RETURN OF HISTORY AS HORROR

The fragility of all positive forms of life is a recurring theme of *Kolyma Tales*. Shalamov is adamant that it is impossible to escape the degradation of one's personality and the only way to avoid it is to die before it reaches its extreme stages. In 'Epitaph', Shalamov fondly remembers his friends who died in the camps, yet the positive image he presents of these friends is due to the fact that they died prior to reaching the final stage of dehumanisation due to cold, hunger and beatings, the stage at which friendship itself inevitably dissolved.

> [Seryozha Klivansky] loved poetry and recited verse by heart while in prison. He stopped doing that in the camp. He would have shared his last morsel, or, rather, he was still at that stage ... That is, he never reached the point where no one had a last morsel and no one shared anything with anyone. ('Epitaph' in Shalamov 1994: 304)

For Shalamov, any belief that adverse conditions could foster or 'temper' friendship, community and solidarity was obscene. The hardships of the camps did not help form any lasting friendships and created no sense of community. The inmates were merely exposed to each other's degradation, forced to observe something obscene and indecent, coming to know something that one should not know: 'We all knew that if we survived we would not want to meet again' ('Dry Rations' in Shalamov 1994: 43).

> In the camp it was each man for himself and I didn't expect any assistance. ('Captain Tolly's Love' in Shalamov 1994: 332)

> Cold, hunger and sleeplessness rendered any friendship impossible, and Dugaev – despite his youth – understood the falseness of the belief that friendship could be tempered by misery and tragedy. For friendship to be friendship, its foundation had to be laid before living conditions reached that last border beyond which no human emotion was left to a man – only mistrust, rage and lies. ('An Individual Assignment' in Shalamov 1994: 22)

> Friendship is not born in conditions of need or trouble. Literary fairy tales tell of 'difficult' conditions which are an essential element in forming any friendship, but such conditions are simply not difficult enough. If tragedy and need brought people together and gave birth to their friendship, then the need was not extreme and the tragedy not great. ('Dry Rations' in Shalamov 1994: 43)

It is important to note that this destruction of friendship and solidarity in the camps is contrasted by Shalamov to the experience of the *prison*, which, at first glance counter-intuitively, he presents as almost a diametric opposite of the camp. While similarly serving as the site of incarceration, the prison differed from the camp insofar as it lacked the conditions that impaired human sociality (cold, hunger, hard labour) and therefore permitted the formation of ties of friendship and solidarity, which Shalamov ironically models on the Bolshevik revolutionary tradition. In the story 'Committees for the Poor' Shalamov describes the practice in the Soviet prisons in the 1930s for the inmates to donate 10 per cent of the money they used to buy things at the prison shop to those who had no money. In this manner, the 'moneyless' were not merely invited to share meals with the 'moneyed', but could buy their own food and supplies in the shop. This tradition received the name of the Committees for the Poor (*kombedy*), the organisations for the poorest peasants during the 'war communism' phase of the Civil War, who redistributed land, cattle and produce in the villages. While the reputation of these committees was and remains at best dubious, what is important is that in the prisons of the 1930s their name was a metaphor for the arrangement that served not merely the task of social justice but also the affirmation of the subjective dignity of the 'moneyless' inmates. It is as if, for Shalamov, the only place where revolutionary egalitarianism could have a place in the USSR in the 1930s was the prison, whose population remained more faithful to the revolutionary tradition than the regime instituted in its name.

> Sausage, butter, sugar, cheese and fresh rolls from the commissary were sheer delight. Everyone enjoyed eating them with tea – not the raspberry-flavoured boiling water issued by the prison, but real tea steeped in a mug and poured from an enormous bucket-sized teapot of red copper, a teapot left over from czarist days, a teapot from which Russian revolutionaries of the 19th century might have drunk. ('Committees of the Poor' in Shalamov 1994: 206)

> Unlike the 'free' world 'outside' or the camps, society in prison is always united. In the committees this society found a way to make a positive statement as to the right of every man to live his own life. Such spiritual forces run contrary to all prison regulations and investigatory rules, but they always win out in the end. (Ibid.: 216)

This is why the narrator ultimately prefers going back to prison even to returning home, reuniting with his family or resuming any contact with them while still in the camp. While prison is viewed as the place in which a new collective subject may be constituted, family reunification would only manifest the subject's loss of its former self to itself and others.

> I wrote that I didn't want any packages. If I survive, it'll be without anyone's help. I'll be obligated only to myself. [There's] nothing noble at all [in this]. You and I are not only beyond good and evil, we are also beyond anything human. After all I have seen, I don't want to be obligated to anyone – not even my own wife. ('Captain Tolly's Love' in Shalamov 1994: 329)

While for Shalamov the restoration of families after a camp term is all but impossible, prison provides the possibility both for individual freedom and the formation of new social ties. Shalamov thus agrees with Solzhenitsyn about the possibility of self-assertion and self-improvement in the conditions of incarceration, yet this is only possible in prison and never in a camp.[2]

> 'You know, fellows, it would be a good thing to go home. After all, miracles do happen ...'. It was Glebov, the horse-driver, speaking. He used to be a professor of philosophy and was famous in our barracks for having forgotten his wife's name a month earlier.
> 'I'll tell you the truth', I answered. 'I'd rather go back to prison. I'm not joking. I wouldn't want to go back to my family now. They wouldn't understand me, they couldn't. The things that seem important to them I know to be trivial. And the things that are important to me – the little that is left to me – would be incomprehensible to them. No man should see or know the things that I have seen and known. Prison is another matter altogether. Prison is freedom. It's the only place I have ever known where people spoke their minds without being afraid. Their souls were at rest there. And their bodies rested too, because they didn't have to work. There, every hour of our being had meaning.' ('Epitaph' in Shalamov 1994: 312)

It is this meaning that is the first to disappear in the camp which shocks the incoming inmates with brute and meaningless violence. 'These types of events are pure hits, tearing and piercing subjective continuity and allowing no justification or recall in the psyche' (Malabou 2012b: 29). Shalamov's account of the camps is strikingly similar to Malabou's theory of the traumatised subject: 'History, having been tragic, returns to us as farce. But there is also a third phenomenon, a third embodiment of a historical pattern – in a senseless horror' (Shalamov cited in Toker 2000: 142). In his harrowing testimony 'What I Saw and Understood in the Camp', not included in the standard English edition of *Kolyma Tales*, Shalamov states tersely that 'Stalin was victorious because he was killing innocent people – an organization that would be ten times smaller in number, but an organization nonetheless would have wiped out Stalin in two days' (Shalamov 2008). In the absence of any genuine anti-Stalin organisation, the regime faced no resistance but only the 'angelic patience and slavish submissiveness of the Trotskyites' ('Major Pugachev's Last Battle' in Shalamov 1994: 242), who could not comprehend the reasons for their plight and therefore could not even conceive of resisting it.[3] Just as Malabou's disaffected subjects of trauma are faced with a destructive event that could not be handled by any version of psychoanalytic negation (repression, denial, disavowal), the subjects of the camp could only respond to their plight by assuming the very impossibility of the flight from their condition as their sole identity.

> The absence of any unifying idea undermined the moral resistance of the prisoners to an unusual degree. They were neither enemies of the government nor state criminals, and they died, not even understanding why they had to die. Their self-esteem and bitterness had no point of support. Separated, they perished in the white Kolyma desert from hunger, cold, work, beatings and diseases. They immediately learned not to defend or support each other. This was precisely the goal of the authorities. The souls of those who remained alive were utterly corrupted and their bodies did not possess the qualities necessary for physical labour. (Ibid.: 242)

The meaninglessness of the Terror also accounts for the fact that very few 'political' prisoners ever tried to escape from the camps. If the inmates had indeed been persecuted for a political cause, they would have been able to count on the help of the other supporters of this cause 'on the outside'. Yet, in the absence of any such 'cause' the escaping prisoners were only likely to endanger their friends and family on the outside.

> An escape by a 'political' is always related to the mood of the 'outside' and – like a hunger strike in prison – draws its strength from its connection with the outside. A prisoner must know, and know well in advance, the eventual goal of his escape. What goal could any political have had in 1937? They might try to escape to their family and friends, but that [would have] been a threat to the very lives of [their] friends and family. Someone would have had to conceal him, render him assistance. None of the politicals in 1938 tried to escape. ('The Green Procurator' in Shalamov 1994: 347)

As we have argued above, what made the Terror particularly difficult to make sense of was the fact that it ultimately made no distinction between the victim and the executioner, nonchalantly transferring the latter into the category of the former for no apparent reason. 'Only by memory did I recognise the red-faced Tartar, Mutalov, who had been the only resident in all Chikment, whose two-storied house had an iron roof, and Efremov, the former First Secretary of the Chikment City Council, who had liquidated Mutalov as a class in 1930' ('The Quiet' in Shalamov 1994: 436). When violence no longer accompanied an ideological project, in which friends and enemies were clearly distinguished (as in the Civil War or even the Great Break), but was emancipated from any relation to an idea, it was impossible for the victims of the Terror to recognise themselves even *as* victims, which precluded even the most elementary forms of solidarity that might have enabled resistance. Instead, the senselessness of the camp contributed to the rapid moral degradation of the inmates.

There were four main forces leading to this degradation. The worst was undoubtedly *work*, whose absence in the prison made it such a blissful place. Shalamov repeatedly accurses senseless physical labour and scorns every attempt to valorise it as a strengthening and ennobling activity.

> In the camp we learned to hate physical labour and work in general. ('Dry Rations' in Shalamov 1994: 40)

> In the camp it is work that kills, and anyone who praises it is either a scoundrel or a fool. ('Captain Tolly's Love' in Shalamov 1994: 326)

The second force was the *cold*, to which the inmates at Kolyma were permanently exposed: 'the greatest method for the corruption of the soul was the cold. In the camps of Central Asia people must have held out for longer, it was warmer there' (Shalamov 2008). The third mechanism of dehumanisation was *hunger*: 'All human emotions – love, friendship, envy, concern for one's fellow man, compassion, longing for fame, honesty – had left us with the flesh that had melted from our bodies during their long fast' ('Dry Rations' in Shalamov 1994: 32). The final force of the corruption of souls was *physical violence*, practised by both camp administrators and the criminal population, whose role in the camp we shall consider in detail below: 'A blow can transform an intellectual into an obedient servant of a petty crook. Physical force becomes moral force' ('Red Cross' in Shalamov 1994: 413).

As a result of hard labour, cold, hunger and beatings 'man becomes beast in three weeks' (Shalamov 2008). This dehumanisation leads to a drastic shift in values in the camp, whereby things considered valuable or important on the outside are reduced to insignificance: 'all that smacked of books was forgotten. No one believed in books' ('Condensed Milk' in Shalamov 1994: 82). Conversely, things we are accustomed to taking for granted or ignoring acquire supreme value: 'Hair in camp is a testimony to importance. Almost everyone was shaved bald, so that anyone who had hair was the object of general envy. Combed hair was a peculiar form of protest against life in the camps' ('Descendant of a Decembrist' in Shalamov 1994: 186). Moreover, the things that we would consider horrid accidents actually become blessings for the camp inmate since they might spare him from hard labour: 'Kolya's happiness began the day his hand was blown off' ('The Businessman' in Shalamov 1994: 321).

> Values shift here, in Kolyma, and any one of our concepts – even though its name may be pronounced in the usual way and spelled with the usual letters – may contain some new element or meaning, something for which there is no equivalent on the mainland. Here everything is judged by different standards: customs and habits are unique, and the meaning of every word has changed. ('The Green Procurator' in Shalamov 1994: 343)

One of the most harrowing descriptions of this shift in values is provided in Shalamov's story 'In the Bathhouse', which probes the question of why camp inmates disliked going to the bathhouse and shows how a hygienic and pleasant procedure becomes in the camp yet another method of dehumanisation. Going to the bathhouse entails the mobilisation of the guards, who do not hesitate to take it out on the prisoners, and the cleaning of the barracks, which entails losing valuable items, such as rags used for keeping warm. The time for the bath is taken out of one's rest time after work and even more time is taken by walking to the bathhouse in the village and waiting for one's turn in the cold. Once inside the bathhouse, one is faced with the lack of water and the threat of criminals stealing one's belongings when one is washing oneself. In short, 'the dream of getting clean in the bathhouse is an impossible dream' ('In the Bathhouse' in Shalamov 1994: 340). The most distressing aspect of going to the bathhouse pertains to the question of underwear. In the camp only 'privileged' prisoners, such as trusties and foremen, were entitled to their own 'individual' underwear. Other inmates were handed out 'common' underwear after bathing without the option of selecting the right size or choosing better quality.

> Clean underwear is a pure lottery, and I felt a strange and terrible pity at seeing adult men cry over the injustice of receiving worn-out clean underwear in exchange for dirty good underwear. Nothing can take the mind of a human being off the unpleasantnesses that comprise life. Only vaguely do the convicts realise that, after all, this inconvenience will end the next bathhouse day, that their lives are what's ruined, that there is no reason to worry over some underwear, that they had received the old, good underwear by chance. But no, they quarrel and cry. This is, of course, a manifestation of those psychoses that are characteristic of a convict's every action, of that same 'dementia' which one neuropathologist termed a universal illness.
>
> The spiritual ups and downs of a convict's life have shifted to the point where receiving underwear from a small dark window, leading into the depths of the bathhouse, is an event that transcends the nerves. Having washed themselves, the men gather at the window far in advance of the actual distribution of underwear. Over and over again they discuss in

detail the underwear received last time, the underwear received five years ago at Bamlag. As soon as the board is raised that closes off the small window from within, they rush to it, jostling each other with their slippery, dirty and stinking bodies. (Ibid.: 341)

This fragment features a rare reference by Shalamov to mental illness, specifically psychosis and dementia as 'universal illnesses' of the camp. Yet, the behaviour of the inmates resembles symptoms of a post-traumatic condition as described by Malabou more than it does psychosis in a strict clinical sense. Having shed all morality and dispensed with books, all its social ties undone and its affections muted, the camp subject is only capable of being excited, pleased, unnerved or disappointed by elementary sensations: pleased by warmth, irritated by dampness, hurt by beatings. Everything else, including the fact that his or her life is ruined, leaves the subject markedly *indifferent*.

> We'd all learned meekness and had forgotten how to be surprised. We had no pride, vanity or ambition, and jealousy and passion seemed as alien to us as Mars and trivial in addition. It was much more important to learn to button your pants in the frost. Grown men cried if they weren't able to do that. We understood that death was no worse than life, and we feared neither. We were overwhelmed by indifference. We knew that it was in our power to end this life the very next day and now and again we made that decision, but each time life's trivia would interfere with our plans. Today they would promise an extra kilo of bread as a reward for good work, and it would be simply foolish to commit suicide on such a day. ('Dry Rations' in Shalamov 1994: 33)

BITTER INDIFFERENCE

Indifference is the key concept in *Kolyma Tales*, occurring in almost every story and attaining a paradigmatic status in Shalamov's work. As we have seen in the previous chapter, Malabou makes 'indifference of life to life' the key feature of her figure of the traumatised subject, irrespective of whether the trauma in question was biological or political (Malabou 2012b: 38). Indeed, in Shalamov's testimony it is impossible to distinguish between the two: while camp imprisonment as such was evidently a 'political' trauma, its effects were the result of physical conditions such as pellagra, resulting from the cold, hunger, hard labour and beatings.

> Envy, like all our feelings, had been lulled and weakened by hunger. We lacked the strength to experience emotions, to seek easier work, to walk, to ask, to beg. External circumstances alone were capable of jolting us

out of apathy and distracting us from slowly approaching death. It had to be an external and not an internal force. Inside there was only an empty scorching sensation and we were indifferent to everything, making plans no further than the next day. ('Condensed Milk' in Shalamov 1994: 80)

Indifference is the outward manifestation of that void of subjectivity that remains when one's form of life is destroyed by the senseless trauma of the camp and the subject remains the bearer of this destruction within itself. The subject is indifferent not as a matter of resistance (for example, concealing its emotions from the guards or the criminals), but simply because that positive form of life, which *could* feel joy or despair, show interest or lack thereof, has become annihilated with nothing positive to replace it. Indifference is what remains to the subject who no longer differs from the others, who cannot be distinguished in terms of some positive predicates, who is like any other because it is no longer a self. In Shalamov's account, this descent into indifference was accompanied by the complete renunciation of subjective autonomy and the subordination to the will of the other: foreman, guards, administrators.

We realised we were at the end of our rope, and we simply let matters take their course. Nothing bothered us any more, and we breathed freely in the fist of another man's will. We didn't even concern ourselves with staying alive. Our spiritual calm, achieved by the dulling of the senses, was always guarded by our subordination to another's will. ('Dry Rations' in Shalamov 1994: 40)

Besides being the paradigmatic mode of the existence of camp inmates, indifference is also projected by Shalamov beyond the camp on two occasions in the text. First, Shalamov's interlocutor in 'The Used Book Dealer', Fleming, an imprisoned NKVD officer, offers a theory about the Show Trials of the 1930s that interprets the defendants' infamous confessions as a result of pharmacological interventions, the use of will-suppressants that rendered the defendants indifferent to their fate.

The trials of the thirties. You know how they prepared them? I was in Leningrad at the time. The preparation of the trials was all chemistry, medicine, pharmacology. They had more will-suppressants than you could shake a stick at. You don't think that if such suppressants exist, they wouldn't use them? It would have been too human to possess chemical will-suppressants and not use them on the 'internal front'. This and only this is the secret of the trials of the thirties, the open trials, open to foreign correspondents and to any Feuchtwanger. There were no 'doubles' in those trials. The secret of the trials was the secret of pharmacology. ('The Used Book Dealer' in Shalamov 1994: 261)

Thus, while the low-level 'Trotskyites' were rendered indifferent to their existence through the senseless deprivations of the camps, the high-level 'Trotskyites' were made similarly disaffected through the medical suppression of will that made them indifferent to their dignity and ultimately their own death. Irrespectively of whether this theory is plausible (and it is at least as plausible as the existing explanations that actually tend to mystify the issue even further), what is more important is the sheer generality of the phenomenon that it seeks to explain: the lack of resistance and indifference to one's situation that characterised the Soviet elite and the underclasses alike.

Second, Shalamov notes the indifference of the wider Soviet society towards those returning from the camps – neither a positive reception, which was still dangerous, nor a negative one, which might have been expected for that same reason, but simply an indifferent acknowledgement of presence not unlike the one the inmates exchanged between themselves in the camp. Since the Terror targeted so many categories of the population for no apparent reason other than their 'counter-revolutionary activity', it was impossible to predict what group would be the next victim and to establish one's relation to this group in advance. Instead, Soviet society indifferently observed sworn enemy states becoming allies and then enemies again, the formerly glorified Soviet party elite executed as hideous enemies of the people, other enemies returning from the camps to unmask those who had sent them there – all of these events having as much or less sense than natural disasters and hence treated accordingly.

> There was another significant factor that might explain the indifference of the populace to those who had returned from the prisons. So many people had spent time in prison that there probably was not a family in the country in which some family member or friend had not been 'repressed'. Once the saboteurs had been eliminated, it was the turn of the well-to-do peasants. After the kulaks came the 'Trotskyites' and the 'Trotskyites' were followed by persons with German surnames. Then a crusade against the Jews was on the point of being declared. All this reduced people to total indifference toward anyone who had been marked by any part of the criminal code. ('The Green Procurator' in Shalamov 1994: 350)

The key question is what remains of the subject after this descent into disaffection: what is it that *is* indifferent? What survives the annihilation of identity? It is evidently nothing but the sheer facticity of existence or, in Agamben's terms, bare life, understood in the precise sense of the remainder of life after all its positive properties have been subtracted

(1998: 6–7). In *Remnants of Auschwitz* Agamben terms this deformed life 'survival', 'a kind of absolute biopolitical substance', in which *zoe* is radically separated from *bios* (1999b: 156).

> It is a matter of dividing animal life from organic life, the human from inhuman, the witness from the Muselmann, conscious life from vegetative life. Biopower's supreme ambition is to produce, in a human body, the absolute separation of the living being and the speaking being, *zoe* and *bios*, the inhuman and the human – survival. (Ibid.: 155–6)

Similarly, Shalamov's texts testify to the emergence, as the effect of the senseless trauma of the camps, of a form of life reduced entirely to bare life, a life that is indifferent to everything except its own survival.

> To live, to survive – that's the task at hand. We mustn't stumble. Life is more serious than you think. ('The Life of Engineer Kipreev' in Shalamov 1994: 465)

> 'If I survive, I'll write a story about it. I even have a title: "The Snake Charmer". How do you like it?' 'It's good but first you have to survive. That's the main thing.' ('The Snake Charmer' in Shalamov 1994: 87)

Yet, the relation of life to its own survival is more complicated than a mere imperative. In fact, survival is not and cannot be posited as an ethical task, because the subject who could have assumed such a task has already been extinguished. It is not a matter of full subjective investment in one's own survival that turns it into a project. According to Shalamov, any such 'exercise of will' is precisely what did *not* take place in the camps: as we have seen, the indifferent inmates 'didn't concern [themselves] with staying alive'. Indifference is general and complete and extends even to survival itself, yet paradoxically it is also what enables survival by, as it were, withdrawing the subject from all possible identities and relations, permitting it to concentrate on *persevering* in its sheer being.

> This moral and spiritual dumbness had one good aspect – I was not afraid of death and could think of it calmly. More than the thought about death I was preoccupied with thoughts about dinner, about the cold, about the difficulty of work, in short, about life. But was it even thought? It was some kind of primitive instinctual thinking. (Shalamov cited in Podoroga 2013)

What desires to survive is not the subject as a rational or affective agent, who, as we have seen, is only present in its absence, but life as such in its auto-affective immanence, its pure givenness to itself.

> I could not afford to lose even the slightest chance in the search for luck – this judgement came from my body and its exhausted muscles, not from experience or intelligence. As in beasts, the will was subordinate to instinct. ('Descendant of a Decembrist' in Shalamov 1994: 185)

> Potashnikov had no fear of death, but he could not rid himself of a passionate secret desire, a last stubbornness – to live. He didn't want to die here in the frost under the boots of the guards, in the barracks with its swearing, dirt and total indifference written on every face. He bore no grudge for people's indifference, for he had long since comprehended the source of that spiritual dullness. The same frost that transformed a man's spit into ice in mid-air also penetrated the soul. If bones could freeze, then the brain could also be dulled and the soul could freeze over. And the soul shuddered and froze – perhaps to remain frozen forever. Potashnikov had lost everything except the desire to survive, to endure the cold and remain alive. ('Carpenters' in Shalamov 1994: 17)

Shalamov inverts the central opposition in the humanist and moralist discourse on the camps, according to which it was precisely the presence of conscience, morality and ethics (or religion) that enabled one to survive in the camps. In his account, conscience, morality and ethics were the *first* to take leave in Kolyma and, yet, one survived, not by suppressing animal instincts but precisely by *expressing* them. Human beings survived longer than animals such as horses, not because they were human, which they no longer were, but because they were physically stronger.

> [A] horse weakens and falls ill much quicker than a human being. It often seems, and it's probably true, that man was able to raise himself from the animal kingdom because he has more physical endurance than any of the other animals. A horse cannot endure even a month of the local winter life in a cold stall if it's worked hard hours in subzero weather. But man lives on. Perhaps he lives by virtue of his hopes? But he does not have any hope. He is saved by a drive for self-preservation, a tenacious clinging to life, a physical tenacity to which his entire consciousness is subordinated. He lives on the same things as a bird or dog, but he clings more strongly to life than they do. His is a greater endurance than that of any animal. ('Snake Charmer' in Shalamov 1994: 88)

On a number of occasions, Shalamov goes even further than attributing survival to animal instincts, extending it to *all* beings, including plants and even stones.

> Something stronger than death would not permit him to die. Love? Bitterness? *No, a person lives by virtue of the same reasons as a tree, a stone, a dog.* It was this that Andreev had grasped, had sensed with every

fibre of his being precisely here at the city transit prison camp during the typhoid quarantine. ('Typhoid Quarantine' in Shalamov 1994: 153; my emphasis).

The reasons in question have nothing to do not only with human will or moral values but also with animal instincts, which evidently are inapplicable to plants and stones. What survives is bare life in the sense of pure being, not being reduced to its natural properties (as Agamben's figure of bare life is often misunderstood), but being stripped of *all* positive properties, including the ostensibly natural ones (Agamben 1998: 182, 188).

It is from this perspective of bare life that we must understand Shalamov's key concept of bitterness. Bitterness is the last affect that remains to the dehumanised subject, the one thing that appears to survive the descent into generalised indifference, so that bitterness itself becomes indifferent.

> In his heart there was nothing but bitterness and his spiritual wounds could not so easily be healed. They were never to heal. ('Typhoid Quarantine' in Shalamov 1994: 154)
>
> Did he think of his family? No. Of freedom? No. Did he recite poetry from memory? No. Did he recall the past? No. He lived in an *indifferent bitterness*, and nothing more. ('Typhoid Quarantine' in Shalamov 1994: 159; my emphasis. Translation modified)[4]
>
> I had little warmth. Little flesh was left on my bones, just enough for bitterness – the last human emotion; it was closer to the bone. ('Sententious' in Shalamov 1994: 284)

At first glance, bitterness and indifference clearly exclude each other: one is not truly indifferent if one is bitter about something. Yet, this is only true if we understand bitterness in subjective and intentional terms as an affect marked by sense or motivated by some cause. However, Shalamov's bitterness must be strictly distinguished from hate or anger, which, as we shall see below, are rather signs of a temporary or tentative *revival* of the subject. In contrast to these, bitterness does not refer to the subject's emotions but to the sheer facticity of its existence amid the assault on its life by the dehumanising forces of the camp. In 'Sententious' Shalamov speaks of 'an existence that had no formula and could not be called life' ('Sententious' in Shalamov 1994: 285). This life that indifferently persists in its abandonment to the deprivations of the camp is indeed only *barely* life, life *as not* life, the zero degree of life, a life that lives its own death but lives it anyway. It is this life that is bitter, but not bitter *about* something – bitter is simply *how it is*, its manner of being in the cold, hunger, violence and exhaustion of the camps.

Shalamov's bitterness consists entirely in the living being's sensation of its own suffering that it cannot (yet or any longer) subjectivise, comprehend or rationalise but simply experiences as given. It is nothing but the sense of survival itself, the sheer fact of the body sensing its own perseverance in being through its suffering (cf. Henry 2003: 200–1). As an elementary experience of life sensing itself as suffering, this ontological tenacity is prior even to indifference, since there is nothing yet in this auto-affective nucleus of subjectivity to be different from or indifferent to. In Shalamov's description of the gradual coming to life of a goner in 'Sententious' bitterness is the threshold that separates the 'almost life' from death. 'Bitterness was the last feeling with which man departed into non-being, into the world of the dead' ('Sententious' in Shalamov 1994: 290). Indifference comes second, when bare life leaves the confinement within its own bitterness, which is 'closest to the bone', and begins to relate itself to its environment. 'And I didn't die. With increasing indifference and without bitterness I began to watch the cold red sub, the bare mountaintops where the rocks, the turns of the river, the trees were all sharp and unfriendly' (ibid.: 286).

THE ETHICS OF SURVIVAL

Insofar as survival unfolds on the level of pure being, it is not attainable by either moral effort or natural instinct, and can therefore not be posited as a task or form the basis of any ethics. A 'quasi-naturalist' ethics that makes perseverance in bare life the supreme task is entirely alien to Shalamov (cf. Des Pres 1980; see also Agamben 1999b: 92–4). First, his camp prose is entirely devoid of any valorisation of nature in any form; in anything, nature is often personified and viewed as complicit in the inmates' suffering: 'Nature in the North is not impersonal or indifferent; it is in conspiracy with those who sent us here' ('A Child's Drawings' in Shalamov 1994: 76). Second, to make of survival an ethical task would entail the valorisation of physical strength that permits one to survive the adverse conditions of the camp. Yet, such a valorisation would be obscenely complicit with the values that constitute the camp as such as a system of forced labour.

> In the eyes of the state and its representatives a physically strong person was better, more moral, more valuable than a weak person. He fulfilled his quota, that is, carried out his chief duty to the state and society and was therefore respected by all. Thanks to his physical advantages, such a person was transformed into a moral force in the resolution of the

numerous everyday questions of camp life. Of course, he remained a moral force only as long as he remained a physical force. ('Dry Rations' in Shalamov 1994: 34)

Thus, if there were such a thing as the morality of survival, it would be the morality *of the camp* and not of the inmates. Finally, there cannot be a naturalist ethics of survival, because survival in the camp is not a 'natural' category that could be contrasted with the 'cultural' constructs of 'good life', culture, civilisation, and so on. On the contrary, for Shalamov the camp is an *extremely unnatural* situation, a horrifying experiment in dehumanisation that can by no means serve as the site for testing one's natural strength. The camp is neither the place where morality may survive against all odds, as in Solzhenitsyn's account, nor a place that could produce its own quasi-morality of survival in adverse conditions, but rather a place that is *as amoral as it is unnatural*. This is why the experience of the Gulag is *totally* negative: all the camp can teach is that it should not exist and the one whom it has taught this should not exist either. This explains why for every reference to 'having to survive' in Shalamov's texts we find a reference to no longer being concerned about staying alive.

This indifference is also explained by the fact that one's survival in the camp was radically contingent and depended more on pure chance than on whatever effort the subject was still capable of. This was the lesson of Shalamov's own experience that he translated into various scenes in *Kolyma Tales*. In 'Handwriting', an inmate named Chris is, thanks to his calligraphic handwriting, 'hired' by the camp investigator to copy files. We gradually come to realise that what he is copying are death sentences during the winter of 1937–8, when hundreds of thousands of camp victims were executed. Chris recognises this fact with the by now familiar indifference.

> Even before no one has ever returned from these journeys, but now no one even gave a thought to these nocturnal affairs. If they were preparing a group, there was nothing to be done. The work was too hard to leave a thought for anything else. ('Handwriting' in Shalamov 1994: 318)

One day Chris's own name appears in the lists but he ends up saved by the investigator who burns his file instead of handing his scribe over for execution.

> Only many years later did [Chris] realise that the burned file had been his own. Many of Chris's friends were shot. The investigator was also shot. But Chris was still alive and at least once every few years he would remember the burning folder and the investigator's decisive fingers as he

> tore up his 'case' – a present to the doomed from the giver of doom. Chris had a life-saving, calligraphic handwriting. (Ibid.: 319)

This gesture of mercy from the giver of doom remains inexplicable to Chris and the reader: it can hardly be due to the investigator's desire to spare someone endowed with calligraphic handwriting. The life-saving event remains as contingent, accidental and senseless as the life-threatening sojourn in the camp. On a number of occasions, however, survival is portrayed as going beyond mere ontological tenacity and becomes almost a subjective achievement, something to take pride in.

> One day Andreev realised with amazement that he had survived. It was extremely difficult to get up from his bunk but he was able to do it. The main thing was that he didn't have to work and could simply lie prone. It was at this precise moment that he realised he felt no fear and placed no value on his life. He also knew that he had passed through a great test and had survived. Everything – love, energy, ability – has been crushed and trampled. Any justification the mind might seek was false, a lie, and Andreev knew this. Only the instinct of the beast could and did suggest a way out.
>
> Precisely here, on these Cyclopian shelves, Andreev realised that he was worth something, that he could respect himself. He was still alive, and he had neither betrayed, nor sold out anyone during the investigation or in the camp. ('Typhoid Quarantine' in Shalamov 1994: 153)

On the one hand, this fragment invokes the already familiar themes of survival being purely instinctive ('beastly'), of the camp victim being overcome by indifference (the lack of fear, no value placed on one's own life), of the inapplicability of all ethical criteria in the camp situation. Yet, we also observe the emergence of a new theme, of survival as a 'great test', after which one could 'respect' oneself as 'worth' something. What merits respect is evidently not survival itself but survival that is not accompanied by betraying or 'selling out' another inmate. We see here the nucleus of an ethics that is never fully explicated in Shalamov's writings but nonetheless pervades all the stories of the *Kolyma Tales* cycle, albeit usually negatively, as the condemnation of or the expression of revulsion before various practices. The sole maxim of this ethics is that *survival is only worth something if it is not attained at the cost of the survival of the other.*

> I could not denounce a fellow convict no matter what he did. I refused to seek the job of foreman, which provided a chance to remain alive, for the worst thing in a camp was the forcing of one's own or anyone else's will on another person who was a convict just like oneself. Our inability to

> use certain types of 'weapons' weakened us in comparison with certain of our neighbours who shared berths with us. We learned to be satisfied with little things and rejoice at small successes. ('Dry Rations' in Shalamov 1994: 34)

This is an ethics that evidently goes beyond the imperative of sheer survival and sometimes even directly contradicts it. At first glance, there is again a tension between this imperative of not surviving in the place of the other and the principle of generalised indifference as the main mode of subjectivation in the camp. A completely indifferent subject would not feel such an aversion to denouncing another convict or becoming a foreman, though he would indeed be indifferent to any hypothetical benefits of such actions. Nonetheless, there is no contradiction between the refusal to denounce others or claim authority over them and Shalamov's persistent invocation of indifference as the paradigmatic mode of existence of the camp subject. On the contrary, it is precisely *because* the subject has become indifferent to everything that it is no longer *tempted* by the benefits of good life that could be gained by denouncing or supervising others. It is precisely *because* of indifference that Shalamov's protagonist can reject the soup with the meat of the puppy killed by the criminals despite his overwhelming hunger ('A Day Off' in Shalamov 1994: 106). It is not the surreptitious return of morality that enables this refusal but rather its *withdrawal*.

On the contrary, unethical action, from killing the puppy in question to killing the inmate to obtain his home clothes, arises not out of indifference but out of the *lack* thereof, of clinging to the comforts or pleasures of life too tightly, of not having abandoned them completely. For Shalamov evil is not a result of moral indifference but of excessive attachment to difference. Ethics as a doctrine of *good* life is entirely useless in the camps, whose subject is *bare* life subtracted from every idea of the good. Any commitment to good life can therefore only weaken one and any hope for a better life can only accelerate the corruption of one's soul. In a hyperbolic form this paradox is presented in the statement of Volodya Dobrovoltsev in *Epitaph*.

> 'As for me,' he said in a calm unhurried voice, 'I'd like to have my arms and legs cut off and become a human stump – no arms or legs. Then I'd be strong enough to spit in their faces for everything they're doing to us.' ('Epitaph' in Shalamov 1994: 313)

It is as if not being completely maimed, wounded or dismembered still creates false hopes (expressed by the other protagonists of the story sitting around the stove on a Christmas night) of returning home, reuniting with family, resuming one's profession, which only serve to corrupt one's soul and undermine one's survival. One is only strong enough to survive, when every thought of rehabilitation and return to good life with its values is revealed as an illusion: 'Hope always shackles the convict. Hope is slavery. A man who hopes for something alters his conduct and is more frequently dishonest than a man that has ceased to hope' ('The Life of Engineer Kipreev' in Shalamov 1994: 468). In contrast, the subject that has abandoned all hope and fully assumed its own devastation, whose life is no longer anything more than indifferent survival, is simultaneously granted strength to survive and spared from the temptation to survive in the place of another.

Survival only assumes the status of an ethics, when it becomes the sole possible *ethos*, that is, dwelling place, of the camp inmate, when there is no longer anything that one survives *for*. Survival is not a means to any end, nor is it an end in itself, in relation to which all means are justified. As the subject with its ends and means, its culture and its nature, is crushed by the camp, what survives this devastation is life itself in its obstinate auto-affection, its persistent sensing itself as suffering. This bitter life does not belong to the subject and cannot be contained within it, but rather traverses its being, comes, goes and sometimes comes back again.

> Life was entering into him and passing out of him, and he was dying. But life came back, his eyes opened, thoughts appeared. Only desires were absent. The dead lived again. And why not? ('Cherry Brandy' in Shalamov 1994: 70)

> Life entered by herself, mistress in her own home. He had not called her, but she entered his body, his brain, she came like verse, like inspiration. (Ibid.: 71)

If what survives is not the subject but the bare life that exceeds and overflows it, then it is impossible to survive in the place of the other, since this life knows neither self nor the other. Survival that lets the other die in one's place extinguishes this bare life as much as one's own death would, and even if it appears to lead to something like a 'good life' for its practitioner, this life remains contaminated by death. Thus, the imperative of not surviving in the place of another is not a vestige of any 'normal' ethics in the abnormal conditions of the camp but rather the nucleus of an ethics attuned to the truth of the destructibility of the subject that the camp has revealed. Every other ethics is grossly inadequate for the camp and the most innocuous ethical norm may reveal itself as obscene or murderous in its conditions. What arouses the greatest contempt in Shalamov is one's attempt to live a *good life*, practising one's code of conduct while ignoring the existence of the camp that has rendered all ethics inoperative. In 'Shock Therapy' the neuropathologist Peter Ivanovich receives the case of one Merzlakov, whose rib was broken during the beating by the guards and who continues to simulate a broken spine by bending himself in two in order not to have to return to the camp, where he would certainly die of hunger, cold or exhaustion. Peter Ivanovich is immediately onto him and seeks to expose him as a faker despite the indifference or even outright hostility of his co-workers to this idea.

> [Peter] Ivanovich spent more than half of his time exposing fakers. He, of course, understood the reasons for their conduct. Peter Ivanovich had himself recently been a prisoner and he was not surprised by the childish stubbornness of the fakers or the primitiveness of their tricks. It was not that he lacked pity for people but he was more of a doctor than a human being; first and foremost he was a specialist. He understood his task of exposing cheaters – not from any lofty, socio-governmental point of view and not from the viewpoint of morality. Rather, he saw in this activity a worthy application of his knowledge, his psychological ability to set traps, into which hungry, half-insane people were to fall for the greater glory of science. In exposing any faker, Peter Ivanovich experienced a deep satisfaction. He regarded it as testimony from life that he was a good doctor who had not yet lost his qualifications, but, on the contrary, had sharpened them, who could still 'do it'. ('Shock Therapy' in Shalamov 1994: 119–20)

Peter Ivanovich is the embodiment of Shalamov's version of Arendt's (1963) famous thesis on the banality of evil. What makes him evil is not any particular cruelty (even though the 'shock-therapeutic' procedure of proof he invents is cruel indeed) or the lack of pity, but precisely his commitment to his profession and concern about maintaining his qualifications, when faced with the bare life of the inmates, the bare life that he had occasion to be reduced to himself. It is precisely his vindication of his ability to 'do it', be a good doctor, return to professional life after having been in the camps, that contrasts so starkly with the indifferent bare life, to which the inmates stick to in trying to delay their return to the camp for another week or even a day. In this affirmation of good life medical science itself is perverted and becomes an instrument of torture, as it was in the camps all over the world during the twentieth century and continues to be today. It is this degradation of their science that so disgusts Peter Ivanovich's peers when they are faced with his enthusiasm in exposing Merzlakov.

'He's a faker, Seryozha,' said Peter Ivanovich, taking the surgeon by the arm as they were leaving the ward.

The surgeon withdrew his arm.

'Maybe,' he said with a disgusted frown. 'Good luck in exposing him. I hope you get your kicks out of it.' ('Shock Therapy' in Shalamov 1994: 121)

What Peter Ivanovich justifies as mere application of professional ethics finally ends in a hideous act of torture, whereby Merzlakov undergoes the injection of camphor oil right into the bloodstream, which produces sudden painful seizures akin to epilepsy. Having undergone this ordeal and failed the test, Merzlakov is 'ready to check out' (ibid.: 125). The border between the camp and the outside world turns out not to be so definitive, as it happens that on the outside doctors can make one's existence as hellish as the guards, simply by following their professional ethics, which, come to think of it, the guards are also following.[5]

Another example of banal evil is Lunin in 'Descendant of a Decembrist', a jovial, good-natured camp doctor (also an inmate but living in much better conditions), who invites the narrator in to reminisce about historic sites of Moscow and boast of his sexual exploits, while completely ignoring the narrator's hunger and the fundamental injustice of the very setting they are both in. Eventually, the story takes a darker turn as Lunin rashly decides to perform ulcer operations on the patients, who are too weak to survive them and eventually die. The title of the story is sadly ironic: Lunin turns out to be the descendant of one of the participants of the Decembrist uprising of 1825, Mikhail Lunin. The Decembrists, young army officers from aristocratic families who rebelled against Emperor Nicholas I due to their disgust at the indignity suffered by Russian peasants and the urban poor, exemplified the universalist disposition, in which one suspends one's own particular interests in order to struggle on behalf of the other. Lunin the descendant is a paradigm of the diametrically opposed disposition of pure particularism that is entirely devoid of any responsiveness, let alone responsibility, toward the other, not only the other inmates, but also his wife, who obtains his early release and reinstatement at the university only to be abandoned by her husband immediately afterwards ('Descendant of a Decembrist' in Shalamov 1994: 197–9).

The third example of survival through pure particularism is the already mentioned ex-NKVD operative Fleming. Finding himself in the camp, Fleming is spared some of the shock by virtue of his prior knowledge of what went on there and his readiness to struggle only for his own life, ignoring the plight of others.

This had been Fleming's defensive reflex against Kolyma – the omnivorous greed. A lack of spiritual fastidiousness acquired behind the desk of a political investigator had also served to prepare him and cushion the shock of his Kolyma fall. As he fell, he perceived no abyss, for he had known all this even earlier and the knowledge saved him by weakening his moral torments, if such torments had ever existed. Fleming experienced no additional spiritual traumas, he witnessed the worst and indifferently watched those next to him perish. Prepared to struggle only for his own life, he saved that life, but in his soul there remained a dark footprint. ('Used Book Dealer' in Shalamov 1994: 273).

These three characters demonstrate the way the camp performs its work of the 'corruption of souls' even on those who are spared its worst privations. What corrupts the souls of these figures is their desire to cling to the existence of the 'normal' world with its ethics and codes, its knowledge and desires, its differences and distinctions. Yet, it is precisely this normal world that ends up obliterated in the camps and acting on its 'norms' turns arguably minor egotistical figures such as Lunin, Fleming or Peter Ivanovich, whose sole sins are 'all too human' vanity, greed and professional pride, into outright monsters whose 'good life' in the camps comes at the expense of the suffering of others and is for this reason irrevocably tainted by death.

THE INHUMAN

Repulsive as these figures as, they are not yet at the bottom of camp life. This is the position Shalamov reserves for the 'thieves' (*vory*), or the criminal population of the camps, which in the 1930s received relatively lenient treatment from the authorities as 'socially proximate' to the victorious proletariat (unlike the bourgeois intelligentsia, kulaks or priests) and were frequently entrusted with supervising the 'politicals' in the camps. One of the most striking aspects of Shalamov's prose is his presentation of the criminal world, which contrasts sharply with the 'humanist' reading that has a long tradition in Russian literature, dating back to Dostoyevsky's *Notes from the House of the Dead* (2004 [1862]) and Chekhov's *Journey to Sakhalin* (2007 [1893]). Shalamov explicitly and starkly contradicts this sympathetic approach, bluntly declaring on many occasions that the 'thieves are not human'.

> In his *Notes from the House of the Dead* Dostoyevsky never knew anyone from the true criminal world. He would never have allowed himself to express sympathy for that world. The evil acts committed by criminals in camp are innumerable. The unfortunates are those from whom the thief steals their last rags, confiscates their last coin. The working man

is afraid to complain, for he sees that the criminals are stronger than the camp authorities. The thief beats the working man and forces him to work. Tens of thousands of people have been beaten to death by thieves. Hundreds of thousands of people who have been in the camps are permanently seduced by the ideology of these criminals and have ceased to be people. Something criminal has entered into their souls forever. Thieves and their morality have left an indelible mark on the soul of each. The authorities are still human beings and the human element in them does survive. The criminals are not human. ('The Red Cross' in Shalamov 1994: 411)

Why does Shalamov so unequivocally deny humanity to the criminals in a statement so completely at odds with most of the Gulag prose? It cannot simply be that he was more exposed to the criminal world than Dostoyevsky, Chekhov or even Solzhenitsyn, although this is also important. In fact, the criminals play a key role in Shalamov's construction of the camp as a negative experience, an experience of utter dehumanisation. The thieves are 'not human' because they *voluntarily engage in their own dehumanisation* and assist in the dehumanisation of others, who are drawn to servitude for the criminals by threats of violence, desire for protection or the attraction of the relative well-being of the thieves in comparison with regular inmates. 'The criminal world, the habitual criminals whose tastes and habits are reflected in the total life-pattern of Kolyma, are mainly responsible for this corruption of the human soul' ('Red Cross' in Shalamov 1994: 413). The thieves make the camp, the site of the production of *bare* life, their ethos, their form of *good life*. The camp, in which every form of life (*bios*) is reduced to the pure facticity of survival (*zoe*), is for the criminals in itself the proper mode of *bios*. They are *at home* in the dehumanising space of the camp and this is why they are, for Shalamov, *logically* not human, since no human being could ever be at home in a place where his or her humanity was annihilated.

The humanist valorisation of or at least sympathy for the criminals arguably arose out of the fascination with their transgressive mode of being, their distancing from the law, which, particularly in nineteenth-century Russia, was widely perceived to be itself at quite some distance from justice. Yet, Shalamov's writings on the criminal world demonstrate the vacuity of such transgression: by breaking the law criminals actually uphold it, proving its normal functioning by taking exception from it. Unlike revolutionaries who want to dispense with the system as it is, the representatives of the underworld do not want the law to cease to exist, but only to benefit from its momentary violation. In the camps the criminals willingly uphold the system they appear to distance themselves from, breaking its prescriptions without questioning their authority and thus making their own existence conditional upon its continued operation. Moreover, in the conditions of the camp, the system which makes the exception its own norm (Agamben 1998: 170), in which 'everything is possible', how can the observance of the law be distinguished from its transgression? 'The law, inasmuch as it simply coincides with reality, is absolutely unobservable, and unobservability is the originary figure of the norm' (Agamben 2005b: 105). The camp makes every discourse of transgression a priori vain.

In his reading of the criminal world in *The Gulag Archipelago* (2007: 201, 261–6, 291, 381) Solzhenitsyn largely agreed with Shalamov's interpretation, yet with an important caveat. While Shalamov's presentation of the thieves is almost metaphysical in its insistence on their absolute, unadulterated evil, Solzhenitsyn opts for a more historical-ideological reading and approaches the participation of the thieves in the running of the camps since the early 1930s as a result of the purposeful policy of the Soviet regime, for whom common criminals were indeed 'socially closer' than pre-revolutionary intelligentsia, priests or bourgeoisie. The 'romantic' valorisation of the criminals that Shalamov observed in the Soviet literature of the period of the Great Break was for Solzhenitsyn not an effect of a misplaced re-invocation of pre-revolutionary humanism and fascination with the marginal and the subaltern, but rather a new and unprecedented phenomenon proper to Soviet history, whereby the ruling regime found its true social base in the underworld, on which it relied in the oppression of the Russian society, culture and tradition. Thus, what was truly criminal for Solzhenitsyn was the Soviet system itself, whose ideology rejected traditional Russian values and forms of life. It is not surprising that such a regime, whose own origins were in the underground party, not averse to engaging in criminal acts to fund its activities, would find more in common with the criminal underworld than with the bearers of the values it rejected. For Solzhenitsyn, the Soviet system's cooperation with criminals revealed the truth of its biopolitical ambition: the New Soviet Person was indeed created and it was a good old criminal.

For an anti-Stalinist communist like Shalamov, Solzhenitsyn's conservative diatribes against the revolution and the valorisation of nation or religion were completely alien and morally suspect (see Soloviev 2011). He did not view the thieves' world as the product of the Soviet system or the policy of reforging, even though he did ridicule their 'governmental function as proletarian friends of the people' ('The Life of Engineer Kipreev' in Shalamov 1994: 467). Instead, he approached it as a 'non-human' way of life that is irreducible to any ideology, system or policy. The criminal was not a product of communist ideology but of the violence that freed itself from all ideological content and constraints.[6] Nonetheless, Shalamov's denial of humanity to the criminals still appears striking. We are accustomed to think that dehumanisation is the most violent gesture there is, practised precisely by the totalitarian regimes that made the camps their *modus operandi*. Yet, if the camp is dehumanising, can the dehumanisers themselves be human? For Shalamov, as we have seen, even the 'authorities' have a 'human element' in them – it may be that despite fulfilling orders they are not themselves 'at home' in the camp and do not enjoy the power it gives them. The thieves, on the other hand, are presented by Shalamov as the true *masters* of the camps, since they enthusiastically engage in the labour of corruption of the inmates through violence, threats or temptations that the guards could never undertake by themselves. In addition to the deprivation of freedom, subjection to slave labour, starvation and cold, within the camp barracks the inmates also were subjected to robbery, rape, torture and murder that facilitated the dissolution of morality, solidarity and empathy, and the descent into the bitter indifference of survival.

> The intellectual convict is crushed by the camp. Everything he valued is ground into the dust while civilization and culture drop from him within weeks. The intellectual becomes a coward and his own brain provides a 'justification' of his own actions. He can persuade himself of anything, attach himself to either side in a quarrel. The intellectual sees in the criminal world 'teachers of life', fighters for the 'people's rights'. A blow can transform an intellectual into an obedient servant of a petty crook. Physical force becomes moral force. ('Red Cross' in Shalamov 1994: 413)

It would therefore be incorrect to view Shalamov's denial of humanity to camp criminals as a gesture of dehumanisation that in a certain sense repeats the logic of the camps. Shalamov simply observes that those who keep the site of dehumanisation running must be always already dehumanised themselves. Moreover, when he makes this statement, we must recall that it comes from someone who has *also* been dehumanised and is himself at least not fully human. As Valery Podoroga (2013) reminds us in his perceptive reading of Shalamov, 'there are no people at all in the Gulag'. Indeed, there are only those whose humanity has been destroyed and those who have destroyed their own humanity and continue to destroy the humanity of others. Perhaps this is all there is to the difference between the human and the inhuman: while the human being suffers its dehumanisation, the inhuman being enjoys it.

Shalamov, or the Negative Experience

REVIVAL

The fervent pages Shalamov devotes to the criminals are furthest away from the indifference discussed and professed in most other camp stories. Instead, in these texts we observe the emergence of a negative affect that testifies to a certain rebirth of the subject, the momentary and tentative ascent from the bitter indifference of survival to the world of differences and distinctions. In the story 'Sententious' Shalamov charts the narrator's 'return from the dead', in which bitter indifference is succeeded by fear and envy.

> Then came fear, not a strong fear, but nevertheless a fear of losing the salvation of this life and world, of losing the tall cold sky and the aching pain in the worn-out muscles. I realised I was afraid of leaving here for the mines. ('Sententious' in Shalamov 1994: 287)

Insofar as it is focused on particular objects, fear is the opposite of indifference: the subject can only fear insofar as it is not indifferent to the world but exists in it by means of making distinctions. What follows fear is envy.

> Envy was the name of the next feeling that returned to me. I envied my dead friends who had died in '38. I envied those of my neighbours who had something to chew or smoke. I didn't envy the camp chief, the foreman, the work brigade leader; that was a different world altogether. (Ibid.: 287)

Similarly to fear, the sentiment of envy emerges as a result of the return of the subject to the world, its heightened awareness of its situation, the difference of its lot from those around it. The resurrection of the goner brings back particular and specific features, the differences that were negated in the subject's withdrawal into the bitter indifference of survival. If indifference was the condition of survival, then the return of the experience of difference (between day and night, work and rest, tastes, smells, colours, and so on) is only possible when survival is at least momentarily no longer at stake.

There are a number of occasions in *Kolyma Tales* of the periodic revival of such sentiments, momentary and fragile reappearances of the human amid general and complete dehumanisation. In 'The Lepers' Shalamov reports a practice of shaving new arrivals in the camps. To add more humiliation to the process, the camp administration assigned men to shave women and the other way round. The male barber at the camp begged his female acquaintance to do it herself: 'He could not accept that his life was ruined, that these amusements of the camp authorities were nothing but dirty foam in a terrible kettle, where he himself was boiled away' (Shalamov 1994: 180; translation modified). The sentiment of shame, which Giorgio Agamben (1999b: 87–135) analysed, notably also in the context of the camps, as the fundamental attunement of the subject, appears in Shalamov's testimony only momentarily, as if instinctively or automatically, as something almost forgotten yet *not quite*, something capable of resurfacing from under the general indifference. It is important to note that for Shalamov these traces do not testify to the 'indestructibility' of the spirit, the survival of the human amid the horrendous experiment in dehumanisation, but rather demonstrate the persistent if also fragile excess of survival, the appearance in the camp of that which should not exist there, since, after all, it is a place 'without people'. The revival of humanity in the camps was so momentary and delicate that it would be more appropriate to speak of the camps being haunted by humans that have become ghosts of themselves.

> People whose lives are ruined, whose past and future have been trampled on, suddenly find themselves in the grip of some trivial prejudice, some nonsense that they for some reason can neither ignore nor deny. And the sudden appearance of shame is the most subtle of human emotions, to be remembered for one's entire life as something real and infinitely precious. ('The Lepers' in Shalamov 1994: 180)

Similarly, the story 'Sententious' ends with the camp chief arriving from Magadan with a record player and records of symphonic music, which, however momentarily, pulled the entire audience out of indifference and into a sense of awe.

> And everyone stood around – murderers and horse-thieves, common criminals and political prisoners, foremen and workers. And the chief stood there too. And the expression on his face was such that he seemed to have written the music for us, for our desolate sojourn in the taiga. ('Sententious' in Shalamov 1994: 291)

These 'excess' sentiments that go beyond mere survival are of course largely negative, arising in response to some specific injustice or humiliation in the camps. In 'Esperanto' the general indifference of the inmates is suspended, when the camp authorities confiscate civilian clothing, which for the inmates was often the sole reminder of 'a different life' outside the camps (Shalamov 1994: 235). This action is met with vocal indignation: the things that one for years struggled to protect against theft by the criminals were now being taken away by the authorities.

> Naïve longing for justice sits deep in man – perhaps even too deep to root out. After all, why be offended? Angry? Indignant? This damn search was just one instance of thousands. But at the bottom of each of our souls something stronger than freedom, stronger than life's experience, was boiling. The faces of the convicts were dark with rage. ('Esperanto' in Shalamov 1994: 236)

This revival of human affects need not necessarily strengthen the subject but may in fact accompany or even condition its renunciation of survival and the embrace of suicide. Shalamov explicitly refutes the existentialist affirmation of suicide as the supreme act of freedom, whose possibility still constitutes the subject as human despite all the dehumanising suffering and privation. The problem with this claim is that it is based on experiences that are simply 'not tragic enough'. Dehumanisation that reduces one's existence to bare life does not merely remove one's will to live, plunging the subject into bitter indifference, but also removes one's will to die, depriving one precisely of the faculty of will, decision and choice required to take one's own life.

> For many years I thought that death was a form of life. Comforted by the vagueness of this notion, I attempted to work out a positive formula to preserve my own existence in this vale of tears. I believed a person could consider himself a human being as long as he felt totally prepared to kill himself, to interfere in his own biography. It was this awareness that gave me the will to live. I checked myself – frequently – and felt I had the strength to die, and thus remained alive. Much later I realised that I had simply built myself a refuge, avoided the problem, for when at the critical moment the decision between life and death became an exercise of the will, I would not be the same man as before. I would inevitably weaken, become a traitor, betray myself. ('The Life of Engineer Kipreev' in Shalamov 1994: 457)

Like fear, envy or shame, the capacity for suicide awakens only when one's state of indifference is suspended. In 'The Quiet' a newly arrived educator undertakes an unconventional experiment of feeding the weaker inmates more than the usual amount in order to ensure better work. After the dinner the narrator's work partner, the unnamed sectarian, walks past the guard into the security zone and is immediately shot dead.

> Suddenly I realised that that night's dinner had given the sectarian the strength he needed for his suicide. He needed that extra portion of kasha to make up his mind to die. There are times when a man has to hurry so as not to lose his will to die. (Shalamov 1994: 442)

Extra food temporarily takes the subject out of the indifference that envelops its entire being, making it possible to reach a *decision* to die, rather than continue to indifferently persist in one's being 'no more alive than dead'. However, the narrator himself remains in this state of indifference – rather than mourn his partner, he is relieved that the latter would no longer irritate him with his chants and hymns: 'I guess I was even happy that it was finally quiet' (ibid.).

While we observe a plethora of human affects reasserting themselves momentarily and rupturing the general indifference of the camp in Shalamov's texts (shame, envy, fear, revulsion, pity), the overwhelming mood of *Kolyma Tales* is understandably negative. In his lectures on Nietzsche, Heidegger spoke of love and hate as two fundamental passions that were different from mere affects: while the latter (fear, envy, anger) arise suddenly and spontaneously, love and hate are always already present in us, 'traversing our Being from the beginning' (Agamben 1999a: 198).

> Hate can explode suddenly in an action or exclamation, but only because it has already overtaken us, only because it has been growing within us for a long time, and, as we say, has been nurtured in us. But something can be nurtured only if it is already there and is alive. In contrast, we do not say and never believe that anger is nurtured. Because hate lurks much more deeply in the origins of our being it has a cohesive power; like love, hate brings an original cohesion and perdurance to our essential being. But anger, which seizes us, can also release us again – it 'blows over' as we say. Hate does not 'blow over'. Once it germinates it grows and solidifies, eating its way inward and consuming our very being. But the permanent cohesion that comes to human existence through hate does not close it off and blind it. Rather, it grants vision and premeditation. The angry man loses the power of reflection. He who hates intensifies reflection and rumination to the point of 'hardboiled' malice. Hate is never blind: it is perspicuous. Only anger is blind. Love is never blind: it is perspicuous. Only infatuation is blind, fickle and susceptible – an affect not a passion. Affect: the seizure that blindly agitates us. Passion: the lucidly gathering grip on beings. Hate and love not only last longer, they bring perdurance and permanence for the first time to our existence. (Heidegger 1991: 48–9)

If we agree with Heidegger's account, then we may understand the experience of the camp in terms of the annihilation of one of these fundamental passions, that is, love. For all the diversity of affects that may traverse the subject of the camp, love is not to be found in Shalamov's texts, at least as regards his own experience (the notable exception being the discussion of the wives who follow their subjects to the camps, cf. Shalamov 1994: 184–99, 343–79). In 'Sententious', as Shalamov recounts the revival of the goner, from elementary bitterness through indifference to fear, envy and even pity for animals, love is something that does not return to the protagonist and generally tends to return last, if at all (Shalamov 1994: 287; see also Podoroga 2013). Just as friendship and solidarity were never strengthened but only destroyed by the camps, so love is only possible for a fully constituted human subject, whose survival is not at stake and whose bare life is safely 'included as excluded' as a foundation of human existence that remains irreducible to it.

> Love didn't return to me. Oh, how distant is love from envy, from fear, from bitterness. How little people need love. Love comes only when all other human emotions have already returned. Love comes last, returns last. Or does it return? ('Sententious' in Shalamov 1994: 287)

Thus, while Heidegger tends to view love and hate as *symmetrically* fundamental passions defining human being and always present within it, in Shalamov's account there is an important asymmetry between them. There is nothing fundamental about love, which evaporates when the conditions that make it possible are not met (when one suffers from hunger, cold, hard labour, beatings and humiliation). In contrast, hate remains even in the state of utter privation in the form of that ontological bitterness that is the last thing that remains to the living. Insofar as the camp operates by reducing all life to the being's sensation of its own being, hate appears closest to being in the bitter tenacity of its holding on to itself, while love, by contrast, appears furthest away from the ontological dimension and closest to that which is 'otherwise than being', a dimension that Emmanuel Levinas (1998) famously characterised as ethical.

WRITING AFTER THE GULAG

Yet, in contrast to Heidegger's argument, the primordial character of hate does not grant it the power of enhancing our perspicuity. If the camp is a totally negative experience, this means that the hate it left one with did not really provide one with anything like a 'lucid grip on beings'. In Shalamov's prose, hate is ultimately debilitating, making the subject lose its grip on the beings around it and its own being. In 'Grishka Logun's Thermometer' Shalamov recounts the first time he was beaten by a foreman for writing a letter to Kalinin on his request that appeared to be too dry and unemotional to the foreman. Faced with this request, Shalamov discovers it has become difficult for him to write letters.

> My fingers were so permanently bent around the handle of a pick and axe that unbending them was unbelievably difficult. I managed to wrap a thick rag around pen and pencil to give them the thickness of a pick or shovel handle. (Shalamov 1994: 449)

Yet, the problem was primarily not physical but mental.

> It was difficult to write because my brain had become as coarse as my hands; like my hands, it too was oozing blood. I had to call back to life – to resurrect – words that, as I then thought, had left my life forever. (Ibid.: 449)

Along with love, culture and morality, language itself takes leave in the camp, leaving one with a 'few dozen words', basic words denoting cold, hunger, work, sleep as well as helpful profanities.

> The camp had dried up my brain, and I could not, I just could not squeeze another word from it. I was not up to the job – and not because my brain was weak and exhausted, but because in those folds of my brain, where ecstatic adjectives were stored, there was *nothing but hatred*. Just think of poor Dostoevsky, writing anguished, tearful, humiliating letters to his unmoved superiors throughout the ten years he spent as soldier after leaving the House of the Dead. Dostoevsky even wrote poems to the czarina. There was no Kolyma in the House of the Dead. ('Grishka Logun's Thermometer' in Shalamov 1994: 450; my emphasis)

In the same story Shalamov provides his own response to the question of the (im)possibility of literature after Auschwitz and the Gulag. It is impossible not merely because the humanist tradition of Russian (and world) literature was no longer credible in the aftermath of the dehumanising experiments of totalitarianism.

> Today the reader is disappointed in Russian classical literature. The collapse of its humanist ideas, the historic crime leading to Stalin's camps, to the furnaces of Auschwitz, have proven that art and literature are zero. (Shalamov cited in Podoroga 2013; see also Shalamov 1965)

> God is dead. Why should art be alive? Art is dead too and no force in the world will resurrect Tolstoy's novel. (Shalamov 1971)

Traditional literature is no longer possible, because the subject of the camp, who remained disaffected and traumatised even in the fortunate case of its survival and liberation from the Gulag, simply *cannot* write such literature, both because the pens and pencils are too thin for the hands accustomed to the handles of picks and axes and because the parts of the brain, where 'literary' language used to be stored, now house nothing but hatred, which cannot give the subject any 'vision and premeditation'. If language is understood in the Heideggerian manner as the 'house of being', then in and after the camps being ends up *homeless*, cast out into the desolate space where it loses all grip on beings and can only survive. Even if hatred could be said to bring 'perdurance and permanence' to the survivor's being, this was the perdurance of trauma that permanently impaired the subject's faculties and, among many other things, affected its potentiality for testimony. The only literature that could be written after the camps had to be expressed in the rudimentary language of hatred and written clumsily by the hand no longer accustomed to writing.

In his reflections on the status of his works Shalamov (1965) called *Kolyma Tales* 'prose *suffered* as a document', neither a collection of memoirs nor a set of short stories but a literary text based entirely on personal experience. In 'The Glove' he describes his near-death experience of suffering from pellagra, when skin could be removed from his hands and feet 'like a glove'. 'With a dead glove you could not write good poems or prose. The glove itself was prose, indictment, document, protocol' (Shalamov 1972). Not only is it impossible to write *with* lumps of shed skin; it is also impossible to write *about* them in a literary text of the classical tradition: the skin glove is always already literature and evidence, prose and protocol that cannot enter into humanist morality tales without being utterly trivialised. 'The Glove', like every other story by Shalamov, has no place for the quest for self-discovery or self-transcendence through hardship and adversity, the elevated pathos of salvation and, perhaps least of all, the ethics of forgiveness.

> The principle of my century, my personal existence, my whole life, the conclusion from my personal experience and the rule learned from that experience may be summed up in a few words. First you must return the blows and only secondly the gifts. One must remember evil before the good, remember everything good for a hundred years and everything evil for two hundred. This is where I differ from all Russian humanists of the 19th and the 20th centuries. (Ibid.: 307)

These are striking words indeed, especially coming from a representative of the Russian literary tradition, albeit the one who insisted most on its having come to an end. Yet, they make perfect sense from the perspective of hate as the sole fundamental attunement that remains to the survivor of the camp. Let us again compare Shalamov's account of the camps with Solzhenitsyn's far more conventionally humanist narrative, in which forgiveness, difficult and almost impossible as it may be, does indeed find its place. For Solzhenitsyn, the camps played a role in his moral education, helping him get rid of all ideological indoctrination and the last remaining illusions about socialism. By revealing to him the truth of communism, the camps made him spiritually stronger, if physically weaker, and it is from this position of strength that one could *both* pass judgement and issue forgiveness (Solzhenitsyn 2007: 312, 385). Since Shalamov was a convinced communist *and* an anti-Stalinist when he was first arrested, he never had illusions about Stalin's regime in the first place and nor did his plight destroy his revolutionary beliefs. Moreover, as we have seen, for Shalamov it was impossible to maintain, let alone increase, spiritual strength in the conditions of utmost physical degradation: whatever strength of spirit remained it was put almost entirely in the service of physical survival. The camp work of dehumanisation was so thoroughgoing that it made humanism, including its ethics of forgiveness, radically inapplicable. It is not merely that the camp survivor would not *want* to forgive his guards, supervisors or torturers, which would also be understandable. It is rather that the being that survives the camp by becoming radically indifferent to everything, ultimately including its survival, is also indifferent to forgiving: what good would it do and for whom? While 'remembering evil' is essential to the work of testimony, whose importance for Shalamov we shall consider below, forgiving evil would have no redemptive value whatsoever. What we are left with is a thoroughly negative experience which cannot be integrated into any ethical system but ruptures any such system once and for all.

Yet, if humanism is so forcefully renounced, why is Shalamov so concerned about the 'souls' that are being 'corrupted' in the camp? In 'Prosthetic Appliances' he describes the situation when his fellow inmates are incarcerated in solitary confinement and stripped of their prostheses: a back corset, artificial arm, leg and eye. When it is the narrator's turn to be processed, he is jokingly asked by the chief guard what he would hand over, perhaps his soul. The narrator's reply is: 'No, you can't have my soul' ('Prosthetic Appliances' in Shalamov 1994: 391). Yet, what is the soul in the camp conditions, where morality and ethics have been stripped away, where the surviving affects are bitterness and indifference, where friendship and solidarity have been rendered impossible? It is nothing but bare life as such, the sheer fact of life as immanent auto-affection. The soul is what bitterly perseveres in being amidst utter deprivation and what indifferently survives the destruction of all its forms. The refusal to surrender one's soul pertains to this persistence in being and is therefore not a morally elevated statement, suggesting something like a spiritual victory of the inmate over his jailors. There is and can be no such victory: the first thing the camp does is break the spirit, which leaves the subject

Shalamov, or the Negative Experience

damaged for the rest of its life. As we have seen, Shalamov's affirmation of survival is entirely non-teleological and deprived of illusions: it is not a matter of surviving the camp *in order to* rejoin one's family, resume one's profession, restore one's dignity. Nothing of the sort is really possible: there is, in a strict sense, *no return from the camps*.

> These changes of the psyche are as irreversible as frostbites. Memory moans like the frostbitten hand at the first cold wind. There are no people who returned from the camps and would live at least one day without remembering the camp and the humiliating and fearful camp labour. (Shalamov 1965)

And yet, this damaged soul that has suffered that which should not be, the living being who has seen things after which 'it is better for him to die', nonetheless clings to its bare existence, refusing to give up this soul even if it is already corrupted beyond repair. The ending of the story affirms this bitter obstinacy and nothing more; yes, one's soul has been destroyed, but it is then appropriated by the subject *as* destroyed, so that it survives to eventually testify to its own destruction. This is the only 'victory' that is possible at the site of Gulag: that the destroyed subject provide testimony of its own destruction, that the *living dead live on*. This is why Shalamov uses the term 'martyr', traditionally reserved for those who sacrificed their lives for some cause, who died in the name of something, to denote the living dead, the goners of the camps (see Ryklin 2007).

> In *Kolyma Tales* we deal with people without a biography, without a past and without a future. Is their present a beastly one or is it a human present? In *Kolyma Tales* there is nothing that could be the transcendence of evil, the triumph of the good. [Theirs] is the fate of martyrs who were not, could not and did not become heroes. (Shalamov 1965)

The martyrdom of the inmates of the Gulag consists solely in their perseverance in bare life, in surviving the totally negative experience. Sacrifice is meaningless in the camp: all the things *in the name of which* one could die are gone in a few weeks of cold, hunger and beatings. If the camp inmate is already dead as a human being, his or her martyrdom consists not in sacrificing but in *living* this death. Shalamov's prose must then be understood as testimony to this deformed life, a life stripped of all predicates and reduced to survival, a life plunged into bitter indifference and only sporadically and tentatively rediscovering various affects amid the fundamental passion of hatred that remains in the subject when the possibility of love has forever gone. What makes such a testimony unbearable and almost impossible for the survivor, whose life can only partially re-form itself by forgetting the violence done to it, is the need to resist this very re-forming and ceaselessly reopen old wounds.

> Suddenly I was afraid and felt a cold sweat form on my body. I was frightened by the terrible strength of man, his desire and ability to forget. I realised I was ready to forget everything, to cross out twenty years of my life. And what years! And when I understood this, I conquered myself. I knew I would not permit my memory to forget everything that I had seen. ('The Train' in Shalamov 1994: 393)

Forgetting is unacceptable because it replicates the logic of the corruption of the soul that Shalamov traced in the camp, whereby the temptation of good life crowds out any concern for the bare life of the other. In 'The Procurator of Judea', we are introduced to head of surgery Kubantsev, who 'forces himself to forget' the steamship *Kim*, where the rebellion of the convicts was put down by hosing down all the holds when the temperature was forty below zero.

> Seventeen years later, Kubantsev remembered the names of each of the convict orderlies, he remembered all the camp romances and which of the convicts 'lived' with whom. He remembered the rank of every heartless administrator. There was only one thing that Kubantsev didn't remember – the steamship *Kim* with its three thousand prisoners. Anatole France has a story 'The Procurator of Judea'. In it, after seventeen years, Pontius Pilate cannot remember Christ. ('The Procurator of Judea' in Shalamov 1994: 176)

While from every perspective of 'good life' 'all this had to be forgotten' (ibid.: 176), Shalamov's texts are devoid of any such perspective and instead insist on testifying to the existence of something that should not exist, the experience that no one should have been subjected to, the life that is in a strict sense as good as death. Let us undertake one final comparison of Shalamov and Solzhenitsyn. *The Gulag Archipelago* is primarily a condemnation of the revolutionary destruction of 'old life' in the name of a chimerical 'new life', which is animated by the somewhat naïve hope for the revival of the old forms of life, be they those of religion, traditional values or local autonomy.

> Solzhenitsyn's path proceeds from the thesis about the blessing of suffering and the need for strong statehood. The good must be strong so that the horrible Soviet evil does not repeat itself; the alternative to Lenin is Stolypin; the alternative to barbarian modernization is the good old conservative archaic. (Bykov 2007)

Shalamov, or the Negative Experience

In contrast, Shalamov has little to say about (and probably little sympathy for) the 'old' forms of life and no particular quarrel with the ideological construct of the 'new' life as it originally appeared in the Bolshevik revolutionary discourse. Shalamov does not compare the 'new' life with the 'old' life and find it wanting. There is in fact neither an old nor a new life in Shalamov's texts: the former was done away with after the revolution and only a few of its traces remain, while the new life promised by revolutionary ideologies was conspicuous by its absence in the camps and, for that matter, around them as well. In Shalamov's texts we hardly ever encounter the figures of new, socialist life familiar to us from the simulacra of socialist realism: the camp was not hospitable to art, even bad art. Shalamov's uncanny discovery is that Stalinism did not really produce any new form of life comparable with the preceding historical forms; instead, it produced nothingness, negativity, the void, death, but as a positive form in itself. The biopolitical product of the camp as the paradigmatic site of Stalinism was a life that was neither old nor new, a bare life of indifferent survival that was neither continuous nor discontinuous with the past but appeared to exist outside time as such.

It is this life alone that could survive the camp after every positive form of life was stripped from the subject and it is this life that made it possible for the subject to eventually provide testimony of its own devastation, finding language again in the same contingent and tentative way as it rediscovered fear, envy, pity and other affects. Indeed, it is only after all these affects come back that Shalamov undergoes the experience of the return of language, poignantly described in 'Sententious'. After years of making do with a simple and crude 'few dozen words', the protagonist suddenly remembers a word that 'was totally inappropriate for the taiga', 'a word [he] did not [himself] understand, not to mention [his] comrades': *sententia*.[7]

> 'Sententia!', I shouted directly into the northern sky, into the double dawn, still not understanding the meaning of the word that had been born within me. And if the word had returned, then all the better! A great joy filled me. [...] The find was enormous. I could not believe myself and was afraid when I went to sleep that I would forget the word that had newly returned to me. But the word did not disappear. For a week I didn't understand what the word meant. I whispered it, amused and frightened my neighbours with it. I wanted an explanation, a definition, a translation. ('Sententia' in Shalamov 1994: 289–90)

Here as elsewhere, Shalamov takes particular care to avoid a morality tale about a return to humanity after surviving the worst in the camp. Yes, the protagonist rediscovers language, yet, just as was the case with fear, envy or pity, this rediscovery is tentative; it is always possible for indifference to set back in and for language to take leave aside from a few crude and simple words. Moreover, the mode in which the narrator reacquires language is highly indicative. The word that returns to Shalamov is important for at least three reasons. First, it is a *foreign* word whose meaning escapes him; he experiences pleasure just from the return of this unfamiliar word to his 'tongue', not his 'mind' (ibid.: 290). No wonder that his companions wonder if he is a 'foreigner' – a dangerous assumption indeed in this world of 'provocations and denunciations, investigations and lengthened sentences' (ibid.: 290). What awakens in the narrator is not any meaningful discourse but the sheer potentiality of signification, the potentiality that is as such glossolalic and devoid of sense (cf. Agamben 1991: 25–6; 1999a: 41–6). According to Agamben, it is precisely in the acquisition of this potentiality for language, which he terms 'infancy', that the experience of human subjectivation consists (2007a: 59). While animals are always already within a 'natural' language, humans are born without language and must acquire it, taking up their place within it. The repetition of this experience of pure language, prior to any meaningful discourse, testifies to the earliest stage of the (re)birth of the subject.

Second, if we do focus on the meaning of the word, the tentative character of the reacquired language is stressed by the fact that 'sententia' originally means 'a sentence', a syntactical unit. What Shalamov recalls is a sentence composed of the word 'sentence', a paradigm of the sentence as such that seems to suspend its own denotation. Again, what returns is language as such, its purely formal semiotic possibilities that are not yet put into play in the production of signifying discourse. Third, the other meaning of the word is of course a legal one, referring to judgement or punishment. Ironically, the first 'non-primitive' word that returns to the protagonist is the very word that describes his predicament of having been sentenced. It is as if at the very moment of his rediscovery of language all that the subject can speak is the fact of its own having been sentenced, the sentence which deprived him of linguistic potentiality beyond a few simple sentences. Yet, slowly this rediscovery proceeds with more and more words, first experienced as pure sounds and only gradually revealing their sense. This is how Shalamov's testimonial prose emerges as the narrative of a life returning to speak of its destruction.

> Many days passed before I learned to call forth from the depth of memory new words, one after the other. Each came with difficulty; each appeared suddenly and separately. Thoughts and words didn't return in streams. Each returned alone, unaccompanied by the watchful guards of familiar words. Each appeared first on the tongue and only later in the mind. ('Sententia' in Shalamov 1994: 290)

With enormous difficulty and with no assurance of any lasting effect, bare life begins to speak, as if for the first time, eventually offering a testimony of its own emergence as the product of a horrendous experiment in the construction of the new subject through its thoroughgoing desubjectivation. This testimony does not redeem anyone or teach anyone anything; this speech is not therapeutic or confessional and does not respond to any recognisable ethical imperative. Moreover, as a result of this testimony its subject does not become other, it does not exorcise the past of its own devastation, which remains its present forever. And yet it speaks, giving voice to the bare life that is not natural, that is in fact the most unnatural thing of all, a life deprived of all positive predicates, whose essence coincided completely with its deprivation: 'In Kolyma there were no people with a colour of the eyes, and this is not an aberration of my memory but the essence of the life back then' (Shalamov 1971). It is this life that stands as the definitive refutation of any claim for the biopolitical productivity of Stalinism. *Kolyma Tales* prove that the new life produced by Stalinism was wholly contained in the destruction of the old life. Yet, they also prove that this destruction was itself *lived*, that the negativity of Stalinism was borne in and by the millions of lives damaged beyond repair by the violence intended to transcend the way they were. It would therefore be too easy to dismiss the biopolitical image of Stalinism by denying it all productivity, reducing it to mere ideological delirium. Shalamov's testimony rather exhibits the full range of the forms of life that Stalinism produced. Pellagra and diarrhoea, shedding skin and lost language, torture and humiliation, and ultimately a deathlike life deprived of a world and withdrawn into bitter auto-affection – this is what the lived reality of socialism looks like.

SHALAMOV IN THE AGE OF ANTICOMMUNISM

While Shalamov's account of the negative experience of the camp clearly resonates with Arendt's insights into the logic of total domination, it also provides an important corrective to Arendt's account of totalitarianism, which is based on ideology as the prime instrument of domination. As we have seen, for Shalamov the experience of the camp was not simply negative in the evident sense of something bad, but also negative in the ontological sense. What the subject experienced in the camp was negativity as such in the sense of the destruction of every anterior form of life, which then became the entire content of the subjectivity produced in the camps, and, insofar as every Soviet subject was somehow touched, or tainted, by the camps, all around them. The camps and their subjective products did not have any 'positive' content, however repulsive that content might be from other ideological perspectives: the subject produced in them was just as negative from any conceivable 'socialist' standpoint as it was from a hypothetical bourgeois, nationalist or Christian standpoint. While the project of reforging in the biopolitical rationality of the Great Break still ventured to produce a model socialist subject out of 'class aliens' or common criminals, to translate ideological precepts into the lived reality of the subject, this task was abandoned as impracticable starting from the mid-1930s. It would indeed be ridiculous to expect a model socialist to emerge after years of hunger, beatings and slave labour in the permanent cold. Rather than function as sites of ideological indoctrination that would replace one *bios* by another, the camps as well as the 'larger zone' of the USSR were the loci of the production of bare life that went on to live its own devastation, indifferent to the minutiae of ideological doctrines.

This is what the anti-totalitarian discourse, even in its most sophisticated version, failed to grasp due to its obsession with the maxims of communist ideology that it perceived, rightly or wrongly, as just as dangerous as arbitrary state violence. When Arendt argued in the final chapter of *The Origins of Totalitarianism* about 'ideology and terror' as together comprising a 'novel form of government' (1973: 460), she approached ideology as the positive obverse of the sheer negativity of terror, the sole foundation that totalitarian power relies on, having abandoned law, tradition and morality. The ideological fictions of the Laws of Nature (for Nazism) and History (for Stalinism) simultaneously expressed and legitimised terror as the *modus operandi* of totalitarian regimes: 'Terror is lawfulness, if law is the law of the movement of some superhuman force, Nature or History' (ibid.: 465). While totalitarian rule could no longer rely on virtue, honour, fear or any other ethical principle, its sole guiding principle remained ideology in the sense of a pseudo-scientific discourse that expressed natural or social laws, from which one could derive a response to any concrete historical situation. In their quest for a total explanation, their independence from all experience and their substitution of logical consistency for any relation to reality Nazi and Stalinist ideologies were, in Arendt's view, a perfect counterpart to terror as the actual method of totalitarian government, preparing its subjects to serve equally well as executioner and victim by subjecting them to the ineluctable logic allegedly governing the historical process (ibid.: 468, 472).

Arendt's account of totalitarian ideology voids it of any positive content by reducing its *ideas* to *logicality* as such, the pure form of argumentative discourse that neither represents the reality as it is nor prescribes the way it should be, but simply offers the logical process of deduction from fundamental premises that is disconnected from reality as such.

> [The] compulsion of total terror on one side, which presses masses of isolated men together and supports them in a world which has become a wilderness for them, and the self-coercive force of logical deduction on the other, correspond to each other and need each other in order to set the terror-ruled movement into motion and keep it moving. Just as terror ruins all relationships between men, so the self-compulsion of ideological thinking ruins all relationships with reality. The preparation has succeeded when people have lost contact with their fellow-men as well as the reality around them; for together with these contacts, men lose the capacity of both experience and thought. The ideal subject of totalitarian rule is not the convinced Nazi or the convinced Communist, but people for whom the distinction between fact and fiction (i.e. the reality of experience) and the distinction between true and false (i.e. the standards of thought) no longer exist. (Ibid.: 474)

It is notable that in her account of totalitarian ideology Arendt elides the very dimension that the Cold War anticommunist discourse found most threatening for Western societies. While it would be preposterous to expect free subjects to sacrifice their freedom to a purely logical system, the 'empty truth' that 'does not reveal anything' (ibid.: 477), the appeal of communist ideology originally lay precisely in the 'great capacity of men to start something new' (ibid.: 473) that Arendt herself famously posited as the true criterion of political action. It is this capacity for a new beginning, which the idea of communism originally promised, that accounted for its continued appeal in Western societies during the Cold War. Against this appeal, the theory of totalitarianism sought to demonstrate how the revolutionary assertion of this political capacity ended up in a horrifying project of total domination. In her analysis Arendt similarly demonstrates this disastrous conversion, yet takes particular care to dissociate totalitarian ideology from anything like a political *idea*, which could have adherents and opponents, whom it could mobilise for political action, where it could be affirmed or denied, enacted in new forms of life or mobilised against old ones. In Arendt's argument, 'the aim of totalitarian education has never been to instil convictions but to destroy the capacity to form any' (ibid.: 468).

Yet, if ideology no longer seeks to produce a convinced communist, but rather destroys the political capacity of the subject to act on the basis of ideas, to what extent may we still speak of *ideology* in any meaningful sense? Isn't the quasi-logical discourse addressed by Arendt rather a form of what we have termed *simulacrum*, a discourse that does not legitimise the reproduction or the transformation of reality but rather crowds it out, derealises it and replaces it with a representation that may be marvelled at or recoiled from in horror but which has nothing to do with thought, ideas and truth. In our view, the simulacrum of socialist realism (and, more generally, the official pseudo-philosophy of 'scientific communism') exemplified the *negation* of ideology understood in the sense of a set of ideas animating political action: individuals and groups subjectivised through socialist realism were not engaged in the struggle between contested ideas or even authoritatively indoctrinated into one victorious idea but simply entered the world in which this idea had already fully passed into the actuality of the real, albeit only in the mode of a simulacrum. After the drive of the Great Break to force ideology into life ended up in a paroxysm of the negation of life, the Soviet regime negated ideological struggle through the construction of the simulacrum of socialism as already attained, which coincided with the actual retreat from its ideological maxims and the dissociation of governmental violence from any ideological content. In the High Stalinist constellation of retreat, simulacrum and terror ideology could survive only as an 'empty truth' incapable of revelation and captivation.

In contrast to Arendt's reading of totalitarianism, Shalamov's prose all but brackets off ideological content, focusing instead on the way the camp strips off every positive form of life and produces the bare life of survival, whose key attribute is indifference, including indifference to any possible ideological indoctrination. While there was a nominally ideological dimension to the Gulag (from the label of 'Trotskyites', which led to even more extreme punishment and humiliation, to the valorisation of common criminals as 'socially proximal'), its *modus operandi* made any ideological indoctrination problematic by attacking precisely the positive forms of life that could be *receptive* to such indoctrination. Shalamov is not merely reticent about the idea of communism himself, but also demonstrates repeatedly and at length why the privileged focus on ideology in any analysis of totalitarianism is misguided. This is why Shalamov's prose is so difficult to subsume under the 'anti-totalitarian' interpretation of Stalinism. Even Solzhenitsyn, whose romantic nationalism and cultural traditionalism were so exasperating for the Western audience, was easier to incorporate into the anti-totalitarian canon due to his unambiguous condemnation of Bolshevism as an idea. This difficulty has nothing to do with the degree of the two authors' anti-Stalinism. Shalamov famously said that every one of his stories was intended as a 'slap in the face of Stalinism' (Shalamov 1971), but, powerful as each of these slaps were, they do not have communist ideology as their target, which distinguishes them both from Solzhenitsyn's conservative version of dissident discourse and the anti-totalitarian liberalism that triumphed at the end of the Cold War.

Shalamov, or the Negative Experience 247

According to this triumphant discourse, revolutionary ideas must be kept at arm's length or further away as safely inaccessible 'regulative ideas' or, preferably, abandoned outright as inevitably yielding violence and oppression, leading the unsuspecting humanity directly to the concentration camp.

> [In] its usual connotation, the category of 'totalitarianism' designates Terror as the inevitable outcome of revolutions whose manifest principle is communism. The underlying argument is that the construction of an egalitarian society is so unnatural an enterprise, so contrary to all the human animal's instincts, that advancing in that direction is impossible without appalling violence. (Badiou 2013: 3)

In Badiou's argument, the claim about terror as the logical consequence of every attempt to realise egalitarian ideas has today become the object of a global consensus, as its original articulation in the anti-totalitarian discourse of the Cold War has now been enthusiastically adopted by the postcommunist elites in China, Russia and other formerly revolutionary states that have no quarrel with the delegitimisation of radical ideas that potentially threaten their own brands of state capitalism.

> The Western interpretation, promoted by the clique of 'new philosophers' in France, actually became the consensus interpretation, especially during the last twenty years of the twentieth century. There was the dissolution of 'actually existing socialism', culminating, as we know, in a Russia embarking upon a version of state capitalism, and a rapidly developing China, under the paradoxical leadership of a party that is still called 'communist' – a ruthless capitalism very similar to that of the nineteenth century in England. As a result, the so-called 'anti-totalitarian' theory, which regards Terror as the inevitable outcome of the communist Idea's coming to power, has no opponents anymore in any countries, none of which defend the Idea any longer. It is as if the communist Idea, definitively associated with Terror, has very rapidly become no more than a dead planet in the historical universe. (Badiou 2013: 5)

It is easy to see why Shalamov's camp prose would be very difficult to incorporate into this discourse: for him, the 'totally negative' experience of the camp, which can have no justification whatsoever, nonetheless does *not* invalidate the communist idea. Let us not forget that Shalamov was the supporter of the Left Opposition at the time of his first arrest and never explicitly abandoned his radical leftist convictions as well as his positive assessment of the revolution and the immediate post-revolutionary period. On the contrary, in his recollections of this period after his release Shalamov claimed that during the early 1920s he had been a 'participant of the grand lost battle for the real renewal of life' (Shalamov 2004).

> Not only the state was stormed furiously, but everything, literally every human decision, was a great trial. October Revolution was definitely a world revolution. The myth of yesterday was becoming real. Why not take this reality one step further, higher, deeper? All of this was of course broken afterwards, cast aside and trampled upon. But there had not been another moment in life when it was so close to international ideals. All that Lenin said about building the state and society of a new type was correct, but for Lenin it was a question of power, while for us it was the air we breathed, believing in the new and rejecting the old. (Ibid.)

This statement evokes nothing other than the desire for biopolitical transformation that translates the ideas of the revolution into lived reality – not merely governing life with the power of new ideas but creating a new life as a reality in its own right. We may recall that the phrase 'renewal of life' (*obnovlenie zhizni*) was used in Bogdanov's *Red Star* as the Martian term for the procedure of blood exchange that produces a communist society. The 'grand battle' for making communism real during the early 1920s was indeed lost and its tentative achievements trampled or cast aside. We can only speculate what the ultimate moment of defeat was for Shalamov: the Great Break that converted the desire for a new life into the violent onslaught on the non-socialist reality or the Great Terror, in which the very ambition of a new life was set aside in the paroxysmal drive for annihilation that produced millions of corpses and tens of millions of the living dead. What matters more is that, unlike Solzhenitsyn who inferred from this lost battle the imperative to oppose every utopia and every revolution, Shalamov never rejected the aspiration for the 'real renewal of life'. While Solzhenitsyn's *Archipelago* waged a struggle against communist ideology in the name of the lost or destroyed pre-revolutionary Russia, ultimately issuing a warning against every attempt at the 'renewal of life', Shalamov's depictions of cruelty, violence, deprivation and dehumanisation in the camps do not discredit the ideology of communism and *especially not* the ambition to transform lived reality.

Instead, *Kolyma Tales* might even be viewed as testimony in support of something like a revolutionary biopolitics. The sheer fact of the Gulag having taken place, of the horrendous experiment in dehumanisation being so successful, of human souls corrupted in weeks, is the best argument there could be *in favour of* a new life, in which such abominations would not take place. It is precisely because something like the Gulag is *possible*, that human evil is so banal and ordinary, that humanity can be destroyed so easily, that a 'real renewal of life' becomes an ethico-political imperative. In Malabou's terms, the evidence of the negative plasticity of the human condition leads to the affirmation of its positive plasticity. After all, every potentiality for destruction, for living one's non-existence, is always also the proof of the potentiality *not to* destroy or be destroyed, the potentiality to take on an infinite number of new forms. What evidently does not follow from the evidence of destructive plasticity is the renunciation of all transformation *as such*, as if the possibility of 'bad' change could somehow be averted by giving up on 'good' change as well.

Shalamov's testimony must thus be rigorously distinguished from every form of anthropological pessimism that is sceptical about the possibility of transforming or improving 'human nature'. Ironically, such a sceptical attitude does not obstruct but may even enable enthusiastic support for the Stalinist violent reforging and deformation of humanity: the human nature that is so difficult to improve, that so persistently lapses into old evil ways, does not really *deserve* pity. From such a perspective, the failure of biopolitical transformation would only prove the correctness of one's pessimism about humanity, while the slightest success in it would be welcome without regard for its costs.[8] If human beings are constitutively imperfect or outright evil, why complain about the attempt to transform them for the better, even if it is likely to end in failure or violence, and probably both?

In contrast, Shalamov is hardly pessimistic about transforming humanity for the better: if a manifestly anti-natural environment such as the camp could destroy the human in a matter of days, there probably are also environments where human existence may be radically improved in accordance with the aspirations of the revolution. Shalamov's presentation of prisons as the place where human solidarity was stronger than on the outside, let alone in the camps, demonstrates the possibility of such a transformation even in relatively adverse conditions: the 'committees of the poor' were closer to the ideals of communism that *any* governmental policy ventured under Stalin or, for that matter, after his death. The problem with Stalinism was not that it *dared* to undertake a biopolitical experiment in transforming human nature but that its biopolitics was *unfaithful* to the emancipatory and egalitarian promise of the revolution and ended up converted into a thanatopolitics of violent reforging of forms of life during the Great Break and the reduction of these forms to bare life or their complete annihilation during the Great Terror. Shalamov's phenomenology of the camps is not to be read as the condemnation of the revolutionary project and even its biopolitical conversion but rather as its *vindication* against the abominations of the Stalinist regime.

The experience of Stalinism makes 'real renewal of life', which is always possible, also *necessary* (cf. Bykov 2007).

In contrast to this vindication, the anti-totalitarian pathos of the renunciation of every 'big idea' as necessarily leading to the Gulag does little more than repeat the violence of the Gulag on the symbolic level. By reducing the inmates of the Gulag to the 'innocent victims' of the ideology many of them actually shared and promoted and whose betrayal and perversion they observed with horror, this discourse, observable, for example, in the half-hearted criticism of Stalinism by the Putin regime during the 2000s, subjects them to a 'second death' as duped victims of their own ideological illusions. It is no coincidence that the TV series based on Shalamov's works, which was produced by the state-owned channel RTR in 2006, was called *Lenin's Testament*. While Shalamov was indeed first arrested for distributing copies of Lenin's last letter, often called his 'testament', the title of the series ironically suggests, contrary to any evidence in Shalamov's own texts, that Lenin's 'true' testament was in fact the Gulag itself, that the revolution ultimately led us straight to the camp. It is of course impossible to kill someone for the second time, but such an interpretation of the Terror certainly comes close to doing precisely that.

> That's what Lenin's testament allegedly is. That's what Lenin left us, this is where all attempts to transform society and the human being inevitably lead. The dichotomy is finally formed: either you love the stability that exists today or you are going to get the Gulag. The authors [of the TV series] are unaware that the Gulag is the other side of stability: while there was stability *here*, there was Kolyma *there*. Shalamov is used to illustrate the theses that he was 100% hostile to. His work was founded on the thirst for the complete and final revolution that would transcend the human being as it was. Now his savage experience, which cannot even be interpreted in human terms, is used to prove the absolute and non-negotiable status of this human being: a step to the left, a step to the right all lead to the Gulag. So [Shalamov] had no luck even after death. (Bykov 2007)

Despite this and other distortions, Shalamov's prose clearly stands in the way of the elevation of the Gulag to the status of the hidden *telos* of every revolutionary transformation. It does not merely insist on keeping the Revolution and the Gulag distinct but forcefully asserts that the Gulag was not a crime *of* the Revolution but a crime *against* it, the suppression of the movement of the 'real renewal of life' already at work in it. And yet, this criminal suppression has itself assumed a positive form, whereby the monstrosity of Stalinism has come to define real socialism

Shalamov, or the Negative Experience

as such. Shalamov's texts are thus furthest away from the naïve ridicule of the totalitarian ambition of producing the New Soviet Person as an alternative form of life. At first glance, the quick scrapping of the socialist ideology and the ardent embrace of Western lifestyles by post-socialist societies testified to the radical impossibility of ever transforming human nature, which would eventually triumph over any attempt to remould it in accordance with the utopian designs of socialist ideology. It is true that few subjects of the kind depicted in socialist-realist novels, paintings or films ever existed in reality, for better or worse. And yet, the New Soviet Person *was* indeed produced in Stalinist biopolitics, even if it bore little resemblance to the heroes of socialist construction. In fact, this new person bore little relation to any ideological system at all, since its being was entirely contained in the deformation of his life in the exposure to senseless violence. This understanding distinguishes Shalamov from the partisans of anti-totalitarianism. He recognised *both* the legitimacy of radical social transformation *and* the fact that the Stalinist effort at such transformation ended up producing millions of the living dead. Shalamov knew that there was nothing naïve about the construction of New Soviet Persons – after all, he *was* one himself for the rest of his life.

This understanding tempers the enthusiasm of post-totalitarian accounts of the resilience of human nature. While this nature might have proven resistant to ideological remoulding, it also revealed itself as extremely fragile and vulnerable to violence and even the threat thereof. If Stalinism teaches us anything, it is *not* the impossibility of changing human nature but its relative ease and even banality, as long as the change in question is entirely negative. It certainly *is* possible to create a new form of life, as long as this form is solely contained in the destruction of anterior forms that erases the subject's past and leaves it incapable of experiencing its own loneliness. It certainly *is* possible to transform human nature, if this transformation is wholly contained in its deformation that destroys the subject's relational and affective capacities. It *is* perfectly possible to produce a socialist subject, provided that this production takes the form of a traumatic shock that the subject can make no sense of. The goner, the criminal, the professional doctor-torturer, Lunin the descendant of the famous Decembrist, Chris the copier and his executed saviour – these are all patently *real* versions of the Stalinist subject, produced by subtraction rather than addition, the subjects whose form of life was exhausted by its deformation. The New Soviet Person was simply the old Soviet person who suffered denunciation, betrayal, resettlement, slave labour, hunger, beatings and rape.

If this is so, then it is also possible that what we observed in the demise of the Soviet system was not the proud reassertion by human nature of its rights against the monstrosity of the New Soviet Person, but simply a new chapter in this person's apathetic existence. The Stalinist subject survived Stalinism and socialism more generally – this is not very surprising since it had, prior to all this, also survived *itself*, that is, went on living its own death. Against the misplaced enthusiasm about the resilience of the human being it is best to reaffirm as the lesson of totalitarianism its own maxim: 'everything is possible', if only in the sense that 'everything can be destroyed' (Arendt 1973: 440; cf. Agamben 1999b: 133–5, 148).

> [The] psyche *can* be destroyed even without the destruction of the physical man; indeed, psyche, character and individuality seem under certain circumstances to express themselves only through the rapidity or slowness with which they disintegrate. The end result in any case is inanimate men, i.e. men who can no longer be psychologically understood, whose return to the psychologically or otherwise intelligibly human world closely resembles the resurrection of Lazarus. The reduction of man to a bundle of reactions separates him as radically as mental disease from everything within him that is personality or character. (Arendt 1973: 441; original emphasis)

We may conclude that the biopolitical productivity celebrated in the postcommunist rehabilitation of Stalinism is not null, as the anti-totalitarian critics of the communist ideology suggest, but is rather a *negative magnitude*. Its subject is real, but its reality coincides with its desubjectivation. Stalinism did succeed in translating the transcendent idea of socialism into the world of the living, yet only at the price at transforming this world itself into the world of the living dead. While it is difficult to see the attraction of such productivity, it is even more difficult to understand why anyone would desire its repetition: after all, the Stalinist 'cool subject' *never really went away*. It is there in the social atomisation and the dissolution of solidarity, in the acceptance of arbitrary and corrupt power as the 'way of the world', in the cynical reproduction of official propaganda without believing a word of it, in the contempt for the truth and those who dare affirm it and, finally, and most unnervingly, in its own manifest indifference to it all. The fruits of Stalin's 'effective management' are still there in postcommunist Russia for all to marvel or shudder at. Peter Sloterdijk once observed that the disenchantment of the postcommunist condition arises out of 'the conviction that the future has already been there and nobody can bear to think of a second visit' (Sloterdijk 2012: 186). Yet, there is no need for this second visit, since the vile fruit of the first still inhabits the present. This is why Shalamov's testimonial prose retains its urgency and exigency today – not in order to remind us of the past in order for it not to be repeated but in order to reignite the desire for the 'real renewal of life'. Shalamov's testimony to the thanatopolitical paroxysm of Stalinism is nothing less than a demand for an affirmative biopolitics.

Chapter 7

A REAL RENEWAL OF LIFE: TOWARDS AN AFFIRMATIVE BIOPOLITICS

LIVING SOCIALISM OTHERWISE

Reading Shalamov's testimony not as a warning against the revolutionary transformation of life but as its vindication raises the question of the possibility of a revolutionary biopolitics that would not end up in the thanatopolitical project akin to Stalinism. Could it all have been different? Could socialist biopolitics have taken a different form or was Stalinism inscribed in the very logic of the revolution? Might there have been a different biopolitics of Trotskyism, Zinovievism or Bukharinism or, why not, even Leninism? Was the Stalinist translation of socialism into biopolitical terms a perversion of socialism or rather the realisation of its true essence? These questions have preoccupied the study of the Russian Revolution and the Soviet period from the very beginning and any attempt to answer them definitively would be entirely premature. Yet, these empirical and historical questions are in our approach also intertwined with questions of a theoretical nature, related to the very notion of biopolitics and its relation to its opposite, the power of death. Given the intertwining of the powers of life and death in every biopolitical project, what would it mean to speak of an affirmative or positive biopolitics? Is it possible to disentangle the political affirmation of life from its subjection to governmental violence often practised in its very name? These questions have been central to the theory of biopolitics since its very inception and continue to be addressed in both historical and contemporary investigations of biopolitical rationalities (Foucault 2003; Agamben 1998, 2011, 2014b; Esposito 2008a, 2011; Cooper 2008; Campbell 2011; Wolfe 2013; Vatter 2014).

Since Stalinist biopolitics was characterised by a highly singular logic arising out of its revolutionary origin and content, our study may also be expected to provide us with a different perspective on these questions. As we have seen, in the liberal and Nazi modes of Western biopolitics violence enters the governmental constellation through the logic of immunity, whereby government takes it upon itself to protect life negatively against its own constituent negativity that places it in danger. In this manner, the natural character of the existent forms of life, which both these modes of biopolitics valorise in different ways, stops being an obstacle to violent interventions, since the latter only strive to protect nature from itself. It is then the excessive force of immunitary violence that transforms biopolitics into thanatopolitics either partially or completely. Accordingly, the attempts at an affirmative biopolitics, developed in the critical analyses of liberalism and Nazism, target precisely this immunitary drive, seeking to temper it by restoring its relation to the communitarian principle from which it arises (Esposito 2008a: 164–94; 2011: 165–77; 2012). Contemporary discourse on affirmative biopolitics therefore targets our desire for security and highlights its corrosive and violent effects on our freedom, equality and democracy: affirmative biopolitics is then a politics that accepts a modicum of insecurity as a means to reactivate or salvage our political communities.

In contrast, Stalinism was from the outset marked by a strong hostility to all things natural, which were to be overcome in messianic revolutionary transformation that abolishes things as they are. When this messianic project leaves the terrain of ideology and is rendered biopolitical, it can only access the immanence of lived reality through the negation of those forms of life that have been ideologically judged as obsolete and dying. Stalinist biopolitics exercises violence not as a matter of protecting reality but explicitly as a matter of changing it. The problematic of immunity never figured in this project and its violence can therefore hardly be theorised as the *excess* of protection. Tempering the drive for protection does not therefore appear to be a reasonable strategy for mitigating biopolitical violence – in fact, it was Stalinism *itself* that was characterised by the withdrawal of protection, be it from the starving peasants in the early 1930s or Soviet society at large in 1937. If we pose the question of the possibility of an affirmative biopolitics in this context, what is the pathway that we should pursue?

At first glance, the answer appears to lie on the surface: the source of the biopolitical violence of Stalinism is not immunity but *ideology*, whose devaluation of existing forms of life in the name of the transcendent ideal of communism led to their negation in the apocalyptic drive of the Great Break and the senseless terror of High Stalinism. As we have seen in the previous chapter, singling out ideology as the root of all evil in Soviet socialism has been the dominant response to the demise of the Soviet order both inside and outside Russia. Summing up our arguments in the preceding chapters, we may list at least four reasons why this move is problematic. First, it is well known that numerous victims of the Stalinist terror, from Zinovievites and Trotskyites in 1936 to West European communists in 1939, were actually supporters (if not the key representative authors) of this ideology, which makes it easy to reverse the anticommunist dogma: it was actually the *commitment* to communist ideology that was statistically most likely to get you killed in Stalin's USSR. Second, as the phenomenon of the Great Retreat demonstrates, Stalinism was not averse to compromising on key ideological issues, abandoning past ideological dogmas in favour of more flexible positions. It would therefore be just as legitimate to attribute the violence of Stalinist biopolitics to its *betrayal* of the ideology of communism, as Trotsky did in the 1930s and his followers continue to do today. Third, as our analysis of Shalamov's prose demonstrates, at its most extreme site of the Gulag, Soviet biopolitics did not operate through ideological indoctrination but rather rendered the latter inoperative by making the terrorised subject indifferent to any doctrinal content. Fourth, as we have seen in the discussion of the postcommunist rehabilitation of Stalinism, the focus on ideology in the process of destalinisation fatally misses its target, leaving precisely the biopolitical aspects of Stalinism immune to criticism, while endlessly and pointlessly bashing the egalitarian promises that it hypocritically displayed on its banners.

Of course, there is an evident limit to the dissociation of Stalinism and communist ideology, since it was precisely *this* ideology that was to be translated into life in 1929–32, *this* ideology that was then retreated from and transformed into a simulacrum of the real in 1934, and so on. While there are arguably good reasons to think of Stalinism in terms of the betrayal of the revolution, there are also good reasons why Stalin never explicitly abandoned communist ideology for conservatism, nationalism or what not. It is also pointless to attempt to purify the idea of communism from the Stalinist abomination by blaming the atrocities committed in its name on the purely contingent factors such as Stalin's paranoia, Bolshevik intolerance or Russian submissiveness. Idiosyncratic as it was, Stalinist biopolitics was a *biopolitics of socialism*: as we have demonstrated in this book, the problematisation constitutive of it is not to be found in any other historical modes of biopolitics. The root of Stalinist violence is precisely the nexus established in the biopolitical passage from ideology into life, whereby the revolutionary aspiration for the new life is transformed into the destruction of the old life and new life lives only a damaged and disaffected life of this destruction.

The difficulty of rethinking revolutionary biopolitics in affirmative terms consists in the fact that this lethal nexus cannot be uncoupled without reproducing the problems that led to the Stalinist biopolitical constellation in the first place. Let us first consider the possibility of abandoning the biopolitical logic and opting for something like a 'pure ideology', making socialism an ideological doctrine without an immediate relation to life. This would mean going back to the constellation that characterised Soviet Russia in the 1920s, when socialism referred to the ideological hegemony established by the dictatorially ruling party and did not yet penetrate the immanence of lived reality, aside from the myriad of minoritarian experiments in new forms of life, to which we shall return. As we have shown, it is precisely this constellation that *led* to the emergence of the Stalinist biopolitical problematisation at the end of the NEP period as an attempt to overcome the schism between the political domination of the socialist idea and its socioeconomic non-existence. As long as ideology is separated from life, that is, remains lifeless in its abstraction from lived reality, there will inevitably be attempts to bring the lifeless to life and these attempts will, in all likelihood, lead to making the living lifeless. It is impossible to oppose biopolitics by the sheer affirmation of the idea, utopia or fable: even 'revolutionary dreamers' eventually get tired of dreaming and want to see their dreams come true.

From this perspective, we must reject as overly facile any attempt to overcome biopolitics by bracketing politics off from life and restricting it to the ideological, ideational or, most generally, 'psychic' dimension. Even if it were possible to separate the dimensions of the ideational and the living, there is no guarantee that this separation would not be once again transgressed from the side of the ideational. After all, is not biopolitics as the politics that translates its idea into life first and foremost itself an *idea* and hence a product of the same ideational politics to which we are asked to return? Moreover, it is difficult to see how it might be possible to remove politics, which has *already* occupied the terrain of life, and, on some accounts, has been occupying it from time immemorial, from the sphere of life. Once life has become an object of politics, any attempt to proscribe the politicisation of life is at best naïve and at worst deceptive: is not the prohibition to intervene into 'life as such' a supremely biopolitical move that defends the existing modes of biopolitics against all possible challengers?

Another way to uncouple the nexus between ideology and life would be to bracket off the ideological dimension as such, to quit dreaming of revolution and get on with 'real life'. In this case, we would end up with something like a 'depoliticised biopolitics' that is content with managing life *as it is*. If revolutionary biopolitics, marked by the paradox of forcing transcendence into immanence, inevitably leads us into ruin and disaster, why not just forget about its messianic and emancipatory exigency and instead affirm a conservative, quasi-naturalist 'managerial biopolitics' that orders and secures what there is. In his *Logics of Worlds* (2009: 1–7) Badiou termed such a biopolitical disposition 'democratic materialism', according to which 'there are only bodies and languages', and all politics can aspire to is to manage, foster and optimise their pluralistic coexistence. Such a design is just as problematic as a purely ideological politics. First, insofar as both bodies and languages are always already suffused with ideas about how best to manage and regulate their existence, 'getting on with real life' simply means giving in to the *existent* mode of biopolitics, e.g. neoliberal biopolitics in today's Western societies. Putting an end to revolutionary dreaming can only take the form of falling into conservative slumber. Second, even if it were possible to reduce politics to the 'non-ideological' management of the vital substrate, the very choice in favour of such a politics would necessarily arise from a certain ideational or ideological perspective: there is no reason why life is to be protected 'as it is' and not 'as it might be', in its potentiality and becoming that perpetually transform and negate 'what is'. A pure biopolitics 'without ideas' is in fact a particularly powerful ideological construct.

Our study of Stalinism permits us to isolate another difficulty with opting for a post-ideological biopolitics as a pathway out of totalitarian terror. The idea of a nihilistic 'pure biopolitics' is uncannily resonant with one of the three negative inflections that characterised High Stalinism, namely the Great Retreat, and, as we have seen, the Great Retreat is never too far from the Great Terror. The Retreat need not be interpreted as a sign of the concealed ideological proximity of Stalinism to Russian nationalism or conservative monarchism (cf. Rogovin 1998: xv–xix, 144–6), but rather as the effect of the fundamental paradox of revolutionary biopolitics as the forcing of transcendence within immanence. If the resources for grand transformation are to be drawn from the same domain that is to be transformed (i.e. the immanence of social life), then what, short of the utter *destruction* of these resources (the possibility realised in different ways during the Great Break and the Great Terror), could possibly be the effect of such transformation, other than the *recycling* of what is? It appears that whatever Stalinism did not *destroy*, for example the lifeworlds of well-off peasants or the non-Bolshevik intelligentsia, it had to leave almost *intact*, for example the pre-revolutionary petty-bourgeois urban lifestyles adopted, in a crude and inane manner, by the newcomers to the cities after the collectivisation. This approach renders problematic every attempt to oppose the ideological extremism of the Soviet project to the nihilism of Russian postcommunism, such as Dmitry Bykov's effort to salvage at least a modicum of justification for

A Real Renewal of Life: Towards an Affirmative Biopolitics

the Soviet project by comparing it favourably to the 'non-historical' traditionalism that preceded it and its nihilistic imitation that succeeded it.

> Communism, wherever it was victorious, led to pretty much the same results. Communist atrocities were not owing to Russian sadomasochism but were common to all totalitarian regimes. But this is where the most frightening thought occurs: what if the Russian were even scarier? What if the choice between the Soviet and the Russian is the hopeless attempt to choose between the horrible ending and horror without end? For all its atrocities, the Soviet project was an attempt to take Russian history out of the endless cycle of repetition that brought nothing but eternal backwardness. However horrible the Soviet project was, to the Russia of the 1910s it brought not only atrocities but also progress. It was Russia's own choice that after 70 years it got rid of the progress while continuing the atrocities. (Bykov 2008: 266)

Yet, if our analysis of the Great Retreat is at all correct, then it makes little sense to compare the Russian tradition and the Soviet project, trying to decide which of them was worse. To cite Stalin's own famous remark, they are 'both worse', simply because they were *both* at work in the Soviet regime as early as the mid-1930s. Russia 'got rid of the progress and kept the atrocities' not after the seventy years of socialism but *during* these years. As soon as the apocalyptic project of the construction of socialism was halted halfway in favour of a compromise with the non-socialist reality, it became no longer possible to choose between the Soviet and the Russian since the 'new' Soviet form of life produced by Stalinist biopolitics was merely a degraded version of the 'old' Russian one. It was *this* society that survived Stalinism and sustained Soviet socialism for the subsequent three decades, during which the gap between the reality of the retreat and the ideological simulacrum became ever greater. It was also *this* society that mockingly abandoned the principles of this simulacrum in the late 1980s, bringing the retreat from socialism to its logical conclusion. Thus, the postcommunist Russian society, whose nihilistic renunciation of all ideas, except those of mindless consumerism and superstitious religiosity, is observed and lamented both within and outside Russia, is the direct descendant and *true heir* of the Stalinist society, formed in the Great Retreat that negated its own biopolitical drive of the Great Break towards the New Soviet Person.

Thus, the non-ideological biopolitics that manages 'life as it is' is not an alternative to totalitarian terror but its possible counterpart. In Nietzschean terms, we may grasp Stalinist biopolitics as unfolding between the two extremes of the *active-nihilist* production of the living dead and the *passive-nihilist* adjustment to what is (Nietzsche 1968: 9–39). While most of us would certainly prefer a life of nothingness to violent death, it makes little sense to oppose the former to the latter as biopolitical rationalities, since both of them emerge from a single source as negative inflections of revolutionary biopolitics. When today's proponents of 'post-ideological' biopolitics of the administration of bodies and languages console themselves by contrasting its dreary reality to the violent paroxysms of Stalinist terror, they should recall that this terror unfolded not on the battlefields of the Civil War or even the 'heroic' campaigns for collectivisation, but rather against the background of stabilisation and the restoration of order, the abandonment of 'excesses' and the relaxation of work norms, the appearance of jovial comedies such as *Volga-Volga* and the opening of the Moscow Luna Park (Schlögel 2012). The retreat into nihilism does not spare us from terror, which is, after all, only another way in which nothingness manifests itself in and takes hold of life. While the choice for the former against the latter is understandable, the case of Stalinism demonstrates how easy it is to end up having *both*. 'The loss of illusions no longer says much about our world. The proximity between the normal disorder of the "disillusioned" order of things and the extreme of destruction or madness tells us much more about it' (Rancière 2013b: 49). Indeed, the rise of terrorism in the contemporary postcommunist world, the world without illusions and big ideas, illustrates the same confluence of retreat and terror as Stalinism showed in the late 1930s.

If it is impossible to uncouple the nexus between ideology and life in favour of either pure ideology or pure administration of life, this means that the alternative to the biopolitical/thanatopolitical constellation of Stalinism must be sought within the biopolitical terrain. Rather than seek to separate ideas and lives or purify one from the other, we ought to conceive of a different *relationship* between them, which does not take the form of the forcing of the transcendence of the idea into the immanence of life. In the following section we shall elaborate one possible version of such a relationship on the basis of Agamben's critique of the ontology of effectiveness and Quentin Meillassoux's distinction between various modes of presence.

DIFFUSE SOCIALISM

In the preceding chapters we have demonstrated how Stalinist biopolitics affirmed the possibility of going beyond 'socialism' as merely institutional and ideological domination of the Bolshevik Party towards socialism as a form of life that really exists. We have then shown that 'real socialism' as the product of Stalinism was constitutively contaminated by negativity, first in the apocalyptic drive of the Great Break that unleashed the paroxysmal destruction of non-socialist forms of life and then in the three negations thereof. Rather than produce socialism as a new form of life, Stalinism ended up producing the *recycling of old life* in the form of the Retreat, the *fake façade* of the new life in the form of socialist realism and the *destruction of life* through the production of the living dead in the Terror. Does this mean that socialism has no real positive presence aside from this proliferation of negativity in various forms, so that the claims of its ideological opponents about its utopian character, incapable of any 'real renewal of life', are ultimately vindicated? This depends on how we understand *real presence*, what we mean by and expect from socialism as 'real'.

As we have seen, Stalinism ventured to make socialism real by forcing the transcendence of the idea into the immanence of life, making new beings real by intervening into the realm of real being. It is this approach to reality as an effect of wilful action, as a project of 'construction', that defines Stalinism and distinguishes it from both liberalism and Nazism. Yet, to insist on this difference is not to attribute to Stalinism the difference from all things Western, let alone subsume it under some specifically Russian 'cultural tradition'. Stalinism certainly differs from the modes of biopolitics that never addressed the question of the constitution of a new life after a social revolution. Yet, while the revolution in question did not take place in the West, the thought of revolution remains an inherent part of the Western ontopolitical tradition. The bio-thanato-political character of the Stalinist project is therefore not a problem for area studies but rather pertains to the metaphysical tradition that the West has not yet surpassed.

In *Opus Dei* (2013) Agamben proceeds from his detailed archaeology of the Christian liturgy to argue for the coexistence of two opposed ontologies in the Western tradition, the 'ancient' (Greek) ontology of being as substance and the (Christian) ontology of duty, command or, most generally, operativity.

> There are two distinct and connected ontologies in the tradition of the West: the first, the ontology of the command, proper to the juridical-religious sphere, which is expressed in the imperative and has a performative character: the second, proper to the philosophical-scientific tradition, which is expressed in the form of the indicative. (Agamben 2013: 120)

While the ontology of substance inquires into what is and therefore founds descriptive (natural) science, the ontology of command addresses being in terms what ought to be and hence founds the domains of law and religion with their prescriptive approach to being. Whereas the former ontology describes a state of affairs in the indicative mood and thus corresponds to the constative dimension of the speech act, the latter ontology constitutes (or at least seeks to constitute) a state of affairs by prescribing it in an imperative mood and thus exemplifies the performative dimension (see Agamben 2005: 131–4; 2009a: 65–72).

In Agamben's reading, Western modernity has been marked by the gradual ascendancy of the ontology of command, demonstrated for example in the prevalence of the juridico-religious paradigm in philosophy from Kant's ethics to Heidegger's ontology (Agamben 2013: 112–25). Two consequences of this ascendancy are of major relevance to our argument. The first is the understanding of being in terms of its *effects*.

> While in the vocabulary of classical ontology being and substance are considered independently of the effects that they can produce, in effectiveness being is inseparable from its effects; it names being insofar as it is effective, produces certain effects and at the same time is determined by them. Effectiveness is the new ontological dimension that is affirmed first in the liturgical sphere and is then to be extended progressively until in modernity it coincides with being as such. (Ibid.: 41)

We have encountered exactly the same logic in Fedorov's projective knowledge whose task is to realise an idea in life. We may also recall that for Fedorov it was precisely the liturgy that offered a model for this mode of knowledge. In the liturgical sphere effectiveness pertained to the presence of Christ in the liturgy, which was neither a mere symbolic, theatrical representation nor real 'flesh and bone' presence (ibid.: 40) but rather a presence coinciding entirely with the effects of grace produced in sacramental rites. For Agamben, this reduction of being to its effects was generalised in modernity to such an extent that

> being and acting today have for us no representation other than effectiveness. Only what is effective and as such governable and efficacious, is real: this is the extent to which office, under the guise of the humble functionary or the glorious priest, has changed from top to bottom the rules of first philosophy as much as those of ethics. (Ibid.: xiii).

It is easy to observe this generalisation of effectiveness in the biopolitical context. Just as being is what must be realised, actualised or effectuated, so politics is what must be *lived*, actualised in real forms of life, and not simply hover above them as an ideological superstructure or an apparatus of security. Politics consists entirely in its effects produced in the domain of life. The Stalinist impatience with mere ideological hegemony and its fateful attempt to force socialism into lived reality is thus not an

A Real Renewal of Life: Towards an Affirmative Biopolitics 263

exception to but the most extreme form of this ontopolitical disposition. The postcommunist designation of Stalin as an 'effective manager', with which we began this study, is certainly a correct designation of at least the ambition of the Stalinist project, which was to make socialism real as an effect of governmental practice. While the naturalist modes of biopolitics, particularly liberalism, were tempered by the fact that their effects were largely conceived in terms of the modulation of the already existent (such as enhanced security, amplified productivity, and so on), Stalinist biopolitics posed for itself the task of producing effects that were hitherto non-existent and, moreover, were antagonistic to the forms of life that did exist. Yet, as we have seen, what made Stalinism extreme is not merely the transcendent character of the ideas that it sought to actualise, but also its own fervour in actualising them – in a different ontopolitical setting, communism might have remained a harmless utopian discourse with no relation to being and no drive to establish such a relation.

The second consequence of the ascendancy of the ontology of effectiveness pertains to the question of the will. In the original liturgical context the effects of the sacraments were produced irrespectively of the character of the priest who administered them, whose presence was nonetheless absolutely necessary for the procedure to be effective (ibid.: 28). In Agamben's argument, the subsequent expansion of the ontology of effectiveness led to the predominance of the metaphysics of the *will* as the principle of the actualisation of potentiality. If potential being is what can both be and not be, then its passage to actuality necessarily presupposes an act of will behind it.

> [The] movement of being is not produced in itself and by nature but implies an incessant 'putting-to-work', i.e. it is thought as an *ergon* that refers to the effectuation on the part of a subject that will be, in the first and last instance, identified with the will. If being is something that must be realised, if it necessarily implies a putting-to-work, it will be necessary to presuppose a will that renders it possible. Will is the form that being takes in the ontology of command and operativity. If being does not exist, but must actualise itself, then in its very essence it is will and command; and vice versa, if being is will, then it does not simply exist but has to be. (Ibid.: 129)

Thus, every biopolitics is from the outset a voluntarist project: it is not life itself that demands either its protection or its transformation. Life is politicised and politics is vitalised by the will of the subject. The extremist character of Stalinism is also observable in this aspect: since the effects of socialist biopolitics belong to the order of the creation of new life rather than protection, maintenance or optimisation of the already existent, the will behind it assumes the status of the demiurge rather than a physician, a shepherd or any other, more modest metaphor of the function of political leadership. We may suggest that the infamous 'cult of personality' around Stalin was not merely an expression of personal vanity or an instrumental ploy to ensure mass obedience, but rather followed, in a bizarrely logical manner, from the character of the Soviet biopolitical project: if this project involved no less than the creation of a new life, then it is hardly surprising that the will behind it would be deified.

From this perspective, the question of affirmative biopolitics ultimately pertains to the possibility of conceiving of real presence otherwise than in the terms of operativity, effectiveness and will, so that politics is no longer viewed as the activity of the governmental construction of forms of life. In his masterful decipherment of Mallarmé's *Throw of the Dice* Quentin Meillassoux (2012) introduced a distinction between three principles underlying various forms of what he calls 'civic religion', 'ceremony' or 'drama', which elevates social life above its everyday banality and gives presence to what lies or goes beyond it. The first principle, familiar to us from Greek theatre and the attempt to revive it in Wagner's opera, is *representation*, which 'renders visible to the masses the principle of their communion with the aid of a narrative embellished with song [and] represents to the people their own mystery' (Meillassoux 2012: 108). For Meillassoux's Mallarmé, this representational option is radically insufficient in the modern age, not simply because the Greek origin is irrevocably lost, but because it is not *our* origin in the first place, since 'Christianity has handed down to us a ritual superior in power to those of paganism – namely the real convocation of a real drama' (ibid.: 109). In contrast to Greek theatre, the Christian Mass does not strive to *represent* Christ's passion but rather to 'produce its true, effective *Presence* to the point where the host is absorbed by the faithful' (ibid.: 109). The Christian ritual goes well beyond the 'communions of total art' in offering a collective communion around a real event.

The decline of Christianity in the late nineteenth century did not entail the disappearance of the desire for such a communion but only marked its absence more explicitly. It is in order to satisfy this desire that Mallarmé, in Meillassoux's reading, ventured to invent a new ceremony, devoid of all transcendence and 'deifying' nothing but Chance as such, the radical contingency of all things.

> The ceremony of the moderns will be a ceremony of hesitation, the sole act capable of comprising in itself the infinite opposites: hesitation to smile with irony, or to believe with sincerity in the possible rebirth of a poetic and political communion. (Meillassoux 2013: 44)

A Real Renewal of Life: Towards an Affirmative Biopolitics

What is important for the purposes of our study is less the content of this new ceremony than the very principle of presence that separates it from its predecessors. In his analysis Meillassoux draws a distinction between the *parousia* and the Eucharist. While the former refers to 'properly speaking, the *presentation* of God, the absolute manifestation of Christ in glory at the end of Times', the Eucharist is a form of presentation that is simultaneously *real* and *incomplete*.

> The Eucharist is thus a paradoxical mode of 'presence in absence': The divine is there, among the elect, in the very host, but not yet returned. It gives itself according to a sufficiently withdrawn mode of reality to leave room for both remembrance (of the Passion) and expectation (of Salvation). It is a presence that is not in the present, but in the past and in the future. We should speak, to signify the Eucharistic mode of presence, of a *diffusion* of the divine, as opposed to its *representation* (the Greek scene) or its *presentation* (Christian Parousia). (Ibid.: 111–12; my emphasis)

In Meillassoux's reading, Mallarmé's poetry liberates this model of diffusion from both representation and eschatology, 'whereby the Eucharistic mode of presence is no longer anticipative but becomes the supreme regime of divine being-there' (ibid.: 112). In such a recasting, Eucharistic diffusion is no longer an indication of what is to come, a teaser of full presence, but a mode of real presence in its own right, whereby something only becomes accessible to us in its diffusion that never assumes a definite or complete form. This mode of presence is evidently most appropriate to Mallarmé's deification of Chance or contingency, since it incorporates contingency in its own unfolding: a hesitant, tentative and fragile process of diffusion, which is always at the risk of discontinuing, embodies within itself the principle of its own possible not-having-been (see Meillassoux 2013: 41–5).

Does Meillassoux's logic of diffusion succeed in surpassing the ontology of effectiveness, duty and will? At first glance, Meillassoux's use of the Eucharist appears to replicate the liturgical logic that gave rise to this ontology in the first place. As Agamben demonstrates, the Christian tradition also interprets Christ's presence in the Eucharist in terms of its effects, as a '[real] presence but of a special type corresponding to the specific goal of the sacrament' (Casel cited in Agamben 2013: 39).

> The liturgical mystery is not limited to representing the passion of Christ, but in representing it, it realises its effects, so that one can say that the presence of Christ in the liturgy coincides totally with its effectiveness. But this implies a transformation of ontology, in which substantiality and effectiveness will seem to be identified. (Agamben 2013: 40)

And yet, insofar as the liturgy is not identical with the *parousia*, the absolute manifestation of Christ, his presence in the effects of the sacraments could not possibly be full or complete. The sacramental host, the priest and the faithful are all *there* at the scene of the sacrament, but Christ is there only in the sense of *not* being there himself but only present *through* the effects of the sacrament; or, conversely, he is absent despite being the primary cause of all the effects produced in the sacrament. His presence is real but *not quite*, since it is not exhausted by its effects, leaving a certain excess of being over effectiveness. This is the only reason why these effects could be produced in the first place and, moreover, produced *repeatedly*: if their primary agent wholly actualised himself in the ceremony rather than partly withdraw from it, there would only ever have been *one* sacramental ritual, in which *parousia* would have been attained definitively. Instead, in Meillassoux's account, the being of Christ is diffused in sacramental effects, which never coalesce into a figure of Christ's full presence in the world. The Eucharistic logic disseminates the being of Christ through its effects without forcing its full actualisation. The transcendent appears in the immanent without being forced into it and without anything being forced out of it.

While the adjudication of the success or failure of Mallarme's strategy (or Meillassoux's interpretation of it) is best left to literary scholars, the three logics of conjuring presence that Meillassoux identifies are highly suggestive for understanding the Stalinist biopolitical rationality and the possibility of its overturning. As we have argued, during the period of the NEP the political dictatorship of the Communist Party was exercised over the underdeveloped agrarian-capitalist society, which entailed that socialism was only present in the sphere of ideological and institutional *representation*. In Meillassoux's terms, pre-Stalinist socialism was embodied by the Party, which represented to the people their own 'mystery' (be it equality, emancipation, Marx's 'generic being', and so on), which was phenomenally inaccessible in their everyday life. Living under socialism was thus difficult to distinguish from living under the socialists in government, a fact that ultimately made little difference to the people, who remained content with the old adage that those in power are all the same, socialist or not. Slavoj Žižek once told a joke about the difference between Stalinist USSR and socialist Yugoslavia: 'in Russia, the members of the *nomenklatura*, the representatives of the ordinary people, drive themselves in expensive limousines, while in Yugoslavia ordinary people themselves ride in limousines through their representatives' (Žižek 1998). As long as we are within the realm of representation, we only ever experience socialism 'through our representatives'.

A Real Renewal of Life: Towards an Affirmative Biopolitics

The apocalyptic drive of the Great Break sought to overcome the limits of representation and produce socialism as a real presence, in which one is incorporated as a living being and not merely as an abstract citizen of an officially 'socialist' state. As we have seen, however, this attempt to force the *parousia* of socialism into the immanence of lived reality ended up in a sociocidal disaster. The destructive dislocations of the Great Break eventually led to the partial negation of this project in the forms of the Great Retreat, the Great Simulacrum and the Great Terror, in which the socialist ideal was respectively recoiled from, faked and replaced by a meaningless fury of destruction. During the post-Stalin period the threat of terror was gradually reduced and the effectiveness of the simulacrum was weakened, leaving the retreat *from* socialism as the sole remainder *of* socialism. The quest for presence ended up producing the void of absence.

Yet, if Meillassoux is correct, the alternative to the apocalyptic forcing of the real presence of socialism need not be the disillusioned return to the logic of representation that renounces the very idea of a biopolitical transformation of life in its immanent reality and remains content with 'superstructural' or 'ideological' governance. If socialism is diffused according to the Mallarméan radicalisation of the Eucharistic model, it is no longer restricted to the domain of representation but is disseminated into the immanence of the real, and yet this real presence never takes an accomplished form of a positive order, but only exists in the mode of its own dissemination. In other words, the biopolitical conversion of the communist idea, whose realisation was so disastrous under Stalinism, need not be conceived in terms of constructing a complete form of life but is rather thinkable in terms of the infinite process of the diffusion of this idea that produces real effects in the forms of life without ever coalescing into a form of life of its own. What is at stake in the idea of diffusion is evidently not any practical 'moderation' of the utopian project of socialism, but the abandonment of the fundamental logic of the *project* itself, of the ontological presuppositions that posit bringing into presence, construction, effectuation as the true criterion of reality.

What attracts us in the logic of diffusion is not its potential status of an alternative model of socialist biopolitics, but rather its resonance with the *actuality* of the pre-Stalinist Soviet reality, captured by Stites's notion of 'experimental lives' addressed in Chapter 3. From a conventional biopolitical perspective, oriented towards the construction of real effects, the sheer myriad of utopian experiments in new 'socialist' forms of life in every possible sphere only testifies to their ultimate inefficacy, their failure to attain a real presence and a real incorporation, so that all we are left with is a plurality of representations, a *theatre* of socialism that conceals the failure to attain socialism itself. This is why it would be naïve to expect these experimental orientations to have succeeded as an 'alternative' to Stalinism on the eve of the Great Break. Once the political discourse is framed in terms of the ontology of effectiveness, 'real socialism' is only thinkable as the project of the full actualisation of the ideal in reality, however violent this actualisation turns out to be. Yet, if, with the invaluable benefit of hindsight, we abandon the desire for the full forcing of transcendence into immanence, we may begin to appreciate the power of the sheer diffusion of the ideal in the undoubtedly incoherent, mutually exclusive and internally contradictory practices of housing and labour communes, new forms of organising work and family life, experimental policies in education and child-rearing, utopian art works and clumsy attempts to imitate them in life.

In this diffusion socialism was certainly present, but never as a complete 'order of things', a transcendentally structured *world* in Badiou's terms (2009). It was only present as a hesitant and uncertain diffusion of the new *amid* the old, that is, amid the 'state capitalist' order of the NEP, which all these experiments opposed in their own ways but did not manage or even attempt to destroy but rather coexisted with and even practised a certain negligence in relation to. Everything depends on how we understand the 'incomplete' character of this diffusion. If we grasp it in the negative terms of deferral and delay, whereby socialism always remains 'to come' but never actually arrives, we are thrown back to the disappointment in 'paralyzed' and 'thwarted' messianism (Agamben 1999a: 171) that inspired the Stalinist Great Break in the first place as the Second Revolution seeking to accomplish what the first one left in abeyance. If the undecidable diffusion of socialism is an indicator of its insufficient or defective reality, then the 'experimental lives' in which it is diffused are indeed reduced to Stites's 'revolutionary dreams'. Yet, why should an actual experiment in *living* in a new way be reducible to *dreaming*? Evidently, the only 'dreamlike' thing about these experiments was the aspiration at their totalisation, whereby a self-consciously minoritarian practice would become universally widespread and institutionalised as the new order of things. It is precisely this dream of the radicalisation of the Eucharist towards *parousia*, of the *fusion* of the diffuse experiments into a positive form of order, that is counter-productive, since it leads to the suspension of this diffusion as such, the gathering together of the disseminated effects into a new unity, in which, quite unsurprisingly, no real presence of socialism could be found, simply because the process of its diffusion has ceased. Conversely, as soon as we stop approaching the diffusion of the idea as a mere pathway towards its actualisation in a form of life and instead understand it as itself its only possible mode

A Real Renewal of Life: Towards an Affirmative Biopolitics 269

of actuality, we are able to recognise that our revolutionary dreams may have already come true.

SOCIALIST LIVES IN THE ABSENCE OF SOCIALISM

The logic of the diffusion of the idea in experimental lives resonates with an influential reinterpretation of the logic of emancipation in Jacques Rancière's political thought. For Rancière, equality, which is the fundamental axiom of any politics worthy of the name and certainly of any 'communist' politics, cannot be posited as the principle of a constituted social order.

> [Equality] turns into its opposite the moment it aspires to a place in the social or state organisation. The two processes must remain absolutely alien to each other, constituting two radically different communities even if composed of the same individuals, the community of equal minds and that of social bodies lumped together by the fiction of inequality. (Rancière 1999: 34–5; see also Rancière 2010: 168–70).

This paradox of equality is addressed in detail in Rancière's masterpiece *The Ignorant Schoolmaster*. The method of intellectual emancipation, developed by Joseph Jacotot in the early nineteenth century, makes it possible to emancipate any individual by teaching him or her what one does not even know oneself, by interrogating and verifying the work of the pupil on the basis of the presupposition of the absolute equality of intelligence of all speaking beings. While it is possible to use this presupposition as a point of departure in the practices of emancipation of concrete individuals, it is impossible to deploy it as a principle of the social order, which accounts for the eventual perversion of Jacotot's method in the practices of education reformers in France and its subsequent oblivion. Against every reformist or revolutionary hope for the possibility of a better society, Rancière somewhat glumly declares that 'there is no such thing as a possible society. There is only the society that exists' (Rancière 1991: 81).

This does not mean that all forms of social order are the same, but that, irrespectively of all possible differences between them, any society that actually exists is necessarily structured in the hierarchical manner that Rancière terms 'police' and hence impossible to govern by the idea of equality. For this reason, a communist society is only thinkable in terms of the expropriation of the emancipation of individuals by the new leaders, who now exercise 'the power of communists over workers', an approach that Rancière traces back to Plato's *Republic* and finds operative in contemporary China (2010: 170). 'One must choose between making an unequal society out of equal men and making an equal society out of unequal men' (Rancière 1991: 133). Equality is a practice that can never yield stable effects that will coalesce into a new social order: 'anybody can be emancipated and emancipate other persons so that the whole of mankind be made of emancipated individuals. But a society can never be emancipated' (Rancière 2010: 169).

Thus, in Rancière's argument, there is an irreducible conflict between communism as the name of a positive social order to be constructed and the factual communism of emancipated workers, whose very emancipation may well make them hostile to the social order that claims to act in their name. Indeed, this conflict may be traced back to the moment of the emergence of Marxism.

> Marx and Engels decided to disband the Communist Party they had created and to wait for the evolution of the productive forces to produce true communist proletarians – instead of those silly asses, who thought they were their equals though they did not catch any of their theory. Communism, they said, is not the gathering of emancipated individuals, attempting to experience collective life as a response to selfishness and injustice. It is the full implementation of a form of universality already at work in the capitalist organization of production. (Ibid.: 170)

Evidently, such an understanding of communism in terms of the full forcing of the presence of a certain positive order erases 'what is at the core of emancipation, namely the capacity of anybody to be where she can't be and do what she cannot do' (ibid.: 171). Instead, one's very subjectivity appears to be a result of the world-historical tendency that one is driven to assume solely as a result of one's own disempowerment as proletarian. Moreover, since the proletarians do not know their disempowerment due to the ideological mystification of the system they inhabit, they must be taught the knowledge of their own ignorance, which further subjects them to the authority of those communists who know best. Thus, for Rancière, communism was *from the outset* (and not only under Stalin or the Bolsheviks) characterised by the tension between its constitutive affirmation of emancipation and its inegalitarian orientation towards those to be emancipated that perpetually suspected them of not being the 'right' kind of workers (that is, trade unionists, anarchists, nationalists, and so on). The eventual triumph of the latter orientation that combined 'its faith in historical necessity with the culture of distrust [in workers] produced a specific kind of communism: communism as the appropriation of productive forces by state power and its management by a "communist" elite' (ibid.: 176).

A Real Renewal of Life: Towards an Affirmative Biopolitics

Given the demise of this form of communism after the Cold War, Rancière suggests that 'the only communist legacy that is worth examining is the multiplicity of forms of experimentation of the capacity of anybody, yesterday and today' (Rancière 2010: 176). Communism is not something that can be *constructed* as a form of social order but rather consists in 'dissensual forms of collective struggle, life and thinking' (ibid.: 176) that need not coalesce into such an order and may well be actualised in opposition to it. In Meillassoux's terms, the experimental diffusion of emancipatory practices need not be accompanied, and may even be hampered, by the attempt to fuse these practices into a form of order that would give full presence to the principle that these practices disseminate. The ontological status of communism is not that of an effect or a construct but rather that of a *movement* of diffusion that is not exhausted in its effects, but rather consists entirely in its own hesitant, undecidable and contingent spreading.

In his later work *Aisthesis* (2013a) Rancière returns to the tension between emancipation as praxis and as a principle of social order, drawing an important analogy between politics and aesthetics. The emergence of the 'aesthetic regime' in arts during the late eighteenth to early nineteenth century was made possible by the break with any hierarchical order regulating representation, paving the way for the radical equality of the objects of art and the radical freedom of its subjects. Art made possible the community of the free and the equal, but only on the condition that this community no longer took the form of a project of constructing a new form of order. Freedom and equality were not conceived as determinate goals of action but as the effects of suspending all end-oriented action in favour of free play.

> [The] aesthetic paradigm was constructed against the representative order, which defined discourse as a body with well-articulated parts, the poem as a plot and a plot as an order of actions. The aesthetic revolution developed as an unending break with the hierarchical model of the body, the story, and action. The free people, says Schiller, is the people that plays, the people embodied in this passivity that suspends the very opposition between active and passive; the little Sevillian beggars are the embodiment of the ideal, says Hegel, because they do nothing; the novel dethroned drama as the exemplary art of speech, bearing witness to the capacity of men and women without quality to feel all kinds of ideal aspirations and sensual frenzies. But it did so at the cost of ruining the model of the story with causes and effects and of action with means and ends. The aesthetic paradigm of the new community, of men free and equal in their sensible life itself tends to cut this community off from all the paths that are normally used to reach a goal. (Rancière 2013a: xiv–xv)

While this idea of gaining freedom and equality through inoperativity may at first glance appear to be an aesthetic utopia entirely at odds with properly political action (cf. Agamben 2011: 197–259), Rancière suggests that exactly the same paradox applies to

> the practices and theories of social emancipation. Emancipated workers could not repudiate the hierarchical model governing the distribution of activities without taking distance from the capacity to act that subjected them to it and from the action plans of the engineers of the future. The fullest expression of the fighting workers' collective was called the general strike, an exemplary equivalence of strategic action and radical inaction. (Rancière 2013a: xv–xvi)

The emancipation from the existing inegalitarian order is not attained by one's submission to the project of the construction of a new order but by the suspension of action in the present one. The fulfilment of the emancipatory promises of communism did not require *building* it as a new form of order and all attempts to do so progressively diminished the degree of the emancipation of the workers until, under Stalinism, there was none left.

> The scientific Marxist revolution certainly wanted to put an end to the workers' reveries, along with utopian programmes. But by opposing them to the effects of real social development, it kept subordinating the end and means of action to the movement of life, at the risk of discovering that this movement does not want anything and does not allow any strategy to lay claim to it. Social revolution is the daughter of aesthetic revolution and was only able to deny this relation by transforming a strategic will that had lost its world into a policy of exception. (Ibid.: xvi)

Rancière's rethinking of communism as an experiment in emancipation clearly goes against the grain of much of communist theory and practice. Yet, for all his acerbic criticism of Marx and Marxism, his understanding of communism is not very distant from Marx's own formula of communism as the 'real movement that abolishes the present state of things' (Marx and Engels 1998 [1846]: 57). Interestingly, there is nothing in this formula that stipulates the construction of a positive order, a form of state or government. On the contrary, Marx and Engels explicitly denied that communism was 'a state of affairs, which is to be established, an ideal to which reality will have to adjust itself' (ibid.: 57). Communism was not defined as a constructible effect actualised in lived reality, produced through the translation of the ideal into the real. However self-evident it appears to us today, the *construction* of socialism as the first stage of communism, undertaken in the USSR under Stalin, was not a necessary project from the standpoint of Marx's definition and indeed contradicted this definition quite explicitly. Yet, if communism is not a matter of the effectuation of the ideal in the real, how are the ideal and the real related to each other in a non-constructionist way? Communism is neither simply an ideal with no relation to life (pure utopia) nor an attribute of lived reality as it is (pure givenness). It is a real movement *within* lived reality that *abolishes* the present order of this lived reality, yet, importantly, not the reality itself. What is it a real movement *of*? What is it that moves within lived reality, abolishing the positive states of affairs within it without itself coalescing into such a state? It is evidently nothing other than the *idea*, insofar as it is diffused in experimental lives. It is in this diffusion that the idea *lives*, not as a matter of forcing, construction or effectuation, but of sheer *spreading*.

The notion of the diffusion of the idea in experimental lives provides us with a mode of problematisation that both belongs to the biopolitical constellation and displaces its foundation in the ontology of effectiveness. An affirmative biopolitics is a politics that does not seek to force its ideal into the real, construct a positive order on the basis of its principles or translate its ideas into life. All that it affirms is solely the life of its ideas as they are diffused in the real. Yet, this formulation still leaves us with a question that must be resolved if affirmative biopolitics is to be anything more than another attempt to force ideas into life by forcing the living out of life. What does it mean to say that an idea *lives* in its diffusion in the real? How can an idea access life without simultaneously negating it? And if it is able to access it, can it also succeed where Stalinism and all forms of constructivist biopolitics failed and actually transform life in the positive way? In the remainder of this chapter we shall address these questions by drawing on Michel Henry's material phenomenology of life.

IMMANENCE AND BARBARISM

Throughout this book we have addressed biopolitics in terms of the government of life in terms of an idea and demonstrated how violent and lethal this process might become when the forcing of an idea into life takes the form of the forcing out of anterior forms of life that conflict with this idea. Yet, why should bringing an idea into life be a problem in the first place? After all, the origin of any idea whatsoever can only be in life itself. In Deleuze's succinct formulation, 'it is the passage of life within language that constitutes Ideas' (Deleuze 1997: 5). Even when they tend to be spelled with a capital 'I', ideas cannot be entirely external to life but are its forms that find their expression in language, just as other forms of life may find their expression in agricultural production, painting, interior decoration or religious rituals. What is it about life that makes it so resistant to the ideas that it itself perpetually generates that these ideas have to be forced into it?

Michel Henry's phenomenological approach begins with a radical disjunction between life and the world, in which ideas dwell. Life is characterised by radical *immanence* and is defined solely in terms of *auto-affection*, the experience of itself, which is withdrawn from being, world and language, the dimensions that Henry terms the Outside (Henry 2003: 13–20). This experience is prior to and independent of all distinctions that ground our being in the world: 'Self-affection, independent of the difference between "subject and object", between "knower and known", independent of Difference as such, constitutes life's essence' (Henry 1993: 164). Furthermore, Henry posits life as prior to being itself: 'Life "is" not. Rather, it occurs and does not cease occurring. This incessant coming of life is its eternal coming forth in itself, a process without end, a *constant movement*' (Henry 2003: 55; my emphasis). Thus, Henry reverses the famous Heideggerian hierarchy that subordinated life, understood in the privative sense, to being, 'under the pretext that it would be necessary for life itself "to be"' (Henry 2008: 3).

> As such, the living would delineate only a region of being, a regional ontology. But the being to which life is submitted is Greek being, the being of a worldly being, which would be thought and conceived starting on the basis of the world. Such a being would still only be a dead being or rather a nonbeing if the ek-stasis in which its proper phenomenality unfolds were not auto-affected in the immediacy of the pathos of Life. So Life always founds what we call 'being' rather than the contrary. (Ibid.: 3)

Before Dasein can experience being thrown into the world and the ecstasis of possibility within it, it must first experience itself as living in the sense of a 'primal suffering that defies every liberty and every possibility of getting rid of oneself in the ek-stasis of a world' (Henry 1993: 127). The essence of life, which is prior to every will and to every action, thus consists in suffering itself, experiencing its own touch.

> [Life] is the force of being, the edifying gathering that presents everything to itself. Such a force, which is neither action nor will, which is not action but its opposite, is the passion of being, the primal suffering in virtue of which the essence of being is also that of life. After immanence and as its ultimate precondition, every philosophy of life inevitably encounters this second essential determination: *affectivity*. (Ibid.: 177)

As entirely contained in self-affection, life is *integral*, that is, not divided or differing from itself. Moreover, it is non-relational in the sense that it only relates to itself, but not to itself as the other. The essence of life is thus interiority and solitude: 'That which has the experience of self, that which enjoys itself and is nothing other than this pure enjoyment of itself, than this pure experience of self, is life. Solitude is the essence of life' (Henry 1973: 285). Life is solitary because it only ever relates to itself: in all its suffering or enjoyment it is itself that life suffers or enjoys. Life gives itself to itself prior to and apart from any opening of the world or any relation to the other.

> [Life] is given in its own way, in a completely unique way, even though this singular mode of givenness is universal. Life is given in such a way that what it gives is given to itself and that what it gives to itself is never separated from it, not in the least. In this way, what life gives is itself. Life is self-givenness in a radical and rigorous sense, in the sense that it is both life that gives and life that is given. No road leads to life except life itself. In life, no road leads outside of itself. Life is absolute subjectivity inasmuch as it experiences itself and is nothing other than this experience. It is the pure fact of experiencing itself immediately and without any distance. By touching each point of its being in the immediacy of its auto-affection, it fills everything. It fills the whole world, as one says figuratively, even though it is not in the world. It is only the whole of being, insofar as it is not in any world and insofar as no horizon overflows it from any side. (Henry 2008: 120)

The immanent auto-affection of life forms the basis of any living being. Yet, as Henry emphasises, this basis is not separable from the living being as something greater than it: the basis of every living being is nothing other than its life.

> The ground on which I stand is never larger than the two feet that cover it. That is the mystery of life: the living being is coextensive with all of the life within it; everything within it is its own life. The living being is not founded on itself; instead, it has a basis in life. This basis, however, is *not different from itself*; it is the auto-affection in which it auto-affects itself and thus with which it is identical. (Henry 2008: 132)

We may recall encountering a very similar understanding of life in Shalamov's camp prose, particularly in the stories dealing with the revival of camp goners, where life was approached in impersonal terms as a force that enters and exits a living being as it pleases, a force irreducible to the living being yet containing all of it. It is also this life that manifests itself in the camps in terms of a bare life of survival, indifferent to the outside world and wholly contained in the bitterness of the sensation of its own suffering. As long as it stopped short of killing, the thanatopolitical destruction of all forms of life in the camps left life reduced to its essence, as *bios* wholly contained in sheer *zoe*. Whereas Henry seeks to demonstrate how a living being is coextensive with its life, how every positive form is still a form of *life*, Shalamov reveals the same figure of life from the other direction, describing a being that is *only* its life, devoid of any form and any content aside from itself. While Henry describes a life that is *prior* to any world, even when it exists in it, Shalamov shows a life that remains *after* each and every one of its worlds has collapsed. In very different ways, Henry and Shalamov affirm the same understanding of life as essentially immanent, affective and internal, contained entirely in its own experience of itself.

What, then, is the relation of this life to the world? After all, living beings, which are all and nothing but life, also exist in the exteriority of the world, in which their lives acquire positive forms. For Henry, life itself does not appear in the world. While in the world we certainly deal with living beings, what we encounter in them is their *being*, not their life. The 'ipseity' of auto-affection that defines life is 'never seen because it is never in a world, because it is not shown in the ek-stasis of being and because it is not a phenomenon in the phenomenological and Greek sense' (Henry 2008: 122). Henry's position is radically different from the phenomenologies of Scheler, Husserl or Heidegger, who, in very different ways, interpreted human existence on the basis of the disclosure of the world, intentionality and sense. In contrast, for Henry life is constitutively outside of this structure and hence inaccessible to intentional phenomenology. In its absolute immanence life is strictly *invisible* (2008: 124), insofar as it withdraws from every representation. Moreover, this invisibility of life in the world is not a contingent feature of the world, but is inherent in life itself as a movement of its own forgetting. Life is not disclosed in the Outside of the world as an object that one could gaze upon, remember and forget. Instead, it is entirely withdrawn from the world and is inseparable from its own experience of itself. For this reason, it is not an object that could be remembered or forgotten, but has always already forgotten itself irreparably.

> In Life there is no 'outside', no space of light into which thought's gaze could slip and perceive anything before itself. Because Life is not separated from itself, because it never places itself at a distance from itself, it is incapable of thinking about itself or even remembering itself. Life is forgetting, the forgetting of self in a radical sense, definitive and insurmountable. Life is without memory not due to distraction or some unfortunate disposition, but instead because no intentionality, no focus

of some *objectum* is capable of taking place in it, of being interposed between Life and itself. (Henry 2003: 147–8)

Thus, while life is the generative *basis* of living beings, it does not *itself* figure in the world in which these beings dwell. Life is constitutively withdrawn from being, world and language, which themselves are only possible on the basis of life. Thus, while ideas are constituted by the 'passage of life within language', this passage onto the outside is both made possible by the forgetting of life proper to life itself and augments this forgetting by the separation of worldly phenomena from their basis in life. The entire constitution of the world, including its political structures, communities and ideologies, is foreign to life, even though it arises on its basis. And yet, despite its withdrawal from the exteriority of the world, life possesses political content of its own. Prior to any worldly political community there is a more fundamental community of life itself, given as an a priori.

> [W]hat is shared in common is not some thing; instead, it is this original givenness as self-givenness. It is the internal experience that brings to life everything that is and makes what is alive in this very experience become alive in and through it alone. (Henry 2008: 120)

All that is shared in common is affectivity itself, which logically entails that this community can never be limited to human beings.

> [T]he community is not limited to humans alone. It includes everything that is defined in itself by the primal suffering of life and thus by the possibility of suffering. We can suffer with everything that suffers. This *pathos-with* is the broadest form of every conceivable community. (Ibid.: 133–4)

This community of life does not stand above worldly communities as a lifeless abstraction; on the contrary, any genuine communities that we observe in the world arise on its basis and are not 'built in and through the world', 'not situated primarily in the world and its representation' (ibid.: 131). While it can be manifested in worldly communities, the community of life cannot be fully translated into intra-worldly categories and for this reason cannot be constructed as a worldly figure.

> The living being is neither for itself nor for the other; it is only a pure experience, without a subject, without a horizon, without a meaning, and without an object. It experiences both itself – the basis of life – and the other, inasmuch as the other likewise has this basis. It thus does experience the other in itself but on this basis, in terms of the other's own

experience of this basis. Both the self and the other have a basis in this experience. But neither the self nor the other represents it to themselves. The community is a subterranean affective layer. Each one drinks the same water from this source and this wellspring, which it itself is. But, each one does so without knowledge and without distinguishing between the self, the other and the basis. (Ibid.: 133)

Yet, if this subterranean basis does not enter the worldly sphere of representation, biopolitics as politics of life appears to be impossible from the outset: after all, it is only in the world that this politics can take place as an attempt to govern life, secure, order or transform it. Indeed, Henry's phenomenology of life may be read as the strongest vindication of the impossibility of biopolitics at least in the more positive, Foucauldian reading. For Henry, the relation between living beings in the exteriority of the world, 'when the living look at one another, represent one another and conceive one another as egos or alter egos', is a different type of experience from life and should not be described either as its 'modification' or its 'superstructure' (ibid.: 133). There is politics and there is life, and while the latter conditions the former, like it conditions everything else in the world, it can never become its object. Power cannot take life as its object because life is not an object and, moreover, does not even appear in the world as something that could be objectified.

However, if we include, as we have done in this book, the negative or thanatopolitical dimension into the concept of biopolitics, things become more complicated and more ominous. While no worldly activity can transform life positively, it can nonetheless affect it *negatively*. Henry (2012) terms such a negative disposition, which asserts the primacy of the world over life and subjects life to the world, *barbarism* and opposes it to *culture*. Culture includes art, ethics and religion and is defined as the representation in the world of life's own auto-affective formation and transformation: 'it is an action that life exerts on itself and through which it transforms itself insofar as life is both transforming and transformed' (Henry 2012: 6). While culture is rooted in life and expresses life's invisible auto-affection in worldly terms, barbarism negates life in favour of the world, which logically also involves the negation of all culture.

The roots of the problem are, not surprisingly, found in Ancient Greece, in the Aristotelian doctrine of the human being as a living being endowed with language.

> [A] *man is more than a living*, a man is a living endowed with *Logos*, that is to say, with reason and language. It follows, reciprocally, that life is less than man, or in any event less than what makes his humanity. (Henry 2003: 50; original emphasis)

From that point onwards, life becomes subordinated to being, humanity and other worldly categories, whose primacy makes it possible to dominate, negate or sacrifice 'life as such' as somehow more deficient than the structures necessarily formed on its basis. 'Never being shown in the world, life can only in fact be denied, as long as the world's truth, extending its reign over everything that is, is posited as the site of any conceivable reality' (ibid.: 263). Biopolitics is thus only possible in the negative sense of the politicisation of life itself, which Agamben described in terms of the inclusive exclusion of *zoe* into *bios* (1998: 5–6). Incapable of being transformed positively, life can only suffer the barbarian assault of worldly politicisation, which finds its auto-affective immanence worthless, approaches it as mere material and seeks to construct some 'proper' form of life out of it. Barbarism consists in making life *have to become* something other than it is, a 'new life', a 'true life', a 'real life', which more often than not is attained by the power of death and itself consists in death. What is ultimately barbaric for Henry is the very presupposition of the constructability of forms of life that we have addressed above with reference to Agamben's notion of the ontology of effectiveness. This ontological disposition ultimately denies being to all that is simply given, to that which is there without being an effect of any project of construction. Yet, what is simply given prior to any possible project and any possible world is nothing but life itself in its auto-affective immanence. Thus, by restricting real being to the effects of construction, this ontology denies real being to life itself, which paves the way for its negation.

The first mode of barbarism that Henry addresses consists in the interpretation of life in biological terms. For Henry, biology is not a science of life but a science participating in the negation of life.

> [It] never encounters life, knows nothing of it, has not the slightest idea of it. *[I]n biology there is no life; there are only algorithms.* Today, despite the marvellous progress of science, or rather because of it, we know less and less about life. Or, more exactly, *we no longer know anything about it, not even that it exists.* (Henry 2003: 38; original emphasis)

Living beings are first reduced to biological objects and then the characteristics of these objects are transferred to life itself, establishing its 'objectivity': 'What is true of living organisms as objective empirical beings appearing in the world is attributed without question to life itself' (ibid.: 45). Biological science takes the worldly appearances of living beings, which are nothing but 'objective displacements in space' (Henry 1993: 139), for the manifestations of life itself and inquires into these objects, deluding itself that it thereby studies life itself. Yet,

> [from] the moment scientific knowledge is taken as the only true knowledge and the Galilean field of the material universe that it apprehends is taken as the sole reality, then what does not appear in such a field, absolute Life, which experiences itself outside the world, the Ipseity of this life that is its 'experience of itself', and finally, any 'me' that is possible only as a self – nothing of that exists. (Henry 2003: 265)

What remains is an automaton, a living being reduced to its external, worldly characteristics (ibid.: 267). Henry's passionate polemic against biology attunes us to the problems involved in the reductionist approaches to biopolitics as directly and immediately 'biological politics'. Any such 'politics', for example Bogdanov's 'renewal of life' through blood exchange, would only ever be able to access worldly biological phenomena and perhaps even be able to modify them without in any way attaining the reality of life.

The same impoverished view of life dominates philosophy and particularly political philosophy, in which life is grasped as something deficient, to which needs to be added some edifying supplement (language, reason, culture, ethics, politics, and so on). Whatever is not worldly is denigrated and subordinated to the rationalities of the world. Focusing in particular on Heidegger's phenomenology, Henry traces the way philosophy refuses life the status of the substrate of all beings and makes it derivative from the world, the openness to which alone gives access to life and its truth.

> [I]t is because the truth is reduced to that of the world, to a horizon of visibility, that life, stripped of truth, of the power of revealing, finds itself reduced to something that shows itself in the truth of the world, finds itself reduced to an entity. (Ibid.: 46)

Similarly to the scientific reduction, life in the sense of immanent auto-affection that reveals and experiences itself is reduced to a series of external phenomena, whose elevation over life permits life itself to be forever sacrificed to ever new forms of 'good life'.

Finally, although at first glance psychoanalysis appears to rehabilitate the auto-affective immanence of life with its notion of the unconscious, the understanding of the unconscious as unknown and unknowable, even to itself, and hence blind and absurd, leads to the negative interpretation of life as a savage and even murderous power, against which worldly protections are required.

> A blind and unconscious life, a life that desires without knowing what it desires and without even knowing that it desires, is an absurd life. An absurd, blind, unconscious power, life can then be charged with every

crime. In its murderous frenzy, entering millions of times into a struggle against itself, it becomes the source of all that ravages the universe. (Ibid.: 49)

These three negations demonstrate that every politics that ventures to govern life immediately becomes thanatopolitical, since it can only negate life but never grasp it as an object of positive transformation. Of course, these three forms are not exhaustive of barbarism, nor are they mutually exclusive. In fact, we may observe elements of all three in the biopolitical rationality of Stalinism: life is first reduced to natural processes, which then are denigrated as obsolete and dying in comparison with the 'true life' in accordance with communist ideology and, finally, every act of life's resistance to its transformation is delegitimised as evidence of its blindness and absurdity. This constellation authorised the destruction of life as the process of the transformation of the old by the new, yet, as we have seen, the entire content of the produced novelty was largely contained in the destruction itself. For Henry, things could never have been otherwise, since every attempt at the transformation of life is conditioned by its prior negation in favour of worldly apparitions that may then be transformed in a myriad of positive ways that all serve to destroy life's originary immanent interiority.

> Everywhere a man or woman is only an object, a dead thing, a network of neurons, a bundle of natural processes – one finds oneself in the presence of what, stripped of the transcendental Self that constitutes its essence, is no longer anything, is only death. (Ibid.: 274)

The worldly government of life appears incapable of producing anything but death.

A CAPTIVATED LIFE

At first glance, Henry's approach is of little relevance to our problematic of affirmative biopolitics since it so categorically denies the very possibility of a non-thanatological politics. Nonetheless, in addition to the barbaric negation of life Henry recognises another, less violent possibility of conceiving the relation between life and politics. Since life as such does not appear in the world, the relations between living beings in the world are mediated by what Henry calls 'images'.

> [When] instead of being carried out 'unconsciously' as a pure affect in the immediacy of life, the relation between the living occurs through the mediation of the world, a new dimension of experience emerges that must be described in its own terms. (Henry 2008: 133)

For Henry, this relation of mediation 'should not be understood on the basis of representation, but on the basis of life' (ibid.: 133), even if this basis itself does not enter the realm of mediation. This is because life is the basis of everything worldly, including the most abstract ideas or images: 'Thought, including rational thought, is only ever given to itself in the pathetic auto-revelation of life' (Henry 2007: 253).

Of course, the barbaric apparitions of science, philosophy and psychoanalysis that we have just considered are *also* images, mediating relations between living beings. These are the images that arise from and aggravate the self-forgetting that, as we have seen, is proper to life itself. Yet, there are also other images that do not negate life but rather translate into worldly terms life's experience and enjoyment of itself: 'the more intensely life experiences itself in the pathos of its suffering and joy, the more lively, the more luminous, the more intelligible are the images in which it projects itself. This world-truth, affectivity's production and radical determination of representation, is brought to light by every form of art' (Henry 1993: 269). Thus, life as self-affection is not only negated by worldly images but can also affect their content, making them more or less lively or luminous. While scientific or philosophical images conceal life, inserting themselves in its place, artistic or more generally cultural images project life's auto-affection and depend on it for their worldly luminosity. The crucial question now is whether the *reverse* relation is also possible: can worldly images or ideas positively affect life in its self-affection, to make it more intense in its suffering and joy? If worldly images can affect life negatively, threatening its very existence, can there also be images so lively and luminous that they make life experience itself *more* intensely? Only if such a possibility is granted, may we speak of a genuinely affirmative biopolitics that does not affect life negatively, yet is not thereby barred from affecting life at all.

While Henry does not address this question explicitly, our idea of a diffused presence of the idea in experimental lives permits us to answer this question affirmatively from Henry's own phenomenological perspective. Worldly ideas or images positively affect life's self-enjoyment if they are able, however momentarily, to move, grip or captivate living beings so that they become, in their very lives, carriers or vehicles of this idea or image. All of us have experienced being moved by a musical piece, seized by a radical idea, taken hold of by an elegant theory – in short, affected to the very core of our existence by what from Henry's perspective is an external, worldly image that, like all things, arises from life but is itself devoid of life. We are all accustomed to saying that this or that symphony, film or novel 'changed our lives', but what does the change actually consist in and how exactly does it operate? What

A Real Renewal of Life: Towards an Affirmative Biopolitics

happens when we are seized by an affirmation of equality, freedom or community? How can a lifeless idea affect our lives in a positive way?

Evidently, these external ideas do not come back to the interiority of life, from which they originally sprang. All that appears in the exteriority of the world remains worldly and cannot itself 'come back to life'. What an idea or image can do, however, is *graft* itself onto the immanent auto-affection of life as a condition for its own diffusion in the world, which is always hesitant, contingent and finite. This can only take place if it succeeds in positively affecting the self-affection of the life of a living being in the world, if it manages to move, seize, fascinate, grip, take hold, captivate – in short, *affect our life in such a way that it enters into its own auto-affection*. Indeed, this is the only way in which anything at all can affect life: since life consists entirely in its auto-affection, to affect life is to participate in the way it affects itself. If life is capable of being moved by worldly ideas in a positive way that augments life's self-enjoyment rather than negate it, some worldly images may graft themselves onto life and diffuse themselves in the world through the lives of those moved by them. Thus, *being moved* by the idea is the condition of this idea's *movement* of diffusion in the world. It is this movement alone that constitutes affirmative biopolitics, a politics of the 'real renewal of life' in accordance with the idea that does not force this idea into life but rather lets it live in the lives that are captivated by it. In this movement of diffusion life and idea become momentarily indiscernible, as if a captivated life consisted entirely in the idea that grips it, while the idea was wholly contained in the vitality of diffusion that the grafting onto life allowed it.[1]

Affirmative biopolitics no longer seeks to replace the immanent auto-affection of life with a new form of life modelled on the transcendent idea (Cosmism), translate this idea into a biological state of affairs (Bogdanovism) or annihilate the auto-affection of life by the forcing of this idea into life's immanence (Stalinism). It is entirely contained in the grafting of the transcendence of the idea onto the immanence of life in the manner that affects the auto-affection of life as the subterranean basis of being. As a result of this grafting the living being finds itself transformed not merely in the superficial modification of worldly practices, habits or conventions, which takes place all the time and usually means precious little, but rather shaken 'in its very being', becoming other in the world as a result of being positively affected by the idea on the 'basic' level of the immanent auto-affection of life.

This life-changing experience is familiar to all of us but remains very difficult to conceptualise, since it cannot be grasped in terms of the familiar oppositions of subject and object, or activity and passivity. When we are captivated by an idea, we are simultaneously the subject and the object of our actions, letting the idea that grips us transform us in each of the worldly actions we engage in. The subject's activity is indistinct from its being acted upon: it *effects* its own being *affected* (cf. Agamben 2014b: 68). The idea is not forced onto an external object but rather acts in and on the subject that lets it captivate itself as well as on the world that this subject furnishes in its actions. The subject and the object are indiscernible in this *movement of being moved*. In the diffusion of the idea the subject acts its own captivation and suffers its own activity and the idea acquires all of its vitality from participating in this movement of auto-affection.

Our notion of the diffusion of the idea in the lives captivated by it is therefore distinct from the logic of 'incorporation' of one's life into the ideational 'body of truth', which Badiou developed in his *Logics of Worlds* (Badiou 2009: 1–9). Badiou advances this logic as an alternative to the nihilistic biopolitics of 'democratic materialism', according to which there are only bodies and languages, with no truths transcending them. His politics of truth presupposes setting aside one's purely natural, animal desires and interests in favour of fidelity to the truth. As a result of this incorporation, the subject is promised an entry into a 'true life' no longer confined to the maintenance of one's bodily and linguistic nature: ' "To live", obviously not in the sense of democratic materialism (persevering in the free virtualities of the body), but rather in the sense of Aristotle's enigmatic formula: "to live as an Immortal" ' (ibid.: 507). It is easy to see that this apparent alternative to biopolitics actually ends up replicating the originary biopolitical move of the inclusive exclusion of bare life (of bodies and languages) as a negative foundation of the political order (the body of truth). Life in the body of truth is a life to be politicised, a proper form of life to be constructed, the mode of being to be realised – in short, it is a worldly simulacrum of life (cf. Prozorov 2015).

In contrast, in the experience of captivation the bodily and linguistic potentialities of life are not set aside, dominated or sublimated in the act of inclusive exclusion, but rather *positively* affected, augmented and amplified by the idea in question. A life seized by an idea both enables this idea's diffusion in the world and derives ever more enjoyment from this diffusion. It therefore does not function as a negative foundation for a politicised form of life, as in Agamben's account of biopolitics or in Badiou's apparent alternative to it, but as something like a 'positive foundation', which *enjoys that which it founds*. The idea of 'good life' is not added to 'mere life' as an external supplement that produces some new form of life. Instead, it is life *itself* that becomes 'good' (or 'better' in the sense of greater enjoyment of itself) by being affected by the worldly idea, which thereby enters, hesitantly and usually temporarily, into life's own auto-affection and can thereby diffuse itself in the life of the being in question.

But what about other beings? In contrast to constructivist biopolitics that, as we have seen, forces its ideas into the immanent interiority of life from the outside, affirmative biopolitics is only conceivable as arising from within the auto-affection of life itself. Now, as we have discussed above, it is precisely this auto-affection that all living beings share *in common*. It is therefore entirely possible that one's being captivated by an idea is shared with others not in the mode of a worldly intersubjective relation but on the level of life itself, on the basis of and in the form of the originary *pathos-with* that characterises life. In such a case, our own fascination with an idea may prove catching or infectious, accelerating and expanding its diffusion in the world. The most fleeting fashions and the most durable cultural trends are both based on this capacity of life to enjoy in common. Of course, this possibility of shared captivation is entirely contingent. As anyone who has ever tried and failed to make another person share in one's fascination with a novel, a symphony or a political programme knows, it is very difficult to transmit one's own captivation to the other, whom the idea in question may well leave cold. In this case the diffusion finds its limit and is redirected elsewhere, without any guarantee for success. What is entirely impossible is forcing this diffusion in the absence of the idea's grip on the living being in question: no socialism, liberalism or nationalism has ever been produced without socialists, liberals and nationalists diffusing these ideas in their lives, and it is doubtful if they have ever had any reality apart from these lives.[2] All that the forcing of an idea into life achieves is the infliction of suffering on life that does not produce anything new and can only eventually lead to a retreat from forcing, the artifice of its success or the senseless destruction of life as such – the three forms of negative biopolitics that we have identified in High Stalinism.

From its very first days in power, the Bolshevik regime was accused of (and vociferously denied) perverting the idea of socialism, degrading what was a radically emancipatory and egalitarian idea into a particularly vicious form of tyranny. Our account of constructivist and diffuse forms of biopolitics permits us to interpret this perversion in ontological terms. While there is nothing a priori violent in the practice of collective organisation of agricultural production, when it is practised by enthusiasts in a voluntary manner as an experiment in working together, its forcing into the lives of decidedly unsympathetic peasants produced the abomination of Stalinist collective farms, whose very constitution was marked by extreme violence: against those forced to work in them, against those forced to flee, against the animals slaughtered by the peasants to avoid surrendering them to the state, against the millions starved as a result of these monstrous policies, and so on. Yet, this was only the beginning, since in order to secure the abominable effects of this forcing it was necessary to organise another, ultimate abomination – the Gulag, in which the ambition of socialist biopolitics to produce a new human being was achieved in a completely negative way as the reduction of the subject to the survival of its own devastation. An apparently innocuous and even somewhat charming idea of agricultural communes became the source of sociocidal violence solely by virtue of being forced into the lives that were hostile or indifferent to it. The perversion in question is then evidently not an inherent feature of the idea itself but rather pertains to its implementation as a constructible project realised by an act of will, bringing misery to the millions held *captive* by it, as opposed to its free dissemination in the lives of those whose *captivation* by this idea amplified their enjoyment of life. One and the same idea may either captivate or force into captivity, with evidently different effects.

The effects of the two forms of biopolitics also differ in terms of their solidity or duration. While constructivist biopolitics attempts to 'build' forms of life as stable structures, for affirmative biopolitics the life of the idea is a matter of *praxis* rather than *poiesis*. It does not produce lasting effects or works, be they forms of life or social orders, but is wholly contained in the movement of its diffusion. The hesitant and undecidable diffusion of the idea, which incorporates within itself the possibility of its own non-being, is *all* the vitality that the idea could ever get from life. All it can attain is a possibility to *live along* with life, as long (and only as long!) as the living beings in question remain captivated by it, act on its basis and enact it in their worldly practices. Life only gives the idea enough to live on and spread on, but never enough to replace, redouble or crowd it out. In other words, the sole possible effect of the idea on life is its own continuing participation in life's auto-affection. We therefore cannot share Badiou's enthusiasm about life in the body of truth as the sole true life, in contrast to mere conservation of physical existence (reactive subjectivity) or its mortification (obscure subjectivity) (2009: 508–9).

> Several times in its brief existence, every human animal is granted the chance to incorporate itself into the subjective present of a truth. The grace of living for an Idea, that is living as such, is accorded to everyone and for several types of procedure. The infinite of worlds is what saves us from every finite dis-grace. Finitude, the constant harping on of our mortal being, in brief, the fear of death as our only passion – these are the

bitter ingredients of democratic materialism. We overcome all this when we seize hold of the discontinuous variety of worlds and the interlacing of objects under the constantly variable regimes of their appearances. We are open to the infinity of worlds. To live is possible. Therefore, to (re) commence to live is the only thing that matters. (Ibid.: 514)

For Badiou, the life attained by the incorporation into the body of truth is the only life worthy of the name since it somehow transcends the finitude that characterises the brute existence of the human animal. Yet, he clearly recognises that the only way this body of truth can be constituted in the first place is on the basis of actual mortal bodies of human animals and takes particular care to protect this animal from the excesses of the truth procedure (Badiou 2001: 84). To live is then only possible for a finite being and an infinite truth may be said to live only on the fragile basis of finitude, which alone is what permits it to produce its immortal effects. While one might live *as* an Immortal, in the sense of the results of one's life, including the truths one participated in, surviving its inevitable end, no one actually *is* immortal, therefore the grand distinction between mere life and True Life, built up by Badiou, is entirely unnecessary and only leads to confusion. There is only *one* kind of life, which may find itself positively affected by ideas to a greater or lesser extent. While the life of the faithful subject is evidently more intense due to its captivation by an idea, it is the *same* life as the life of the reactive subject preoccupied with the conservation of its animal existence or even the obscure subject involved in the mortification of life in the name of its simulacrum (cf. Badiou 2009: 54–61). The body of truth is simply the body of the human animal, whose life has become gripped by an idea that thereby acquires the potentiality for diffusion.[3]

In this manner, affirmative biopolitics breaks with the ontology of effectiveness that only confers reality on the actualised, the realised and the constructed, whereby any life worthy of the name is always an effect of a politicisation in accordance with a certain idea. Affirmative biopolitics does not and cannot construct anything; no socialism, communism or any other -ism is 'built' in it, since it is entirely contained in the movement of the diffusion of its ideas that is made possible by these ideas first moving, gripping or fascinating the lives of those upholding them. From a standpoint based on the ontology of effectiveness this might appear to be a lesser, somewhat defective form of biopolitics, failing to fully translate the ideal into the real. In fact, this 'lesser' biopolitics attains much more than any constructivist project of forcing transcendence into immanence, which, as our analysis of Stalinism demonstrates, is forever doomed to fail in its hubristic attempts to build a form of life out of an idea, negating the former in the name of the latter and ending up retreating from life, faking its transformation or simply destroying it. In contrast, affirmative biopolitics is capable of endowing its ideas with a modicum of vitality, precisely and only because what it affirms is not only the idea but first and foremost life itself, the auto-affection that makes all diffusion possible. Any affirmation of a *bios* as a positive form of life that does not remain a mere verbal utopia or relapse into paroxysmal destruction must take place on the basis of this prior affirmation of the unqualified life of *zoe*. Bare life is not something to be politicised, transformed or negated in the vain hope of making 'good life' out of it. The idea of good life is only given a chance to live by grafting itself onto bare life as the only life there is.

That is all there is to affirmative biopolitics. No socialism was ever *built* anywhere: there were only ever *socialists* who were driven by the grip that the idea of communist revolution exerted on their lives. Yet, these socialists responded to their captivation by this idea in different ways. While some of them were busy experimenting with the forms of life this idea authorised, diffusing it in their everyday practices and thus endowing it with life, others were more interested in forcing this idea into the lives of others and forcing out all the forms of life that conflicted with it. While they were at it, they also forced out all those socialists, whose manner of diffusing the idea conflicted with their privileged model. The uncertain diffusion of the socialist idea in experimental lives that might have been naïve, clumsy or vulgar gave way to the proliferation of barbaric apparitions (collective farms, agricultural exhibitions, concentration camps, and so on), which had nothing to do with life, other than in the sense of its negation, and therefore testified, in their very existence, to the lifelessness of the idea they embodied. There is little point in trying to adjudicate whether this second group of socialists were genuinely moved by the idea of socialism or were in fact gripped by some other idea. It also matters little whether the first group of socialists were in possession or, better, possessed by a more authentic, pacific or better idea of socialism. What matters is less the content of the idea than the manner in which it comes to presence in the world, that is, as a contingent diffusion in the lives of those captivated by it or as an effective construct in which lives are held captive. By opting for the latter, Stalinism made sure that socialism could no longer be enjoyed but only suffered.

CONCLUSION

What are the implications of this account of affirmative biopolitics for our case of Soviet socialism? If we no longer approach socialism in terms of either an impotent representation of life or its impossible presence in life, but rather conceive of it as a real movement of diffusion in which, in full accordance with Marx and Engels, existing states of affairs are abolished, we must conclude that the *only* instance of real socialism in Soviet history was the experimental movement of the 1920s: housing communes, the Militant Godless, science fiction, Proletkult, Godbuilders, dis-urbanists and super-urbanists, and so on. In these experiments, many of which now strike us as hopelessly naïve or outright daft, the lives of their practitioners were *trans*formed as a result of their being captivated by the idea of communism without ever consolidating into fixed *forms* of a new state of affairs or a social order. Moreover, there was nothing dreamlike about these experiments, since they had a clear material basis in the lives of those engaged in them, yet only insofar and as long as they continued to be so engaged. What *was* a dream, or rather a nightmare, was the attempt to fix the always tentative and contingent effects of such experiments into a determinate form of order, invading the interiority of life from the outside of the 'new world' and forcibly making it the basis of the latter.

The attempt of Stalinism to render the idea of communism alive in its own right, rather than diffused in the experimental practices of living beings, ended up negating life as such and thereby deprived socialism of any access to it for the remainder of the Soviet project. The annihilation of the non-socialist ways of life of the peasantry and the intelligentsia during the Great Break and the indiscriminate bloodbath of the Great Terror are only the most extreme examples of the thanatopolitical negativity that annihilated *both* the lives it targeted and the force of the idea in the name of which this annihilation took place. We must also pay attention to the ways in which the relatively *non*-violent inflections of Soviet biopolitics, that is, the Retreat and the Simulacrum, were directly complicit in the gradual loss of the vitality of the idea of socialism, the former by making empirically observable socialism frequently indistinct from the more impressionable descriptions of nineteenth-century capitalism and the latter by eventually making of socialism a thoroughly lifeless artefact that neither the regime nor the society even pretended to believe in.

Born of life but then externalised into the world, ideas may temporarily and contingently 'come back' to life, if they succeed in captivating living beings so that they can then spread in the world in their practices. Yet, when this movement of diffusion gives way to the project of forcing the idea into life in a hubristic quest for full presence, the destruction of life also inevitably leads to the expiry of the idea's vitality, which is what happened to Soviet socialism already in the late 1930s. This explains why the eventual demise of socialism was a traumatic affair in practically every aspect *except* the ideological one. By the 1980s, the official Soviet ideology, whose core had remained unchanged since the Stalin period, was literally a dead letter and its hurried abandonment during Perestroika brought noticeable relief to all those involved in its reproduction (see Prozorov 2009: ch. 3; Yurchak 2006).

This is why, as we have seen in Chapter 1, the postcommunist rehabilitation of Stalinism under Putin did not take the form of the revaluation of socialist ideology, which could hardly be resuscitated, but instead focused on the biopolitical dimension of the construction and 'effective management' of new forms of life. It is precisely the ambition of *building* the socialist order as a lived reality that defines Stalinism and, as this book has shown, defines it as a *failure*, since its biopolitical productivity is grossly overrated and in fact limited to three kinds of products. First, Stalinism achieved the rehabilitation and entrenchment of many pre-revolutionary peasant and petit-bourgeois forms of life that were deformed and degraded by their forced and hypocritical insertion into the ostensibly socialist context. Second, it established the simulacrum of socialism in the official style of socialist realism, which yielded a myriad of artworks that served to crowd out the reality of this retreat from socialism. Finally, in the exterminist drive of the Great Break and the purges of the 1930s it destroyed the traditional forms of life of the peasantry, intelligentsia, national minorities and other social groups, annihilated millions of their representatives and transformed millions more into the disaffected 'living dead'.

Millions of corpses, restored old norms and practices, and an abundance of mediocre artworks – *this* is the true heritage of Stalinism. Just as the traumatised subject of Stalinism was formally a 'new' subject yet the content of its novelty was exhausted in the negation of the old forms of life, Soviet society was established as a positive reality only at the cost of being utterly pervaded by negativity, biopolitics and thanatopolitics becoming completely indistinct in it. It is this catastrophic failure to 'build' socialism as a form of life that any possible third destalinisation in Russia and the former USSR must target in order to challenge the myth of the 'effective manager' that survives the death of the ideology, whose conversion into life this manager aspired to.

As we have argued throughout this book, the violent paroxysms of Stalinism were not directly attributable to the contents of communist ideology but were rather the result of the conversion of its messianic aspiration towards transcendence into the biopolitical project of effectively producing this transcendence within the immanence of lived reality as a new social order upheld by a new kind of subject. While it certainly matters that this ideology was characterised by the aspiration to transcend the world as it is, what accounts for the horrendous violence of Stalinism is not this aspiration as such, which is arguably one of the nobler features of the human condition, but rather its recasting into the governmental project of the construction of socialism, in which transcendence took the form of negation and, all too frequently, physical annihilation.

Nonetheless, the constructivist logic of Stalinism remained obscure throughout the two attempts at destalinisation. While Stalinism was rejected as either a personal or an ideological deviation, the destalinising regimes themselves continued to engage in projects of the construction of new forms of life, first as a matter of a return to authentic Leninist socialism (1956–64, 1986–8), then as a matter of a wholesale reinvention of socialism as a 'social market' system (1988–91) and, finally, as a matter of the explicit restoration of capitalism (after 1991). While none of these attempts were marked by the apocalyptic violence of Stalin's Great Break, they shared its basic presupposition about the susceptibility of life to a governmental reconstruction, of the basic *constructability* of forms of life. It is not so surprising, then, that despite their ideological heterogeneity to the Stalinist vision of socialism, the post-Stalinist and post-Soviet regimes could not really make a complete break with Stalinism and even retained a perverse fascination with this period. After all, for all their ideological differences, they shared the approach to government as biopolitical construction, the effective realisation of ideas in life, without wanting or daring to pursue it to its logical conclusion that Stalin arrived at during the Great Break: for a new world to be built, the old one must be destroyed; and for a new life to start, the old one must end. Yet, the same lack of daring or desire to engage in the negation of life has also spared the successors of Stalin the drawing of one more conclusion: the negation of the existing forms of life in the project of building new ones does not really succeed in producing anything positive, the new form of life being wholly contained in the ruins of the old one.

While it is certainly essential to any hypothetical destalinisation, the problematisation of the constructivist principle of biopolitics has a rather more general significance. During the late Perestroika and the early Yeltsin period, the anticommunist intelligentsia repeatedly mocked the idea of 'building communism' while enthusiastically embracing the project of 'building capitalism', which proceeded from the very same presuppositions of the amenability of life to governmental intervention and reordering. The similarity did not escape the early Western critics of the neoliberal reforms of the Yeltsin presidency in 1992 that were criticised as a case of 'market Bolshevism' (Reddaway and Glinsky 2001). Yet, the efficacy of this critique was undermined by the fact that alternatives to these policies were *also* framed in terms of the construction of positive orders and forms of life, be they 'Nordic socialist', 'socialist with a human face', 'Chinese', 'Ordoliberal' and so on. While 'building communism' certainly sounded ridiculous in the early 1990s, building other forms of life apparently did not. When politics as such appeared to have been hijacked by the metaphor of construction, it was not so surprising for the Stalinist discourse to reassert itself in the 2000s by countering every criticism of the Soviet system with the demand that their opponents first build a system of their own and only then start criticising other builders.

In this attachment to the presupposition of constructability, the late- and post-Soviet political class and intelligentsia missed or misinterpreted the lesson of Andrei Platonov, the author of the Stalin era, whose key works only began to be published during Perestroika. Platonov's novels *The Foundation Pit* (1930), in which the construction of socialism never leaves the preparatory stage of digging the foundation pit, and *Chevengur* (1927–9), in which socialism is declared already attained in 'one village', were interpreted in the late 1980s as warnings against naïve attempts to translate utopian ideology into reality. Indeed, Platonov's descriptions of both the preparatory stage of socialism and its already attained status were far from tantalising. *The Foundation Pit* depicts scenes of hard labour in adverse conditions, whose sense escapes its protagonists as well as the reader. Furthermore, the project of the construction of the better future appears marred from the outset because of the death of the orphan child adopted by the novel's protagonists, to whom their entire work was explicitly dedicated. As the foundation pit continues to be burrowed, the process of the construction of socialism only takes negative forms, such as the liquidation of the remaining kulaks of the village and other acts of senseless violence and destruction.

Conclusion

In contrast, in *Chevengur* communism has apparently already been attained, yet looks suspiciously similar in its devastation to the foundation pit. The protagonists of the novel proceed from the eschatological interpretation of Marxist teaching to institute heaven on earth in the village of Chevengur. Whereas *The Foundation Pit* envisioned a long and tortuous process of construction of communism, whose completion was not assured, the protagonists of *Chevengur* ventured to attain communism in the here and now through something like an eschatological shortcut. As a condition defined by the abolition of the exploitation of labour, communism would presumably be achieved by the respective abolition of both the exploiters and labour itself. The transcendence of communism appears in the immanence of the village of Chevengur in the form of the negation of life and labour, that is, extermination and idleness. As a result, the significantly diminished population of the village, as well as the nomads and cast-offs lured into Chevengur, ends up idle yet hardly content and even somewhat disappointed, since the attainment of the eschaton did not seem to change anything in their lives, at least for the better. While in *The Foundation Pit*, written during the Great Break, Platonov appears to question the possibility of attaining a new form of life through slavish labour and senseless violence, in *Chevengur*, written on the eve of the Second Revolution, he seems equally sceptical about the possibility of a shortcut to communism that takes place through the simple termination of labour and negation of life. Both working one's way to communism and getting there through the suspension of work appear to leave nothing but dead bodies in their wake. For the readers of the Perestroika era, it was as if Platonov demonstrated the futility of communism both as an eschatological utopia and as a practical project.

And yet, such interpretations ignored the fact that Platonov was manifestly *not* an anticommunist, eager to portray the dire consequences of translating utopia into reality. It took remarkable hermeneutic insensitivity to enlist Platonov in the group of 'anti-utopian' authors who issued warnings about the dangers involved in the realisation of the communist idea. Even less sensitive was the use of Platonov in the critical discourse that inferred from the difficulties of the construction of socialism the imperative of constructing capitalism, while ignoring Platonov's subtle critique of the paradigm of *construction* as such. Platonov's prose struggles, on a literary and philosophical terrain, with the same problem of the translation of socialism into lived reality that defined the power struggles in the Bolshevik Party in 1925–7, which ended with the triumph of the Stalinist line. The fundamental tension in his writings is between a radical idealism evident in his characters' quest for the transformation of their existence combined with perpetual doubt and anguish and an equally radical materialism evident in his well-known attention to living and inorganic matter, his penchant for graphic physiological description and the focus on the experiences of bare life not far removed from death. Platonov seeks to resolve this tension by articulating the two dimensions, overcoming every separation of ideas from life, yet at the same time problematises any attempt at such an articulation (cf. Wark 2015: ch. 2).

The effective actualisation of ideas in life is always at the risk of degenerating into mere violence, negativity and destruction of the kind observed both in the endless deferral of socialism in the senseless labour of *The Foundation Pit* and its disastrous attainment in the shortcut of *Chevengur*. Socialism may be forever deferred in the dreary routine of its 'construction' or it might be claimed to be already attained by purely negative and destructive means. Indeed, the experience of Stalinist biopolitics resonated with the premonitions of both of these novels, insofar as the 1936 Stalin Constitution declared as already achieved the 'socialism' which consisted in nothing but the sedimentation of the practices involved in its construction during the Great Break. Thus, the suffering and sacrifices that Soviet workers and peasants went through in order to 'build' socialism, from poor working conditions to harsher discipline, from lower salaries to the perennial shortages of consumer goods, became permanent features of the newly built socialism itself. Any attempt to construct a real form of life out of socialism *or any other idea* always risks collapsing into disaster that can endanger and ultimately destroy both the idea and the lives into which it is to be forced. And yet, in the absence of some kind of actualisation, this idea is bound to remain a mere utopian abstraction that can do little more than entertain or sedate. Platonov's characters are thus faced with a double imperative of persisting in the quest to realise their ideas and pausing to problematise this quest itself: this is why they are simultaneously enthusiastic and tired, confident and doubtful, active and passive, all their efforts perpetually suspended in their efficacy.

And yet, as we have seen, it is this very suspension, undecidability and withdrawal from presence that characterises the authentic mode of the diffusion of the idea, socialist or otherwise, in the immanence of life. The movement of the idea in the world through its grafting onto the lives that are captivated by it and sustain it in their practices is a radically contingent process that can expire at any moment simply because even good ideas have a tendency to lose their grip. And yet, this hesitant process of diffusion is the only way we can bring our ideas to life. This is the reason why Platonov's works have enjoyed a renaissance in the postcommunist period: the hazardous quest for a new life, the quest that is always at the risk of ending too early or leading nowhere, is a genuine alternative to both the passive-nihilist gesture of recoiling from radical change due to the risk of failure and the active-nihilist move of plunging into this very failure with a forced enthusiasm. Even if Platonov's vision of socialism remains suspended between the frustrated labour of the not-yet and the inevitable disappointment of the already-there, this very suspension makes possible a different kind of movement, the undecidable diffusion of the idea as a result of its fragile and tentative grip on living beings. The sheer heterogeneity of Platonov's quest to make socialism real to the Stalinist 'real socialism' demonstrates the possibility of an affirmative biopolitics that continues to aspire to what Shalamov called the real renewal of life while renouncing the task of building a 'new life' as a stable state of affairs. Perhaps this is how we should understand Platonov's subtitle to *Chevengur*: *Travels with an Open Heart*. Rather than being built in Chevengur or any other determinate location, communism exists only in the travels of its practitioners and only as long as their hearts remain open to this idea. As a form of life, communism is not a mode of government, a socioeconomic or a geopolitical entity – as its founders recognised, it is a real movement that is only real as long as it moves us.

NOTES

CHAPTER 1

1. Although Filippov's interpretation of Stalinism has come to be known in the Russian and international media as the discourse of the 'effective manager', the phrase itself does not appear in the textbook. The first use of this phrase in relation to Stalin may be traced back to the 2005 book by the left-nationalist economist Mikhail Delyagin (2005: 211), who nonetheless used the term ironically, noting that Stalin's proverbial efficiency ultimately led to the administrative crisis of the late 1940s. While Filippov (2015) disowns the term itself, his reading of Stalinism is entirely compatible with it. See Brandenberger (2009) for a more detailed discussion.

CHAPTER 2

1. See David-Fox 2006 for the critical discussion of the use of the concept of modernity in the 'modernity school' in Soviet studies. David Hoffmann's definition of modernity in terms of state interventionism and mass politics is perhaps the most widely used in this literature (2003: 7). Similarly, Stephen Kotkin defines modernity in terms of 'mass production, mass culture and mass politics' (2001: 111–64). These definitions subsume such distinct cases as interwar Britain, France, Nazi Germany and Soviet Russia under the aegis of modernity, the remaining differences explained by their respective ideologies that assume the status of superstructural (epi)phenomena. 'Whatever features of Russia/USSR do have parallels with other modern societies confirm its modernity, while those it lacks are simply an indication of its own path to its own "distinctive" modern form' (David-Fox 2006: 17). Other conceptualisations of modernity, stressing, for example, capitalism, democracy or the rule of law, would of course make the subsumption of the Soviet case more problematic. While this is not the place to attempt to adjudicate the debate between the modernity school and its neo-traditionalist or neo-totalitarian challengers in Soviet studies, we shall merely point out that our biopolitical interpretation of Stalinism cannot

be easily fitted into this opposition, since we shall demonstrate that Soviet biopolitics *is* fundamentally different from the Western forms, yet precisely *as* modern and not traditional. The difference of Stalinism from Western modernity does not have much to do with its 'pre-modern', traditionalist features, which may of course also be observed in Stalin's USSR, but rather with the post-revolutionary constellation, which, while most certainly 'modern', posed rather different problems from those faced by other modern European societies at the time – most importantly, the problem of the institution of socialism as a form of life.

2. The understanding of biopolitics in terms of the regulation of biological aspects of existence is simultaneously too general and too specific. It is too general, insofar as political power has *always* concerned itself with this aspect, *among other things*. It would be impossible to find a period of human history in which the governance of life in the aspects of sexuality, child-rearing, hygiene, and so on was entirely absent. On the other hand, if this concern is elevated to the fundamental principle of political practice, prescribing and determining practices of government in every domain, we end up with a model that would be applicable neither to the liberal tradition nor, for that matter, to Soviet socialism, which, after all, renounced grounding social behaviour in biological factors, opting instead for the environmentalist approach to the causes of crime, deviance, degeneration, and so on (Hoffmann 2011: 33–4, 158–9). Such a concept of biopolitics would *only* be applicable to regimes explicitly founded on biological principles, such as German Nazism that Esposito defined as 'political biology' (Esposito 2008a: 110–44). While there are certainly good reasons to approach the phenomenon of Nazism as the *pinnacle*, the extreme point of the biopolitical tendency, it is less productive to make it a *paradigm* of biopolitics, since it does not exemplify but rather contradicts the biopolitical tendencies observed in other regimes.

3. It is not at all certain that there is such a thing as a 'biological understanding of life'. As Agamben reminds us, in the discipline of biology 'discussions on the meaning of the words "life" and "death" are signs of a low level conversation' (Agamben 1998: 164). The so-called 'biological concept of life', which would be so general as to be both useless and inaccessible to biological science, is in fact a political concept that derives its power from its ostensibly non-political content. See also Henry (2003) for an even more decisive rejection of biology as a science of life from a phenomenological perspective. We shall return to Henry's philosophy of life in Chapter 7.

4. For a similar account that emphasises the irreducibility of biopolitics to mere governance of biological aspects of life through the techniques derived from biological science see Forti 2015: ch. 4. Against the interpretations that view such extremely naturalist modes of biopolitics as Nazism as 'applied biology' with no positive ideological or ethical content (Esposito 2008a: 110–44), Forti argues that all biopolitics (and especially its extreme versions) is 'hypermoral', suffused by ideational content that qualifies *zoe* in specific ways arising from moral, religious, mythological or scientific

discourses (Forti 2015: 149–50). 'Far from achieving the "beyond good and evil", the return to life, to nature, and to biological laws was promptly reworked into an axiological alternative, in which good and evil returned to their rigid normative positions' (ibid.: 151). Since it is not life as such that biopolitical rationalities valorise but always already Life in some positive form (economic, racial, mythical, class, and so on), the confluence of biopolitical and thanatopolitical practices becomes easier to understand: individual lives may be dispensed with as superfluous, heterogeneous or even dangerous to the privileged Life, which governmental rationalities both construct and protect.

CHAPTER 3

1. This canonical formulation raises a well-worn problem of the distinction between socialism and communism that has accompanied the Soviet regime for its entire existence and has yielded diverse discussions in the theoretical literature, Marxist and otherwise. See Van Ree 2002: 25–9, 104–9, 137–42; Tucker 1992: 541–5. Without delving into this almost inexhaustible field, let us merely note that the biopolitical perspective permits us to distinguish between communism as an ideological project and socialism as its 'first stage' in real existence. To venture a quasi-mathematical definition so beloved by Bolshevik leaders, *socialism is communism plus biopolitics*. We shall therefore use 'communism' to refer to the ideological dimension of the Revolution and post-revolutionary politics and 'socialism' to refer to the biopolitical project of the (first stage of the) translation of this ideology into life. While communism as a transcendent ideal could only exist in the modality of 'being built' and hence be manifested in its heroic 'builders' (from Stakhanovites to NKVD operatives), socialism was something that would be 'already built' by the mid-1930s, at least 'in its foundations' and could therefore boast a real existence that communism never succeeded in attaining. There was a 'real socialism' in the USSR and its East European satellites, but there never was a 'real communism' anywhere on Earth. On the other hand, this infinite deferral of actualisation may well have been to communism's advantage: while the Soviet model of socialism remains profoundly discredited worldwide, the idea of communism continues to exert some attraction precisely as a transcendent ideal of messianic redemption, whose actualisation remains deferred. Yet, as long as this transcendent ideal is translated into immanence in political projects, its biopolitical conversion of the Stalinist kind remains a permanent possibility.
2. Since Buldakov's perspective does not take note of this biopolitical conversion, he does not single out the period of Great Break, viewing the Stalinist period as somehow all of a piece. To the extent that he discusses the policies of the Great Break, it is as a cynical move by the regime to cultivate mass support by recourse to egalitarian rhetoric (2013: 455–8). As we shall argue below, his account is far more appropriate for the *aftermath*

of the Great Break, specifically the policies known as the Great Retreat, which indeed were oriented towards a conservative stabilisation that in the argument of many amounted to the betrayal of the revolution, for better or worse.

3. In his reading of Stalinism David Roberts (2006: 261–9) offers a similar interpretation, addressing the Soviet regime as a failed experiment in the 'great politics' that mobilises collective action to a hitherto unprecedented degree in order to attain an 'alternative modernity'. For Roberts, this aspect of mobilisation was even more important for the Soviet project than the specific ideological content that the regime ceaselessly modified to suit its needs. Roberts's reading comes closest among all theories of Soviet socialism to isolating the biopolitical dimension: his 'great politics' is only great to the extent that it manages to transform life, and its poverty, alluded to in the subtitle of Roberts's book, consists precisely in its ultimate failure to do so, in the 'dissipation' of this life-transforming mode of collective action.

4. In his biography of Stalin Stephen Kotkin argues for the constitutive character of the Civil War for the Soviet regime. 'The new state [not only] owed its existence to civil war, as most states do, but it remained in peacetime a counterinsurgency. Civil war was not something that deformed the Bolsheviks: it *formed* them, indeed it saved them from the near oblivion of 1918' (Kotkin 2014: 290; my emphasis). This claim challenges the earlier revisionist readings of the Civil War as a tragic accident that somehow perverted the course of the Revolution that could otherwise have yielded a more democratic or at least less violent regime (Fitzpatrick 2008: 71–2).

5. While the resistance of Soviet biopolitics to any biologism may be surprising at first glance, it follows logically from its transformative orientation, whose valorised form of life is yet to be constructed, which makes all living beings little more than the material for transformation. Any biological determinism would evidently jeopardise the very intention of the construction of socialism, while a non-deterministic biology, for example the one emphasising chance and contingency in the process of evolution, would contradict the radically voluntarist character of this project. Nonetheless, the irreducibility of the episteme of biopolitics to biological knowledge is true not only of socialism but also of the more familiar liberal and Nazi governmentalities, in which biological knowledge was ideologically processed and transformed in various ways (Forti 2015: 142–79). Whereas liberalism identified its 'nature' with the decidedly non-natural practices of economic exchange, Nazism articulated biological knowledge with archaic mythology. No form of biopolitics was ever reducible to, let alone guided by biological knowledge, if only because biology as the science of living beings is entirely indifferent to these beings' very existence: there is no strictly biological reason why this or that species or race should survive, be protected or be allowed to perish. The problematisation of life that defines biopolitics in our approach is not something peculiar or proper to biological knowledge but is always articulated in the ideological domain, even if

this articulation mobilises the science of biology as one of the means of the construction of the privileged form of life.

6. Another instructive example of an alternative problematisation of socialism is the ideological orientation of the Menshevik wing of the Social Democratic party that split from the Bolsheviks during the 2nd Congress in 1903 and eventually formed their own party in 1912. The Mensheviks, led by such figures as Julius Martov and Pavel Axelrod, were doctrinal Marxists that were in principle just as supportive of socialism as the Bolsheviks, but, in line with the more conventional reading of Marx, denied the possibility of a socialist revolution in Russia due to its backwardness and the underdevelopment of capitalism. Instead, they focused on the promotion of the bourgeois-democratic revolution that would eventually create the conditions for socialist revolution. Thus, in contrast to the Bolsheviks, for whom socialism was a vision of the future to be actualised in the present through the revolutionary negation of the present into the past, for the Mensheviks socialism *remained* a vision of the future even in the case of a successful revolution. While the Socialist Revolutionaries ventured to construct socialism on the basis of the existing forms of life and the Bolsheviks did so on the basis of their complete negation, the Mensheviks did not have a project of the construction of socialism in real life *at all*, thus remaining outside the biopolitical constellation altogether.

7. The sole exception to this tendency might be the sphere of 'high culture', which Bolshevik leaders such as Lenin and Trotsky sought to preserve and defend against the attacks of the more extremist factions of the avant-garde and the partisans of 'proletarian culture'. See Stites 1989: 76–8; Clark 1995: 143–60. Nonetheless, despite this conservatism with regard to the cultural heritage, the regime never abrogated the wider task of cultural revolution but rather incorporated conventional 'cultural development' into the ideologically defined project of the emergence of 'proletarian culture' (see Fitzpatrick 1974; Hoffmann 2003: 38–45; Rosenthal 2002: 88–9, 156–64). The thoroughgoing rehabilitation of pre-revolutionary culture only began in the mid-1930s as a retreat from the logic of the Cultural Revolution of 1928–32.

8. From this perspective, the ceaseless debates about the counterfactual possibilities of Soviet socialism becoming less violent in the event of Lenin's longer life, Stalin's earlier death, the victory of the Left Opposition or the maintenance of the Right policy line, would certainly benefit from the biopolitical perspective. While the *exceptional* degree of state violence is certainly due to Stalin's extraordinary persistence in carrying out the Great Break against peasant resistance and party opposition (Kotkin 2014: 739), recourse to violence was a priori inscribed in the very policies of the Great Break. To avoid the violent paroxysms of the latter, the Soviet regime would have had to abandon the biopolitical project of the construction of socialism altogether, opting instead for the uneasy coexistence of communist party dictatorship with a semi-capitalist economy or, ultimately, transforming this dictatorship into an altogether different form of regime.

Notes

9. For the discussion of Bogdanov's philosophical position see Rosenthal 2002: 70–9; Krementsov 2011: 34–8; Wark 2015: ch. 1. Bogdanov's empiriomonism or empiriocriticism, famously lambasted by Lenin, was derived from the works of Ernst Mach and Richard Avenarius. It was a monistic and positivist philosophy that aimed at a universal explanation of nature at every level. In this monistic scheme the economic base and the sociocultural superstructure obey the same general principles derived from labour. Just as capitalism governs both economy and society according to the principles of individualism, socialism must be collectivist not only in economic but also in cultural matters. It is therefore up to the proletariat, who already embraces collectivism, to develop this new form of culture. Throughout his life Bogdanov ventured to develop a universal 'organisational science' of *tectology* based on these philosophical principles, which some view as a precursor to systems theory.

10. Shlapentokh (1996: 448–9) goes so far as to label Bolshevism and specifically Stalinism a 'Fedorovian' project or regime, rather than, for example, a Marxist or Leninist one. Of course, Fedorov's own ideology was remarkably conservative, monarchist and Orthodox-Christian, marked by thorough disdain for socialism, liberalism or any other form of progressivism. The identification of the two is only possible on the basis of a reading of Stalinism that downgrades or outright ignores the ideological content of this project. Moreover, such an interpretation tends to exaggerate the authoritarian and technocratic aspects of Fedorov's project and downgrades his central idea of universal resurrection, reducing it to something like totalitarianism *avant la lettre* (1996: 459). Shlapentokh recognises these difficulties in claiming that Stalin's version of Fedorovism was more demonic than Christian (1996: 453), which nonetheless leaves the question of whether the label 'Fedorovian' is then at all appropriate.

11. Slavoj Žižek (2014: 6) refers to 'biocosmism' as the 'occult shadow ideology' or 'obscene secret teaching' of Soviet Marxism. 'Biocosmism', represented by such figures as Aleksandr Svyatogor and Pavel Ivanitsky, was a minor and relatively short-lived group within the Cosmist movement, active in 1921–2 and distinguished by a pronounced leftist or anarchist orientation that recontextualised the familiar Cosmist themes of immortality, resurrection of the dead and the conquest of space (see Young 2012: 197–9). Rather than pertain specifically to biocosmism, Žižek's argument appears to refer to the Cosmist movement in its entirety, since more moderate Cosmists such as Tsiolkovsky, Chizhevsky or Vernadsky were rather more influential in the early USSR than the biocosmists. Yet, even with this caveat, Žižek's argument is problematic in its opposition between the frontal ideological edifice of Soviet Marxism and the 'obscene' or 'shadow' Cosmist teaching as its underside. In our view, Stalinism was not a 'front' for Cosmism but its *successor*, which succeeded, in its own way, where Cosmism failed, that is, in the actual translation of its grand transformative projects into governmental policies. There was never any need to make Cosmism into an occult or

shadow teaching, since its ideals of active evolution, rephrased in the official ideological idiom, were quite openly displayed on Soviet propaganda posters that called on the population to heroically fulfil five-year plans, build the bright future, conquer nature, and so on. What was conspicuous by its absence was of course the Fedorovian theme of the resurrection of the dead, an ideal that was probably somewhat embarrassing for the Soviet regime given its mass murder record.

12. Of course, the Nazi vision of the Third Reich as a racially purified and racially ordered empire may be considered a utopia, yet a utopia of a particularly morbid and gruesome kind. Insofar as it was characterised by the extreme intensification of immunitary protection, this utopian order would never have attained homeostatic stability but would go on killing so as to prevent death. It is more difficult to imagine the Nazi Reich in terms of paradisiacal bliss enjoyed by perfectly healthy and racially pure Aryans than it is to imagine it as a bureaucratic hell, in which these very Aryans are subjected to perpetual biopolitical interventions that persistently try to find in them some biological defect, a concealed disease or racial impurity – any excuse to kill them.

13. Of course, limitless exercise of power was also characteristic of the Nazi rule as well as, with some caveats, other fascist regimes in Europe of the 1930s, yet in these cases it arguably arose from a different mode of problematisation: due to their construction of social reality in strictly biological terms and the subjection of politics to racial-biological principles, Nazi policies could be construed as no longer political but rather *themselves* biological, lacking any distance from the reality they governed. As exercises in applied biology, these policies could evidently not be limited by biology. While in Stalinism the absence of limits to government was due to the gap between the transcendent Good and the quasi-natural immanence of society, in Nazism it was rather a result of the removal of any such gap, whereby government itself acted as a 'force of nature'.

14. See Žižek 2008: 202–3 on the ambiguity involved in the identity of the 'kulak'. Originally the term referred to the most wealthy peasants who relied on hired labour, as opposed to the 'middle peasants' (*serednyaki*), who owned their land but employed no outside labour, and the poor (*bednyaki*), the village proletariat who did not own land and sold their labour power. In the context of massive resistance to collectivisation the term quickly lost its socioeconomic meaning and began to signify one's political stance (refusing to join collective farms), which was increasingly independent of one's actual socioeconomic position. In order to designate potential or actual opponents to collectivisation among the poor peasants, the new term 'subkulak' (*podkulachnik*) was introduced, covering anyone suspected of any 'counter-revolutionary' intentions. '[The] art of identifying a kulak was no longer a matter of objective social analysis; it became a kind of complex "hermeneutics of suspicion", of identifying an individual's true political attitudes hidden beneath his or her deceptive

public proclamations. The "subkulak" names political division as such, the Enemy whose presence traverses the entire social body of the peasantry, which is why he can be found everywhere' (ibid.: 203–4). We shall return to the transformations of enmity under Stalinism in the following chapter.

15. In his methodological treatise *The Signature of all Things* Agamben defined the paradigm as an example that illuminates the set to which it belongs, a 'singular object that, standing equally for all others of the same class, defines the intelligibility of the group of which it is a part and which at the same time it constitutes' (Agamben 2009b: 17). Insofar as paradigms illuminate something beyond themselves, their normal denotative use must be suspended in order to enable the constitution of a new ensemble. For instance, the very word 'paradigm' may itself be used paradigmatically as an example of an English noun for which its own specific denotation must be suspended. And yet, 'it is precisely by virtue of this nonfunctioning and suspension that it can show how the syntagma [of other English nouns] works and can allow the rule to be stated' (ibid.: 24). This is the function of the numerous paradigmatic figures that we encounter in Agamben's works: *homo sacer*, the *Muselmann*, Bartleby, angels are all historically concrete phenomena used in the paradigmatic manner, making intelligible the wider ensemble from which they stand out due to the suspension of their own denotation. What makes Agamben's paradigmatic method so controversial is that the figures he chooses are usually *hyperbolic* examples, that is, extreme manifestations of principles that are at work elsewhere in a much more mitigated form. When Agamben uses *homo sacer*, the being that can be killed with impunity, or the *Muselmann*, the emaciated inmate on the brink of death, as paradigms of the modern biopolitical subject, he evidently does not claim that these figures are somehow typical or representative, but rather that these extreme cases apparently illuminate most clearly the more general state of affairs. Whether they indeed do so remains a contested question. Nonetheless, the Soviet camp of the Great Break period is paradigmatic of Soviet biopolitics in a much more conventional sense, since for all its violence its logic was strictly homologous to the governmental rationality in society at large. For a more general discussion of Agamben's paradigmatic method see Prozorov 2014: 31–2.

16. For this reason, Stalinist USSR is also a paradigm of the tendency towards the integrated spectacle that we discussed in Chapter 2. This tendency does not consist in the mere proliferation of exceptional spaces, in which one is exposed to governmental violence, but rather in the disappearance of the very difference between the exceptional and the normal, when there is no longer any possibility of 'perpetual flight' or 'foreign land' to escape to, when escape is meaningless since one only ever flees *into* another camp (see Agamben 1998: 183). Agamben's gloomy premonition of the destiny of global biopolitics is more understandable in terms of the universalisation of the Gulag rather than of Auschwitz.

CHAPTER 4

1. The term 'High Stalinism' is often used to refer to the postwar period (1945–53). In this study we opt for a different periodisation, distinguishing between early Stalinism (1927–34), High Stalinism (1934–41) and late Stalinism (1941–53). The specificities of World War II and the postwar period are outside the scope of this study. In terms of the three negative inflexions of the biopolitical project that we identify in this chapter these periods were distinguished by the intensification of the Retreat and a modification of the Simulacrum that linked the canonical image of socialism to the pre-revolutionary imperial past. While both of these tendencies are highly interesting and deserve a study of their own, they do not form a biopolitical rationality in their own right, hence we shall subsume them under our account of High Stalinism.
2. The earliest date for this interruption given in the literature is Stalin's 1931 'New Conditions' speech, while the latest is the passage of the Stalin Constitution in 1936. In the aftermath of Timasheff's argument about the Great Retreat (1946), most scholars opt for a date in the middle, using 1933 or 1934 as a symbolic marker for the abandonment of the Great Break.
3. For other influential readings that posit High Stalinism as a partial retreat from the socialist project see Tucker 1977: 95–99 and Lewin 1994: 274. For the contemporary debate on the Great Retreat see Van Ree 2002: 8–17; Dobrenko 2004; Lenoe 2004; Hoffmann 2004; Brooks 2004; Brandenberger 2012.
4. The celebration of the one hundredth anniversary of Pushkin's death in 1937 was arguably the key turning point in the regime's reappropriation of pre-revolutionary culture and its abandonment of iconoclastic intentions. See Schlögel 2012: 144–59; Clark 2011: 79; Hoffmann 2003: 161–3.
5. Until the 1930s the science of history was not even part of the official Soviet school curriculum. To the extent that it was taught or practised as an academic discipline in the 1920s, it was in the 'sociological' mode of applying the insights of Marxism, the practice decried personally by Stalin in March 1934 as 'good for nothing' (Brandenberger and Dubrovsky 1998: 874). From the perspective of the neo-katechontic turn after the Great Break the re-appreciation of history is easily understandable: the past may only become a matter of interest and concern when the *present* order of things acquires at least some stability and is not undergoing radical negation by a future-oriented project. While the victory of the Revolution and its resumption in the Great Break were marked by the messianic sense of the end times, in which the historical process was to be brought to a standstill, the turn towards stabilisation and security of the Soviet order in the mid-1930s extended the period of dwelling within history, thereby making history of interest once again and enabling the positive revaluation of past historical events, from the Christianisation of Russia to the colonisation of Central Asia. While the revalorisation of Russian history is usually interpreted in terms of Stalin's desire to

establish historical continuity between the Imperial and Soviet periods (ibid.: 874; see also Hoffmann 2003: 164–75), our approach helps illuminate why this continuity was sought in the first place: after all, the revolutionary project of the Bolsheviks was initially characterised by the affirmation of *discontinuities* of every possible kind and Stalin's own General Line during the Great Break did not require any such continuity for its legitimacy. It is precisely the fact that after 1934 it became possible to justify Soviet policies with reference to historical continuity that testifies to the Great Retreat being a genuine shift in governmental rationality rather than a mere rhetorical manoeuvre.

6. The reasons for the Great Retreat may certainly be manifold. Timasheff (1946) originally offered two related explanations for this process: the concessions to the population, among whom the socialist ideals have not yet fully taken hold, and the threat of the new world war that made it necessary to bolster popular patriotism even at the cost of a partial retreat from prior policies. In the context of our discussion of the inherently violent nature of the biopolitics of the Great Break these two explanations converge: the persistence with the sociocidal course of the Great Break would have threatened the very existence of the Soviet society and hence its capacity or willingness to defend the regime against any external threat. The catastrophic failures of the Soviet state in the first two years of the German invasion in 1941, most notably mass desertion and collaboration with the Nazis in the occupied areas, demonstrate the way the biopolitical project of the Great Break actually undermined the territorial security of the Soviet state. The German invasion may well be viewed as the advent of the very Antichrist that the Soviet katechon was supposed to delay and hold back. Instead, the Great Break only succeeded in 'accelerating' it, augmenting the scale and scope of the catastrophe. From this perspective, it is notable that after 1941 no Soviet government ever attempted any project of transformation comparable to the Second Revolution of 1928–32, choosing to remain in the katechontic role. The sole exception is Gorbachev's attempt to democratise socialism, the disastrous results of which are well known. See Kotkin 2008 for a more detailed discussion.

7. There is an ongoing debate about the extent to which the doctrine of socialist realism was actually *imposed* on Soviet society. Dobrenko (1995) demonstrates through a study of the literary preferences of Soviet readers that socialist realism largely corresponded to the people's vision of what 'true literature' should be, as distinct from both the pulp fiction of romantic and criminal genres so widespread in the 1920s and the impenetrable experimental prose of the avant-garde. On the other hand, Groys (2011) argues that socialist realism did not appear as the reflection of public tastes but as an attempt to mould those tastes along with their bearers: 'Socialist realism did not seek to be liked by the masses – it wanted to create masses that it could like. Generally, the public gets the art that it deserves. But socialist realism tried to produce the public that would deserve it' (Groys 2011: 124). Whether socialist realism was alien to the Soviet masses or

developed according to their demands, its status as a simulacrum of the already attained socialism is not in doubt.

8. This argument evidently resonates with Boris Groys's already classical account of the similarities between the aesthetic-political project of the avant-garde and the Stalinist project of social transformation. Yet, Groys's reading ultimately affirms the comparative *advantage* of Stalinism over its avant-garde predecessors (2011: 72–4) with regard to its capacity to realise that, of which the avant-garde utopians could only write, sing, paint, and so on. In our biopolitical approach, the very comparability of the Stalinist simulacrum of socialist realism with the project of the avant-garde rather points to its weakness. If, as Groys argues, 'the highest goal in the building of socialism is aesthetic and socialism itself is regarded as the supreme measure of beauty' (Groys 2011: 74), this can only mean that the biopolitical productivity of Stalinism is minimal and it remains within the century-old tradition of utopianism, which, even when fortified by the immense repressive apparatus, remains distinct and disjointed from lived reality.

9. In Stephen Kotkin's interpretation, the use of violence was a structural feature of the Soviet regime, arising from its ideological orientation, rather than a personal deviation of any of its leaders. From its very inception the regime responded to every challenge as the threat of counter-revolution, behind which were external or internal enemies. Thus, the Stalinist terror was only the most extreme version of the politics of 'demonisation' that 'inhered in Bolshevism': 'The problems of the revolution brought out the paranoia in Stalin and Stalin brought out the paranoia inherent in the revolution' (Kotkin 2014: 597). See also Kotkin 2014: 649–52.

10. Of course, party purges and show trials of alleged oppositionists took place before 1936 and often ended with (frequently commuted) death sentences, yet they never reached the scope or intensity of what was to come after the assassination of Kirov in 1934. Among these earlier purges we must note the Shakhty trial of 1928 (in which 'bourgeois specialists', including foreigners, were accused of sabotage and wrecking), the Industrial Party trial of 1930 (in which leading Soviet economists were accused of plotting a coup against the government), the Ryutin Affair of 1932 (in which a covert opposition group within the party was put on trial). Immediately preceding the Great Purges were the two more routine purges within the Party, the 1935 verification of party documents and the 1936 exchange of party documents. See Getty and Naumov 2010: 45–94; Priestland 2007: 304–32; Kotkin 2014: 634–5, 687–96 for a detailed account of the events leading up to the Terror.

11. The contradiction between the development of Soviet carnival culture and the purges is only apparent if we recall Mikhail Bakhtin's (2009) famous reading of the carnival which was written precisely during the period of the purges. In Bakhtin's argument, elaborated by such contemporary authors as Giorgio Agamben (2007a: 73–95) and Slavoj Žižek (2005: 416, note 19, 2008: 246–59), the carnival exemplifies a temporary reversal in power

relations, whereby 'what was nothing becomes everything', the sacred rituals are profaned and the order of things overturned, yet only for a *limited period of time*, after which the old order is restored and arguably strengthened precisely by its controlled transgression. Rather than point to a popular-democratic resistance to sovereign power, the carnival rather indicates the classical sovereign gesture of the declaration of the state of exception in order to avert its own overthrow in a 'real state of exception' from below. In their targeting of the Soviet elite, particularly the top levels of the Party, the Stalinist purges exemplified precisely this logic of the carnivalesque suspension of order that ultimately strengthened it.

12. This is not to say that the three types of purges were entirely unrelated. As Priestland demonstrates, mass operations were often used by the regional party leaders to deflect the threat of the purges away from themselves and their patron–client networks. Engaging in an overzealous hunt for ex-kulaks, priests or beggars, regional authorities initiated a bloodbath that they thought could save them. See Priestland 2007: 388–91; Getty and Naumov 2010: 184–5.

13. The changed status of the camps during High Stalinism renders them rather more similar to the Nazi extermination camps than the reforging camps of the Great Break. While, as we have argued, the camps of the Great Break were paradigmatic sites of the project of the construction of socialism, the camps of the Great Terror no longer had any *exemplary* function: despite all the slave labour, no socialism was constructed in them in the sense of a form of life, no reforged subject was ever supposed to emerge *back* from them into the Soviet society. Yet, as we shall argue in Chapter 5, while the camps of High Stalinism were no longer paradigmatic as models of the Soviet project, the subject produced in them may still be considered a paradigm of the Stalinist mode of subjectivation.

CHAPTER 5

1. For the sake of fairness, we must recall that these heroes were never posited as perfect superhumans either. As Kaganovsky (2008) argues, the physically damaged, maimed or injured male body was precisely the ideal cultivated by the Stalinist discourse of male subjectivation in socialist realism. The heroic figures of shock workers, Stakhanovites, pilots, explorers and soldiers were simultaneously *both* hyperbolically strong or virile *and* disabled from fully actualising this strength due to sustained injuries, wounds, diseases, work accidents, and so on. From Pavel Korchagin in Nikolai Ostrovsky's *How the Steel was Tempered* to Alexei Maresiev in Boris Polevoi's *Story of a True Man* we observe the proliferation in socialist-realist art and literature of 'heroic invalids', emasculated masculinities, whose potentialities are barred from actualisation. There was only *one* New Soviet Person for whom full, unimpaired subjectivity was possible and that was Stalin himself – quite an achievement for a short sickly man with a scarred face and a damaged arm (Kaganovsky 2008: 4–10). While Kaganovsky operates

with a psychoanalytic framework of symbolic castration to interpret this prevalence of physical damage in socialist heroes, our Malabouan reading focuses on the material impact of the trauma that ontologically precedes the formation of the unconscious. Whereas her approach focuses on the physical disabilities of the symbolic characters of the Soviet discourse, we focus on the traumatic character of the subjectivation of real individuals.

2. In Slavoj Žižek's interpretation of Malabou, this paradigmatic status is extended much further, whereby the 'new wounded' become the paradigm of the subject as such, of the *zero degree* of subjectivity. 'The properly philosophical dimension of the study of the post-traumatic subject resides in this recognition that what appears as the brutal destruction of the subject's narrative substantial identity is also the moment of its birth' (Žižek 2011: 311). The 'pure externality of the meaningless real' (the shock of the trauma) is converted into the 'pure internality of the "autistic" subject, detached from external reality, disengaged, reduced to a persisting core deprived of all substance' (ibid.: 311). For Žižek, Malabou's key lesson consists in the refutation of any theory of the subject that reduces it to a 'social construct', a positive product of the symbolic order, a thoroughly historico-cultural-discursive entity: 'When all this is taken away, something (or, rather, nothing, but a form of nothing) remains, and this something is the pure subject of the death drive' (ibid.: 311). As a pure form giving presence to absence, the subject even goes beyond the unconscious, insofar as it completely lacks any libidinal investments. As a result of this interpretation, Žižek is able to restore the Freudian thesis that a trauma always involves the resonance of the past: in the case of the 'empty' post-traumatic subject, it is evidently not *this* subject's past, which has become fully erased or estranged, but rather the impersonal birth of subjectivity *itself* as a pure form. '[What] remains after the violent intrusion which erases all substantial content is the pure form of subjectivity, a form which must have already been there. This then is the subject at its zero level: like an empty house where "no one is home"' (ibid.: 312).

3. The notion of pure living substance resonates with Arendt's harrowing description of totalitarianism as driven by the ambition to 'organise the infinite plurality and differentiation of human beings as if all of humanity was just one individual' (1973: 438). This task, which at first glance appears entirely absurd, becomes more intelligible if we recall the argument made in Chapter 2 about the constitutive tension between *zoe* and *bios* (life and Life) at the heart of every biopolitical rationality. While it is evidently impossible to merge individual lives into a single individual being, it is possible to reduce these lives to a single form of life, especially if this form is wholly contained in its own formlessness. All of humanity becomes a single individual when the diverse plurality of forms of life is annihilated in governmental violence that devalues them as obsolete. This reduction is a mirror image of the elevation of the figure of the totalitarian leader to the status of the Life that wholly embodies the ideal *bios* in its very *zoe*. Totalitarianism ends up producing a dualistic scene, in which the sovereign,

whose life is always already all form, faces the undifferentiated substance, whose only form is its life.

CHAPTER 6

1. In both Russian and English studies *Kolyma Tales* is used as the conventional title for the entire collection of Shalamov's camp prose. Yet, strictly speaking, *Kolyma Tales* is only the title of the first volume of the series, followed by *The Left Bank*, *The Artist of the Spade* (also known in the English translation as *The Virtuoso Shovelman*), *Resurrection of the Larch* and *The Glove* (also known as *Kolyma Tales 2*). The Penguin Edition of *Kolyma Tales* reproduces most of stories from the first four volumes with some important omissions. In our analysis in this chapter we shall focus primarily on this text, introducing additional stories not included in this translation or not translated into English at all, whenever necessary for our argument. For the reader's convenience we shall indicate the title of the story in question in the references, unless it is already indicated in the sentence or the reference in question pertains to the entire volume. Shalamov's complete works are available in Russian at <http://shalamov.ru/library/>.
2. From this perspective, the difference between the two authors' positions might be due to the fact that Solzhenitsyn never experienced the camps of Kolyma or Central Asia but was largely confined to the 'first circle' of a special prison facility that actually resembled Shalamov's prison more than the Kolyma camp.
3. It is notable that active resistance and even rebellion in the Gulag only began in the post-World War II period, when many of the inmates were 'bourgeois nationalists' from the newly annexed territories of Eastern Ukraine, Moldova and the Baltic States. In contrast to the hapless 'Trotskyites' of the 1930s who had not the slightest intention of fighting Stalinism when they were free and did not develop such intentions in the camps, this new group of inmates were open enemies of the Soviet regime that knew perfectly well what kind of system they had been fighting and what awaited them in the camps. See Barnes 2011: 155–99, 219–25 for a detailed discussion.
4. In the English edition of *Kolyma Tales*, Glad translates '*s ravnodushnoi zloboi*' as 'with distracted bitterness', which introduces the connotations lacking in the Russian '*ravnodushie*' (indifference). Given the importance of the theme of indifference for Shalamov's texts, we have chosen to modify the translation.
5. We have already seen how different Shalamov's construction of the universe of the camps is from Solzhenitsyn's. Another good example of this difference is the role played by professional morality in their accounts of camp life. In Solzhenitsyn's *In the First Circle* a group of scientists imprisoned in a prison research facility (*sharashka*) are working on technical solutions to enable more effective surveillance, phone tapping and scrambling. In a key episode of the novel, one of the scientists, Gerasimovich, an otherwise timid and 'unpolitical' inmate, eager to obtain early release and rejoin his wife,

bluntly declines to cooperate when his supervisor insists that the work on optic surveillance is 'exactly his field'. It is precisely this humble suggestion that Gerasimovich is unable to accept, leading to his scornful reply to the 'degenerate' who dared to insult his profession: 'No, it is not what I was trained to do. Putting people in prison is not my trade. I am not the fisher of humans. It is enough that we have been imprisoned ourselves' (Solzhenitsyn 2009: 633). While other characters of *In the First Circle* eventually yield to the secret police out of desire to be 'useful' in 'their field', Gerasimovich is able to see what Shalamov's Peter Ivanovich blinded himself to: in the presence of the dehumanising machine of the camp every positive ethics turns into an indignity and there is no longer any justification for acts made 'in the name of science', when they ultimately serve the purpose of 'catching humans'. In his refusal to gain freedom at the cost of the freedom of others, Gerasimovich follows Shalamov's imperative, yet in his case his continuing respect for his science actually *helps* him to arrive at this decision. In contrast, in Shalamov's camp universe there is no longer any place for science (or morality, or religion) – nothing but bare life itself can provide any guidelines for existence.

6. This is why Shalamov's hatred for the criminals is unconditional, while Solzhenitsyn's account is rather more ambivalent. Despite his staggering account of the cruelty and treachery of the criminal world, Solzhenitsyn credits it with non-cooperation and self-distancing from the Soviet system that other camp inmates, including the 'politicals' described by Shalamov, were not capable of. For Solzhenitsyn, despite all their viciousness the criminals who refused cooperation with the system deserved more sympathy than those among the politicals, who, even in the camps, continued to worship the Party and even Stalin himself. See Ryklin 2008 for a more detailed discussion.

7. In the English edition of *Kolyma Tales*, the Latin word '*sententia*', which remains untranslated in the Russian original, is translated as 'sententious', an English adjective denoting 'given to excessive moralising'. The Latin word has no such connotation in Russian. We shall therefore amend the translation.

8. This position has been attributed to the two key authors of the Stalinist period, Maxim Gorky (Bykov 2008: 288–95) and Leonid Leonov (Prilepin 2010: 272–6). Both Gorky and Leonov were deeply sceptical about every utopian design of the transformation of human existence, which they viewed in rather bleak and unforgiving terms. Yet, this did not stop them from enthusiastically embracing the Stalinist project of producing socialism as a new form of life and the 'New Soviet Person' as its subject. On the basis of our analysis in the preceding pages, we may suggest that this was precisely because the latter project was *not* simply utopian: having no illusions about human beings voluntarily building the utopia prescribed for them, Stalin was fully prepared to exercise the violent measures necessary for such a construction. The enthusiasm of Gorky, Leonov and other representatives of the Soviet intelligentsia about the Great Break had to do less with their belief that this project of reforging would ever succeed than

with the appreciation of Stalin's audacity in pursuing it. See also Rosenthal 2002: 78–86.

CHAPTER 7

1. The concept of captivation is significant in the biopolitical context due to its centrality to the distinction between humanity and animality, theorised by Heidegger (1995) and more recently taken up by Giorgio Agamben (2004). In his *Fundamental Concepts of Metaphysics* Heidegger posited captivation (*Benommenheit*) as the defining feature of animal life, whose 'poverty in world' he contrasted with the 'world-forming' character of human Dasein. The animal always remains closed in the circle of its 'disinhibitors', that is, the elements of the environment that interest it and on which its receptive organs are focused. In Heidegger's argument, insofar as the animal is completely absorbed in its disinhibitors, it cannot truly act in relation to them *as* beings but only 'behave' with regard to them as if 'taken' by them (1995: 242). The animal is certainly open to beings that captivate it but insofar as it cannot disclose them for what they are, it is only ever 'open to a closedness' (Agamben 2004: 65). And yet, as Agamben argues in his reading of Heidegger, what distinguishes the world-forming human from the captivated animal is nothing positive, but simply the human capacity to *suspend* the animal relationship to its disinhibitor in an experience of 'being held in limbo', whereby the human grasps the inaccessible *as* inaccessible. While the animal is poor in world due to its captivation by worldly beings that remain inaccessible to it, the human awakens '*from* its captivation *to* its captivation' (ibid.: 70; original emphasis), resolutely standing in the opening to the closed. Besides bringing the human much closer to the animal, this understanding of captivation and its suspension is highly fruitful for grasping the relation between life and being (or the world) in Henry's phenomenological perspective. One cannot be properly captivated in the world, which is the open space where beings are disclosed in their being. The worldly being is always already world-*weary*: it knows the nullity of all there is, and worldly phenomena, be they objects, ideas or images, attract it only ephemerally, if at all. True captivation is only possible when the phenomenon in question gets a hold on one's very life in its immanence of auto-affection. Superimposing Heidegger's argument onto Henry's we end up with an at first glance paradoxical claim: the captivation by an idea that characterises affirmative biopolitics is entirely 'otherwise than being', at odds with the anthropological theme of world disclosure, and instead pertains to the aspect of our existence, originally theorised in the privative terms of animality. The subject of affirmative biopolitics is, in a strict sense, *an animal that has got an idea*. This formulation connects the discussion of affirmative biopolitics ventured in this book with the growing literature that rethinks biopolitics from the perspective of a Nietzschean or Deleuzian reaffirmation of animality. See, for example, Garrido 2012; Wolfe 2013; Lemm 2009.

2. A late-Soviet era joke sums up this point succinctly: 'Is it possible to build a Swedish model of socialism in the Soviet Union? – Of course not. Where would we get so many Swedes?' A model, even one as attractive as the Swedish one, is useless without the beings sufficiently captivated by it to practise and diffuse it in their lives. A more ominous version of the same joke illustrates the violent logic of constructivist biopolitics that ventures to overcome this obstacle through the forcing of the idea into life: a local party committee is entrusted with the experiment of constructing a Swedish model of socialism in the USSR. In a few weeks it sends a telegram to Moscow: 'The model has been built. Send in the Swedes.'
3. Badiou arguably arrives at a similar conclusion, insofar as the content of his truths is explicitly posited as *generic*, pertaining to the sheer being of the situation and devoid of any particular predicates (Badiou 2005: 371; 2009: 321–4). Badiou's biopolitics avoids a thanatopolitical inflexion of the kind analysed in this book by flattening the difference between life and truth through reducing the content of the truth to the affirmation of the consequences of the ontological status of every situation as inconsistent multiplicity. See Prozorov 2015 for a detailed discussion.

BIBLIOGRAPHY

Adams, M. (1990), 'Eugenics in Russia', in M. Adams (ed.), *The Wellborn Science: Eugenics in Germany, France, Brazil and Russia*, Oxford: Oxford University Press.

Agamben, G. (1991), *Language and Death: The Place of Negativity*, Minneapolis, MN: University of Minnesota Press.

Agamben, G. (1998), *Homo Sacer: Sovereign Power and Bare Life*, Stanford, CA: Stanford University Press.

Agamben, G. (1999a), *Potentialities: Selected Essays in Philosophy*, Stanford, CA: Stanford University Press.

Agamben, G. (1999b), *Remnants of Auschwitz: The Witness and the Archive*, New York: Zone Books.

Agamben, G. (2000), *Means without End: Notes on Politics*, Minneapolis, MN: University of Minnesota Press.

Agamben, G. (2004), *The Open: Man and Animal*, Stanford, CA: Stanford University Press.

Agamben, G. (2005a), *State of Exception*, Chicago: The University of Chicago Press.

Agamben, G. (2005b), *The Time that Remains: A Commentary on the Letter to the Romans*, Stanford, CA: Stanford University Press.

Agamben, G. (2007a), *Infancy and History: On the Destruction of Experience*, London: Verso.

Agamben, G. (2007b), *Profanations*, New York: Zone Books.

Agamben, G. (2009a), *The Sacrament of Language: An Archaeology of the Oath*, Stanford, CA: Stanford University Press.

Agamben, G. (2009b), *The Signature of All Things: On Method*, New York: Zone Books.

Agamben, G. (2011), *The Kingdom and the Glory: For a Theological Genealogy of Economy and Government*, Stanford, CA: Stanford University Press.

Agamben, G. (2013), *Opus Dei: An Archaeology of Duty*, Stanford, CA: Stanford University Press.

Agamben, G. (2014a), *The Unspeakable Girl*, New York: Seagull.

Agamben, G. (2014b), 'What is a Destituent Power?', *Environment and Planning D: Society and Space*, 32: 1, 65–74.

Amis, M. (2003), *Koba the Dread: Laughter and the Twenty Million*, London: Vintage.

Amis, M. (2014), *The Zone of Interest*, London: Jonathan Cape.

Arendt, H. (1963), *Eichmann in Jerusalem: A Report on the Banality of Evil*, New York: Penguin.

Arendt, H. (1973), *The Origins of Totalitarianism*, New York: Harcourt.

Arutyunyan, A. (2013), 'Russians Favour Authoritarian Leaders', *The Moscow News*, 22 May, http://themoscownews.com/russia/20130522/191535253.html (accessed 10 May 2014).

Badiou, A. (2001a), *Ethics: An Essay on the Understanding of Evil*, London: Verso.

Badiou, A. (2001b), *Saint Paul: The Foundation of Universalism*, Stanford, CA: Stanford University Press.

Badiou, A. (2009), *Logics of Worlds*, London: Continuum.

Badiou, A. (2010), *The Communist Hypothesis*, London: Verso.

Badiou, A. (2013), 'The Communist Idea and the Question of Terror', in S. Žižek (ed.), *Idea of Communism 2*, London: Verso.

Bakhtin, M. (2009), *Rabelais and his World*, Indianapolis, IN: Indiana University Press.

Barnes, S. (2011), *Death and Redemption: The Gulag and the Shaping of Soviet Society*, Princeton, NJ: Princeton University Press.

BBC Editorial (2013), 'Stalingrad Name to be Revived for Anniversaries', *BBC News*, 1 February, http://www.bbc.co.uk/news/world-europe-21291674 (accessed 10 May 2014).

Benjamin, W. (1978), 'Moscow', in P. Demetz (ed.), *Reflections*, New York: Schocken Books.

Benjamin, W. (2003), *The Origin of German Tragic Drama*, London: Verso.

Berdyaev, N. (1937), *The Origin of Russian Communism*, New York: Geoffrey Bles.

Bernstein, J. M. (2004), 'Bare Life, Bearing Witness: Auschwitz and the Pornography of Horror', *Parallax*, 10: 1, 2–16.

Bernstein, F. (2005), 'Panic, Potency and the Crisis of Nervousness in the 1920s', in C. Kaier and E. Naiman (eds), *Everyday Life in Early Soviet Russia: Taking the Revolution Inside*, Indianapolis, IN: Indiana University Press.

Bogdanov, A. (1984), *Red Star: The First Bolshevik Utopia*, Indianapolis, IN: Indiana University Press.

Bowring, B. (2014), *Law, Rights and Ideology in Russia: Landmarks in the Destiny of a Great Power*, London: Routledge.

Bibliography

Brandenberger, D. (2002), *National Bolshevism: Stalinist Mass Culture and the Formation of Modern Russian National Identity, 1931–1956*, Cambridge, MA: Harvard University Press.

Brandenberger, D. (2009), 'A New *Short Course*? A. V. Filippov and the Russian State's Search for a "Usable Past"', *Kritika: Explorations in Russian and Eurasian History*, 10: 4, 825–33.

Brandenberger, D. (2012), 'Simplistic, Pseudo-socialist Racism: Debates over the Direction of Soviet Ideology within Stalin's Creative Intelligentsia: 1936–1939', *Kritika: Explorations in Russian and Eurasian History*, 13: 2, 365–93.

Brandenberger, D. and Dubrovsky, A. (1998), '"The People Need a Tsar": The Emergence of National Bolshevism as Stalinist ideology, 1931–1941', *Europe-Asia Studies*, 50: 5, 873–92.

Brooks, J. (2004), 'Declassifying a "Classic"', *Kritika: Explorations in Russian and Eurasian History* 5: 4, 709–19.

Brovkin, V. (1998), *Russia after Lenin: Politics, Culture and Society 1921–1929*, London: Routledge.

Brzezinski, Z. (1967), *Ideology and Power in Soviet Politics*, New York: Praeger.

Brzezinski, Z. and Friedrich, C. (1965), *Totalitarian Dictatorship and Autocracy*, Cambridge, MA: Harvard University Press.

Buck-Morss, S. (2002), *Dreamworld and Catastrophe: The Passing of Mass Utopia in East and West*, Cambridge, MA: The MIT Press.

Buldakov, V. (2013), *Utopia, Aggressia, Vlast: Psihosotsialnaya Dinamika Postrevolutsionnogo Vremeni. Rossiya: 1920e-1930e*, Moskva: Rossiyskaja Politicheskaya Entsiklopedia.

Burchell, G. (1991), 'Peculiar Interests: Civil Society and Governing the "System of Natural Liberty"', in G. Burchell, C. Gordon and P. Miller (eds), *The Foucault Effect: Studies in Governmentality*, London: Harvester Wheatsheaf.

Burchell, G. (1996), 'Liberal Government and Techniques of the Self', in A. Barry, T. Osborne and N. Rose (eds), *Foucault and Political Reason: Liberalism, Neoliberalism and Rationalities of Government*, London: UCL Press.

Bushkov, A. (2011), *Stalin: Krasny Monarkh*, Moskva: Olma Media.

Bykov, D. (2003), *Opravdanie*, Moskva: Vagrius.

Bykov, D. (2005), *Boris Pasternak*, Moskva: Molodaya Gvardiya.

Bykov, D. (2007), 'Imeyushy Pravo', *Russkaya Zhizn*, 22 June, http://www.rulife.ru/old/mode/article/103 (accessed 20 February 2014).

Bykov, D. (2008), *A Byl li Gorky?*, Moskva: Astrel.

Campbell, T. (2011), *Improper Life: Technology and Biopolitics from Heidegger to Agamben*, Minneapolis, MN: University of Minnesota Press.

Chekhov, A. (2007 [1893]), *Sakhalin Island*, New York: OneWorld.

Chubais, A. (2003), 'Missiya Rossii v 21-m Veke', *Nezavisimaya Gazeta*, no. 209.

Chukovskaya, L. (1994), 'Afterword', in L. Chukovskaya, *Sofia Petrovna*, Chicago: Northwestern University Press.

Clark, C. (1995), *Petersburg: Crucible of Cultural Revolution*, Cambridge, MA: Harvard University Press.

Clark, C. (2011), *Moscow: The Fourth Rome*, Cambridge, MA: Harvard University Press.

Collier, S. (2009), 'Topologies of Power: Foucault's Analysis of Political Government beyond "Governmentality"', *Theory, Culture and Society*, 26: 6, 78–108.

Collier, S. (2011), *Post-Soviet Social: Neoliberalism, Social Modernity, Biopolitics*, Princeton, NJ: Princeton University Press.

Colta Editorial (2015), 'Pochti Polovina Rossiyan Opravdyvaet Stalinskie Repressii', *Colta*, http://www.colta.ru/news/6822 (accessed 1 May 2015).

Conquest, R. (1987), *The Harvest of Sorrow: Soviet Collectivization and the Terror-Famine*, Oxford: Oxford University Press.

Conquest, R. (2007), *The Great Terror: A Reassessment*, Oxford: Oxford University Press.

Cooper, M. (2008), *Life as Surplus: Biotechnology and Capitalism in the Neoliberal Era*, Seattle, WA: University of Washington Press.

Danilov, A., Utkin, A. and Filippov, A. (eds) (2008), *Istoriia Rossii, 1945–2008: 11 klass. Uchebnik dlia Uchashchikhsia Obshcheobrazovatelnykh Uchrezhdenii*, Moskva: Prosveshchenie.

David-Fox, M. (1999), 'What is Cultural Revolution?' *The Russian Review*, 58, 181–201.

David-Fox, M. (2004), 'On the Primacy of Ideology: Soviet Revisionists and Holocaust Deniers', *Kritika: Explorations in Russian and Eurasian History*, 5: 1, 81–105.

David-Fox, M. (2006), 'Multiple Modernities vs. Neo-Traditionalism: On Recent Debates in Russian and Soviet History', *Jahrbücher für Geschichte Osteuropas*, 55: 4, 535–55.

De Waal, T., Lipman, M., Gudkov, L. and Bakradze, L. (2013), 'The Stalin Puzzle: Deciphering Post-Soviet Public Opinion', *Carnegie Endowment for International Peace Report*, 1 March, http://carnegieendowment.org/2013/03/01/stalin-puzzle-deciphering-post-soviet-public-opinion (accessed 10 May 2014).

Deacon, R. (2000), 'Theory as Practice: Foucault's Concept of Problematization', *Telos*, 118, 127–43.

Dean, M. (1999), *Governmentality: Power and Rule in Modern Society*, London: Sage.

Dean, M. (2002a), 'Liberal Government and Authoritarianism', *Economy and Society*, 31: 1, 37–61.

Dean, M. (2002b), 'Powers of Life and Death Beyond Governmentality', *Cultural Values*, 6: 1–2, 119–38.

Debord, G. (1994), *The Society of the Spectacle*, New York: Zone Books.

Debord, G. (2011), *Comments on the Society of the Spectacle*, London: Verso.

Des Pres, T. (1980), *The Survivor: An Anatomy of Life in the Death Camps*, Oxford: Oxford University Press.

Deleuze, G. (1997), *Essays Critical and Clinical*, Minneapolis, MN: University of Minnesota Press.

Delyagin, M. (2005), *Rossiya posle Putina: Neizbezhna li v Rossii Oranzhevo-Zelenaya Revolutsia*, Moskva: Veche.

Derrida, J. (1994), *Spectres of Marx: The State of the Debt, the Work of Mourning and the New International*, London: Routledge.

Derrida, J. (1998), *Of Grammatology*, Baltimore, MD: Johns Hopkins University Press.

Dobrenko, E. (1995), 'The Disaster of Middlebrow Taste, or Who "Invented" Socialist Realism?', *South Atlantic Quarterly*, 94: 3, 773–805.

Dobrenko, E. (2004), 'Socialism as Will and Representation, or What Legacy Are We Rejecting?', *Kritika: Explorations in Russian and Eurasian History*, 5: 4, 675–708.

Dobrenko, E. (2007), *The Political Economy of Socialist Realism*, New Haven, CT: Yale University Press.

Dostoevsky, F. (2004 [1862]), *Notes from the House of the Dead*, New York: Dover.

Duncan, P. (2000), *Russian Messianism: Third Rome, Holy Revolution, Communism and After*, London: Routledge.

Dunham, V. (1990), *In Stalin's Time: Middle Class values in Soviet Fiction*, Durham, NC: Duke University Press.

Edele, M. (2011), *Stalinist Society: 1928–1953*, Oxford: Oxford University Press.

Ekho Moskvy Editorial (2014), Ekho Moskvy, *Golosovania*, 3 August, http://echo.msk.ru/polls/1398454-echo.html (accessed 5 September 2014).

Engelstein, L. (1993), 'Combined Underdevelopment: Discipline and the Law in Imperial and Soviet Russia', *American Historical Review*, 98: 2, 338–53.

Esposito, R. (2006), 'Interview with Timothy Campbell', *Diacritics*, 36: 2, 49–56.

Esposito, R. (2008a), *Bios: Biopolitics and Philosophy*, Minneapolis, MN: University of Minnesota Press.

Esposito, R. (2008b), 'Totalitarianism or Biopolitics? Concerning the Philosophical Interpretation of the 20th Century', *Critical Inquiry*, 39, 633–45.

Esposito, R. (2010), *Communitas: The Origin and Destiny of Community*, Stanford, CA: Stanford University Press.

Esposito, R. (2011), *Immunitas: The Protection and Negation of Life*, London: Polity.

Etkind, A. (2005), 'Soviet Subjectivity: Torture for the Sake of Salvation?', *Kritika: Explorations in Russian and Eurasian History*, 6: 1, 171–86.

Etkind, A. (2013), *Warped Mourning: Stories of the Undead in the Land of the Unburied*, Stanford, CA: Stanford University Press.

Fainsod, M. (1959), *How Russia Is Ruled*, Cambridge, MA: Harvard University Press.

Fedorov, N. (1970), *Filosofia Obshego Dela: Statji, Mysli i Pisma Nikolaia Fedrovicha Fedorova*, 2 vols, Farnborough: Gregg.

Filippov, A. (2015), 'V 101-raz ob Effektivnom Menedzhere Staline', *Svobodnaya Pressa*, 19 January, http://svpressa.ru/blogs/article/110256 (accessed 14 April 2015).

Fitzpatrick, S. (1974), 'Cultural Revolution in Russia: 1928–1932', *Journal of Contemporary History*, 9: 1, 33–52.

Fitzpatrick, S. (1992), *The Cultural Front: Power and Culture in Revolutionary Russia*, Ithaca, NY: Cornell University Press.

Fitzpatrick, S. (2002), *Everyday Stalinism: Ordinary Life in Extraordinary Times*, Oxford: Oxford University Press.

Fitzpatrick, S. (2008), *The Russian Revolution*, Oxford: Oxford University Press.

Forti, S. (2015), *New Demons: Rethinking Power and Evil Today*, Stanford, CA: Stanford University Press.

Foucault, M. (1977), *Discipline and Punish: The Birth of the Prison*, New York: Knopf.

Foucault, M. (1980a), 'Power and Strategies', in M. Foucault, *Power/Knowledge: Selected Interviews and Other Writings: 1972–1977*, ed. C. Gordon, New York: Knopf.

Foucault, M. (1980b), 'Questions of Geography', in M. Foucault, *Power/Knowledge: Selected Interviews and Other Writings: 1972–1977*, ed. C. Gordon, New York: Knopf.

Foucault, M. (1982), 'The Subject and Power', in H. Dreyfus and P. Rabinow, *Michel Foucault: Beyond Structuralism and Hermeneutics*, Chicago: The University of Chicago Press.

Foucault, M. (1988a), 'Confinement, Psychiatry, Prison', in M. Foucault, *Michel Foucault: Politics, Philosophy, Culture. Interviews and Other Writings: 1977–1984*, ed. L. D. Kritzman, London: Routledge.

Foucault, M. (1988b), 'The Concern for Truth', in M. Foucault, *Michel Foucault: Politics, Philosophy, Culture. Interviews and Other Writings: 1977–1984*, ed. L. D. Kritzman, London: Routledge.

Foucault, M. (1988c), 'Politics and Reason', in M. Foucault, *Michel Foucault: Politics, Philosophy, Culture. Interviews and Other Writings: 1977–1984*, ed. L. D. Kritzman, London: Routledge.

Foucault, M. (1990a), *History of Sexuality, Volume One: An Introduction*, Harmondsworth: Penguin.

Foucault, M. (1990b), *History of Sexuality, Volume Two: The Use of Pleasure*, New York: Random House.

Foucault, M. (1990c), *History of Sexuality, Volume Three: Care of the Self*, New York: Random House.

Foucault, M. (1991), 'Questions of Method', in G. Burchell, C. Gordon and P. Miller (eds), *The Foucault Effect: Studies in Governmentality*, London: Harvester Wheatsheaf.

Foucault, M. (1994a), 'Crimes et châtiments en U.R.S.S. et ailleurs', in M. Foucault, *Dits et Écrits, tome III: 1976–1979*, Paris: Gallimard.

Foucault, M. (1994b), 'La Philosophie analytique du pouvoir', in M. Foucault, *Dits et Écrits, tome III: 1976–1979*, Paris: Gallimard.

Foucault, M. (2003), *'Society Must be Defended': Lectures at the Collège de France 1975–1976*, London: Picador.

Foucault, M. (2006), *The Hermeneutics of the Subject: Lectures at the Collège de France 1981–1982*, London: Picador.

Foucault, M. (2007), *Security, Territory, Population: Lectures at the Collège de France 1977–1978*, Basingstoke: Palgrave.

Foucault, M. (2008), *The Birth of Biopolitics: Lectures at the Collège de France 1978–1979*, Basingstoke: Palgrave.

Foucault, M. (2011), *The Courage of Truth: Lectures at the Collège de France 1983–1984*, Basingstoke: Palgrave.

Furet, F. (1981), *Interpreting the French Revolution*, Cambridge: Cambridge University Press.

Furst, J. (ed.) (2006), *Late Stalinist Russia: Society between Reconstruction and Reinvention*, London: Routledge.

Garrido, J.-M. (2012), *On Time, Being and Hunger: Challenging the Traditional Way of Thinking Life*, New York: Fordham University Press.

Gellately, R. (2013), *Stalin's Curse: Battling for Communism in War and Cold War*, Oxford: Oxford University Press.

Gessen, M. (2012), 'The Stalin in Putin', *Latitude, International Herald Tribune*, 13 August, http://latitude.blogs.nytimes.com/2012/08/13/the-stalin-in-putin (accessed 12 October 2014).

Gessen, M. (2015), 'Is it 1937 Yet?', *New York Times*, 5 May, http://www.nytimes.com/2015/05/06/opinion/masha-gessen-putin-russia-is-it-1937-yet.html?ref=opinion&_r=1 (accessed 6 May 2015).

Getty, A. (2013), *Practicing Stalinism: Bolsheviks, Boyars and the Persistence of Tradition*, New Haven, CT: Yale University Press.

Getty, A. and Naumov, O. (2010), *The Road to Terror: Stalin and the Self-Destruction of the Bolsheviks: 1932–1939*, New Haven, CT: Yale University Press.

Goldman, W. (2007), *Terror and Democracy in the Age of Stalin: The Social Dynamics of Repression*, Cambridge: Cambridge University Press.

Goldman, W. (2011), *Inventing the Enemy: Denunciations and Terror in Stalin's Russia*, Cambridge: Cambridge University Press.

Gorbachev, M. (1987), 'Oktyabr' i Perestroika: Revolutsiya Prodolzhaetsa', *Pravda*, 3 November: 2–5.

Gordon, C. (1980), 'Afterword', in M. Foucault, *Power/Knowledge: Selected Interviews and Other Writings: 1972–1977*, ed. C. Gordon, New York: Pantheon Books.

Gordon, C. (1991), 'Governmental Rationality: An Introduction', in G. Burchell, C. Gordon and P. Miller (eds), *The Foucault Effect: Studies in Governmentality*, London: Harvester Wheatsheaf.

Gregory, P. (2003), *The Political Economy of Stalinism: Evidence from the Soviet Secret Archives*, Cambridge: Cambridge University Press.

Grossman, V. (1989), 'Vse Techet ...', *Oktyabr'*, 6, 30–108.

Groys, B. (2010), *The Communist Postscript*, London: Verso.

Groys, B. (2011), *The Total Art of Stalinism*, London: Verso.

Groys, B., and Hagemeister, M. (eds) (2005), *Die Neue Menschheit: Biopolitische Utopien in Russland zu Beginn des 20. Jahrhunderts*, Berlin: Suhrkamp.

Halfin, I. (1999), *From Darkness to Light: Class, Consciousness and Salvation in Revolutionary Russia*, Pittsburgh, PA: University of Pittsburgh Press.

Halfin, I. (2009), *Stalinist Confessions: Messianism and Terror at the Leningrad Communist University*, Pittsburgh: University of Pittsburgh Press.

Halfin, I. and Hellbeck, J. (1996), 'Rethinking the Stalinist Subject: Stephen Kotkin's "Magnetic Mountain" and the State of Soviet Historical Studies', *Jahrbücher für Geschichte Osteuropas*, 64, 456–63.

Hardt, M. and Negri, A. (2000), *Empire*, Cambridge, MA: Harvard University Press.

Head, M. (2008), *Evgeny Pashukanis: A Critical Reappraisal*, London: Routledge

Heidegger, M. (1991), *Nietzsche*, vols 1 and 2, New York: HarperCollins.

Heidegger, M. (1995), *The Fundamental Concepts of Metaphysics: World, Finitude, Solitude*, Bloomington, IN: Indiana University Press.

Bibliography

Hell, J. (2009), 'Katechon: Carl Schmitt's Imperial Theology and the Ruins of the Future', *The Germanic Review*, 84: 4, 283–326.

Hellbeck, J. (2006), *Revolution on my Mind: Writing a Diary under Stalin*, Cambridge, MA: Harvard University Press.

Heller, L. (1995), 'A World of Prettiness: Socialist Realism and Its Aesthetic Categories', *South Atlantic Quarterly*, 94: 3, 687–714.

Henry, M. (1973), *The Essence of Manifestation*, The Hague: Martinus Nijhoff.

Henry, M. (1993), *The Genealogy of Psychoanalysis*, Stanford, CA: Stanford University Press.

Henry, M. (2003), *I Am the Truth: Toward a Philosophy of Christianity*, Stanford, CA: Stanford University Press.

Henry, M. (2007), 'Phenomenology of Life', in C. Cunningham and P. Candler Jr. (eds), *Transcendence and Phenomenology*, London: SCM Press.

Henry, M. (2008), *Material Phenomenology*, New York: Fordham University Press.

Henry, M. (2012), *Barbarism*, London: Continuum.

Hindess, B. (1996), 'Liberalism, Socialism and Democracy', in A. Barry. T. Osborne and N. Rose (eds), *Foucault and Political Reason: Liberalism, Neoliberalism and Rationalities of Government*, London: UCL Press.

Hindess, B. (2001), 'The Liberal Government of Unfreedom', *Alternatives*, 26: 2, 93–112.

Hoffmann, D. (2003), *Stalinist Values: The Cultural Norms of Soviet Modernity*, Ithaca, NY: Cornell University Press.

Hoffmann, D. (2004), 'Was There a "Great Retreat" from Soviet Socialism? Stalinist Culture Reconsidered', *Kritika: Explorations in Russian and Eurasian History*, 5: 4, 651–74.

Hoffmann, D. (2011), *Cultivating the Masses: Modern State Practices and Soviet Socialism: 1914–1939*, Ithaca, NY: Cornell University Press.

Hoffmann, D. and Timm, A. (2009), 'Utopian Biopolitics: Reproductive Policies, Gender Roles and Sexuality in Nazi Germany and the Soviet Union', in M. Geyer and S. Fitzpatrick (eds), *Beyond Totalitarianism: Stalinism and Nazism Compared*, Cambridge: Cambridge University Press.

Hoffmann, M. (2014), *Foucault and Power: The Influence of Political Engagement on the Theories of Power*, London: Bloomsbury.

Holquist, P. (2002), *Making War, Forging Revolution: Russia's Continuum of Crisis 1914–1921*, Cambridge, MA: Harvard University Press.

Inkeles, A. and Bauer, R. (1959), *The Soviet Citizen: Daily Life in a Totalitarian Society*, Cambridge, MA: Harvard University Press.

Istoria Vsesoyuznoi Kommunisticheskoi Partii (Bolshevikov) (1954), *Kratky Kurs*, Moskva: Gospolitizdat.

Kaganovsky, L. (2008), *How the Soviet Man was Unmade: Cultural Fantasy and Male Subjectivity under Stalin*, Pittsburgh, PA: University of Pittsburgh Press.

Kaier, C. (2005), 'Delivered from Capitalism: Nostalgia, Alienation and the Future of Reproduction in Tretiakov's *I Want a Child*', in C. Kaier and E. Naiman (eds), *Everyday Life in Early Soviet Russia: Taking the Revolution Inside*, Indianapolis, IN: Indiana University Press.

Kalashnikov, M. (2013), 'Pochemu Putin ne Stalin', *Forum.Msk.ru*, http://forum-msk.org/stalin/9619876.html (accessed 10 June 2014).

Kharkhordin, O. (1999), *The Collective and the Individual in Russia: A Study of Practices*, Berkeley, CA: Berkeley University Press.

Kharkhordin, O. (ed.) (2001), *Michel Foucault i Rossiya*, St Petersburg: Letni Sad.

Khlevniuk, O. (2015), *Stalin: Zhizn Odnogo Vozhdya*, Moskva: Corpus.

Khmelnitsky, D. (2015), 'Blef Veka: Tseli i Itogi Pervogo Pyatiletnego Plana', *Gefter.ru*, 2 March, http://gefter.ru/archive/14406 (accessed 2 May 2015).

Khruschev, N. (1956), *Speech at the 20th Congress of the Communist Party of the USSR*, 25 February, English translation published at *Guardian.co.uk*, http://www.guardian.co.uk/theguardian/2007/apr/26/greatspeeches2 (accessed 20 February 2014).

Kiva, A. (1990), 'Krizis Zhanra', *Novy Mir*, 3, 206–16.

Klyamkin, I. (1987), 'Kakaja Doroga Vedet k Khramu', *Novy Mir*, 11, 150–88.

Kojève, A. (1969), *Introduction to the Reading of Hegel: Lectures on the Phenomenology of Spirit*, Ithaca, NY: Cornell University Press.

Kojève, A. (2001), 'Colonialism from a European Perspective', *Interpretation: A Journal of Political Philosophy*, 29: 1, 115–30.

Kotkin, S. (1995), *Magnetic Mountain: Stalinism as a Civilization*, Berkeley, CA: The University of California Press.

Kotkin, S. (2001), 'Modern Times: The Soviet Union and the Interwar Conjuncture', *Kritika: Explorations in Russian and Eurasian History*, 2: 1, 111–64.

Kotkin, S. (2008), *Armageddon Averted: The Soviet Collapse 1970–2000*, Oxford: Oxford University Press.

Kotkin, S. (2014), *Stalin: Paradoxes of Power 1878–1928*, London: Allen Lane.

Kozlova, N. (2005), 'The Diary as Initiation and Rebirth: Reading Everyday Documents of the Early Soviet Era', in C. Kaier and E. Naiman (eds), *Everyday Life in Early Soviet Russia: Taking the Revolution Inside*, Indianapolis, IN: Indiana University Press.

Krementsov, N. (1996), *Stalinist Science*, Princeton, NJ: Princeton University Press.

Krementsov, N. (2011), *A Martian Stranded on Earth: Alexander Bogdanov, Blood Transfusions, and Proletarian Science*, Chicago: The University of Chicago Press.

Bibliography

Kremlev, S. (2011), *Veliky Stalin*, Moskva: Yauza Press.

Krylova, A. (2000), 'The Tenacious Liberal Subject in Soviet Studies', *Kritika: Explorations in Russian and Eurasian History*, 1: 1, 119–46.

Lahusen, T. (1995), 'Socialist Realism in Search of Its Shores: Some Historical Remarks on the "Historically Open Aesthetic System of the Truthful Representation of Life"', *South Atlantic Quarterly*, 94: 3, 661–86.

Latsis, O. (1988), 'Perelom', *Znamya*, 6, 123–78.

Latynina, Y. (2013), 'Pikseli Odnoi Kartinki', *Gazeta*, 31 May, http://www.gazeta.ru/comments/column/latynina/5363817.shtml (accessed 20 February 2014).

Lefort, C. (1986), *The Political Forms of Modern Society: Bureaucracy, Democracy, Totalitarianism*, Cambridge, MA: The MIT Press.

Lefort, C. (2007), *Complications: Communism and the Dilemmas of Democracy*, New York: Columbia University Press.

Lemke, T. (2001), 'The Birth of Biopolitics – Michel Foucault's Lecture at the Collège de France on Neo-Liberal Governmentality', *Economy & Society*, 30: 2, 190–207.

Lemke, T. (2011), *Biopolitics: An Advanced Introduction*, New York: New York University Press.

Lemm, V. (2009), *Nietzsche's Animal Philosophy: Culture, Politics and the Animality of the Human Being*, New York: Fordham University Press.

Lenin, V. (1967 [1908]), *The Development of Capitalism in Russia*, Moscow: Progress Publishers.

Lenoe, M. (2004), 'In Defense of Timasheff's *Great Retreat*', *Kritika: Explorations in Russian and Eurasian History*, 5: 4, 721–30.

Lepeshinskaya, O. (1954), *The Origin of Cells from Living Substance*, Moskva: Foreign Languages Publishing House.

Levi, P. (1991), *If This is a Man* and *The Truce*, New York: Abacus.

Levinas, E. (1998), *Otherwise than Being, or Beyond Essence*, Pittsburgh, PA: Duquesne University Press.

Lewin, M. (1994), *The Making of the Soviet System: Essays in the Social History of Interwar Russia*, New York: The New Press.

Losurdo, D. (2004), 'Towards a Critique of the Category of Totalitarianism', *Historical Materialism*, 12: 2, 25–55.

Losurdo, D. (2011), *Liberalism: A Counter-History*, London: Verso.

Lowe, K. (2012), *Savage Continent: Europe in the Aftermath of World War II*, New York: St. Martin's Press.

Malabou, C. (2012a), *The New Wounded: Neurosis and Brain Damage*, New York: Fordham University Press.

Malabou, C. (2012b), *Ontology of the Accident: An Essay on Destructive Plasticity*, London: Polity.

Malevich, K. (1971), 'On the Museum', in K. Malevich, *Essays on Art*, vol. 1, New York: George Wittenborn.

Malia, M. (1996), *The Soviet Tragedy: A History of Socialism in Russia 1917–1991*, New York: The Free Press.

Martin T. (2000), 'Modernization or Neo-Traditionalism? Ascribed Nationality and Soviet Primordialism', in S. Fitzpatrick (ed.), *Stalinism: New Directions*, London: Routledge.

Martynov, K (2014), 'Stalin Protiv Bandery -2: Istoricheskie Idealy Liderov DNR', *Slon*, http://slon.ru/russia/stalin_protiv_bandery_2_istoricheskie_idealy_liderov_dnr-1109341.xhtml (accessed 10 September 2014).

Marx, K. (1881), *First Draft of Letter to Vera Zasulich*, http://www.marxists.org/archive/marx/works/1881/03/zasulich1.htm (accessed 10 July 2013).

Marx, K. and Engels, F. (1998 [1846]), *The German Ideology*, New York: Prometheus.

Medvedev, D. (2010), 'Eksklyzivnoje Interview Prezidenta Rossii Dmitria Medvedeva Gazete "Izvestia"', *Izvestia*, 7 May, http://izvestia.ru/news/361448 (accessed 10 September 2014).

McCarland, E. (1998), 'The Politics of History and Historical Revisionism: De-Stalinization and the Search for Identity in Gorbachev's Russia: 1985–1991', *The History Teacher*, 31: 2, 153–79.

Meier, H. (1998), *The Lesson of Carl Schmitt: Four Chapters on the Distinction between Political Theology and Political Philosophy*, Chicago: The University of Chicago Press.

Meillassoux, Q. (2012), *The Number and the Siren: A Decipherment of Mallarmé's Coup de Dés*, London: Urbanomic.

Meillassoux, Q. (2013), 'Badiou and Mallarmé: The Event and the Perhaps', *Parrhesia*, 16, 35–47.

Miks, J. (2013), 'Putin's Nod to Stalinism', *CNN Global Public Square*, 8 May, http://globalpublicsquare.blogs.cnn.com/2013/05/08/putins-nod-to-stalinism (accessed 23 July 2014).

Molotov, V. (2007), *Molotov Remembers: Inside Kremlin Politics*, Chicago: Ivan Dee.

Nad, N. (2011), *Stalin i Hristos*, Moskva: U Nikitskih Vorot.

Naiman, E. (2001), 'On Soviet Subjects and Scholars who Make Them', *Russian Review*, 60: 3, 307–15.

Newton, S. (2014), *Law and the Making of the Soviet World: The Red Demiurge*, London: Routledge.

Nietzsche, F. (1968), *The Will to Power*, New York: Vintage.

Ojakangas, M. (2012), 'Michel Foucault and the Enigmatic Origins of Bio-politics and Governmentality', *History of the Human Sciences*, 25: 1, 1–14.

Bibliography

Oshlakov, M. (2010), *Stalin-Pobeditel: Svyashennaya Voina Vozhdya*, Moskva: Yauza Press.

Pasquino, P. (1991), 'Theatrum Politicum: The Genealogy of Capital – Police and the State of Prosperity', in G. Burchell, C. Gordon and P. Miller (eds), *The Foucault Effect: Studies in Governmentality*, London: Harvester Wheatsheaf.

Pavlova, I. (2013), 'Nashei Yunosti Polet', *Grani*, 30 May, http://grani.ru/opinion/m.215146.html (accessed 10 May 2014).

Pipes, R. (2003), *Communism: A History*, New York: Random House.

Plamper, J. (2002), 'Foucault's Gulag', *Kritika: Explorations in Russian and Eurasian History*, 3: 2, 255–80.

Podoroga, V. (2013), 'Derevo Mertvyh: Varlam Shalamov I Vremya GULAGa', *Novoe Literaturnoe Obozrenie*, 120, http://magazines.russ.ru/nlo/2013/120/v10.html (accessed 10 February 2014).

Popov, G. (1987), 'S Tochki Zrenia Ekonomista (O Romane Aleksandra Beka "Novoe Naznachenie")', *Nauka i Zhizn*, 4, 54–65.

Priestland, D. (2007), *Stalinism and the Politics of Mobilization: Ideas, Power and Terror in Interwar Russia*, Oxford: Oxford University Press.

Prilepin, Z. (2010), *Leonid Leonov*, Moskva: Molodaya Gvardiya.

Prokhanov, A. (2013), 'Putinskaya Rossiya eto Zamorozhennaya Meduza', *Svobodnaya Pressa*, 21 February, http://svpressa.ru/online/article/64392 (accessed 10 February 2014).

Prozorov, S (2008), 'Russian Postcommunism and the End of History', *Studies in East European Thought*, 60, 207–30.

Prozorov, S. (2009), *The Ethics of Postcommunism: History and Social Praxis in Russia*, Basingstoke: Palgrave.

Prozorov, S. (2012), 'The Katechon in the Age of Biopolitical Nihilism', *Continental Philosophy Review*, 45: 4, 483–503.

Prozorov, S. (2013), *Theory of the Political Subject: Void Universalism II*, London: Routledge.

Prozorov, S. (2014), *Agamben and Politics: A Critical Introduction*, Edinburgh: Edinburgh University Press.

Prozorov, S. (2015), 'Badiou's Biopolitics: The Human Animal and the Body of Truth', *Environment and Planning D: Society and Space*, 32: 6, 951–67.

Rancière, J. (1991), *The Ignorant Schoolmaster: Five Lessons in Intellectual Emancipation*, Stanford, CA: Stanford University Press.

Rancière, J. (1999), *Disagreement: Politics and Philosophy*, Minneapolis, MN: University of Minnesota Press.

Rancière, J. (2010a), 'Communists without Communism?', in C. Douzinas and S. Žižek (eds), *The Idea of Communism*, London: Verso.

Rancière, J. (2010b), *Dissensus: On Politics and Aesthetics*, London: Continuum.

Rancière, J. (2013a), *Aisthesis: Scenes from the Aisthetic Regime of Art*, London: Verso.

Rancière, J. (2013b), *Bela Tarr: The Time After*, Minneapolis, MN: Univocal.

Reddaway, P. and Glinsky, D. (2001), *The Tragedy of Russia's Reforms: Market Bolshevism Against Democracy*, Washington, DC: US Institute of Peace Press.

Ree, E. van (2002), *The Political Thought of Joseph Stalin: A Study in Twentieth-Century Revolutionary Patriotism*, London: Routledge.

Rittersporn, G. (1991), *Stalinist Simplifications and Soviet Complications: Social Tensions and Political Conflicts in the USSR 1933–1953*, London: Routledge.

Roberts, D. (2006), *The Totalitarian Experiment in Twentieth-Century Europe: Understanding the Poverty of Great Politics*, London: Routledge.

Rogovin, V. (1998), *1937: Stalin's Year of Terror*, Oak Park, MI: Mehring Books.

Rogovin, V. (2009), *Stalin's Terror of 1937–1938: Political Genocide in the USSR*, Oak Park, MI: Mehring Books.

Rose, N. (2001), 'The Politics of Life Itself', *Theory, Culture & Society*, 18: 6, 1–30.

Rosenthal, B. (2002), *New Myth, New World: From Nietzsche to Stalinism*, University Park, PA: The Pennsylvania State University Press.

Rybas, S. (2010), *Stalin*, Moskva: Molodaya Gvardiya.

Ryklin, M. (2007), *Iskusstvo kak Prepyatstvie*, Moskva: Ad Marginem.

Ryklin, M. (2007), 'Proklyaty Orden: Shalamov, Solzhenitsyn i Blatnye', *Otechestvennye Zapiski*, 2, http://shalamov.ru/research/9 (accessed 10 February 2014).

Sanchez-Sibony, O. (2014), 'Depression Stalinism: The Great Break Reconsidered', *Kritika: Explorations in Russian and Eurasian History* 15: 1, 23–49.

Said, E. (1988), 'Michel Foucault, 1926–1984', in J. Arac (ed.), *After Foucault: Humanistic Knowledge, Postmodern Challenges*, New Brunswick, NJ: Rutgers University Press.

Sakharov, A. (1991), 'Revolutsionny Totalitarizm v Nashei Istorii', *Kommunist*, 5, 65–6.

Service, R. (2006), *Stalin: A Biography*, Cambridge, MA: Harvard University Press.

Schlögel, K. (2012), *Moscow 1937*, London: Polity.

Schmitt, C. (1995), *Staat, Grossraum, Nomos. Arbeiten aus den Jahren 1916–1969*, Berlin: Duncker und Humblot.

Schmitt, C. (2003), *The Nomos of the Earth in the International Public Law of the Jus Publicum Europaeum*, New York: Telos Press.

Scott, J. (1998), *Seeing Like a State: How Certain Schemes to Improve the Human Condition Have Failed*, New Haven, CT: Yale University Press.

Shafarevich, A. (1990), 'Ostajus' Dissidentom', *Vestnik Akademii Nauk*, 11, 89–96.

Shalamov, V. (1965), 'O proze', *Shalamov.ru*, http://shalamov.ru/library/21/45.html (accessed 10 February 2014).

Shalamov, V. (1971), 'O Moei Proze', *Shalamov.ru*, http://shalamov.ru/library/21/61.html (accessed 10 February 2014).

Shalamov, V. (1972), 'Perchatka', *Shalamov.ru*, http://shalamov.ru/library/7/1.html (accessed 10 February 2014).

Shalamov, V. (1994), *Kolyma Tales*, London: Penguin.

Shalamov, V. (2004), 'Shturm Neba', *Shalamov.ru*, http://shalamov.ru/library/18/5.html (accessed 10 February 2014).

Shalamov, V. (2005), 'Berzin', *Shalamov.ru*, http://shalamov.ru/library/26/6.html (accessed 10 February 2014).

Shalamov, V. (2008), 'Chto Ja Videl i Ponyal v Lagere', *Shalamov.ru*, http://shalamov.ru/library/29 (accessed 10 February 2014).

Shlapentokh, D. (1996), 'Bolshevism as a Fedorovian Regime', *Cahiers du Monde Russe*, 37: 4, 429–65.

Sholokhov, M (1933), 'Letter to I.V. Stalin', *Fundamentalnaja Elektronnaya Biblioteka*, http://feb-web.ru/feb/sholokh/texts/shp/shp-1054.htm (accessed 10 February 2014).

Shuster, S. (2009), 'Rehabilitating Joseph Stalin', *Time*, 22 December, http://content.time.com/time/world/article/0,8599,1949500,00.html (accessed 10 June 2013).

Simon, J. (1971), 'A Conversation with Michel Foucault', *Partisan Review*, 38: 2, 196–201.

Sloterdijk, P. (2012), *Rage and Time: A Psychopolitical Investigation*, New York: Columbia University Press.

Smith, S. (2011), *Captives of Revolution: The Socialist Revolutionaries and the Bolshevik Dictatorship, 1918–1923*, Pittsburgh, PA: Pittsburgh University Press.

Smith-Spark, L. (2013), 'Putin Defends Russia's Record on Freedom of Speech', *CNN International*, 25 April, http://edition.cnn.com/2013/04/25/world/europe/russia-putin-questions (accessed 24 September 2013).

Solzhenitsyn, A. (1968), *The First Circle*, New York: Harper.

Solzhenitsyn, A. (2007), *The Gulag Archipelago: An Experiment in Literary Investigation*, New York: Harper Perennial.

Solzhenitsyn, A. (2009), *In the First Circle*, New York: Harper Perennial.

Soloviev, S. (2011), 'Posledstvia Osventsima: Svoboda kak Soprotivlenie', in D. Gasparyan (ed.), *Filosofia Svobody*, Sankt Peterburg: Aleteia.

Starks, T. (2009), *The Body Soviet: Propaganda, Hygiene and the Revolutionary State*, Chicago: The University of Wisconsin Press.

Steele, J. (2004), 'Putin Warns of Security Backlash', *The Guardian*, 6 September, http://www.theguardian.com/world/2004/sep/06/chechnya.russia2 (accessed 10 June 2013).

Stites, R. (1989), *Revolutionary Dreams: Utopian Vision and Experimental Life in the Russian Revolution*, Oxford: Oxford University Press.

Szakolczai, A. (1998), *Max Weber and Michel Foucault: Parallel Lifeworks*, London: Routledge.

Talmon, J. (1970), *The Origins of Totalitarian Democracy*, New York: Norton.

Taubes, J. (2004), *The Political Theology of Paul*, Stanford, CA: Stanford University Press.

Tertz, A. (1960), *The Trial Begins, and On Socialist Realism*, Berkeley, CA: The University of California Press.

Timasheff, N. (1946), *The Great Retreat: The Growth and Decline of Communism in Russia*, New York: E. P. Dutton and Company.

Tismaneanu, V. (2012), *The Devil in History: Communism, Fascism and Some Lessons of the Twentieth Century*, Berkeley, CA: University of California Press.

Toker, L. (2000), *Return from the Archipelago: Narratives of Gulag Survivors*, Bloomington, IN: Indiana University Press.

Trotsky, L. (2004 [1937]), *The Revolution Betrayed*, New York: Dover.

Tsipko, A. (1988), 'Istoki Stalinizma', *Nauka i Zhizn*, 11, 45–55.

Tsipko, A. (1990), *Nasilie Lzhi ili Kak Zabludilsya Prizrak*, Moskva: Progress.

Tsvetkov, A. (2010), 'Stalin v Gorode: Zharkie Spory o Staline', *Russky Zhurnal*, 24 February, http://www.russ.ru/pole/Stalin-v-gorode (accessed 21 September 2013).

Tucker, R. (1973), *Stalin as Revolutionary*, New York: Norton.

Tucker, R. (1977), 'Stalinism as Revolution from Above', in R. Tucker, *Stalinism: Essays in Historical Interpretation*, New York: W. W. Norton.

Tucker, R. (1992), *Stalin in Power: The Revolution from Above 1928–1941*, New York: W. W. Norton.

Vatter, M. (2014), *The Republic of the Living: Biopolitics and the Critique of Civil Society*, New York: Fordham University Press.

Viola, L. (1999), *Peasant Rebels under Stalin: Collectivization and the Culture of Peasant Resistance*, Oxford: Oxford University Press.

Virno, P. (2008), *Multitude between Innovation and Negation*, Los Angeles: Semiotext(e).

Wark, M. (2015), *Molecular Red: Theory for the Anthropocene*, London: Verso.

Weiner, A. (1999), 'Nature, Nurture, and Memory in a Socialist Utopia: Delineating the Soviet Socio-Ethnic Body in the Age of Socialism', *The American Historical Review*, 104: 4, 1114–55.

Wemheuer, F. (2014), 'Collectivization and Famine', in S. A. Smith (ed.), *The Oxford Handbook of the History of Communism*, Oxford: Oxford University Press.

Werth, N. (2007), *Cannibal Island: Death in a Siberian Gulag*, Princeton, NJ: Princeton University Press.

Wolfe, C. (2013), *Before the Law: Humans and Other Animals in a Biopolitical Frame*, Chicago: The University of Chicago Press.

Wood, A. (2005), *Stalin and Stalinism*, London: Routledge.

Young, G. (2012), *The Russian Cosmists: The Esoteric Futurism of Nikolai Fedorov and his Followers*, Oxford: Oxford University Press.

Zemskov, V. (2014), *Stalin i Narod: Pochemu ne Bylo Vosstania*, Moskva: Algoritm.

Žižek, S. (1998), 'The Interpassive Subject', *European Graduate School*, http://www.egs.edu/faculty/slavoj-zizek/articles/the-interpassive-subject (accessed 10 August 2013).

Žižek, S. (2002), *Did Somebody Say Totalitarianism: Five Interventions into the (Mis)use of a Notion*, London: Verso.

Žižek, S. (2005), *The Parallax View*, Cambridge, MA: The MIT Press.

Žižek, S. (2008), *In Defense of Lost Causes*, London: Verso.

Žižek, S. (2011), *Living in the End Times*, London: Verso.

Zubov, A. (2014), 'Eto Uzhe Bylo', *Vedomosti*, 1 March, http://www.vedomosti.ru/opinion/news/23467291/andrej-zubov-eto-uzhe-bylo (accessed 10 September 2014).

Zyuganov, G. (2004), *O Russkih I Rossii*, Moskva: Molodaya Gvardiya.

Zyuganov, G. (2008), *Stalin i Sovremennost*, Moskva: Molodaya Gvardiya.

Zyuganov, G. (2009), 'Stalin kak Revolutsioner i Patriot', *Communist Party of the Russian Federation*, 8 September, http://kprf.ru/rus_soc/70545.html (accessed 16 July 2013).

INDEX

abortion, prohibition of, 60, 69, 131–2
'accelerator', concept of, 119–20
Agamben, Giorgio, 7–8, 11–12, 50–6, 65, 69–70, 118–19, 124, 158, 189, 200, 217, 220, 229, 232, 234, 242, 261–3, 265, 279, 284, 297, 303, 311
apocalypticism, 118–21, 129–31, 269
Arendt, Hannah, 11, 57, 124, 158, 189–96, 225, 243–6, 252, 308
auto-immunity, 101, 155
avant-garde, 73, 110–11, 117, 130, 147–8, 300, 305, 306

Badiou, Alain, 96, 151–3, 247, 258, 268, 284–7, 312
barbarism
  and biopolitics, 278–81
Benjamin, Walter, 72, 118

biopolitics
  affirmative, 254–69, 278–88
  and biology, 58–9, 66, 69, 86–92, 199–200, 279–80, 297, 299, 302
  and ideology, 61–6
  as a mode of problematisation, 67
  concept of, 43, 64, 67–70, 278
  transformative and securitarian, 6, 85–6, 104–5, 119, 123, 299, 301
Bogdanov, Alexander, 111–18, 248, 280, 283, 301
Bolshevism, 93, 99, 176, 246
Buldakov, Vladimir 72–3, 76, 113, 129, 141
Bulgakov, Mikhail, 115–17
Bulgakov, Sergei, 106, 107
Bykov, Dmitry, 95, 103, 125, 158–9, 240, 250, 258–9

331

Camus, Albert, 145
captivation
  and affirmative biopolitics, 282–8
  and animality, 311
Chukovskaya, Lydia, 191–2
Civil War, in Russia, 5, 21–22, 71–4, 79, 81, 83, 104, 113, 150–5, 162, 209, 260, 299
class enemy
  and racial enemy, 48, 87–9, 162
  concept of, 82, 162
  reforging of, 88–124, 159–64, 202, 229, 244, 249, 307, 310
collectivisation, 9, 14, 26, 29, 39, 82–4, 88, 91, 104, 121, 127–9, 138, 162–3, 194–5, 258, 302
collectivism, 112–17
Collier, Stephen, 66–8, 79–80
constituent power, 8, 54–6
constructivism, in biopolitics, xii, 39, 104, 273, 285–7, 291–2, 312
Cosmism
  as a precursor to Soviet biopolitics, 9, 105–10, 117, 283, 301
Crimea, annexation of, 28, 32
Cultural Revolution, in the USSR, 29, 81–2, 89, 92, 103, 128–9, 139, 142, 300

Debord, Guy, 53–4
democracy
  and biopolitics, 8, 59–60, 255
  and totalitarianism, 8–9, 43, 51–6, 58–9
Derrida, Jacques, 93, 98
destalinisation
  in the 1950s, 13–19
  in the 1980s, 19–22
diffusion, of ideas in life, 12, 265–9, 271, 283–8
Dobrenko, Evgeny, 85–6, 90, 124, 130, 142–8, 160, 305
Dunham, Vera, 173

'enemy of the people'
  concept of, 15, 158, 162–4, 197
Engels, Friedrich, 270, 272, 289
Esposito, Roberto, 8, 36, 56–60, 67, 96, 98, 100–1, 118, 119, 255, 297
Etkind, Alexander, 166, 177–80, 189, 197
eugenics
  in the Soviet Union, 64, 88–92

family policy
  under Stalinism, 60, 89, 105, 131–3, 136, 153
famine (1932–3), 39, 83, 90–1, 121–3, 127, 134

Index

Fedorov, Nikolai, 105–11, 117, 125–6, 262, 301, 302
Filippov, Alexander, 13–14, 296
Fitzpatrick, Sheila, 30–1, 81–2, 121, 134, 135, 150, 173, 299
Foucault, Michel, viii–ix, 4, 7, 36–7, 40–50, 62–4, 66–70, 84, 87, 122, 139–40, 146, 156, 171, 179–80, 186, 254

genetics
  in the Soviet Union, 88–92
Getty, Arch, 14, 150, 155, 158, 163
Girkin, Igor, 28, 32
Gorbachev, Mikhail, 19–22, 138, 200, 305
Gorky, Maxim, 85–7, 108, 110, 124–5, 310
Great Break, the
  biopolitical rationality of, 78–84, 102–5
  negative inflections of, 128–9
Great Retreat, the
  concept of, 129–35
  critique of, 136–42
Great Terror, the
  and Soviet constitutional reform, 151–2
  explanations of, 158–9, 161–2
  mass operations, 155–6
  national operations, 156–8
  party purges, 153–5

Grossman, Vasily, 20
Groys, Boris, 4, 38, 86, 111, 117, 147, 161, 169, 305, 306
Gulag
  and Nazi concentration camps, 303
  during High Stalinism, 160–1, 182–4, 195–6, 309
  during the Great Break, 124–5
  Foucault on, 40–3
  Shalamov on, 201–41

Halfin, Igal, 146, 164, 171, 175, 178
Heidegger, Martin, 187, 234–5, 237, 262, 274, 280, 311
Hellbeck, Jochen, 171, 175–9
Henry, Michel, 220, 273–82, 297, 311
High Stalinism, 127–8, 304
Hoffmann, David, 61–5, 102, 132, 136–41, 156, 161–2, 296, 297, 300

ideology
  and biopolitics, 38, 41–3, 57–9, 60–9
  and logic, 244–6
  and terror, ix–x, 19–23, 35–6
immanence
  and transcendence in Soviet biopolitics, 96, 102, 119, 124, 146
  of life, 273–6

immunity
  in liberal biopolitics, 98, 101–2, 255
  in Nazi biopolitics, 101–2, 255
  renunciation of, under Stalinism, 119
indifference
  as the feature of Soviet subjectivity, 185, 187, 193–4, 214–20, 309
industrialisation, during the Great Break, 9, 26, 29, 77, 79–81, 121, 127

Kaganovich, Lazar, 14, 123, 141
katechon, 9, 93–8, 101, 118–21, 152, 305
Kharkhordin, Oleg, 42, 142, 182
Khruschev, Nikita, 7, 14, 16, 19, 21, 24, 164, 203
Kirov, Sergei, 151, 153, 306
Kotkin, Stephen, 62, 71–2, 76–9, 83, 94, 100, 121–2, 128, 157, 174–6, 296, 299, 300, 306
Krasin, Leonid, 72, 111, 113
Krylova, Anna, 173–5, 179
kulak, concept of, 82–3, 94–5, 122, 195, 302–3

Lenin, Vladimir, ix, 1, 2, 13, 16, 19, 29, 71–2, 78, 83, 100, 111, 112, 132, 143, 154, 202, 240, 248, 250, 254, 300

Lepeshinskaya, Olga, 199–200
liberalism
  biopolitical rationality of, 84–6, 120, 140
  governmental intervention in, 97–105
life
  and the world (in Henry's philosophy), 276–8, 280–1
  as auto-affection, 273–5
  community of, 277, 283
  in the theory of biopolitics, 68–70
  phenomenological concept of, 273–9
liturgy, 12, 110, 261–2, 265–6
Lunacharsky, Anatoly, 111, 112
Lysenko, Trofim, 90–4, 199

Malabou, Catherine, 185–90, 192–3, 196–7, 204–6, 210, 214, 249, 308
Mallarmé, Stéphane, 264–7
Marx, Karl, vii, 2, 92, 100
Marxism, 15, 23, 41, 44–5, 58, 62, 64, 65, 71, 86, 91, 93, 99, 105, 133, 270, 272–4, 300, 301, 304
Meillassoux, Quentin, 264–7, 271
Menshevism, 300
messianism, in Soviet socialism, 85, 93, 96, 120, 131, 255, 268, 291, 304
Michurin, Ivan, 90
Mikoyan, Anastas, 134–5, 148

Index

modernity
  and biopolitics, 50–4, 66–70
  the concept of, in Soviet studies, 61–6
Molotov, Viacheslav, 1, 71, 157, 197
Moscow Trials, 154–5

Naiman, Eric, 177–80
naturalism
  in Western biopolitics, 6, 57, 84
  renunciation of, in the Soviet Union, 87–92, 99–105
Naumov, Oleg, 150, 158, 163, 166–7, 306, 307
Nazism, 6, 8, 38–9, 44–5, 49, 51–60, 69, 84, 100–5, 162, 171, 199, 244, 255, 261, 297, 299, 302
Negri, Antonio, 55–6, 67
Neoliberalism, 38, 66, 258, 292
New Economic Policy (NEP), 19, 31, 71–4, 76, 78, 93–4, 113, 121, 128, 134–5, 138–40, 165, 257, 266, 268
Nietzsche, Friedrich, 86, 234, 259–60, 311
nihilism, 8, 51, 53, 158, 258, 260

paradigm, 36, 42, 62, 98, 124, 183, 186–7, 193, 214, 223, 241, 297, 303, 307
Pashukanis, Yevgeni, 134–5
Perestroika, 1, 17–21, 76, 115, 120, 138, 142, 290, 292–4

planning
  genetic and teleological approaches to, 79–80, 85
plasticity, 186–7, 196, 206, 249
Platonov, Andrei, 292–5
Priestland, David, 82, 131, 165
pro-natalism, in Soviet family policy, 10, 105, 131–2
Prokhanov, Alexander, 23–5, 28, 31
Putin, Vladimir, 1, 2, 7–8, 25–30, 32–5

racism
  and biopolitics, 36, 40–4, 47–9
  and socialism, 44–6, 60, 70, 87, 90, 139, 156
Rancière, Jacques, 158, 260, 269–73
re-stalinisation
  and Putinism, 25–32
  in the 1970s, 18, 27

St Paul, 93–4
Schmitt, Carl, 94, 119–20
Security, as a biopolitical rationality, 97–8, 140
Shalamov, Varlam
  and affirmative biopolitics, 11, 249–3
  on hate, 233–5
  on indifference, 214–20
  on language, 214–43

Shalamov, Varlam (*Cont.*)
  on literature, 235–7
  on prison, 209–10
  on survival, 220–5
  on the camp as a negative experience, 203–6
  on the destruction of subjectivity, 207–14
  on the inhuman, 227–30
  on the October Revolution, 248
  postcommunist reappropriation of, 250–1
Sloterdijk, Peter, 104, 158, 252
socialism
  and communism, 298
  as a form of life, 73–4, 78–80, 118–25
  in one country, theory of, 35, 77, 94, 119, 121, 131, 152
  real socialism, concept of, xi–xii, 5, 12, 21, 63, 93, 136, 142, 144–7, 166, 168–9, 250, 261, 268, 289, 295
socialist realism
  as a simulacrum of socialism, 144–9
  as an aesthetic doctrine, 142–4
  as anti-naturalism, 143
Socialist Revolutionaries (political party), 100, 300
socio-cide, 122
Solzhenitsyn, Alexander, 11, 16, 30–42, 196, 204, 210, 221, 228–30, 237–8, 240, 246, 248, 309, 310

'Soviet exhaustion', 113, 115
Stalinism
  as a construct of destalinization, 13
  biopolitical rationality of, 84–92, 118–22
  emergence of, 71–7
  in the postcommunist period, 21–34
Stites, Richard, 61, 72–5, 267–8, 300
Stolypin, Petr, 100, 240
subjectivity
  and indifference, 196–8
  and loneliness, 196, 251
  and terror, 181–5, 191–8
  and trauma, 185–90
  in Soviet studies, 171–81

Timasheff, Nicholas, 25, 129–30, 136–41, 304, 305
Toker, Leona, 17, 183–4, 194
totalitarianism
  and democracy, 56–60
  and the destruction of the subject, 180–91
  concept of, 56–8
  critique of, 39, 59, 86, 124
transcendence
  and immanence in Soviet biopolitics, 96, 102, 119, 124, 146
  the forcing of, 124–5, 257–8, 287–9
trauma, 185–97, 200, 210, 214, 217, 227, 236, 251, 290, 308

Index

Trotsky, Lev, 14, 22, 55, 76, 78, 83, 88, 95, 121, 134, 141, 300

Vavilov, Nikolai, 91
Virno, Paolo, 94, 98
voluntarism, 17, 85, 165, 263, 299

Witte, Sergei, 100

Zasulich, Vera, 100
Žižek, Slavoj, 39, 77, 122, 168, 266, 301, 302, 306, 308
Zyuganov, Gennady, 22–5, 29

EU representative:
Easy Access System Europe
Mustamäe tee 50, 10621 Tallinn, Estonia
Gpsr.requests@easproject.com

www.ingramcontent.com/pod-product-compliance
Lightning Source LLC
Chambersburg PA
CBHW061706300426
44115CB00014B/2576